The
GUNKS
GUIDE

The GUNKS GUIDE

Third Edition

Todd Swain

FALCONGUIDES •

GUILFORD, CONNECTICUT
HELENA, MONTANA

AN IMPRINT OF ROWMAN & LITTLEFIELD

WARNING: CLIMBING IS A SPORT WHERE YOU MAY BE SERIOUSLY INJURED OR DIE.

READ THIS BEFORE YOU USE THIS BOOK.

This guidebook is a compilation of unverified information gathered from many different climbers. The author cannot assure the accuracy of any of the information in this book, including the topos and route descriptions, the difficulty ratings, and the protection ratings. These may be incorrect or misleading and it is impossible for any one author to climb all the routes to confirm the information about each route. Also, ratings of climbing difficulty and danger are always subjective and depend on the physical characteristics (for example, height), experience, technical ability, confidence and physical fitness of the climber who supplied the rating. Additionally, climbers who achieve first ascents sometimes underrate the difficulty or danger of the climbing route out of fear of being ridiculed if a climb is later down-rated by subsequent ascents. Therefore, be warned that you must exercise your own judgment on where a climbing route goes, its difficulty and your ability to safely protect yourself from the risks of rock climbing. Examples of some of these risks are: falling due to technical difficulty or due to natural hazards such as holds breaking, falling rock, climbing equipment dropped by other climbers, hazards of weather and lightning, your own equipment failure, and failure or absence of fixed protection.

You should not depend on any information gleaned from this book for your personal safety; your safety depends on your own good judgment, based on experience and a realistic assessment of your climbing ability. If you have any doubt as to your ability to safely climb a route described in this book, do not attempt it.

The following are some ways to make your use of this book safer:

1. Consultation: You should consult with other climbers about the difficulty and danger of a particular climb prior to attempting it. Most local climbers are glad to give advice on routes in their area and we suggest that you contact locals to confirm ratings and safety of particular routes and to obtain first-hand information about a route chosen from this book.

2. Instruction: Most climbing areas have local climbing instructors and guides available. We recommend that you engage an instructor or guide to learn safety techniques and to become familiar with the routes and hazards of the areas

described in this book. Even after you are proficient in climbing safely, occasional use of a guide is a safe way to raise your climbing standard and learn advanced techniques.

3. Fixed Protection: Many of the routes in this book use bolts and pitons which are permanently placed in the rock. Because of variances in the manner of placement, weathering, metal fatigue, the quality of the metal used, and many other factors, these fixed protection pieces should always be considered suspect and should always be backed up by equipment that you place yourself. Never depend for your safety on a single piece of fixed protection because you never can tell whether it will hold weight, and in some cases, fixed protection may have been removed or is now absent.

Be aware of the following specific potential hazards which could arise in using this book:

1. Misdescriptions of Routes: If you climb a route and you have a doubt as to where the route may go, you should not go on unless you are sure that you can go that way safely. Route descriptions and topos in this book may be inaccurate or misleading.

2. Incorrect Difficulty Rating: A route may, in fact, be more difficult than the rating indicates. Do not be lulled into a false sense of security by the difficulty rating.

3. Incorrect Protection Rating: If you climb a route and you are unable to arrange adequate protection from the risk of falling through the use of fixed pitons or bolts and by placing your own protection devices, do not assume that there is adequate protection available higher just because the route protection rating indicates the route is not an "X" or an "R" rating. Every route is potentially an "X" (a fall may be deadly), due to the inherent hazards of climbing – including, for example, failure or absence of fixed protection, your own equipment's failure, or improper use of climbing equipment. **THERE ARE NO WARRANTIES, WHETHER EXPRESS OR IMPLIED, THAT THIS GUIDEBOOK IS ACCURATE OR THAT THE INFORMATION CONTAINED IN IT IS RELIABLE. THERE ARE NO WARRANTIES OF FITNESS FOR A PARTICULAR PURPOSE OR THAT THIS GUIDE IS MERCHANTABLE. YOUR USE OF THIS BOOK INDICATES YOUR ASSUMPTION OF THE RISK THAT IT MAY CONTAIN ERRORS AND IS AN ACKNOWLEDGEMENT OF YOUR OWN SOLE RESPONSIBILITY FOR YOUR CLIMBING SAFETY.**

FALCONGUIDES

Copyright © 1995 by Todd Swain.
Previously published by Falcon Publishing, Inc.

Falcon, FalconGuides, and Chockstone are registered
trademarks of Rowman & Littlefield.

Cover photo by Michael S. Miller
Front cover: Dan Teng on *Foops,* Sky Top.
Back cover: French Connection, the second pitch of
The Zone, The Trapps.

Library of Congress Cataloging-in-Publication Data is
available

ISBN 978-0-7627-3836-6

Manufactured in the United States of America

Distributed by NATIONAL BOOK NETWORK

Preface

With this third edition of *The Gunks Guide* I have again tried to fix previous mistakes without making any further ones. All of the new routes and variations that were reported to me since 1990 have been included in this updated edition. Ivan Rezucha has been my most important correspondent, providing me with page after page of corrections, additions, and comments. This guidebook would not be anywhere near as complete and accurate if it weren't for Ivan's untiring help.

I also want to thank John Thackray, who has revised and updated his climbing history of the area. While this is only a brief treatise, it will provide you with a good overview of the important climbs and climbers in Shawangunk history. For those interested in trivia as well as the history of the area, I have prepared a new group of trivia questions. Unlike the previous two guides, I have included the answers in this edition (no cheating).

Once again, George Meyers and the staff at Chockstone Press are responsible for the layout and publishing of this guidebook. Without their skills, the information I had amassed would still be in my Powerbook.

Because of their significant help with the last two editions (upon which this third edition is based), I would again like to thank the following people: Joe Bridges, Mike Dimitri, Mike Freeman, Rich Gottlieb, Jeff Gruenberg, Annie O'Neill, Ivan Rezucha, Sue Rogers, Dave Saball, Andy and Randy Schenkel, Thom Scheuer, Donette Smith, Mike Steele, Iza Trapani, Paul Trapani, and Dick Williams.

To Earl and Gail Swain

Who have good-naturedly supported my climbing
endeavors despite their unflagging mystification.

Earl Swain, age 68, on his first climb, *Easy Overhang* 5.2, May 1994

Table of Contents

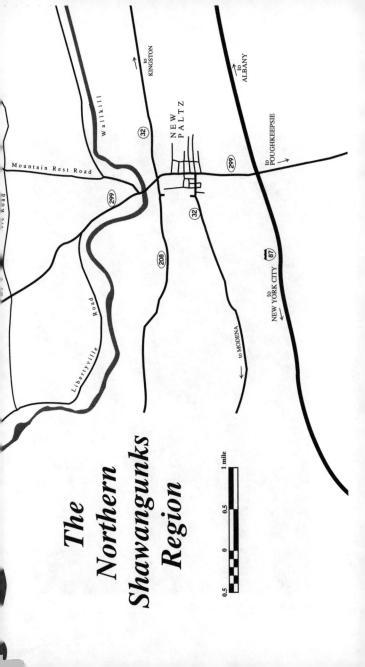

The Northern Shawangunks Region

to KINGSTON

to ALBANY

NEW PALTZ

to POUGHKEEPSIE

Wallkill

Mountain Rest Road

32

299

299

32

208

87

Libertyville Road

to MODENA

to NEW YORK CITY

Road

0.5   0   0.5   1 mile

Ivan Rezucha on *Twisted Sister* 5.8+

Introduction

Shawangunk rockclimbing guides have always limited descriptions to the four major cliffs in the area—The Trapps, Near Trapps, Millbrook, and Sky Top, and this edition of *The Gunks Guide* is no exception. Numerous other crags will be found in the vicinity, but due to long-standing local tradition, these do not appear in any guide.

If you have never visited the Gunks, you are in for a treat. The rock is generally excellent, and there are a multitude of classic routes from 5.1 to 5.13. Enjoy the area, and please help preserve it for future generations.

The Shawangunk Ridge (pronounced Shon-gum) is located just 90 miles north of New York City in Ulster County, New York—eight miles west of New Paltz. While only a short distance from millions of people, the area is surprisingly unspoiled. The cliffs provide wonderful views, while the numerous carriage roads and trails lead to solitude and frequent sightings of wildlife.

The best time to visit the Gunks is in the fall. The seasons run something like this: September, October, and early November is cool and less humid (55°-75°). While this is peak visitation time for the area, the beautiful colors of fall foliage tend to compensate for the circus-like atmosphere. Try to avoid weekends during this time if at all possible. By mid-November the weather turns too cold to climb comfortably. While the winters are cold (0°-40°), there is only enough snow to cross-country ski about five weekends out of the season. The spring climbing season begins in mid-March and runs until the end of May. Spring brings warmer weather (55°-75°), as well as fantastic displays of mountain laurel, shadbush, and wildflowers. The summers are hot and humid (80°-95°). While it's rarely too hot to climb, the humidity makes climbing somewhat unpleasant.

Since this is a wilderness area, there are some nasties to look out for. During the warmer months wasps are active and nest under overhangs on the cliffs. Climber traffic usually keeps the classic routes wasp-free, but caution should be used. Snakes are somewhat common in the area. While the majority are harmless, there have been climbers bitten by the poisonous copperhead while on climbs. Ticks may be found in the area, and may be carrying Lyme disease. Mosquitoes and black flies will be encountered in the spring, but can easily be controlled with insect repellent. The Mohonk Preserve rangers and staff can answer any natural history questions you may have, and the Preserve also publishes books and brochures about the area.

The Land and Its Owners

First-time visitors are amazed at how unspoiled the area is. This is primarily due to the foresight of the Smiley family. In the mid-1800s, members of the Smiley family first visited the New Paltz area in search of land to build a family summer house on. They were directed to the Stokes Tavern on Mohonk Lake, which they purchased soon afterwards.

Over the next fifty years the Smileys acquired thousands of acres of land along the ridge, stretching as far south as Kerhonkson and Ellenville. It was during this time of expansion that the extensive network of carriage roads was built (Undercliff Road was built in 1903, Overcliff in 1931). By the late 1950s, the family members operating the Mohonk Mountain House could not justify maintaining the enormous areas of land that they had purchased.

In the early 1960s members of the Smiley family and friends of the Mohonk Mountain House founded a non-profit land preserve to manage the wilderness that they had purchased along the ridge. The Mohonk Trust was formed in 1963, with the purpose of acquiring lands formerly owned by the Mohonk Mountain House. The Trust considered the protection of the now famous Gunks climbing area a high priority.

Today, the Trust is known as Mohonk Preserve, Inc., and manages over 6,000 acres on the Shawangunk Ridge. It is a completely separate entity from the Mohonk Mountain House (officially known as Smiley Brothers Inc.), and is host to nearly 100,000 visitors each year. In addition, the Preserve has over 18 miles of carriage roads and 26 miles of hiking trails. The Mohonk Mountain House owns and regulates Sky Top, and they have a set of regulations that differ slightly from those that govern the cliffs on Preserve land.

The Mohonk Mountain House

The protection of the Gunks and the whole Shawangunk Ridge as a major climbing area and as open space is still a high priority of the Preserve. Only with your help and cooperation can climbing continue. With increased use of the land, erosion, trash, and overcrowding are becoming bigger problems. Since 1958, in order to generate funds to pay for maintenance and protection of the Preserve as a natural, open space available to the public on a daily basis, payment of a day use fee is charged, or annual membership has been required. Climbing, running, biking, skiing, hiking, deer hunting, et cetera are all considered compatible uses of the land. The day fee is collected by Preserve rangers while on patrol, or there is a self-service fee collector with envelopes on the east side of Trapps Bridge (the steel bridge over Route 44-55). To obtain membership information, trail maps, copies of the climbing instruction policy, or other information, please write to Mohonk Preserve, Mohonk Lake, 1000 Mountain Rest Road, New Paltz, NY, 12561 (Telephone: 914-255-0919), or visit its headquarters just below the Mountain House Gatehouse (see map on pages x and xi).

The Mohonk Preserve and the Mohonk Mountain House (which owns about 2000 acres, including Sky Top) have a reciprocal arrangement whereby climbers, hikers, bikers and such are allowed use of the lands of the Mountain House without paying an additional fee (as long as they abide by the rules and regulations of the Mountain House). These include, but are not limited to the following:

1) The hotel and all its facilities are reserved for hotel guests. Day visitors are not allowed in the hotel or use of Mohonk Lake.

2) Dogs are not allowed on hotel grounds, and must be leashed at all times on Preserve land.

3) Bicycles are restricted around Sky Top and the Mountain House. There are "No Biking" signs posted at most carriage road intersections indicating where bicycles are allowed and where they are restricted. Bikes may only be ridden on carriage roads, not trails, and must now have a permit to be ridden on Preserve land.

4) Climbers entering at the Mohonk Gatehouse must have an annual membership, otherwise they will be required to pay the daily fee charged by the Mountain House. Annual members will still have to pay $1 per person to park at the Gatehouse parking lot. A day pass bought from one of the Preserve rangers is not adequate to enter via the Gatehouse, unless on foot.

5) Climbers should not expose their climbing gear while hiking to and from Sky Top on Hotel lands, as climbing is not officially sanctioned by the Hotel.

6) Climbers are required to wear shirts, and refrain from loud, abusive, and/or obscene language while climbing at Sky Top.

7) From Memorial Day to Columbus Day, on Friday, Saturday, and Sunday no climbing is allowed to the left (west) of **The Crevice**. This includes **Foops** and **Sound and Fury**.

8) **The Crevice** is not to be used as a descent route during the above times.

9) No climbing instruction or guiding is allowed on Mountain House lands.

Remember, The Mountain House is in business to please hotel guests, not climbers. Climbing at Sky Top is a very special privilege and unless the Mountain House rules are adhered to, that privilege could be withdrawn at any time. Please do not be the person that causes Sky Top to be closed to climbing.

The Mohonk Preserve also has policies that affect climbers. These include but are not limited to:

> **Mohonk Preserve, Inc. does not maintain the rocks, cliffs, or other natural features of the terrain, does not provide supervision or instruction, is not responsible for the condition of the terrain or the acts of persons who may be on Mohonk Preserve property and has not placed or maintained climbing or safety aids on or about the cliffs (for example, bolts, pitons, and rappel slings and rings) and is not responsible for the placement of maintenance of such devices by others.**

1) No new bolts or pitons may be placed, except to replace those installed prior to November, 1986. When replacing a bolt, every effort must be made to use the existing hole. (This is best left to the local climbing community.)

2) Chipping or improving holds is forbidden, as is rock trundling.

3) Cutting or removing trees is forbidden.

4) Climbing and/or rappelling instruction or guiding is regulated in New York State, and even more strictly controlled on Preserve land. On the Preserve this includes scout groups, schools, college groups, camps, church groups, professional guides, et cetera. Any group planning to instruct climbing on the Preserve needs to contact the Preserve prior to their trip. A copy of the guiding policy can be obtained from the Preserve at the address above.

5) The Preserve recommends the use of natural colored webbing when left as retreat or rappel slings.

6) It is also recommended that if chalk is used, it is of a color natural to the area.

7) Dogs are required to be on a leash at all times.

8) Glass containers are not allowed on the Preserve.

9) Radios are not permitted, unless used with earphones.

10) Bicycles may only be ridden on carriage roads, and bikers should observe the "No Biking" signs. All bikes must now be registered with the Preserve.

11) Fires and high impact camping are not allowed on the Preserve or Hotel grounds. See the section "Where to Sleep" for details.

After reading through all of these rules and regulations, it may appear that the Gunks is run like a police state. This is far from the truth. The important thing to remember is that without the Preserve there would be no climbing. The Preserve's mission is to protect a unique mountain ecosystem for future generations, as well as allow compatible and appropriate public visitation at present. Please cooperate with the Preserve rangers!

The Shawangunks is blessed to have such an enlightened steward. Many of the nation's climbing areas are not so fortunate. The Access Committee of the American Alpine Club was formed to help mitigate disputes that threaten access to good climbing. They can negotiate, organize, and even litigate closures of climbing areas. In addition, should litigation fail, what is now called the Access Fund

provides funds to purchase or preserve problem areas. Your tax deductible contribution to the Access Fund is a concrete way of giving something back to climbing and making a real difference in the effort to save the rich diversity of climbing resources throughout the United States. To contact The Access Fund or to send your donation (of any amount) they can be reached at The Access Fund; Post Office Box 17010; Boulder, Colorado 80308.

The Friends of the Shawangunks is a not-for-profit corporation working for open space preservation in the Shawangunk Mountains. They are not a climbers' organization but are interested in maintaining public access for all sensitive outdoor enthusiasts. They welcome members and contributions and can be reached at: Friends of the Shawangunks, Post Office Box 177, Accord NY 12404.

The Gunks: A History
by John Thackray

Aspects and fragments of history are everywhere at the Gunks—in the names of climbs that speak to the history of pop music, soap operas, books and film; the 50-year-old soft iron pitons on many classics; the ancient Senior Ranger who has seen five or six generations of climbers pass by. There are in fact many histories of the Gunks: first ascents, gear, access, ethics, guidebooks, etiquette, et cetera. What follows is one old timer's scatter-shot impressions of a few highlights.

Prehistory

Long before there was technical climbing on these cliffs, guests at Minnewaska and Mohonk House—two popular grand resorts built at the end of the last century—rambled and scrambled up a few breaks in the seven miles of vertical cliffs. Locals from New Paltz did likewise, without leaving any record or indeed imagining their deeds had significance. These were aesthetes, not climbers. All they sought were sublime views and inspiring "prospects."

The Patriarchs

Seven years after New Hampshire's Cannon, White Horse and Cathedral Crags were first climbed with roped techniques imported from the Alps, the Gunks was discovered by technical climbers. One clear spring day in 1935, a group of New Yorkers climbing Breakneck Ridge, which rises on the flanks of the Hudson River, looked north and saw a band of white cliffs.

One of these gazers was the German émigré Fritz Wiessner. The following weekend he arrived at the base of Millbrook, and with characteristic boldness, put up a fine line now called **Old Route**. In 1940, another first-rate European climber arrived on the scene, Hans Kraus, an orthopedist with experience in the Dolomites which then had the most advanced rock climbing standards in the world. Kraus put up the first route in the then highly-vegetated Trapps, **Northern Pillar.** The following year Wiessner and Kraus free-climbed **High Exposure**, one of the jewels of the Gunks, placing only three pitons on the upper pitch. With other seconds, Wiessner and Kraus put in new routes for almost a decade. Both climbed to a high standard well past middle age.

Old Styles

The pioneers of the forties set a style that was to last roughly thirty years. They viewed the crags as fragments of major mountains that had magically landed in the rolling woodland of Ulster County. They dressed as for the mountains, in climbing breeches and sweaters, parkas and stiff soled heavy boots. They tied on with bowlines around the waist. Typically they left their packs at the entrance to the cliffs and climbed always from the bottom to the top, then walked the crest back to the starting point. A bona fide new route had to reach the cliff top.

Appies' Ascendance

Until the mid-sixties, most climbers not affiliated with the few college outing clubs, climbed with the rock climbing section of the Appalachian Mountain Club (AMC), known throughout New England as "Appies." Ostensibly for reasons of safety, the AMC imposed a strict behavior code. All leaders had to be "certified" route by route. Seconds too. Every climbing party had to sign out and sign back in with the club. When a few climbers tried to operate independently, the club unsuccessfully petitioned the cliff's

landowners to banish them. Although the Gunk's Appies were on the wrong side of history, they selflessly ran an excellent introduction to rock climbing program which set hundreds of beginning climbers on the right path.

Vulgarian's Arise

Ever hear that quote about the sixties? "If you remember it then you weren't there." It fits those legendary rock children of the Gunks in the sixties. Who and what were The Vulgarians is lost in the mist of time and the haze of cannabis, hallucinogens and hangovers. The Vulgarians' posture was one of outrageousness at any price. Inevitably it became their historic mission to liberate the Gunks for the Appies' uptightness.

Among the tribe were a handful of exceptional climbers like Jim McCarthy and Richard Goldstone who led a surge in standards and new route activity. But it was The Vulgarians' strident unconventionality that attracted the first Western visitors and for which they are best remembered. Two relics of that time are a poster of Dick Williams climbing **Shockley's Ceiling** nude, and Elaine Mathews topless with climbing rack on the glossy cover of ***The Vulgarian Digest***, a short-lived but remarkably good magazine. The Vulgarian phenomenon was something you had to be there for—without the context of the sixties, much of their behavior looks juvenile or, worse, offensive (which is why some of their routes named after reproductive organs have fallen to revisionism).

Guidebooks

In pioneering days climbers carried mimeographed sheets of the few dozen classics. In 1964, *A Climber's Guide to the Shawangunks* by Arthur Gran, containing 249 routes, was co-published by the American Alpine Club (AAC) and the AMC. For the time it was one of the finest guides in the country being the first to use aerial photographs of a crag. It also set a pattern followed by all subsequent guidebook authors of describing climbs on the four largest cliffs only. Information on Lost City, Bonticou, Bayards and other outlying cliffs was (and remains) with the grapevine. Two successive Gunks guidebooks were published by the AAC (1972 and 1980), written by Richard Williams, one of the preeminent new route setters in the history of the cliff.

To keep abreast of the flurry of new route activity in the early eighties, locals used loose-leaf supplements privately published by Ivan Rezucha. In 1986, Todd Swain privately published *The Gunks Guide*, which documented 881 routes and introduced to the area the three-star quality rating and the G-PG-R-X protection rating—a standard ever since. A second edition of *The Gunks Guide* was brought out by Chockstone in 1990. In 1991 Williams' new version appeared, again under the escutcheon of the AAC, the three-volume *Shawangunk Rock Climbs.* The Gunks thus became one of the few cliffs in the U.S. with rival guidebooks in print.

Local Heroes

Richard Goldstone used to say, "Wanna know how tough Jim McCarthy was? Try **Tough Shift**." Much of the enjoyment of a "traditional" area like the Gunks is the connection it offers with the legends of the past, their style, their ethics, and the routes that defined each new generation. In this limited space there is room for mentioning only a sprinkling of local heroes. After the Vulgarian heyday, a strong new wave was led by John Stannard who free climbed the great **Foops** roof in 1967, not repeated until Henry Barber six years later. Stannard's achievements were based on an ascetic's attitude towards intoxicants and in a mid-week training schedule that was far more demanding than customary. His one-time protégés Henry Barber, Steve Wunch and John Bragg evolved into climbers every bit as good. Other notables in the next new-route surge were Kevin Bein, Rich Perch, Russ Raffa, Mark Robinson, Mike Sawicky, Mike Freeman, Rich Romano, Todd Swain, Ivan, Rezucha, Russ Clune, Jack Mileski and Jeff Gruenberg, Jim Damon, Hugh Herr, and Lynn Hill, who would eventually leave the Gunks to become the world champion in competition climbing. Scott Franklin, Al Diamond, Jordan Mills and Jeff Morris were not the last to put in good lines, but by the mid- to late-eighties the amount of virgin and protectable rock was clearly scarce.

Gunslingers

The first wave of Western climbers trying out the Gunks included Layton Kor, Royal Robbins, Yvon Chouinard, Steve Roper and later

Ron Kauk, who made the second ascent of Wunch's **Supercrack**.
They left impressed by the exposure and difficulties and severe
grading. The next wave of gunslingers was not so overawed. It
included the Australian Kim Carrigan, Brits Peter O'Donovan and
Jerry Moffatt, German Wolfgang Gullich and French star Patrick
Edlinger. After their fairly easy triumphs on Gunks' testpieces,
locals concluded their standards were no longer leading edge.

Ethics

One reason the Gunks is unusually cluttered with old pins is that
most early climbs involved aid. By the seventies, the pendulum had
swung toward free climbing—often reaching a ethical rigor that
seems archaic today. When, for instance, some leaders took a fall,
they would be lowered all the way to the ground, pull the rope
through all the protection in place, then start up the climb again. (An
even purer idea of form: to equate a fall with failure and abandon
the entire climb, to return another day.) This ethic proved to be too
demanding to prevail with the masses. By the eighties hangdogging
and toproping were widespread: so was chalk, despite the bellyach-
ing by older climbers that it was an eyesore.

In the late eighties, the Gunks was beset by an ethical crisis over
bolting, chiseling nut placements, chipping and enlarging holds.
Although bolts existed on a dozen climbs and their use had raised
no furor when placed, a debate now raged between younger
climbers who wanted to apply maximum technology and the old
guard who feared the consequences. At a noisy climber meeting,
arranged by the Mohonk Preserve in 1986, the consensus was that
existing bolts and fixed pins should be grandfathered, but no new
ones placed, and that all chipping and other alterations of the environment such as tearing out trees should be outlawed. Bolts contin-
ued to be placed by a handful of climbers, and were quickly torn
out by their opponents. At two further meetings sponsored by the
Preserve, the conflict was again aired. The pro-bolters argued the
Gunks was exhausted of new route possibilities with leader-placed
protection and that only by adopting Euro-style tactics could the

Gunks develop and attract world class talent. To which the status quo proponents replied: "So what? Who cares?"

In 1988 the Preserve issued its first climbing policy, prohibiting the placement of new bolts and pins and any alteration of the rock or its vegetation. Compliance has been extremely good. That same year Mohonk Preserve issued its first rules regulating guides and guiding, and Mohonk House banned all guides from Sky Top.

Historical Sources
If you want more history read Laura and Guy Waterman's *Yankee Rock and Ice* (Stackpole Books).

Crowding
When I fist climbed here in the mid-seventies, the locals wanted to keep the Gunks a secret. Articles publicizing the Gunks in magazines were frowned upon, even when their authors made it impossible for outsiders to find the cliffs. New guidebooks were received with ambivalence. Climbers supported the Preserve's policy against commercial use of the land.

Perhaps we all sensed that the secret could not be kept: that the magic we shared would attract others just like us, waiting in the wings of history. So it has turned out. What I didn't recognize in the beginning was that I was an interloper in the space of others. The first recorded complaint of overcrowding at the Gunks came from Kraus in 1951, when there were 50 climbers on the busiest days!

I believe that knowing the Gunks is a very ancient place, one that played a key role in the development of U.S. climbing for half a century, should help today's climbers be more sensitive to others in the 500 plus weekend horde, more aware of our impact on the rock and vegetation and approaches. So remember: keep your voice low, tread softly. This is for many hallowed ground.

John Thackray

Services
Located just below the cliffs at the intersection of Routes 44-55 and 299 are two restaurants and a small convenience store. Only eight

miles to the east is New Paltz—a college town that has to be seen to be appreciated. Numerous restaurants and bars will be found in the town, the most popular with climbers being the Plaza Diner, the Gay '90s, Bacchus, and David's Cookies (who says climbers eat only health food?). Motels are plentiful, with most located by the NY State Thruway (Route 87). Two large grocery stores will also be found near the Thruway, and the town also has a health food store, Earthgoods. For rainy days or long nights, there is a movie theater and a very nice village library and indoor climbing walls. (See also climbing gym information in "What To Do on a Rainy Day" section.)

The local climbing shop, Rock and Snow, is located on Main Street in the center of New Paltz, and carries a good supply of gear and clothing. They can answer any questions you have about the area.

While in New Paltz, a trip down Huguenot Street is a must. Some of America's oldest homes, wonderfully restored, are along this street.

Rules of the Game

As stated before, Mohonk Preserve regulations allow no new bolts or pitons, except to replace those installed prior to November, 1986. Top-roping has become an accepted form of climbing as protectable new route possibilities dwindle. Many of the recent first ascents have been top-roped, preprotected on rappel, then led. While this is obviously not as challenging as an on-sight lead, the remaining new route possibilities generally do not lend themselves to much protection.

Local standards define free ascents as starting on the ground and climbing to the belay without weighting the rope or protection (hence hangdogging, pulling on slings, et cetera are not free climbing techniques). If you want to discuss the merits of redpointing, pinkpointing, flashing, and other stylistic issues go to the Uberfall on a crowded weekend and ask others.

The bottom line is to respect the environment, show courtesy towards others, and have fun. If all three points are met, everyone should be happy.

Where to Sleep

Mohonk Preserve has a strict policy against high impact camping and fires. Climbers are currently allowed to sleep out in two places:

Wawarsing Turnpike: Directly below the hairpin turn on Route 44-55 is a dead end, dirt road. Climbers are allowed to sleep in their vehicles or set a tent up next to their vehicles. No fires, parties, or loud music. Also, a private residence is located at the end of the road. Please keep the road passable and respect their privacy.

Trapps Tenting Area (also known as Camp Slime): On the west side of Trapps Bridge (the steel bridge over Route 44-55) is a small area where climbers are allowed to tent. The limits of this area are clearly posted—please abide by them. No fires, radios, or parties allowed. Outhouses and a trash can are located on the opposite (east) side of Trapps Bridge. There are also outhouses located across from the Uberfall on Route 44-55, on Wawarsing Road, and at Coxing Picnic Area (the local swimming hole—see the map on pages x and xi).

In addition to these two places close to the cliffs, there are private campgrounds in the area, and many motels. Should you have questions about where to camp, contact one of the Preserve rangers.

How to Use the Book

The four major Shawangunk cliffs described in this book, The Trapps, Near Trapps, Millbrook, and Sky Top, define the various chapters of the book. A page-top mini-map will show the position of the information on the current page relative to the entire cliff. In addition, a periodic display of cliff photos will help locate the routes to follow. In two chapters, "The Trapps," and "The Near Trapps," a series of topo maps will help you approach the cliff through the ever-present trees that characterize these areas.

Once again, I have used the Yosemite Decimal System (currently 5.0-5.14) with + and – to signify climbs that are considered difficult or easy for their grade. Remember, no rating system is 100% accurate. Height, reach, finger size, flexibility, et cetera will change a climb's character. If the climb seems too hard for its grade, don't "go for it" just because the guide says it's only a 5.7. The route will be there next weekend for another try.

Protection ratings have been used to give you an idea of what a climb is like. Again, just because the guide says a climb is well protected (G), doesn't mean you should forge ahead hoping you'll

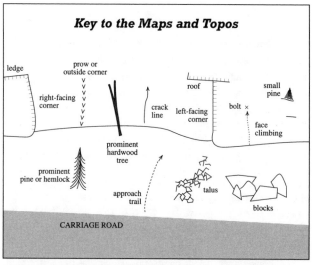

Key to the Maps and Topos

ledge

prow or outside corner

right-facing corner

roof

small pine

crack line

left-facing corner

bolt ×

face climbing

prominent hardwood tree

prominent pine or hemlock

approach trail

talus

blocks

CARRIAGE ROAD

find protection. The protection rating system is as follows, and is based on Jim Erickson's *Rocky Heights, A Guide to Boulder Free Climbs* (1980, pages 6 and 7):

G   Protection is commonly considered excellent. A falling leader probably will suffer no injuries in a fall, assuming he/she is competent in the grade and at placing protection.

PG   Protection is commonly considered adequate. A falling leader may fall up to 15 feet, but probably will suffer no injuries, assuming he/she is competent in the grade and at placing protection.

PG13 A sporty PG. Formerly PG/R.

R   Protection is commonly considered inadequate. A falling leader will probably fall in excess of 15 feet and/or suffer injuries.

X   Protection is commonly considered extremely poor (you're soloing). A falling leader will probably suffer major injuries or death.

Examples:

	(5.8)	*(5.11)*
G	**Bonnie's Roof**	**Climb and Punishment**
PG	**Broken Sling**	**Criss** (P2)
R	**Ape Call** (P1)	**Abracadaver**
X	**Sudden Death** (P1)	**Skeletal Remains**

The quality rating system is based on a one to three star system (★ to ★★★) three being best. If your favorite route didn't get all the stars you think it deserves, pencil some more in.

Finally, the following climbing terms have been used throughout the text:

FA	First Ascent
FFA	First Free Ascent
FRA	First Recorded Ascent
FRFA	First Recorded Free Ascent
(TR)	Top Rope

Generally, the person whose name appears first was the person who led the crux section of the climb. I've also included nationality if known.

Directions (left, right, et cetera) are assuming you are facing the cliff.

Routes at The Trapps and Sky Top are described from left to right. At The Near Trapps, routes are described from right to left, following the natural access to the area. Millbrook is approached by a centrally located rappel, and the two halves of the cliff are treated separately, first the right side (left to right), then the left side (right to left).

V1, **V2** refer to variations to the standard line, and are noted in the text where the variation route begins. Where possible, I have given credit to the variation first ascent party.

P1, **P2**, etc. refer to pitches.

A check list of routes is provided at the back of the book, where climbs are arranged by rating.

This is, after all, only a guide, and some of what appears in this book may not be fully accurate. In order to make future editions of this book more accurate, I encourage all to send any corrections, comments, and new route information to me care of the publisher, Chockstone Press, PO Box 3505; Evergreen, CO 80439.

Equipment

With the advent of Friends, RP Nuts, Tri-Cams, and Three Cam Units (TCUs), protection at the Gunks is generally very good. Racks at the Gunks tend to be smaller than at other areas (like Devils Tower, Yosemite), with a set of Friends, TCUs, RPs, and small stoppers fitting most routes. Extra carabiners, quickdraws and full-length runners round out the rack. In the text I have tried to note routes that may require "specialty gear." While a single 10.5 or 11mm rope will suffice, many climbers use double 9mm ropes to reduce rope drag through overhanging sections.

As a general rule, the fixed protection at the Gunks should be considered suspect until proven otherwise. Many fixed pins have been pulled out by hand. Check all rappel stations and webbing—many have been there for years without being replaced.

Should you choose to rappel from ledges and the top of climbs, always check to make sure people are not below you. There have been many near accidents due to rocks and ropes hitting those below.

Accidents and Rescues

If a ranger is not available, a first aid cache is located at the Uberfall at The Trapps, and is stocked with litters, backboards, and basic first aid equipment. In case of accident or fire, the nearest telephone is located at the intersection of Routes 44-55 and 299 (by the store and restaurant). Call 255-1323 (New Paltz Emergency Communications Center) or 255-1000 (Mohonk Mountain House). Both numbers are manned 24 hours.

The nearest hospitals are in Poughkeepsie (Vassar Brothers and St. Francis hospitals) and Kingston (Kingston and Benedictine).

Rainy Day Routes

Short of a torrential and continuous downpour, the following routes are usually dry:

The Trapps

No Man's Land	The Sting
Tiers for Fears	Lisa and variations P1
Yellow Wall	Counter Strike P1
Carbs and Caffeine	Sudden Death P1
Airy Area P1	Trigger Point and variations
Uphill All the Way P1	

The Near Trapps

Easy Rider	Le Plié P1
Outer Space P1	

Millbrook and Sky Top

None, although both dry out quickly once it stops raining.

Other things to do when it rains:

Movies in New Paltz, Rosendale, Kingston and Poughkeepsie.

Library in New Paltz.

At present there are two indoor climbing walls in New Paltz. Check at Rock and Snow for locations and hours.

There are three National Park Service historic sites in Hyde Park just north of Poughkeepsie including Franklin Delano Roosevelt's home, Vanderbuilt Mansion and Eleanor Roosevelt National Historic Site.

West Point is approximately 45 minutes south along the Hudson River and well worth a visit.

Trivia Page

As with the last two *Gunks Guides*, I have included a number of trivia questions concerning Gunks climbing history. Trying to correctly answer each question should help pass at least one rainy day. Good searching! Answers on page 387.

1) *The Lord of the Rings* trilogy including *The Hobbit* were very popular in the 1970s. Can you name the 12 Gunks routes or variations that pertain to Tolkien's world?

2) How many climbing guidebooks and supplements have been commercially produced for the Gunks? (This doesn't include photocopy type supplements such as Dave Ingalls' [1962] or Joe Kelsey's [1966].)

3) At least 13 Gunks first ascentionists have written commercially available guidebooks. Can you name the authors, and what areas they wrote guidebook(s) for?

4) Gary Brown's best FFA effort was probably his lead of **New Frontier** at Millbrook. On what other Gunks FFAs did he take part?

5) Herb Laeger, an active first ascentionist since the sixties, used to live on the East Coast. Where did he live, and what Gunks FAs did he do?

6) At least fourteen Mohonk Preserve Rangers have participated in Gunks first ascents. Can you name the rangers?

7) At least seven foreign countries have had residents do first ascents at the Gunks. What countries are represented?

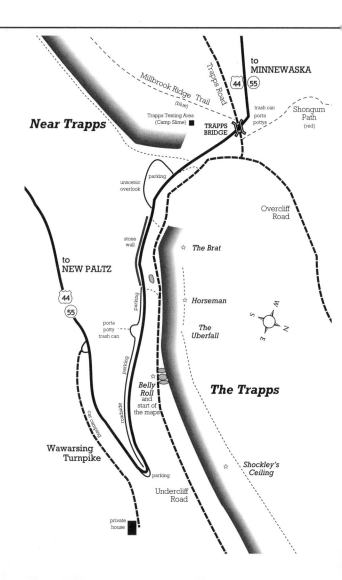

to
MINNEWASKA

Millbrook Ridge Trail
(blue)

Trapps Road

44 55

Near Trapps

Trapps Tenting Area
(Camp Slime) ■

TRAPPS
BRIDGE

trash can
porta
pottys

Shongum
Path
(red)

parking

unscenic
overlook

Overcliff
Road

stone
wall

☆ The Brat

parking

to
NEW PALTZ

44
55

☆ Horseman

The
Uberfall

W
N S
E

porta
potty
trash can

parking

The Trapps

roadside

☆ Belly
Roll
and
start of
the maps

car camping

Wawarsing
Turnpike

☆ Shockley's
Ceiling

parking

Undercliff
Road

private
house ■

The Trapps

The Trapps cliff is by far the most popular cliff for climbing in the Gunks. Ranging in height from 30-200 feet and extending nearly 1.5 miles, it hosts over 600 routes and variations from 5.0-5.13. It is believed the word Trapps comes from the Dutch *treppen*, meaning stairs. Slightly more than halfway up the cliff is the Grand Traverse Ledge (GT ledge). This ledge system—with minor breaks—traverses the cliff from **Easy Overhang** (**Easy O**) to **Emilietta**. Undercliff Carriage Road runs below the cliff, with marked trails leading up to the crag itself. Please stay on the marked trails (shown in the maps of the cliff base and marked with yellow blazes).

There are four marked access trails from Route 44-55 to Undercliff Road between Trapps Bridge (the steel bridge over Route 44-55) and the Hairpin Turn. All are clearly signed and marked with yellow blazes. At present, parking is only allowed on the downhill lane side of Route 44-55 between Trapps Bridge and the Hairpin Turn. Below the Hairpin Turn and south of Trapps Bridge (over the crest of the ridge), cars may park on both sides of the road, but they must be completely inside the white line, or they will be ticketed and/or towed. This arrangement may change soon, with parking banned altogether on Route 44-55. Users will then need to park in the designated parking lots, such as the one just beyond Trapps Bridge.

The Uberfall is the gathering place of the Gunks. If you are looking for a partner, ranger, information, potable water, or first aid equipment, it's the place to go. A well-worn trail leading up to the Uberfall from Route 44-55 will be found about halfway between the Hairpin Turn and Trapps Bridge (see map). The times given on the approach topos assume a steady, moderate pace from the Uberfall.

Running along the summit of the Trapps is the Top O' The Trapps Trail. When finishing a climb, simply follow the trail in either direction to the nearest descent route. For climbs left of **Dirty Gerdie**, descend down the south (**Brat**) end of the cliff. The **Uberfall Descent** is normally used for climbs right of **Dirty Gerdie** and left of **High Exposure**. For climbs between **High Exposure** and **Simple Suff** the usual descent is **Silly Chimney**. **Roger's Escape Hatch** is used for climbs right of **Simple Suff**. In addition, numerous rappel routes are marked on the cliff photos.

Finally, various sections of the cliff are named (i.e.: McCarthy Wall, The Yellow Wall, Sleepy Hollow, etc.). When thumbing through the guide, look for the section names and overhead map to find your location.

1   The Great Wall of China 5.9 R
FA: Ken Nichols, Dave Rosenstein, May, 1987
This complete girdle traverse of The Trapps stays below the GT ledge, has 67 pitches, and is about 9,000 feet long. It may be the longest rock climb in the world. Other girdles of The Trapps have been done, but have always involved the GT ledge (traversing this is a good winter outing). Since the description is eight double-spaced, typewritten, 8x11 pages, I'm leaving it out. The two crux sections are across **Retribution–Nosedive**, and in **The Yellow Wall** area. A scary section will be encountered crossing the High Exposure Buttress. Have fun.

2   Short and Simple 5.7+ G
FA: Todd Swain, Judy Paddon (Can), June, 1981
Start at the south (left) end of the cliff at a blocky arête. Climb the easy arête to a ledge, then up a short, steep crack (crux) to the summit.

3   Birthday Biscuit Boy 5.9 G
FA: Harvey Arnold, Kevin Bein, June, 1979
Done on Arnold's birthday. On top of a boulder pile 50 feet from the left end of the cliff are two short right-leaning cracks. Climb the right one.

4   Keyhole 5.7 PG
FA: Doug Kerr, 1951
Slither up the 4" crack to the alcove (crux, V1), then up and right the top.

V1 For a harder start, climb the cracks to the left; 5.9.

5   Katzenjammer 5.7 PG
FA: Jim McCarthy, Jack Hansen, 1958
Not for kids. Romp up the left side of the white and yellow **Brat** face (V1) along thin cracks and a short flake.

V1 5.11+ FA John Gill, 1969. Start to the left and climb the very difficult crack and face to join the regular route at mid-height. Gill also did a very difficult problem out the center of the overhanging, egg-shaped boulder near the start of **Short and Simple**. This boulder is known as the Gill Egg.

6   Little Rascals 5.9– PG ★
FA: Unknown, circa 1960
Sneak straight up the middle of the face between **The Brat** and **Katzenjammer**. Good face climbing.

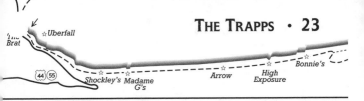

The Brat

☆Uberfall

44 55   ☆Shockley's   ☆Madame G's   ☆Arrow   ☆High Exposure   ☆Bonnie's

2	Short and Simple 5.7+	8	Handy Andy 5.7
5	Katzenjammer 5.7	9	Easy Keyhole 5.2
7	The Brat 5.7	11	Black Fly 5.5

7 The Brat 5.7 PG ★★

FA: Bonnie Prudden and partner, 1946

A popular face climb that is often top-roped (as can all of the climbs in this neighborhood). Near the right edge of the white and yellow face is a vertical crack in black rock. Climb the crack (5.7, V1) to the slab above. Whine your way past a blast hole (5.6; this was once filled with cement), then traverse left under the headwall to a vertical crack, and up this to the top.

V1 An easier start can be done, by wandering up left, then back right above the black crack; 5.6.

8   Handy Andy 5.7 PG
FA: Jim and Louise Andress, 1956. FFA: Gerry Bloch, 1956
In 1987 Gerry Bloch became the oldest person to date to climb The Nose on El Capitan in Yosemite Valley. Just around the corner to the right of the **Brat** face is another, smaller, white face. Starting at a thin vertical crack on the right edge of the face (V1,2), climb up five feet, then traverse left above an overhang (V3,4) to the arête. Follow a hidden crack to the top.

V1 5.10+ FA: Dick Williams, 1964. Begin under a ceiling halfway between the starts of **The Brat** and **Handy Andy**. Climb past the ceiling to black rock, then move up and right to join the regular route.

V2 5.10 FA: Steve Larsen, 1964. Begin about eight feet left of the normal **Handy Andy** start and climb up the face just left of a thin seam to join the regular route on the traverse line.

V3 Climb straight up from midway along the traverse; 5.8.

V4 Climb up and right from the start of the traverse to a large horizontal. Escape left (5.9), or persevere straight up (5.10).

9   Easy Keyhole 5.2 G
FA: Hans Kraus, Bonnie Prudden, 1950
Popular, and easy after the first 15 feet. Struggle up the wide crack in a corner just uphill from the carriage road and **Handy Andy**. Most people climb only P1, but P2 climbs behind the pinnacle, while P3 moves left from its top, and up a short dihedral to the summit.

10   Astro Traveler 5.10+ G
FA: Unknown FFA: Ron Matous, circa 1975
Ron worked as a Mohonk Preserve ranger in the 1970s, and is now a climbing guide in the Tetons. A short but sweet crack climb above **Easy Keyhole** and **Black Fly**. Approach by scrambling up ledges right of **Black Fly** or from above and then launch up the overhanging crack. 2.5 Friend and RPs needed.

11   Black Fly 5.5 G
FA: Gardiner and Mary Perry, Carol Mahen, 1958
Starting just right of **Easy Keyhole**, wander up the face left of an obvious crack (V1) to a large pine tree above an overhang. Most people rappel from the tree, but another 100 feet of easy climbing will put you on top.

V1 Climb directly up the nice crack; 5.5.

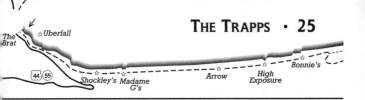

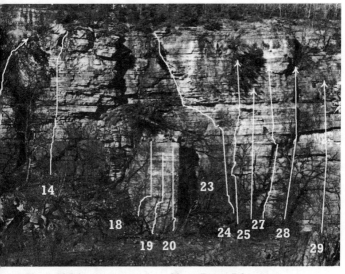

13	69 5.3	24	Bunny 5.4
14	No Picnic 5.4+	25	Retribution 5.10
18	Herdie Gerdie 5.6+	27	Nosedive 5.10
19	Dirty Gerdie 5.8+	28	Double Chin 5.5
20	Nurdie Gerdie 5.10+	29	Something Scary 5.10
23	Fancy Idiot 5.6		

12 Short Job 5.4 G

FA: Willie Crowther, Gardiner Perry, 1958

About 125 feet right of **Black Fly** is a right-facing corner that is fairly clean. Up right into the corner, then exit left (crux) at the top to a belay. P2 walks a bit right, then climbs a ramp up and left, exiting right. P3 ascends a thin crack, then angles right to the woods.

13 69 5.3 G

FA: Dick and Marilyn DuMais, 1969

Crawl up a short slab 20 feet right of **Short Job**, left around a nose, back right around an overhang, then up a face to the ledge (see route name for history of ledge). Scramble to the woods.

14 No Picnic 5.4+ PG
FA: Willie Crowther, Gardiner Perry, 1958
Starting 55 feet right of **Short Job**, climb a slab and white left-facing corner to overhangs. Continue straight on through the hangs to a pine tree and the summit.

15 Shit or Go Blind 5.8+ PG
FA: Steve and Corey Jones, 1976
Dirty. Most of the route was climbed in 1974 by Joe Ponte and Ivan Rezucha. Climb ten feet right of **No Picnic** past two overhangs, the second one passed on the right at a block, then up to a belay. Climb an overhang at an arête, then up the face to the top.

16 Sudoriferous 5.2 G
FA: John D'Arcy, Bruce Miller, Rich Kast, 1975
This obscure route climbs the left-facing corner that is the left side of the large, detached block (the **Dirty Gerdie** block). Ascend the large corner, then climb a dihedral on the right for 25 feet. Angle left under a tree and roof to the top.

17 Heel, Hook, and Hack-it 5.10– R/X
FRA: Michael Emelianoof, Brian Anderson, Jerry Grupo, 1987
Begin this extravaganza atop the **Dirty Gerdie** block at the highest tree on the ledge. Pull past a low overhang (scary) then up the face to the top.

18 Herdie Gerdie 5.6+ PG
FA: Dick Williams, Dick DuMais, 1965
On the left front of the large, detached block just above the carriage road, climb the right-leaning crack (crux at top of crack), then straight up the face to the top. This and the next two climbs are very popular to top-rope or lead.

19 Dirty Gerdie 5.8+ PG ★
FA: Thom Scheuer, Jim Andress, Fall, 1963. FFA: Thom Scheuer, 1964
Saunter up the center of the block past many horizontals to the top. Crux at about 15 feet.

20 Nurdie Gerdie (aka Dogs In Heat) 5.10+ PG
FRA: Rich Ross, 1975
Crank up the thin vertical crack on the right edge of the block, avoiding the arête (using the edge makes it about 5.9). Often top-roped, as it was by Ross before being led.

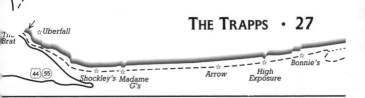

21	Red Cabbage 5.9–	33	Doug's Roof 5.11+
22	Friday the 13th 5.7+	34v	Lower Eaves 5.9+
30	Eyebrow 5.6	35	Horseman 5.5
31	Double Clutch 5.9+	36	Apoplexy 5.9

21 Red Cabbage 5.9– G ★
FA: Unknown. FFA: Joe Kelsey, Dick DuMais, 1969
A good face route up the overhanging, north facing, red colored, and vertically fractured side of the block.

V1 If you start up the crack on the left edge of the face and then climb directly up the left center of the face, it's solid 5.9.

V2 If you climb the right side of the face, connecting the disjointed cracks, it's 5.10.

22 Friday the 13th 5.7+ R
FRA: Joe Bridges, Faith Aubin, 1983
Climb a crack ten feet right of the **Dirty Gerdie** block to a ledge (5.7). Continue straight up the blank face (scary) to connect with

Fancy Idiot at the belay. Climb the corner for ten feet, traverse right through the roof above (crux), then climb up the face just right of the arête to the top (the face right of the arête had been climbed earlier).

23 Fancy Idiot 5.6 PG

FA: Ann Church, Krist Raubenheimer, 1955

A tricky climb up the green face left of the **Bunny** crack. Climb up the face past a small right-facing flake (crux) to a ledge, move left, then back right to the belay at the base of a huge left-facing corner. Up the corner (5.4) to the top (watch for bees).

24 Bunny 5.4 G ★★★

FA: Ann Church, Krist Raubenheimer, Fall, 1955

The first, first ascent by an all female party in the Gunks. A popular and classic excursion. Starting 25 feet right of the **Dirty Gerdie** block, hop straight up the obvious crack system to a small roof at 40 feet. Move left (V1), then back right above the roof and up to a belay at a huge pine tree. Scramble to the top.

V1 Bunny's Roof 5.6– G FA: Unknown. Climb directly over the roof.

25 Retribution 5.10 G ★★

FA: Art Gran, Peter Himot, 1958. FFA: Jim McCarthy, 1961

The first 5.10 for many people, but a hard move past the roof nonetheless. Ascend the left of two appealing crack systems right of **Bunny** (V1) over a roof at 20 feet (crux), then up the crack and steep face to the summit.

V1 Retro-rabbit 5.10 PG FRFA: Jim Thompson, circa 1975. Climb the face and arête just left of **Retribution**. Bring extra #0 TCUs to supplement the bad fixed pins. Scary towards the top.

26 No Solution (aka Retro-dive) 5.12– X

FA: (TR) Kevin Bein, late 1970s. FA: (lead) Sebastian Scherwertner (German), August, 1988

Originally tried by Stannard on the lead, he made it over the first ceiling, then got scared and traversed off. Bein later top-roped the route. Top-roped and gear placed on rappel before its first complete lead. Climb the face between **Retribution** and **Nosedive**.

27 Nosedive 5.10 G ★★★

FA: Ted Church, Krist Raubenheimer, 1956. FFA: Jim McCarthy, 1961

Easier than its sister climb **Retribution**, but not to be taken lightly.

Many people have taken "the dive". Climb up the left-facing corner, and the crack system above past a bulge (crux, V1) to the trees.

V1 Many people climb the face just right of the crack to the bulge.

28 Double Chin 5.5 G
FA: Norton Smithe, Doug Kerr, 1954
In the early 1950s, Smithe made the first angle pitons used in the Gunks. Some of these soft iron relics are still on climbs today. Climb up the large right-facing corner system ten feet right of **Nosedive** past trees, and two roofs, to the top.

29 Something Scary 5.10 PG
FA: Hardie Truesdale, Chris Monz, 1979
Monz worked as a Mohonk Preserve Ranger in the mid-1980s. At the left edge of the large ceiling over the carriage road, climb a short crack then wade up the dirty face, following thin seams to the large roofs above. Swing over the lower hang, then over the upper ceiling, ten feet left of the pointed block on **Double Clutch** (crux). Continue on to the trail, or rappel.

30 Eyebrow 5.6 PG
FA: Gary Hemming, Claude Suhl, 1959
Hemming was involved in first ascents of many now-classic routes in the Alps. Start as for the previous climb, then diagonal up right, crossing **Double Clutch** ten feet below the pointed second hang. Over the roof just right at a thin vertical crack (5.5), then on upwards from there.

NOTE: Across the carriage road from the cliff is a large boulder known as the Mental Block. At least nine routes have been done on it, the most famous of which is **Stupid Crack** 5.12– PG13, the hardest looking crack on the downhill side.

31 Double Clutch 5.9+ G
FA: Dick Williams, John Hudson, Pete Geiser, 1964
Very height related—if you are short, it's hard! Start as for the last two climbs, but hand traverse right under the roof over the carriage road, and through the roof at the first break (crux). Continue up to the next roof, and over this right of the pointed block (5.9). The first crux is a popular top-rope problem. The famous boulderer, John Gill, did several very difficult problems under the roof between **Double Clutch** and **Doug's Roof**.

Uberfall Area

33	**Doug's Roof 5.11+**	46	**Shitty Mitty 5.11**
35	**Horseman 5.5**	47	**Mitty Mouse 5.8+**
39	**Dirty Chimney 5.0+**	49	**Low Exposure 5.11–**
43	**Rhododendron 5.6–**		

32 Ralph's Climb 5.8 A3

FA: Ralph Worstfold, 1964

A little known aid route out the largest part of the ceiling between **Double Clutch** and the obvious crack of **Doug's Roof**. Above, go to a pine tree, then climb the face and a thin crack, keeping right of **Eyebrow**.

33 Doug's Roof 5.11+ G

FA: Doug Kerr, Stan Gross, 1954. FFA: Bob Jahn, 1972

Even more height-related than **Double Clutch**. Dean Giftos was the first to reach the holds at the lip, Jahn the first to be able to hang on to them! At the left end of the Uberfall area, swing over the big over-hang at a thin crack. Either rappel off at a pine tree above the roof, or bushwhack straight up the face to the summit.

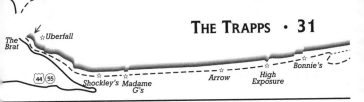

The Brat
Uberfall
44 55
Shockley's Madame G's
Arrow
High Exposure
Bonnie's

34 The Bridle Path 5.7+ PG

FRA: Joe Bridges, Dick Williams, May, 1988

Climb the first 30 feet of **Horseman** (V1-3), then traverse out left along a horizontal that is just above the giant roof to the front face. Climb the face and arête until just below the hanging belay on **Horseman**, then angle up left. Follow a left-facing, left-curving corner, then climb straight up to the trees.

V1 Lower Eaves 5.9+ G FA: Unknown Canadians, 1960s. Climb out left along the lip of the lowest roof (crux, old pins), then up the very grassy face to connect at the traverse.

V2 Upper Eaves 5.8 R FA: Unknown, circa 1960s. Climb above **Lower Eaves** to the giant roof then angle up and left to the nose. Climb the grassy face above as for **Lower Eaves** to connect with **The Bridal Path**.

V3 Upper Upper Eaves 5.9 PG FA: Ivan Rezucha, Keith LaBudde March, 1992. Start at the stance after traversing around the nose on **Upper Eaves**. Move left about eight feet then climb straight up to the top staying between **Eyebrow** and **The Bridal Path**.

35 Horseman 5.5 G ★★★

FA: Hans Kraus, Fritz Wiessner, 1941

A classic Gunks climb. Named for a horseman who rode by during the FA and shouted "It looks hard" or, "Is this the way to Minnewaska?" (or something like that). Gallop up the huge right-facing corner at the right edge of the low roofs above the carriage road. At mid-height and 15 feet below the ceiling (V1), move out left (possible belay here), then straight up the face to the bushes (150 feet).

V1 Climb directly up the corner/ceiling instead of traversing left; 5.5.

36 Apoplexy 5.9 PG

FA: Jim McCarthy, 1960

A little sandy, but a good face climb. Scramble straight up the face ten feet right of **Horseman**, passing a loose flake at 40 feet (scary 5.8), then up and over an overhang (crux) into the left chimney. Follow this to the top.

37 Coronary 5.10– R

FA: Jim Kolocotronis, 1973

Turn your pacemaker up a notch for this one. Climb the thin vertical seam 15 feet right of **Horseman** (crux) to the blank face (scary). Continue up the right-facing corner above.

Uberfall Area

---

38 Pony Express 5.6 PG
FA: Ted Church, Krist Raubenheimer, 1957
Starting at the base of **Coronary**, climb up, then left to the middle of the **Horseman** corner. Diagonal back right crossing **Apoplexy** (crux) to a belay on a ledge at a pine tree. Finish as for **Coronary** up the corner.

39 Dirty Chimney 5.0+ G
FA: Krist Raubenheimer, 1957
The right-leaning chimney/corner system 20 feet right of **Horseman**. Good access to set up top-ropes for **Laurel** and **Rhododendron**.

40 Junior 5.9+ PG
FA: Bob Gilmore, pre-1964
A popular boulder problem, not to be taken lightly. Climb the steep, white face just left of **Laurel**.

41 Laurel 5.7+ G ★
FA: Thornton Read, Norton Smithe, Lester Germer, circa 1950
The most often done 5.7 in the Gunks. After you succeed, don't rest on your laurels! Climb the obvious crack 30 feet right of **Horseman** to the large tree at 50 feet. Most people rappel from here.

NOTE: A Mohonk Preserve Ranger can usually be found near here on weekends during the climbing season to obtain passes and information.

42 Clover 5.7+ PG
FA: Paul Rubin, Marc Cassler, 1974
Top-roped then led. The initial climbing was done previously. Climb a flake between **Laurel** and **Rhododendron** to the ledge (5.7), then up past a difficult bulge (crux) to the top.

43 Rhododendron 5.6– G ★
FA: Unknown, 1950s
Scamper up the vertical crack right of **Laurel** to the tree. Rappel.

44 Birch (aka Streats of Fength) 5.10+ X
FA: (TR) Kevin Bein, 1970s. FA: (lead) Russ Clune, Jeff Gruenberg, 1983
A long-standing top-rope problem that was finally led. Waltz up the steep face just right of **Rhododendron**.

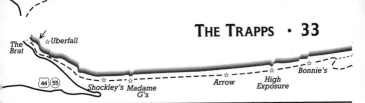

45 Das Wiggles 5.3 PG
FA: Hans Kraus, Dick Hirschland, 1946
Wiggle up the chimney facing left, just uphill from the **Low Exposure** roof.

46 Shitty Mitty 5.11 PG
FA: (TR) Unknown, 1973 FA: (lead) George Willig , Jim Thompson, 1973
Previously top-roped by other parties before Willig did the first lead. May be a bit easier if you're tall. Starting at a short hand crack, climb the overhanging green wall right of **Das Wiggles** past a bulge (crux) to the top.

47 Mitty Mouse 5.8+ PG
FA: Todd Swain, Ivan Rezucha, November, 1984
Climb up the hand crack as for **Shitty Mitty**, hand traverse out right onto the arête (crux), then up that to the summit. Small wires needed.

48 Walter Mitty 5.8+ PG
FA: Steve Larsen, Dick Williams, Fall, 1963
A worthwhile face climb. Starting at the **Shitty Mitty** hand crack, angle up right (avoiding the chimney), then up the steep face facing the carriage road. Crux at mid-height.

49 Low Exposure 5.11– G
FA: John Stannard, 1969
Seldom done with grace. Struggle out the roof via an obvious, flaring crack, then up the face above.

NOTE: Under the roof are a number of popular boulder problems above what used to be the frog pond.

50 Jiggles 5.1 G
FA: Unknown, 1950s
15 feet left of the spring at the **Uberfall** and just right of **Low Exposure** is a dirty dihedral with a tree at the top. Numerous boulder problems are on either side.

51 Squiggles 5.4– PG
FA: Peter Himot, Bill Meyer, 1959
A popular climb to lead or top-rope. Start as for **Jiggles** (V1, 2),

Uberfall Area

The Uberfall area, Trapps cliff

then follow a ramp out right around the roof. Straight up the easier face above.

V1 Squiggles Direct 5.10 R FA: Dick Williams, John Hudson, 1963. FFA: Dick Williams, 1963. Layback the vertical seam just right of the spring. This is usually top-roped.

V2 Squiggles Redirect 5.11 R FA: Unknown, 1960s Climb the face five feet right of the vertical seam on **Squiggles Direct**.

52 Dislocation 5.9 R
FA: Jim Thompson, 1973
An eliminate climb crossing **Squiggles**. Thompson dislocated his shoulder on the first ascent. Up the bulge just right of **Squiggles**, then up the arête on the left past the roof. Usually top-roped.

53 Jacob's Ladder 5.10 R
FA: Phil Jacobus, 1960
A popular top-rope up the face directly above the spring. At the

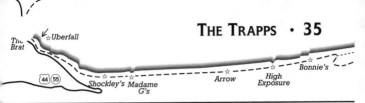

time of the first ascent, a small tree afforded some protection, and the crux section had a bigger hold. Climb out left on a ramp (crux, V1,2), then up the easier rock to the woods.

V1 No Pro 5.8 R FRA: Todd Swain, Andy Schenkel, May, 1984. Plod straight up the face from the start of **Jacob's Ladder** to connect with a very shallow corner near the top.

V2 Devine Wind 5.12- (TR) FA: Barbara Devine, 1985. Begin at the lowest section of the face and climb straight up the face, finishing just left of the **Jacob's Ladder** ramp.

54 Greasy Kid Stuff 5.5 G
FA: Unknown, 1950s
Climb the mungy corner at the right edge of the **Jacob's Ladder** face.

55 Crowberry Ridge 5.6 PG
FA: Todd Swain (solo), July, 1981
Climb directly up the clean arête to the left of the **Uberfall Descent Route**. Worthwhile.

56 Uberfall Descent Route
At least three different ways up or down are collectively known as the **Uberfall** (to fall across). The original **Uberfall Descent** went across to the top of the **Susie A** block, then down the chimney behind.

57 Trashcan Overhang 5.11– PG
FA: John Hudson (top-roped, possibly led), 1963. FFA: (definite lead) Pete Livesy (UK), August, 1978.
Also known as Hudson's Boulder Problem, this large overhang lies 50 feet right of **Jiggles** and just to the right of the broken area used for descent. Layback and undercling up the vertical flakes to the roof (V1, 2), then Tarzan to the lip. At least the first aid equipment is handy if you blow it!

V1 Trashcan Direct 5.12 (TR) FA: Dick Cilley, 1978. Start on the boulder to the right and climb out left through the blankest part of the roof.

V2 Garbage Can Overhang 5.10+ FA: Steve Wunsch, 1973. Start on the boulder just to the right and climb out the right side of the overhang.

Uberfall Area

58 Susie A 5.11– R
FA: Roddey Miller, Jim Andress, 1958. FFA, P1: Ants Leemets, circa 1965. FFA, P2: Rich Romano, July, 1975.
Boulder up the yellow, front side of the detached block at the right end of the **Trashcan** roof (5.10+), then climb a thin, angling crack on the main cliff to the top.

59 The Flake 5.1 PG
FA: Unknown, pre-1964
The obvious left pointing, vertical flake, left of a beautiful finger crack.

60 Ken's Crack 5.7 G ★★
FA: Ken Prestrud, Lucien Warner, 1951
Why can't this crack be two pitches long? Cruise up the obvious, right-leaning finger crack to the trees.

V1 The faces just left and right have been top-roped.

61 Phoebe 5.10 + R
FA: Dick Williams, 1963 (top-roped then led).
Climb the face ten feet right of **Ken's Crack** (V1) past a bolt and a small hang to the top.

V1 Freebie 5.11 (TR) FA: Mike Freeman, 1978. Climb the face just right of **Phoebe**.

62 Boston 5.4+ PG
FA: Dick Hirschland, Bonnie Prudden, 1950
Named for a portion of Bonnie Prudden's anatomy, while describing the relative locations of Portland and New York with her knees. Snake up the all-too-obvious chimney/offwidth 20 feet right of **Ken's Crack**.

63 Fitschen's Folly 5.7+ X
FA: Joe Fitschen, 1961
Fitschen is still climbing, and has at least one other route named for him in Yosemite. On this route, his belayer refused to follow! Dance up the face ten feet right of **Boston** (V1), staying out of the corner on the right. Once you reach the flake up high, you're probably safe. Usually top-roped.

V1 Charie 5.10- R FA (TR): Dave Craft, 1963 FA (lead): Unknown, 1960s. An eliminate line up the face just right of **Boston**. Usually top-roped.

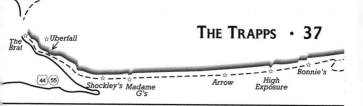

The Brat ☆ ☆ Uberfall

44 55 · Shockley's · Madame G's · Arrow · High Exposure · Bonnie's

64 Alphabet Arête (AA) 5.10+ PG
FA: (TR) Todd Swain, Bob Hostetter, August, 1986. FA: (lead) Todd Swain, Dave Levenstein, Bob Hostetter, September, 1986
Easier if tall. Angle left above a ceiling to the arête left of **DD Route** past one fixed peg (crux above peg).

65 DD Route 5.10 R
FA: Unknown, 1970s
Up the steep face left of **CC Route** following a thin crack. There are two ways to climb the crux—both are usually top-roped.

66 CC Route 5.7– PG
FA: John Turner, Al Alvarez, 1955
CC stands for the Climbers Club, of which Briton John Turner was a member. Up the left-facing corner 25 feet right of **Boston** to an overhang, then exit out left. The beam on top was used for belay tests by the Appalachian Mountain Club (AMC).

67 BB Route 5.8 G
FA: Unknown, 1960s
Better than it looks. Follow the crack right of **CC Route** up to the large roof, then exit out right to salvation.

68 The Star Route 5.4 G
FA: Unknown, pre-1964
Start up the crack as for the **BB**, then at 20 feet, escape out right around the nose, and up a short crack to the bushes.

69 Crimson Corner 5.0 G
FA: Unknown, circa 1950
Originally named Meshugina Ek. Climb the low-angled, rounded arête left of **Yale** to the top.

70 Yale 5.3 PG
FA: Unknown, pre-1964
Continue along the carriage road past a lower-angled broken area to a point where the cliff rears up again. From the top of boulders 20 feet left of **Harvard**, climb up the left edge of the face.

71 Eyesore 5.6+ G
FA: Unknown, pre-1964
Climb a vertical crack system up the wall just left of the **Harvard** chimney. This can be split into two pitches.

Uberfall Area

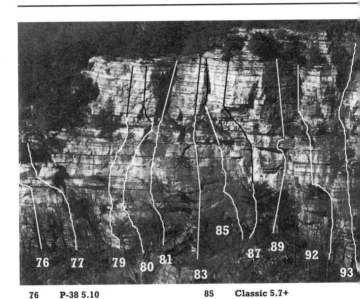

76	P-38 5.10	85	Classic 5.7+
77	Radcliffe Class 4	87	Pink Laurel 5.8+
79	Dennis 5.5	89	Ape Call 5.8
80	Belly Roll 5.4	92	RMC 5.5
81	Roddey 5.2	93	Raubenheimer Special 5.6+
83	Jackie 5.5		

72 Harvard 5.3 G

FA: George Evans, Robert Graef, 1953

Start 100 feet right of **Boston** and 30 feet right of a low angled, broken area. Climb the steep face below a chimney (crux) to reach a ledge. Either continue up the chimney, or tunnel through to Radcliffe.

73 Trapped Like a Rat 5.7 G

FA: Unknown, 1974 or earlier

Struggle up the short dihedral right of **Harvard** to the ledge (5.7). Step right, climb onto the arête, and follow weaknesses (5.7) through the overhangs to the conclusion.

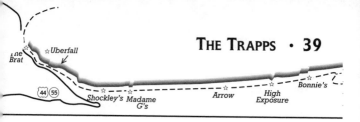
74 Silly Dickin' 5.12– PG

FA: (TR) Dick Cilley, 1978. FA: (lead) Hugh Herr, December, 1981
A short testpiece. Romp up the shallow, left arching corner on the arête right of **Harvard**. Usually top-roped.

75 Stirrup Trouble 5.10 PG ★★★

FA: Bill Goldner, 1960s. FFA: John Stannard, 1973
Legend has it Goldner did stir up trouble when he aided this line. It supposedly was being saved for a free ascent! From the top of a block 25 feet right of **Harvard**, climb a shallow groove (V1, 2) to a horizontal. Traverse left and up to a roof. Move left around the overhang, up a corner, then climb past another roof to the top. Sustained.

V1 The Mohel 5.12 (TR) FA: Russ Clune, Jeff Gruenberg, 1985. A real tip eater. Climb the blank, white face left of **Stirrup Trouble**. It may help to be tall.

V2 5.11 G FA: Jeff Gruenberg, 1984. Climb the short, thin crack just left of the start.

76 P-38 (aka Shady Lady) 5.10 G ★★

FA: Dave Craft, Jim Andress, 1962. FFA: Dick Williams, 1964
The first ascent party supposedly used 38 pins for aid. A key hold has broken off, making this a bit harder. Fifteen feet right of **Stirrup Trouble** is a left-angling crack. Up the crack, then left ten feet (V1) and up to the top.

V1 Climb straight up over the bulge above the first crack; 5.9+ R.

77 Radcliffe Class 4

FFA: pre-1964
Twenty feet right of **P-38** is a hidden crack/gully leading up left. Useful for descent.

78 Badcliffe 5.10 PG

FRA: Todd Swain, Patty Lanzetta, October, 1981
Follow the thin vertical seam just right of **Radcliffe** (V1) to the easier face above.

V1 If you start on the blocks and traverse out, or use the large tree, the climb is easier.

Uberfall Area

79 Dennis 5.5 G ★★

FA: Gardiner and Mary Perry, Ann Buffin, 1960

A good introduction to a 5.5 roof. **Dennis** is located behind the left edge of two huge boulders touching the carriage road and 30 feet right of **P-38** at a nose. Ascend the menacing roof right off the ground (crux), then up left to a ledge. Continue to the GT ledge (85 feet). The next pitch climbs around a pointed ceiling to a corner and the summit.

80 Belly Roll 5.4 PG

FA: Doug Kerr, Norton Smithe, 1955

The name says it all. Roll into the obvious left leaning crack/chimney right of **Dennis** (V1), then up to a ledge. Climb the left-facing corner (crux) to the GT ledge (70 feet). Move up and around right of a roof, then up an easy groove to finish.

V1 It is possible to tunnel inside the **Belly Roll** chimney and exit out a different way.

81 Roddey 5.2 PG

FA: Roddey Miller, Jim Andress 1958

Starting 15 feet right of **Belly Roll**, climb up a corner to the left

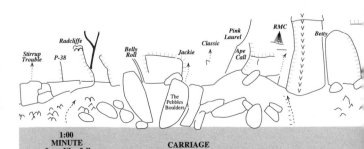

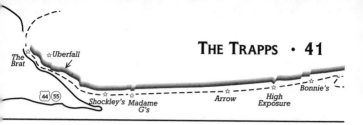

The Brat
☆ Uberfall

44 55 Shockley's Madame G's Arrow High Exposure Bonnie's

edge of the huge roof (5.2, V1, 2), then left around roof, and up the trough to the GT ledge. Climb the easy corner above.

V1 Slightly Roddey 5.10 R FA: Marguerite Baumann, Bill Kemsley, Bill Goldner, 1959. FFA: Kevin Bein, 1969. A hold has broken since the FFA, making the climb harder. Muscle out the enormous roof just right of **Roddey**'s start. Usually top-roped.

V2 The roof just left of **Slightly Roddey**, is 5.11+ and was first toproped by Kevin Bein in 1978.

NOTE: The boulders on the carriage road below the previous climbs are home to a host of popular boulder problems. There are also worthwhile top-rope routes on the right boulder (Pebbles).

82 Daydream 5.8 PG

FRA: Rich Ross, Mike Robin, 1985

Climb to the top of large blocks under the right edge of the **Slightly Roddey** roof. Pull the roof just left of **Jackie** (contrived crux), then angle left (V1) under a bulge to a left-facing corner. Follow the corner to the GT ledge.

V1 Climb straight over the bulge, then up along a thin crack; 5.7+ R.

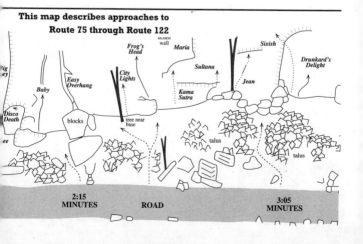

This map describes approaches to
Route 75 through Route 122

bench wall Maria Sixish
Frog's Head
City Lights Sultana Drunkard's Delight
Easy Overhang Jean
Baby Kama Sutra
Disco Death blocks tree near base
talus talus

2:15 MINUTES ROAD 3:05 MINUTES

Uberfall Area

83 Jackie 5.5 G ★★★
FA: Jack Taylor, Lester Germer, 1952
Climb the face just right of the **Slightly Roddey** overhang to a thin
vertical crack. Follow the crack past a couple of roofs (cruxes), to
the GT ledge. Climb left to a corner and the end of a great climb.

84 Jasmine 5.9+ PG
FA: Ivan Rezucha, Annie O'Neill, 1984
Climb straight up the face between **Jackie** and **Classic**, passing a
roof at its right tip. Continue up to the GT ledge (5.8). From the
ledge, move up right to a vertical seam. Up the seam (contrived
crux) to finish.

85 Classic 5.7+ G ★★
FA: Mike Borghoff, Brownell Bergen, 1960
Be careful on the opening moves! Finesse up a thin crack five feet
left of **Pink Laurel**, then move up and left, following weaknesses
past a notch in the roof and belay. Climb an easy corner (as for
Jackie) to the top.

86 Classy 5.8 PG
FA: Unknown, 1970s
Starting up **Classic** or **Pink Laurel**, climb the left-facing flake/corner

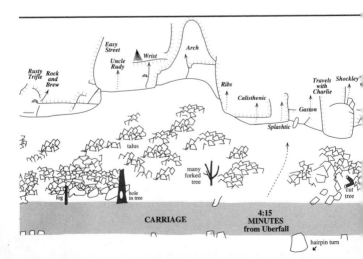

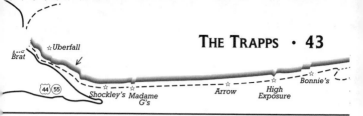

system that is just left of the **Pink Laurel** corner. At the roof, traverse left (crux; #2.5 Friend) and exit over the roof at a finger crack. Rappel, or slog to the summit.

87 Pink Laurel 5.8+ G ★★

FA: Ted and Ann Church, 1955. FA: (final roof) Doug Kerr, 1950s
A popular route. A bit harder since rockfall in 1971. Climb the very obvious left-facing, pink corner 20 feet right of **Jackie** (V1) to a belay under a roof (but on the same ledge as for **Classic**, 5.8+). P2 hand traverses right on a long flake (V2-4), then moves far right to a corner. Up the corner past a roof to an arête and the woods.

V1 Triple Bypass 5.6 PG FA Ivan Rezucha, Annie O'Neill, September, 1990. Using creativity, it's possible to climb this section of cliff at only 5.6. You'll bypass the crux of four routes (**Pink Laurel**, **A-Gape**, **Apecall**, and **RMC**) and end at the **RMC** belay in two pitches.

V2 Above the flake, move left above the roof; 5.7.

V3 Climb directly above the flake. Extremely loose 5.10.

V4 Move right, then back left below a roof; 5.9.

This map describes approaches to Routes 126 to 181

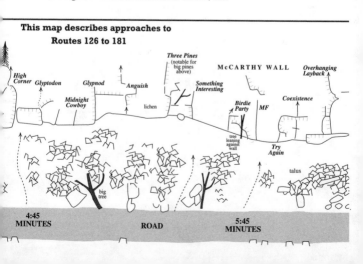

88 A-Gape 5.11 PG

FA: Dave Loeks, Joe Bridges, 1973

No longer 5.10, since the horn broke off on pitch two. Climb a short vertical crack 15 feet left of the **Ape Call** chimney to a bulge. Move right, then follow weaknesses to a ledge and the **Ape Call** belay (5.9). Move out left and over the roofs (crux), then along the arête to end it all.

89 Ape Call 5.8 R ★

FA: Jim McCarthy, Jim Andress, Ants Leemets, Spring, 1962

The second pitch is great. Climb up the face 40 feet right of **Pink Laurel** and left of a flaring chimney (V1) until you can move right (5.8 R) to the left-facing corner/crack. Belay above on a ledge in a left-facing corner. Stem up to the roof, bellow like Tarzan, then swing over on huge jugs to the GT ledge (5.7+). Climb easy rock on the left side of the face to the jungle.

V1 Bumwad 5.9 PG FA: Dick Williams, Dave Craft, 1961. Climb the flaring chimney, then join the regular route.

90 Ape and Essence 5.9+ PG

FA: Jim McCarthy, Laura Brant, 1973

A good alternate first pitch to **Ape Call**. On the arête right of the **Ape Call** chimney, climb a vertical crack, move right (crux), then up

**This map describes approaches to
Routes 181 to 218**

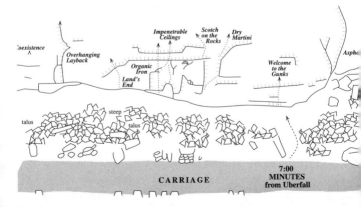

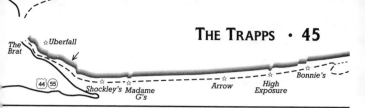

to big holds and the belay. Climb the corner right of the **Ape Call** roof, then up easy rock to the shrubs.

91 Jane 5.8 PG

FA: Jim Kolocotronis, Tom Rosecrans, 1973
Rosecrans wrote the 1976 climbing guidebook to the Adirondacks. Climb the thinning crack just left of the **RMC** chimney. When the crack ends, continue straight up the face (crux). Finish at will.

92 RMC 5.5 G ★

FA: Ralph Clapp, Grant Oakley, 1948
So named for the Rensselaer Mountain Club. Popular. Scramble up a left-facing chimney/corner, 35 feet right of **Ape Call** until it is possible to traverse left to a pine, then up (crux) to the belay ledge. Walk left and finish up the middle of an easy, white face.

93 Raubenheimer Special 5.6+ PG ★

FA: Ted Church, John Lomont, pre-1964
Named after a popular sandwich at what is now the Brauhaus. Ascend the arête 20 feet right of **RMC**, and ten feet left of **Betty** (V1) to easier rock and the GT ledge. Scamper up the broken rock to the top.

V1 5.8+ PG Climb the obvious vertical seam right of the arête on P1.

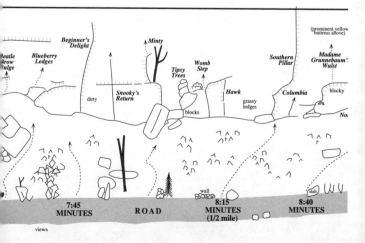

Uberfall Area

94 Betty 5.3– G ★★
FA: Betty Woolsey, Fritz Wiessner, 1941
This route involves all types of climbing, making it many people's
first real rock climb. Clamber up an obvious wide crack that is 30
feet right of **RMC** and visible from the carriage road, to a belay
ledge beneath a chimney (50 feet). Climb the chimney (crux, V1) to
the highest ledge, then angle left up the face just left of a second
chimney (V2) to the trees.

V1 From the top of the first chimney, traverse straight left (exposed),
then up easy rock.

V2 Climb the right chimney to the top.

95 The Blackout 5.9 R ★
FA: Dick Williams, Dave Craft, Dick DuMais, 1968
Three worthwhile pitches. The bolt was added on a later ascent.
Climb a nice left angling thin crack 20 feet right of **Betty** to a belay
ledge (5.7+). Up the corner (V1), then hand traverse right to the
nose (keeping right of the **Betty** chimney) (5.7+) and up to the GT
ledge. Take a deep breath and climb orange rock to a bolt at the
roof. Clip the bolt, let out a sigh of relief, traverse right then over the
hang to easy rock (5.9).

V1 Climb over the hang at a crack to the start of the hand traverse;
5.8.

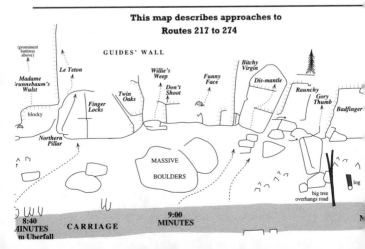

**This map describes approaches to
Routes 217 to 274**

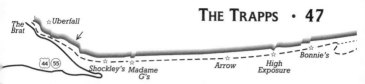

The Brat
☆Uberfall
44 55
☆ Shockley's
☆ Madame G's
☆ Arrow
☆ High Exposure
Bonnie's

89	Ape Call 5.8	103	Baby 5.6
94	Betty 5.3–	105	Easy Overhang 5.2
97	Matinee 5.10+	107	Son of Easy O 5.8
99	Big Chimney 5.5	108	Heather 5.9
102	Fetus 5.9+		

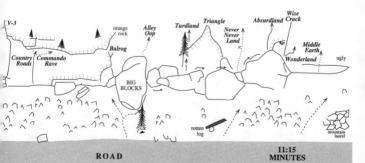

V-3
orange rock
Alley Oop
Turdland
Triangle
Never Never Land
Absurdland
Wise Crack
Country Roads
Commando Rave
Balrog
BIG BLOCKS
Middle Earth
Wonderland
ugly
rotten log
mountain laurel
ROAD
11:15 MINUTES

Uberfall Area

96 The Late Show 5.12– PG13
FA: Steve Levin, Kevin Bein, 1977
The second pitch was the original **Matinee** aid line. It's harder now that a hold has broken. Climb a thin vertical crack (scary) to the left edge of the roof on pitch one of **Matinee**. Belay as for **Matinee**. Climb the roof ten feet left of **Matinee** (V1), into the **Matinee** corner. At the top, step left and climb the ceiling at a crack, then finish on **Matinee**.

V1 Kinky Claw 5.11 R FA: Hugh Herr, Russ Clune, July, 1983.
Climb the steep face left of the second pitch of **The Late Show** to a roof. Left around this and up a crack to the GT ledge. Finish on **The Blackout**.

97 Matinee 5.10+ G ★★
FA: Yvon Chouinard, Jim Andress 1961. FFA: Jim McCarthy, John Hudson, 1963
A free climb way ahead of its time. Still considered hard. The first pitch is popular by itself and stays dry in light rain. Starting 40 feet right of **Betty**, climb a left-facing corner to a roof, then traverse left under the roof (5.10), to a comfortable belay. The second pitch climbs the obvious left-facing corner above the left edge of the first

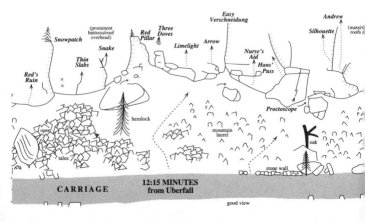

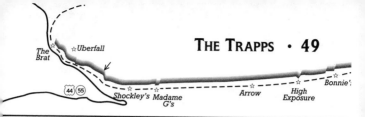

pitch roof. At the top of the corner, move right, then left past roofs to the GT ledge. Finish on **The Blackout**. Set up a good directional before leading pitch two!

98 Creature Features 5.11 PG

FA: Kevin Bein, Mark Robinson, 1976. (top-roped, then led by Bein)
The direct start still hasn't quite gone yet. Start up **Big Chimney**, then hand traverse left (V1, 5.10+) to gain the left-facing corner system left of the chimney. Follow the corner to a roof, move left (V2) and swing over the roof to a belay in a right-facing corner. Pitch two wanders up and over the ceilings above to the GT ledge. Finish at will.

V1 Traverse in from the right via the lip of the **Matinee** P1 roof (watch for rope drag); 5.9.

V2 Escape right under the roof and then up the face; 5.9 (but 5.10+ to get to the escape).

99 Big Chimney 5.5 G

FA: Fritz Wiessner, Edward and Ann Gross, 1942
Once known as Double Chimney. An obvious left-facing chimney 45 feet right of **Betty** and about 150 feet right of the Pebbles boulders on the carriage road. Up the chimney to its top, then move right and

This map describes approaches to
Routes 277 to 336

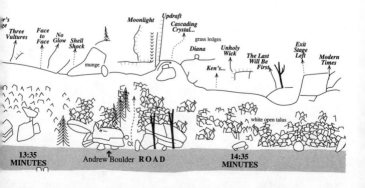

Uberfall Area

belay. Climb another chimney (loose and filled with pigeon poop). Belay on the GT ledge above. The third pitch climbs a loose right-facing corner (V1).

V1 Move left and climb an overhanging right-facing corner past steep rock to the top; 5.7.

NOTE: This climb marks the line between the Uberfall section of cliff (ledges and lower angle rock), and the steeper, cleaner main section of The Trapps.

100 Miss Bailey 5.6 G
FA: Dave Noyes, Eric Schiffman, pre-1964
Climb **Big Chimney** to the second chimney and belay. Move out left onto the face, then up past a right-facing corner. Continue up a crack, go right and up through a roof, then up to the woods.

101 Barking Up the Wrong Tree 5.8 X
FA: Henry Barber, John Bragg, Rich Perch, 1976
Just right of **Big Chimney** is a huge roof with a very dead tree that used to touch the cliff at the lip of the roof. You guessed it—climb the tree (crux, V1) until you can reach the cliff above the roof, then follow a corner (5.6) to the GT ledge.

V1 Disco Death March 5.10+ G FA: Don Perry, Mike Burlingame, Cheyenne Wills, 1977. Climb the all too obvious undercling/offwidth

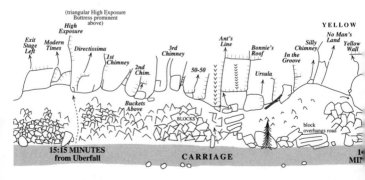

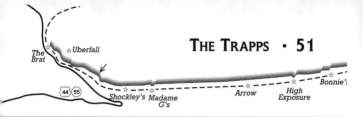

The Brat
☆ Uberfall
44 55
Shockley's Madame G's
Arrow
High Exposure
Bonnie'

joining **Big Chimney. Swing** around right to finish on **Barking Up the Wrong Tree**. Bring the usual offwidth protection gear.

102 Fetus 5.9+ PG
FA: John Lomont, Francis Coffin, 1959. FFA: Dick Williams, 1965
Start left of **Baby** at a short right-facing flake. Hard moves up the flake lead to easier climbing. From the GT ledge, either rappel, or finish on another climb.

103 Baby 5.6 G ★★★
FA: Fritz Wiessner, Mary Cecil, Betty Woolsey, 1941
The second most popular 5.6 crack climb at the Gunks. Climb the obvious widening crack on the left end of the Frog's Head Wall (High Exposure Buttress) (crux) to the GT Ledge. Up the distinct left-facing corner above. Beware of the loose blocks on the GT ledge in this section, and of sand on pitch two.

104 Twisted Sister 5.8+ G
FA: Ivan Rezucha, Annie O'Neill, 1984
Climb the vertical flake just left of **Easy O**, then up the face to the GT ledge (5.8+). Walk left of **Baby**, and climb the face and roof just right of a small left-facing corner, then up an easy runout left of a left-facing corner, past a block to the woods (5.6).

This map describes approaches to
Routes 336 to 416

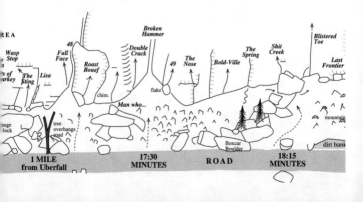

105	Easy Overhang 5.2	114	Maria 5.6
107	Son of Easy 5.8	114v1	Maria Direct 5.9
109	Pas de Deux 5.8	117	Scungilli 5.7+
111	City Lights 5.7	118	Jean 5.9
112	Frog's Head 5.5	119	Precarious Perch 5.9
113	Sundown 5.9	120	Sixish 5.4+

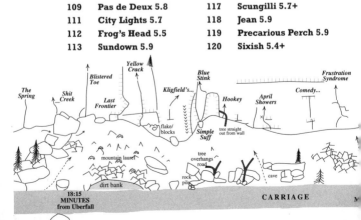

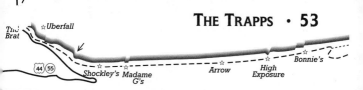

105 Easy Overhang (aka Easy O) 5.2 G ★★★

FA: Hans Kraus, Susanne Simon, 1940

A very exciting beginner climb. Start 15 feet right of **Baby** and 45 feet right of **Big Chimney**. Slither up a wide, leaning crack to the GT ledge (V1) DON'T KNOCK OFF ROCKS ONTO THOSE BELOW. Walk right then climb up the left-facing corner past an overhang (V2, 3), until it is possible to exit right around the arête, and up the face to the summit.

V1 Move onto the face right of the leaning crack at mid-height and up to the ledge; 5.3.

V2 Easy Baby 5.6 PG FA: Bill Shockley, Steve Jervis, June, 1952. Attempted previously before Shockley succeeded with Jervis. Exit left at the top of the corner and join **Baby**.

V3 Indecent Exposure 5.4 G FA: Ted Church, circa 1955. Traverse out right to connect with **Son of Easy O** above the roof.

106 Queasy O 5.9+ R

FA (TR): John Stannard, 1960's. FA (lead): Russ Raffa, Russ Clune, Dick Williams, 1981

Climb the face between **Easy O** and **Son of Easy O** on pitch one. The crux is off the ground.

This map describes approaches to Routes 408 to 449

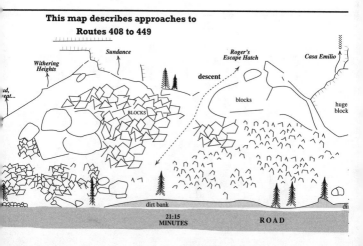

107 Son of Easy O 5.8 G ★★★

FA: Jim McCarthy, Al DeMaria, Fall, 1962

One of the best 5.8s on The Trapps. Both pitches will keep you thinking! Start 15 feet right of **Easy O** below a thin crack. Ascend the face, step left and follow the thin crack to the GT ledge (5.8). From the right end of the ledge, move up and right to an inside left-facing corner that cleaves the overhangs. Go up the corner, swing right, then race to the top (5.8).

108 Heather 5.9 R

FA: Henry Barber, Pete Ramins, Ric Hatch, 1974

A solid 5.9. Wander up the weaknesses 15 feet right of **Son of Easy O** to the left edge of the tiny **Pas de Deux** ledge ten feet up. Step left (5.9, scary), and up a thin crack to easier rock and the GT ledge. Traverse right of **Son of Easy O** on ledge under the roof and then up to roof at a thin seam (5.9, loose). Continue on to the bushes.

109 Pas de Deux 5.8 PG ★★

FA: Jim McCarthy, Jack Hansen, 1950s. FFA: Jim Geiser, 1959

A classic first pitch that was first led after pins were placed on rappel. The second pitch has been switched with **City Lights** to create

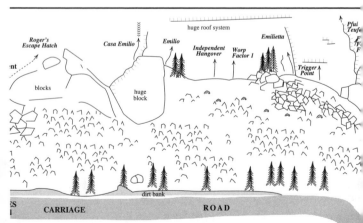

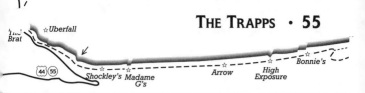

a straight line. At a short corner 25 feet right of **Son of Easy O**,
dance up and right, then back left (crux, V1), and follow a crack up
right to the GT ledge. From the ledge climb a right-facing corner,
then exit left and wander up to the trail above.

V1 Climb straight up the initial crack; 5.10.

110 Patty Duke 5.9 PG
FA: Ivan Rezucha, Annie O'Neill September, 1985
A bit squeezed in. Climb the thin vertical seam just right of **Pas de
Deux**. Step right for protection at the flake on **City Lights**, then
climb the face left of the flake (crux) to a bucket on **City Lights**.
Cross to the right of **City Lights**, and up to the GT ledge (5.9 PG).
Climb the steep face right of **Pas de Deux** to a short right-facing
corner. At the top of the corner, move right and up to the ledge (5.8
PG). Climb the face and overhang above a pine tree to the woods.

111 City Lights 5.7 G ★
FA: Dick Williams, Art Gran, 1965
An enlightening first section leads to easier climbing. Technique (or
thrash) up a short, triangular pod 40 feet right of **Son of Easy O** to a
ledge (15 feet, crux). Move left to a flake, then climb the flake and
face above to the GT ledge. Traverse left to a belay on **Pas de Deux**.
Pitch two diagonals right, then follows a corner and face to the top.

**This map describes approaches to
Routes 448 to 505**

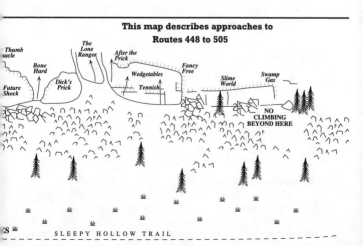

112 Frog's Head 5.5 G ★★★

FA: Fritz Wiessner, Lorens Logan, 1941

A ribbiting climb. Both pitches are sustained for their grade. Follow the crack system 25 feet right of **City Lights** (crux at bulge 25 feet up) to a belay at a flake on the GT ledge. Jump up steep rock above the flake (5.4), then move up and right to a corner. Up this to the next ledge, where you can escape left (V1).

V1 Climb the final hang; 5.6.

113 Sundown 5.9 PG

FA: Ivan Rezucha, Annie O'Neill, 1984

Don't wait until the end of the day for this one. The crux is protected off to the side of the route, making it a little scary. Struggle up the right side of the initial **Frog's Head** block, then straight up the yellow face above (crux at 40 feet, #3 Friend on left) to the **Frog's Head** ledge. Move right, then straight up past an overhang (keeping left of lichen) to small trees on the GT ledge. Climb the roof above on the right edge.

114 Maria 5.6 PG ★

FA: Maria Millar, Fritz Wiessner, 1946

Quality, but make sure to protect the second on the traverse! Start on **Frog's Head** and climb past its crux (V1, 2), then traverse far right to the base of the huge left-facing corner and belay. Up the corner to another belay ledge, then pull the final roof above the corner at an obvious crack (crux), or escape right.

V1 **Maria Direct 5.9 G ★** FA: John Turner, 1956 (may have been done on aid previously). Climb the small right-facing corners 20 feet right of **Frog's Head**. It is also possible to climb the small left-facing corners ten feet left of **Maria Direct** (5.9 G).

V2 **Maria Redirect 5.11 R** FA: Ants Leemets, circa 1968 (possibly top-roped, and probably done with aid first). Up the vertical crack right of the **Direct**.

115 Kama Sutra 5.12– R

FA: Ants Leemets, Dick Williams, 1964 FFA: John Stannard, 1974

A large mattress is required equipment on this on. Often top-roped. Using your best karma, climb the face ten feet right of the **Frog's Head** block to a horizontal, then slightly right to a belay on

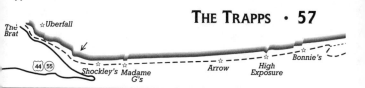

the **Maria** traverse. Most people call it quits here. The rest of the climb stays left of the **Maria** corner (5.8).

116 Sultana 5.8– PG
FA: Dick Williams, John Hudson, Fall, 1963. FFA: Dick Williams, 1964
Begin 55 feet right of **Frog's Head** at a right arching flake. Up the flake (crux) to a ledge. Move right, then up the steep face to an overhang. Swing over this at a weakness, then up **Scungilli** along a crack to another hang. Traverse left under the ceiling and belay just right of the **Maria** corner (90 feet). Climb the face above, staying right of the arête to the top. Finish on **Maria**'s roof .

117 Scungilli 5.7+ PG
FA: Art Gran, Jack Hansen, 1958
Eight arms might be helpful on the crux traverse. Start atop blocks 85 feet right of **Frog's Head** (V1). Climb a crack atop the blocks to flakes. Traverse left 20 feet (crux), then up a crack and over an overhang to a belay on right (100 feet). Continue up the face above to the GT ledge. Finish on **Maria**.

V1 5.9 PG FA: Ivan Rezucha, Annie O'Neill, Randy Schenkel, Keith LaBudde, June, 1992. Start just left of the normal start. Angle left, then up to the right edge of a grassy ledge. Angle slightly right along a flake to the **Scungilli** hand traverse (the flake is obvious if you look). Step left a few feet (the further left you go, the easier it gets), then straight up and past a ceiling. Move left to the **Scungilli** belay.

118 Jean 5.9 PG ★
FA: Art Gran, Phil Jacobus, John Hudson, 1960. FFA: Dick Williams, 1964
A good 5.9 roof problem. Start right of **Scungilli**, up, right, and up an orange, left-facing corner ending at a roof. Pump the roof to the belay slings (most people rappel from here). The second pitch climbs a corner on the left, then wanders up to a belay ledge. The last pitch climbs a face and a roof, then up right to the shrubs.

119 Precarious Perch 5.9 PG ★
FA: Rich Perch, Mike Sawicky, 1981
Similar to, and slightly easier than **Jean**. Named for the bus that ran through the wall on the hairpin turn below. Originally named Macho Do About Nothing—until Perch left town. Climb up right on orange

rock from the base of **Jean** to a stance (V1) under the roof. Swing over the roof ten feet right of **Jean**, then belay (5.9). Either rappel, or continue on up to connect with **Sixish** at the GT ledge.

V1 One can also start on the **Sixish** block to the right, and climb up left to the same point.

120 Sixish 5.4+ G ★★
FA: Hans Kraus, Dick Hirschland, 1951
A classic route with varied climbing. A bit hard for 5.4, hence the name? Start just right of **Jean** at a huge right-facing corner on top of boulders. Climb a left-facing flake, then easier rock up the corner, until you are forced out left to an exposed belay (5.4+). Step up and slightly left around a ceiling, then back right and up a crack to the GT ledge. Climb the face just left of the corner to a roof (V1), then move right and on to the summit.

V The original aid line 5.10 G FFA: Art Gran early 1960s. Starting by the huge pine on the GT ledge, climb a short face (crux) to the big ceiling. Hand traverse left around the roof, and rejoin the regular line.

121 One Blunder and It's Six Feet Under 5.10 X
FA: P1, P2 Todd Swain, Matt Jasinski, John Goobic, 1985; P3 Bill Shanaman, Mike Freeman, 1978
The last pitch was originally entitled Sometimes You Feel Like a Nut. Whimper up the clean face between **Sixish** and **Drunkard's Delight** to a belay under the **Drunkard's** roof (5.9 X). Climb over the roof on the left at a corner (5.6), then on to the GT ledge. Climb the small, white dihedral above the GT ledge, exiting left at the ceiling to the top (5.10 R).

122 Drunkard's Delight 5.7+ PG ★★★
FA: Jim Andress, Jim McCarthy, 1959
Not to be missed—although the initial moves are scary. Starting 25 feet right of **Sixish**, stagger up a right-angling crack (crux), then up to a belay under the big roof. Swing out the roof at a crack (5.6, wild), move left, then up to the GT ledge to belay. Follow an obvious corner to the top.

123 Five Tendons 5.10+ R
FA: P1 Felix Modugno, Norman Schenck, 1984; P2 Will Chen, 1981
Climb the face between **Drunkard's** and **Morning After**, connecting with a right-facing flake on **Morning After** (5.10 R). Climb the overhang right of **Drunkard's** at a thin crack (crux).

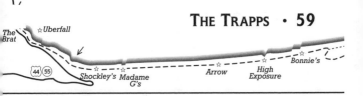

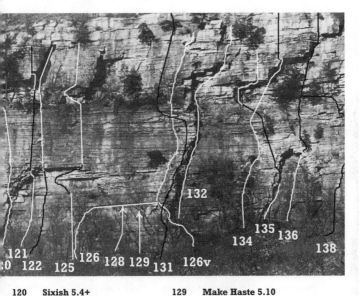

120	Sixish 5.4+	129	Make Haste 5.10
121	One Blunder and It's Ten	131	Trusty Rifle 5.9
	Feet Under 5.10	132	Easy Street 5.7
122	Drunkard's Delight 5.7+	134	Wrist 5.6
125	Bloody Mary 5.6+	135	Invitation to Hell 5.10
126	Rusty Trifle 5.4	136	Arch 5.4
129	Rock and Brew 5.9	138	Ribs 5.4

124 Morning After 5.8– PG ★★

FA: Jim Andress, Doug Tompkins, 1964

Starting 40 feet right of **Drunkard's** and just left of **Rusty Trifle**, stumble up to a right-facing corner that is about 20 feet up. At the corner's top, move left to flakes, climb up and then back right to a belay at trees (under a left-facing corner in the roof above, 5.7+). The second pitch avoids the roof on the right, and climbs up to the GT ledge (5.7). Pitch three skirts another ceiling on the right, then follows a white layback crack to the woods (5.8-).

125 Bloody Mary 5.6+ PG
FA: Walter Baumann, Dick Williams, Cherry Merritt, 1972
Climb an obvious crack for 30 feet (V1), then move left to a right-facing corner. Angle left at the top of the corner, past another right facing corner to a belay under the middle of the roof. Pitch two traverses up and right out the roof (5.6+), then up to the GT ledge. The final pitch walks left (V2), ascends a short right-facing corner, then up left to the trail.

V1 Start on **Rusty Trifle** and climb straight up a crack to the trees.

V2 Move right 20 feet to a right facing corner, which is ascended to the summit; 5.8.

126 Rusty Trifle 5.4 G ★
FA: Hans Kraus, Bonnie Prudden, 1950
A very popular beginner climb with two starts. The most popular start begins 65 feet right of the **Sixish** corner at the base of large, left-facing blocks (V1). Scamper up right on the blocks from the base of the last two climbs until it is possible to traverse far right (crux), almost to the right arête of the buttress. Follow a short right-facing corner, then weaknesses to a belay at a pine tree (100 feet). Continue on up to the GT ledge, moving left through a roof enroute. Finish up an easy face by weaving up right, then back left to a corner, which is followed to the top. Protect the second on the first pitch traverse!

V1 **Alternate Start 5.3** From the **Easy Street** corner (55 feet right of the regular start) move out left onto the front of the buttress to join the route after the crux traverse.

127 Arc of a Diver 5.9– G
FA: Ray Dobkin, Joe Ferguson, October, 1985
Climb a crack ten feet right of **Rusty Trifle** past a tree to a left-facing corner above the **Rusty Trifle** traverse. Up the corner past a roof to a belay ledge (5.8). Straight up a shallow left-facing corner past a double overhang, then angle left to the GT ledge (5.7). Climb the obvious (and previously climbed) right-facing corner to the top (5.9–).

128 Rock and Brew 5.9 PG
FA: Dick Williams, Dave Loeks, 1973
Named for the corporation that founded the Rock and Snow climbing

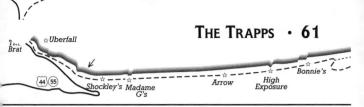

shop and what used to be the North Light bar. The next three routes all start on the steep wall below **Rusty Trifle**'s traverse line. Boulder up to the left edge of a low roof, 20 feet left of an off width, then up right to a thin seam. Move left through a bulge (crux, #2 Friend) to a belay on the **Rusty Trifle** traverse. Continue straight on up to the GT ledge. End the climb by passing a bulge and crack line to a tree and the top.

129 Make Haste, or Tomato Paste 5.10 PG
FA: Todd Swain, Neil Harvey (UK), September, 1985
Climb the difficult face right of **Rock and Brew** over the roof at a seam, then up right past a bulge (crux, .5 Tri-cam, # 4 Friend) to belay on the **Rusty Trifle** traverse. Traverse off right, or climb to the GT ledge staying left of **Rusty**, then finish on **Trusty Rifle** (5.8).

130 Crusty Waffles 5.10 PG
FA: Herman, Ivan Rezucha, Bill Ravitch, September, 1991
Begin just left of the obvious, right-leaning offwidth that is the first pitch of **Trusty Rifle**. Over a ceiling at its right edge, then angle a bit left to a grass bog and a right-leaning crack. Up to a wide horizontal (large Friend), then angle left to easier climbing.

131 Trusty Rifle 5.9 G
FA: P1 Rick Cronk, Matt Munchkin, Kevin Bein, John Bragg, Rich Perch, 1975; P2 and P3: Todd Swain, Dave Saball, Andy and Randy Schenkel, November, 1984
While doing the FA of what was to become **Rusty Trifle**, Kraus saw a hunter on the carriage road below, and mixed up his words while commenting to Prudden about the hunter's gun. Start below an obvious offwidth crack down and left from **Easy Street**. Struggle up the offwidth (5.9) to a ledge. Follow a thin seam (crux) up the arête left of the **Easy Street** corner to the GT ledge. Move left 20 feet, and climb cleaned rock past a small left-facing corner to the top (5.8).

132 Easy Street (aka Bloody Bush) 5.7 G
FA: P1 Unknown, pre-1960. FA: Dick DuMais, John Stannard 1972
Begin 55 feet right of **Rusty Trifle** at a large right-facing corner. This is the alternate start for **Rusty Trifle** and the beginning of **Easy Street**. Climb the corner to the GT ledge (5.5). From the GT ledge, diagonal right through roofs (crux) to the top.

133 Uncle Rudy 5.8 PG
FA: Mike and Pete Werner, September, 1975
A dirty route that has good climbing. Start 15 feet right of **Easy Street** at a right-facing corner. Climb over an orange roof (5.7+), then up a thin face (crux) to easier climbing and the GT ledge (120 feet). Climb up and left to a large overhang. Climb easily over the roof at the corner, go past another small ceiling, then on to the descent trail.

134 Wrist 5.6 G
FA: Bonnie Prudden, Hans Kraus, 1953
Varied climbing. Begin just left of the huge arch and 25 feet right of **Easy Street**. Follow cracks and a left-facing corner to the GT ledge. The last pitch climbs a corner to a roof, hand traverses left (crux) to a ledge (beware of rope drag), and then up a crack in a white face or the clean face on the right (harder).

135 Invitation to Hell 5.10 G
FA: Mike Steele, October, 1984
A good crux ceiling. Climb the left side of the arch almost to the top, swing left and climb past a white bulge just above a wide horizontal (5.9) to the GT ledge. Move left 30 feet to a pine tree. The crux pitch goes out the large roof above, moving slightly right, then on up a small right-facing corner (fixed peg). Climb easy rock from there.

136 Arch 5.4 PG ★
FA: Hans Kraus, Bonnie Prudden, 1953
Starting at a small right-facing flake/corner in the center of the huge arch, wander up the face until you can traverse right (5.4, V1) under a roof out of the arch to a belay. Clamber up easy rock to the GT ledge and another belay. Move up and right to a roof and climb through it at a notch. Weave left (V2), then right and follow a corner to the top.

V1 Arch Direct (aka Wick's Banana) 5.9 G FA: Dick Williams, Bill Goldner, 1962. Climb out the top of the arch following a wild crack. Usually wasp infested.

V2 Climb left around the overhangs above; 5.5.

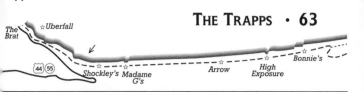

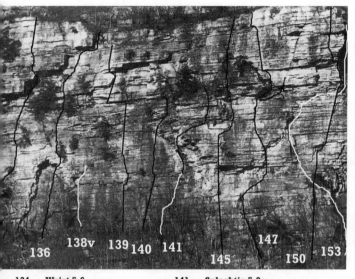

134	Wrist 5.6	141	Splashtic 5.9
136	Arch 5.4	145	Strictly from Nowhere 5.7
138v	Spare Ribs 5.6	147	Shockley's Ceiling 5.6
139	Calisthenic 5.7	150	Grim-Ace Face 5.9
140	Gorilla My Dreams 5.7	153	High Corner 5.5

137 Billy Shears 5.8+ G

FA: Ray Dobkin, Joe Ferguson, Max Strumia, August, 1982
Named for the man Dobkin borrowed pruners from as well as the character mentioned in a Beatles song. Follow the right corner of the arch (V1) crossing the **Arch** traverse, then past an overhang at a hand crack that is down and right of **Arch Direct** (crux). Belay on **Arch**, then wade up to the GT ledge and walk right 20 feet to another belay. The final pitch had been climbed earlier, and follows an obvious right-facing corner system to the top, passing ceilings enroute (5.8).

V1 Viscious Rumors 5.11+ PG FA: Darrow Kirkpatrick, Frank Minunni, November, 1985. A scary lead. Climb the thin, overhanging crack and face at the bottom right wall of the arch.

138 Ribs 5.4 PG
FA: Hans Kraus, Bonnie Prudden, 1953
After stepping out right around the right outside corner downhill of **Arch**, (V1) wander up the face on the right to a belay on the same ledge as **Arch** (5.4; 75 feet). Continue up steep rock right of **Arch**, then finish on P3 of **Arch**.

V1 Spare Ribs (aka Ribless) 5.6 PG FRA: Todd Swain, Dave and Marie Saball, 1985. Climb directly up the arête to the belay.

139 Calisthenic 5.7 PG
FA: Phil Jacobus, John Hudson, 1962
Named for the jump needed to start the climb, if you are short. Starting 35 feet right of **Ribs**, pull over the low overhang just right of a tree touching the rock. Move left and climb straight up to the belay on the GT ledge (140 feet). Climb a crack above to the roof, then move left to easier climbing and the shrubs.

140 Gorilla My Dreams 5.7 PG
FA: Dick Williams, Ants Leemets, Jim McCarthy, 1966
Ape Call Jane for the **Gorilla My Dreams**. Start 60 feet right of **Ribs** and climb the leftmost of two corners facing right, then up the face right of a small corner to the belay (70 feet). Up then angle right to a large inside left-facing corner and continue left through loose, blocky overhangs to the GT ledge at a tree. Walk left a bit then follow an obvious orange left-facing corner straight past a ceiling (small cedar tree above) to the trees.

141 Splashtic 5.9 R ★
FA: Dick Williams, Ants Leemets, 1966
A wild route, especially if you come off on pitch two! Climb the clean face 12 feet right of the previous route (and just left of a shallow right-facing corner), then up right to a belay in the main corner system. Up the corner, then traverse out right (crux) at the bottom of a clean white face around the arête. Continue up through a notch in a roof to the GT ledge. Finish on **Strictly From Nowhere**.

142 Gaston 5.7+ PG
FA: Ken Prestrud, Lucien Warner, 1952
An interesting first pitch beginning 15 feet right of **Splashtic**. Climb a ramp up right past a bulge (threaded runner to protect bulge), move up and left on thin climbing, then right to a belay at the base of the huge corner (5.7+). Up the corner to the GT ledge. Follow

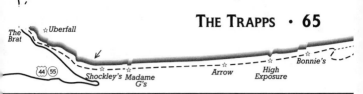

The Brat, ☆Uberfall, Shockley's, Madame G's, Arrow, High Exposure, Bonnie's, 44, 55

the corner to ceilings (V1, 2), then traverse far left, until the top is gained easily.

V1 Gaston Direct 5.10 G FA: Unknown, 1970s. Over the roof partway along the traverse left.

V2 Climb straight up to **V1**; 5.8.

143 Travels With Charlie 5.7+ R ★
FA: Dave Ingalls, Charlie Bookman, 1968
The only trip you'll take on this one, is a trip to the hospital if you blow the crux! Starting 25 feet right of **Splashtic**, climb the obvious corner and face above to a belay on **Gaston** at the base of a huge corner (5.7; 80 feet). Climb flakes to a roof, traverse out right (scary crux), then around the corner. Up the face, then right to a right-facing corner and more overhangs, which are climbed on the right to the GT ledge. Scamper through a notch in the ceiling above.

144 Revenge of the Relics 5.10– PG
FA: Ivan Rezucha, Chris Monz, August, 1991
A little intimidating, but good climbing. Begin right of the arête of the **Travels With Charlie** corner. Up past a bulge (5.9, much harder if short), past a bush to a belay at a small pine tree (where **Travels** exits the corner). Climb straight up to the base of a left facing corner. Get pro, step right, then up a steep orange face just right of the arête (pro halfway up on the arête: #1 Friend, .5 Tri-cam) to a large horizontal. Hand traverse right (V1) about six feet then up over double ceilings (this is about six feet left of the **Strictly's** crux). Either join **Splashtic/Travels** or traverse right and down to the **Strictly's** tree to rappel (#1 Friend for a directional to protect the second).

V1 Move left and up to join **Travels** on the scary traverse.

145 Strictly from Nowhere 5.7 G ★★
FA: Art Gran, Jim Andress, 1959
Good training for **Son of Easy O** as both climbs are similar. Begin 20 feet right of **Travels** in the center of a small buttress. Climb up and around right of a roof to nice face climbing and a great belay ledge below an overhanging, left-facing corner (5.6). Up through the corner (crux), to easier climbing and a short vertical seam. Follow the seam to the right (possible belay here at a pine), then up and through a roof at its narrowest point to the GT ledge. The last pitch ascends an inside left-facing corner to the top (5.4).

146 Epiclepsy 5.10 X

FA: Kevin Bein, Barbara Devine, Mark Robinson, Roy Kligfield, 1976 (top-roped in 1972, led in 1976)

Serious climbing on pitch two. Wander up the face 20 feet right of **Strictly** to the belay platform (5.7+). Fire out the roof above at the widest point (crux) and belay at a pine. Up right on the face above, go through overhangs at a crack near the right side and continue to the GT ledge (5.9+). Finish as desired.

147 Shockley's Ceiling 5.6 G ★★★

FA: Bill Shockley, Doug Kerr, 1953

Shockley avoided the now classic third pitch roof on his first attempt by climbing **Shockley's Without**. He came back with Kerr to climb the roof a short time later. A classic either way. Start 40 feet right of **Strictly** and directly above the hairpin turn on the public highway. Scramble out left from a blocky right-facing corner and up an easy chimney to a great belay ledge (5.3, same belay as for **Strictly**). Traverse right off the ledge (5.3), then up to a ledge below ceilings (possible belay here). Swing through the ceilings to a right-facing corner system (5.3) and up this to its top. Angle right to a belay on the GT ledge (130 feet). Power through the roof above at the obvious crack (crux, V1), and climb the inside corner above to its top. Move right, then go past another ceiling with a crack to the finish.

V1 Shockley's Without 5.3 G ★★★ FA: Bill Shockley, Ian Ross, 1953. By following a crack in nice white rock left of the belay, the climb stays at 5.3 difficulty. At the top of the crack, move left, and up a short corner to the trees.

148 Mister Transistor 5.10+ PG

FA: P1 (flake) 5.7 Raivo Puusemp, 1960; Ivan Rezucha, Todd Swain, November, 1984.

Named for Shockley, the man who invented the transistor, which of course began the computer age. A linkup of previously climbed sections that is harder since Maury Jaffe accidentally broke the crux hold in 1986. Climb the large flake just left of **PR** , then a thin crack passing a bulge on the right (crux) to a belay under the roof above (75 feet). Over the hang ten feet left of **Shockley's** P2 corner into a left-facing corner (5.8), then up right to a roof. Climb this by traversing out left, then up to the belay. Finish by climbing the face between the **Shockley** finishes (previously climbed as Shockley's Within, 5.6 R).

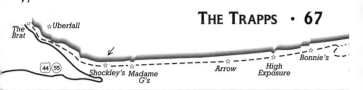

The Brat · ☆Uberfall · 44 · 55 · Shockley's · Madame G's · Arrow · High Exposure · Bonnie's

149 PR 5.11+ R

FA: Skip King, 1972. FFA, P1, P2: John Stannard, 1974. FA, P3: Jim McCarthy, 1960s

Originally a variation named Shock-King Barrier. The PR stands for Public Relations—a name given by Stannard after the original aid ascent was reported in a climbing magazine. The initial crack is a serious piece of climbing and difficult to protect. Usually top-roped. Climb the thin, vertical seam 20 feet right of **Shockley's** to a belay as for **Mister Transistor**, then on to the GT ledge, to a belay right of the **Shockley's** crack. The final pitch climbs the roof above a short corner at a notch (5.9), then up steep rock to the finish.

150 Grim-Ace Face 5.9 R ★

FA: Jim McCarthy, Royal Robbins, 1966

The last pitch is what Gunks climbing is all about. Climb a steep, blocky face 35 feet right of **Shockley's** (5.8) to easier rock and a belay. From a tree (V1), climb to an overhang, swing around right (5.8+ R, loose), then up to the GT ledge. Climb up the edge left of **High Corner**, then traverse left through a roof (exposed, 5.9 PG) to easier climbing and the summit.

V1 5.10 R FA: Pete Thexton (UK), Dick Williams, 1982. Begin left of the tree and climb straight up past a ceiling. Continue up the face to the GT ledge.

151 No Belle Prize 5.10 R

FA: Ivan Rezucha, May, 1980

Named for Nobel Prize winner Shockley. Start as for **High Corner**, but after the initial corner, climb straight up the steep face (5.7) to the base of **High Corner**. Move left, climb a right-facing corner and the ceiling above (crux, biscuit shaped hold) to the top.

152 Hi Coroner! 5.9 PG ★

FA: Todd Swain, Pat Barlow, Ray Dobkin, October, 1984

Three good pitches make this a popular climb. Start just left of **High Corner** below a short, yellow dihedral. Climb the steep, clean hand crack in the dihedral past a difficult exit move (5.9) to the base of a chimney and the belay (40 feet). Up the squeeze chimney (5.7), then directly up the steep face above the chimney to the GT ledge. Climb the imposing left wall of the **High Corner** following a shallow corner system to the trees (creepy 5.9).

153 High Corner 5.5 PG
FA: Fritz Wiessner, Roger Wolcott, 1942
Decent protection with intimidating climbing. Climb a dirty right-facing corner 80 feet right of **Shockley's**, until you can move out left below a squeeze chimney to the main face. Climb up and slightly left to a belay (75 feet; 5.3). Angle up right to the GT ledge and another belay (5.5). Pitch three climbs the final, north facing, pigeon frequented corner (crux).

154 Glyptomaniac 5.8+ PG
FA: Ivan Rezucha, Don Lauber, Annie O'Neill, August, 1982
Climb the face just right of the start of **High Corner** to a ledge, then climb the rightmost right-facing corner past a ceiling. Move right, then over another ceiling and continue to the GT ledge. Wander up the face ten feet right of the **High Corner**, then right a bit, passing a small roof to the bushes.

155 Glyptodon 5.8+ R ★
FA: Helmut Microys (Can), Eric Marshall, 1970
A great first pitch if you use double ropes, bring lots of gear and slings. Begin 35 feet right of **High Corner** at a right-facing corner. Up the easy corner, exit left and up a thin face (5.8 R) to the base of another corner. Up this corner, then swing out left (5.8) and up a face to another roof, which is also passed on the left (crux, possible to belay under this roof). Belay on the GT ledge above (150 feet). Follow a crack up right around a roof to join **Simple Ceilings** then traverse right at the final ceiling to the bushes.

156 Nemesis 5.10- PG
FA: Jim McCarthy, Phil Jacobus, Pete Vlachos, Steve Larsen, John Hudson, Dick Williams, 1966
A hard boulder problem up a thin seam ten feet right of **Glyptodon** leads to easier climbing right around overhangs and the belay (5.10–). P2 climbs flakes and a right-facing corner and ceiling to a ledge, then moves left and through a notch to the GT ledge (5.8). The final pitch climbs up to an overhang (V1), hand traverses right around an arête, and then climbs to the summit.

V1 5.8 PG FA: Ivan Rezucha, Andy Schenkel, September, 1991. From the GT ledge go up a bit then traverse right above a roof to a nose. Climb the arête and face just left of the arête (crossing the regular route) to the top.

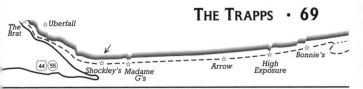

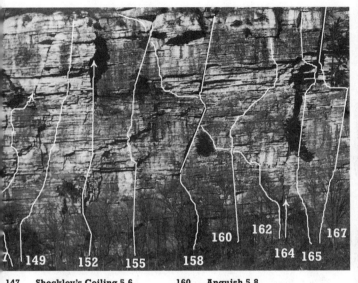

147 Shockley's Ceiling 5.6	160 Anguish 5.8
149 PR 5.11+	162 Simple Ceilings 5.5
152 Hi Coroner! 5.9	164 Three Pines 5.3+
155 Glyptodon 5.8+	165 Something Boring 5.9
158 Glypnod 5.8	167 Something Interesting 5.7+

157 Midnight Cowboy 5.10– R
FA: Rich Goldstone, Dick Williams, 1968

Another hard boulder problem. Start 20 feet right of **Nemesis** at the right-hand seam on the short, smooth face. Up the thin seam, then right past a ledge, to easy rock and the belay below steep rock (5.10–, V1). Move left, then up exciting rock past a ledge. Up right, with more thrills, past a bulge to the GT ledge (5.8). Climb to the roof above (as for **Simple Ceilings**), then whimper out right around the nose and below a roof to the summit (5.9).

V1 1 O'Clock Cowgirl 5.10 FA: Bob D'Antonio, Mike Freeman, 1979. Unclear if this was top-roped or led. Climb the face just right of **Midnight Cowboy**'s first pitch.

McCarthy Wall

158 Glypnod 5.8 G ★

FA: P1 John Wharton, Dave Isles; P2: Hans Kraus (done before P1)
FFA: John Turner, Craig Merrihue, pre-1964

Kraus aided the last pitch and named it Suspenders. Wharton and
Isles aided the first pitch and repeated Kraus' pitch and called it all
Adam's Preamble. Turner and Merrihue freed the entire climb and
renamed it **Glypnod**! Harder if you are short. Climb the obvious
right-facing crack/corner system 120 feet right of **High Corner** and
80 feet left of **Three Pines**, passing a roof near the top (crux).

159 Yesterday's Lemonade 5.10 R

FA: Charlie Rollins, John Stannard, 1970s

Climb the tricky, yellow face 20 feet right of **Glypnod** (5.9 R) past a
low roof (crux, two different possibilities) to a belay. Traverse off left
and rappel, or wander up the dirty face to the GT ledge (5.7). Finish
as desired.

160 Anguish 5.8 PG ★

FA: Jim McCarthy, Burt Angrist, 1965

Named for a spectacular fall taken by Angrist after he smashed his
finger with a piton hammer on the first ascent. Climb a flake and
left-facing corner 40 feet right of **Glypnod**, then move right to a
right-facing corner. Up the corner to a ceiling, climb around it on
the left and belay (80 feet). Diagonal right to the GT ledge and
another belay. Sneak up the face to tackle the imposing roof above
at a right-facing corner (crux), swinging left around the roof to
easier climbing.

161 Ruby Saturday 5.9– PG

FA: Jim McCarthy, Ants Leemets, 1966

Named for a fiery lawn mower incident McCarthy was involved in.
Climb a vertical seam 30 feet left of **Three Pines**, then a right-facing
corner to a small tree and the belay (5.8). Hike up left on **Simple
Ceilings**, then straight right through a roof above the belay (crux,
#3 Friend). Follow weaknesses up the face to the GT Ledge. Finish
on any climb of your choosing.

162 Simple Ceilings 5.5 PG

FA: Willie Crowther, Gardiner Perry, Paul Peterson, 1957

The last pitch is pretty good. Starting at **Three Pines**, climb up left
to join **Ruby Saturday**'s first pitch. Traverse up left and belay on the

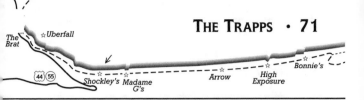

GT ledge under **Glypnod**'s crux roof (150 feet; 5.5). Move past a pine and up to some overhangs, which are bypassed on the left. Continue up steep rock to a ledge, then climb a corner and traverse left across beautiful white rock (crux), to the trail.

163 Raspberry Sundae 5.9 PG

FA: Ivan Rezucha, Don Lauber, Annie O'Neill, July, 1982

Up the face left of **Three Pines**, passing a ceiling even with the first pine, then continue on to the GT ledge. Move up left just left of the nose, and climb the roof right of **Anguish** (crux).

164 Three Pines 5.3+ G ★★★

FA: Hans Kraus, Roger Wolcott, Del Wilde, 1941

A very popular beginner climb that is many people's first lead. Start 80 feet right of **Glypnod**, at a very distinct corner system facing right with pine trees. Climb the corner in one or two pitches, to the GT ledge. Move right on the GT ledge, and up a left-facing corner (5.3, V1), until you can traverse out right (V2), around to a ledge (possible belay here). Follow a crack to a grassy ledge, then traverse left (V3), across a slab to the top.

V1 The Dangler 5.9 G FA: Kevin Bein, circa 1977. Up the corner, then hand traverse right along the lip of the roof to the ledge.

V2 Jam up the vertical handcrack in the middle of the traverse to the upper grass ledge; 5.6.

V3 Climb either of the thin and tricky cracks directly up to the top; 5.6.

165 Something Boring 5.9 X

FA: Walter Baumann, Jim McCarthy, Beth Stannard, Laura Brant, Christian Leroyer, 1971

The leftmost of the McCarthy Wall climbs and probably the most serious for its grade. Climb the face right of **Three Pines** to a bush, then up the bulge (5.7 R) to easier rock and a belay on **Three Pines**. Climb just right of **Three Pines** straight up the wall over a small ceiling (5.9– X) to the GT ledge. Over the roof in the right-facing corner above, diagonal up and left, move left around the corner and finish straight up (5.9).

McCarthy Wall

166 Something Or Other 5.10– PG
FA: Russ Raffa, Steve Beccio, Russ Clune, November, 1982
Climb the first section of **Something Boring** (5.7 R) to a ledge, then move right and up easy rock to the GT ledge. Start up **Something Interesting**, then climb the right-center of the ceiling above at a flake (crux). Angle right to the trees.

167 Something Interesting 5.7+ G ★★★
FA: Hans Kraus, Ken Prestrud, Bonnie Prudden, 1946. FFA: Art Gran, 1960s
Interesting no matter what grade you climb at. Climb the delightful crack 30 feet right of **Three Pines** past a bulge (crux) to a belay ledge. Up slightly easier climbing along a left-facing corner to the GT ledge. Climb the left-facing corner above, swing around right, then angle left to the large right-facing corner and follow it to the top.

168 Higher Stannard 5.9– PG ★
FA: Jim McCarthy, John Stannard, 1967
The first pitch is not well defined, but the climbing is intricate and continuous. Climb a blank face 30 feet right of **Something Interesting** to a thin crack that starts at 20 feet and diagonals left. At its end, head right (crux), then up and slightly left to the roof. Pump the hang, then hand traverse right around a corner (V1), and up to join **MF** and **Birdie Party** to the trees. There is a rappel station at the top of the first pitch.

V1 At the end of the hand traverse, angle left past a bulge to the GT ledge (5.8). This is a cleaner and better finish.

169 Birdie Party 5.10– PG ★★
FA: Jim McCarthy, Doug Tompkins, 1959. FFA: Kevin Bein, 1966
When Bein freed the crux roof, he thought he was on **MF**! Maybe the first roof climb in the Gunks done using a heel hook. Start 40 feet right of **Something Interesting**. Climb a thin crack up, right and up then head right to a large, pointed flake under the roof. Hand traverse right to the belay as for **MF** and **Interstice** (5.9, excellent pitch). Swing out the big ceiling above at a flake (crux), then wander up near **MF** to the top.

170 Interstice 5.10+ PG
FA: John Stannard, 1975
The most popular line, climbs P1 of **Mother's Day Party**, then P2 of **Interstice**. Climb a one-foot roof (5.10) at a left-facing corner eight

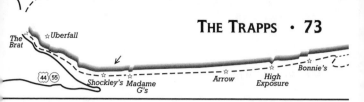
feet left of **Mother's Day** to a thin seam. Follow a shallow left-facing arch/groove up, step right out of the arch, then up to the pointed flake on **Birdie Party**. Belay to the right with the other routes. Climb the roof at a thin crack (5.10+, scary) left of **Birdie Party**, then join **MF** to the shrubs.

171 Mother's Day Party 5.10 PG
FA: Jim Kolocotronis, Herb Laeger, 1973
Climb a series of left-facing inside corners 70 feet right of **Something Interesting** to a thin, vertical crack. Climb up right above the first **MF** roof to the common belay (5.9+). Climb up to the flake on **Birdie Party**, then hand traverse right, and pull the roof left of **MF** (5.10, contrived).

172 MF 5.9 G ★★★
FA: Jim McCarthy, Roman Sadowy, Claude Suhl, Spring, 1960
The climb that brought solid 5.9 to the Gunks. Climb thin cracks 80 feet right of **Something Interesting** to an overhanging left-facing corner. Swing out around the roof to the right (5.9, V1), then follow a steep crack (5.9) to a belay under the roof. Move right around the left facing corner, then climb the roof above (5.9), then angle a bit right to the GT ledge. Climb a right-facing corner to the bushes.

V1 At the first hanging corner climb straight over the roof (avoids the swing out right and the finger crack above); 5.10.

173 Water King 5.10+ R
FA: John Myers, Mike Freeman, 1980
Named for a hilarious boating episode. The first pitch climbs the face between **MF** and **Men At Arms**. Climb up and left, then traverse straight right until below a notch (crux, #2.5 Friend); continue up, keeping about ten feet left of **Men At Arms** (5.9, not as bad as it looks). Swing left through an overhang and continue up steep rock (5.8), staying left of the nose. Join **Men At Arms** at the easy ceilings near the top.

174 Men At Arms 5.10– PG13
FA: Jim McCarthy, Dick Williams, 1966
A rather necky lead that wanders up the face right of **MF**. Start at a large left-facing corner 95 feet left of **Overhanging Layback** and 110 feet right of **Something Interesting**. Climb the corner, weave left up the face then hand traverse back right (V1) to a belay below the **Try Again** ceiling. Traverse out left to a stance (fixed peg), then

McCarthy Wall

up right along a small right-facing corner (5.9, scary) and the face above. Move left and up to overhangs which are passed on the left, and on to a belay at the GT ledge. Up a face to a ceiling, skirt it on the left to the trail.

V1 Men At Arms Direct 5.10+ R FA: Henry Barber, circa 1974. From the middle of the hand traverse right, climb straight up to rejoin the route at the stance out left.

175 Try Again 5.10 PG ★★
FA: Jim McCarthy, Hans Kraus, 1955. FFA: Rich Goldstone, Jim McCarthy, Raymond Schrag, 1967
More than twenty seven years later, people still fail on this well-named route. Climb the inside corner as for **Men At Arms**, but move right and follow a corner leaning right over a triangular roof (crux, one can belay under the roof as for **Men At Arms**). Follow thin cracks up right to the common belay of **Coexistence**, **Fly Again**, and **Star Action**. Most people rappel off here, but if you desire, continue up to the GT ledge via some corners, then easy rock to the path.

176 Fly Again 5.11+ R ★★
FA: Russ Clune, Mike Law (Australian), May, 1983
Climb the face left of **Coexistence**, then follow a beautiful thin verti-cal crack to the belay on **Try Again** (5.10). Step right past a bulge and climb the ceiling at a thin seam left of **Coexistence** (TCUs below, #3 RP up left, crux) to the communal belay. Rappel off.

177 Coexistence 5.10+ PG ★★★
FA: Jim McCarthy, Phil Jacobus, John Hudson, Peter Armour, 1962. FFA: Rich Goldstone, Jim McCarthy, 1967
Another climb that firmly established hard 5.10 at the Gunks. Still a climb to be reckoned with. Dash straight up over a roof 20 feet right of **Try Again** to a ledge at 40 feet. Follow a great, thin crack to the roof and over this (crux) to the belay. Rappel, or continue upwards.

178 Star Action 5.10+ PG ★★
FA: Bob Richardson, Dick Saum, Ivan Rezucha, 1974
Named for a pinball machine frequented by the FA party. Zoom up a corner and crack 30 feet left of **Overhanging Layback**, then tra-verse left to the **Coex** ledge and belay (40 feet). Follow a thin crack right of **Coex** to the roof. Launch over the roof, into the corner on

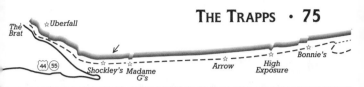

The Brat ☆Uberfall
44 55 Shockley's Madame G's Arrow High Exposure Bonnie's

163	Raspberry Sundae 5.9	177	Coexistence 5.10+
164	Three Pines 5.3+	179	Graveyard Shift 5.11–
167	Something Interesting 5.7+	180	Tough Shift 5.10
169	Birdie Party 5.10–	181	Overhanging Layback 5.7
172	MF 5.9	183	Scene of the Climb 5.11–
174	Men at Arms 5.10–	184	Land's End 5.9
175	Try Again 5.10		

the left (crux), then easily up and left to the communal belay (90 feet). Rappel, or continue up the **Overhanging Layback** corner, then right and roll over a large ceiling at a left-facing corner (5.9, done previously).

179 Graveyard Shift 5.11– PG ★★

FA: Russ Raffa, Rich Ross, 1978

You'll probably end up working overtime on this one. Small wires needed. Climb an obvious thin crack through a bulging wall right of **Star Action**, then step left and up a small left-facing corner. Over

McCarthy Wall

---

the ceiling, then right to flake and up to the roof (scary crux). Climb the roof left of **Tough Shift** (5.7), then finish as for **Tough Shift** or traverse left to the communal belay.

V1 Don't Shift 5.11+ (TR) FA: Kevin Bein, 1986. Climb the face between this route and **Tough Shift**.

180 Tough Shift 5.10 PG13 ★★
FA: Jim McCarthy, Ants Leemets, 1961
This shift is not for the nine-to-five crowd. Start 20 feet left of **Overhanging Layback** below a thin crack and right-facing corner. Race up the thin crack and right-facing corner to a ceiling. Get good pro at the ceiling (V1), shift gears, and traverse out left onto the face and a right-facing flake. Sputter up the face (scary crux) to a roof and belay at a stance. Either rappel, or follow **Overhanging Layback** to the top.

V1 5.11 PG FA: Russ Clune, circa 1986. Climb straight up above the right facing corner over the ceiling with difficult pro (TCUs above roof).

181 Overhanging Layback 5.7 PG ★
FA: Fritz Wiessner, Bill Shockley, 1946
A good climb and aptly named. This climb marks the right edge of the McCarthy Wall. Climb up a very obvious, right-facing corner with a huge right pointing flake a short way up. Undercling/layback partway out the flake then back left and up to a belay in the big corner (5.7). Up the corner to a tree, traverse out left onto the face to another corner, then up the face (V1) to a roof. Move far right around a roof, and on to the GT ledge. Climb to the path.

V1 Follow the face just left of arête up past loose flakes to a roof, then left through the roof near its right side to the GT ledge; 5.7.

182 No Existence 5.9+ R
FA: Jim McCarthy, Sam Streibert, 1964
A scary first pitch leads to more difficult climbing above. Starting ten feet right of **Overhanging Layback**, climb the face above a triangular block, wandering up and left to a belay in the **Overhanging Layback** corner (5.9 R, #3 Friend in pocket on the face). Follow a corner system up and over a roof at a notch (crux) to the GT ledge. Waddle to the summit.

183 Scene of the Climb 5.11– G ★
FA: P1 Kevin Bein, Steve Amter, Barbara Devine, Roy Kligfield, Steve Levin, Mark Robinson, Ron Sacks, 1976; P2 Ron Sacks, Kevin Bein,

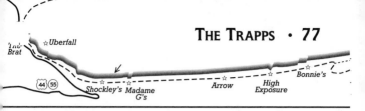

1976; (complete) Russ Raffa, 1976

A popular face climb that is often wet. The first pitch had the most
people on an FA at the Gunks to date. Start 25 feet right of
Overhanging Layback below a seam with a fixed peg. Climb up to
the seam and up this (crux), angling left over an overhang to a
belay. Rappel off, or climb to the right edge of some roofs. Reach
over, move left to a right-leaning corner, then pull three ceilings
(5.10) to the GT ledge and a very easy finish above.

184 Land's End 5.9 PG ★

FA: Art Gran, Jim McCarthy, 1960

The first pitch is popular, but slightly runout above the crux. It's not
named for the popular mail order clothing company! Tackle a short,
right-facing arch 40 feet right of **Overhanging Layback** (crux), to a
stance to the left. Diagonal way right from here (scary, V1) over
steepish rock then back left to the belay. Follow a crack (V2) over a
ceiling to an arching right-facing corner and the GT ledge (5.8).
Crawl to the summit.

V1 Climb straight up orange rock past flakes to a right facing corner. Undercling right on a ceiling then up to the belay; 5.10.

V2 Before reaching the crack at an overhang, escape out left and
jugbash to the GT ledge.

185 Land Ho! 5.9+ PG

FA: Ivan Rezucha, Keith Buesing, March, 1992

The first section of this route is an old variation to **Land's End**.
Climb the face to the start of the **Land's End** crux. Undercling a
flake out right (hands above, feet below roof), then climb over a
small ceiling to rejoin **Land's End**. Angle right to a short left facing
corner, then straight up the face to a belay stance (5.9 PG). Climb a
small overhang to a roof at a flake. Climb the roof (5.9+ G), then
straight up to the right edge of another roof. Step right, then angle
left to pass the final overhang to the GT ledge.

186 The Jane Fonda Workout 5.12 (TR)

FA: Russ Clune, Summer, 1986

Start about 40 feet right of **Land's End** and climb past a small ceiling to thin face moves up a bulging wall (crux). A 5.10+
variation—The Jane Fonda Workout for Pregnant Woman—has also
been top-roped, but the exact location isn't known.

187 Organic Iron 5.12+ PG

FA: Ivan Rezucha, January, 1982. FFA: Lynn Hill, Russ Raffa, 1984

If you can hang out to protect the crux, it's pretty well protected. If not. . . . Tiptoe up flakes 50 feet right of **Land's End** then pull over a ceiling. Continue past more flakes, fire the second roof (crux), then angle right to belay on **Impenetrable Ceilings**, below the **Scotch on the Rocks** roof. The second pitch moves left around a corner, then up and over a roof at a right-facing corner. Scamper up and right to the trees.

188 Impenetrable Ceilings 5.11 PG

FA: Ivan and Paul Rezucha, 1978

Up a small left-facing corner 130 feet right of **Overhanging Layback**, then follow a flake through big overhangs (crux) straight on to **Scotch on the Rocks**, and eventually the summit.

189 Scotch on the Rocks 5.10 G

FA: Ivan Rezucha, Paul Potters, 1974

Start at a left-facing corner 150 feet right of **Overhanging Layback** and 190 feet left of **Asphodel**. Up the corner to the roof, exit right, then over another ceiling. Angle left to a diagonal crack, and the belay at a corner, below a roof. Follow a crack system through the roof (crux) and on to the GT ledge. Skip to the trail.

190 Dry Martini 5.7 G ★

FA: Hans Kraus, Bonnie Prudden, Lucien Warner, 1955

A popular route, that wanders a bit. Start as for **Scotch on the Rocks** at a left-facing corner that is just right of some blocks. Scamper part way up the left-facing corner, then traverse far right and up to a belay in a corner (5.6). Move left, and up past a bulge with a bolt (crux), to a corner on the right and the belay just above. The third pitch follows a fissure to a corner, then exits up left to the GT ledge. Ramble to the brambles above.

191 Tequila Mockingbird 5.7+ G ★

FA: Rich Perch, Ivan Rezucha, 1975

What do you get when you cross Gregory Peck with Jose Cuervo? Perch, a Mohonk Preserve ranger in the late seventies, now works at Canyonlands National Park. Start just right of **Dry Martini** at a left-arching crack. Climb up the crack and past the right edge of a ceiling to the belay on **Dry Martini** (5.6+). Follow a right-arching corner/flake until you can step left and up the face (crux) to the second

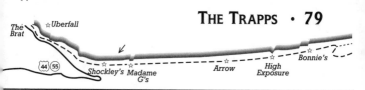

Dry Martini belay. Continue up the right-facing corners right of **Dry Martini** to the summit (watch for wasps).

192 PT Phone Home 5.10+ PG

FA: Russ Raffa, Russ Clune, Jeff Gruenberg, Pete Thexton (UK), December, 1981

Named for Thexton, who died later on Broad Peak in the Himalayas. Climb a crack 70 feet right of **Dry Martini** and just left of **Co-op**, to the left end of the **Co-op** traverse at a left-facing corner. Step right and climb the roof above (crux, TCUs, V1), then on to a belay. Follow **Co-op** past left-pointing flakes, then over a small hang and out left through more ceilings to the GT ledge and the woods (5.8).

V1 Tits Like Orange Fireballs 5.11 PG FA: Jeff Morris, Jim Damon, 1988. Instead of stepping right at the roof, it is possible to hand traverse left past two fixed pegs and up around the left side of the roof.

193 Co-op 5.9– PG

FA: Jim McCarthy, Dave Bernays, Spring, 1954. FFA: Art Gran, pre-1964

A very confusing line that is not particularly interesting, even if you can stay on route! Start 90 feet right of **Dry Martini**, and 100 feet left of **Asphodel**. Climb past a block and bulge, then wander left around a roof (V1), then way back right and through a ceiling at a notch to a corner and the belay above. If you make it this far, follow your nose to the top.

V1 Co-op Direct 5.10- PG13 FA: Unknown, 1970s. Good climbing, but really scary. Start between a giant oak tree and a block. Climb basically straight up along thin seams through an overhanging wall to a slab. Continue up past ceilings at a short left-facing corner.

194 Fall From Grace 5.11 PG

FA: Dick Williams, Tom Spiegler, 1990

Rope up 15 feet left of **Welcome to the Gunks** below a short, right facing corner that begins on a mossy ledge. Climb the corner and face above through a bulge to a thin, white seam that runs through two small ceilings. Climb left-facing flakes, then right-facing flakes, then an overhang. Climb past two more overhangs that are left of the **Co-op** notch, then angle up right to a rappel station.

195 Welcome to the Gunks 5.10 PG13 ★★

FA: Jim Kolocotronis, Andy Cairns, 1973

The initial roof is popular, but the scary 5.9+ climbing above isn't. Start 70 feet left of **Asphodel** in the center of a low roof with two crack/flake systems. Climb out the leftmost of the two flake systems (5.10–, V1). Move left and climb a steep orange face (5.9+) to a cramped stance below a left-facing corner in a ceiling. Up the corner (5.10–) to the belay (many people rappel just above the corner). Climb on up past two more ceilings (5.8+) to the bushes.

V1 Laughing Man 5.10 PG FA: Rich Pleiss, 1970s. Swing left out the right hand flake system (crux), then up a left-facing corner. Rappel off, or traverse right at its top to join **Credibility Gap**.

196 Tree's a Crowd 5.9 G

FA: Ivan Rezucha, Mike Sawicky, February, 1981

If you're into hugging trees, this is the climb for you. Diagonal up left past the right edge of the **Laughing Man** ceiling, squeezing behind a tree. Climb up a few feet, then branch out right under a roof and up a right-facing corner to a belay on **Credibility Gap** (5.8). Follow a left-leaning crack past a roof, then up to the GT ledge (5.9, done previously). The final pitch climbs overhangs right of some pines to the top.

197 Credibility Gap 5.6 G

FA: Jim McCarthy, Joe Kelsey, Dick Williams, 1968

A good-looking pitch up the clean cracks left of **Asphodel** leads to less interesting climbing above. At the top of the cracks, move left to a corner, and up this to a belay under a roof. Climb the ceiling, then continue past the GT ledge, and on to the woods.

198 Asphodel 5.5 G

FA: Hans Kraus, Bonnie Prudden, 1953

Named for a white and yellow flower in the lily family, that according to Homer's *Odyssey* grows in abundance in the hereafter. Start at a large, yellow right-facing corner, 190 feet right of **Dry Martini**, and 120 feet left of **Beginner's Delight**, then exit left across loose rock to a belay. Jog left, then right, and on past the GT ledge, to the shrubs.

V1 The obvious handcrack through the roof above pitch one has been climbed, but no more is known.

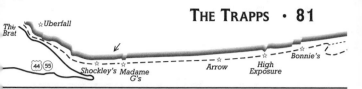

184	Land's End 5.9	193	Co-op 5.9–
188	Impenetrable Ceilings 5.11	195	Welcome to the Gunks 5.10
189	Scotch on the Rocks 5.10	196	Tree's a Crowd 5.9
190	Dry Martini 5.7	197	Credibility Gap 5.6
191	Tequila Mockingbird 5.7+	198	Asphodel 5.5
192	PT Phone Home 5.10+		

199 Beatle Brow Bulge 5.9+ PG

FA: Jim McCarthy, Matt Hale, Jim Alt, 1966. FFA: John Stannard,
Henry Barber, 1973

A fun roof problem, that is now well protected with Friends and Tri-cams. Climb up easy rock 70 feet right of **Asphodel** to a belay
under an overhang. Out the roof at a left-facing flake/corner (crux),
then angle right up a steep little face (Friends, Tri-cams) to a belay.
Rappel, or climb up to the GT ledge and then up a dirty left-facing
corner past a roof to the top (watch for wasps).

V1 The face to the left of pitch one has at least one hard route up it
(past the pointed block), but no more is known.

200 Blueberry Wine 5.11– PG13

FA: John Stannard, 1970s

Climb just right of **Beatle Brow Bulge** past a roof at a left-facing corner, to a second, and more difficult roof. Rappel, or climb up and connect with **Seldom Mustard, Never Relish**. This route is runout on easier rock.

201 Blueberry Ledges 5.4+ PG

FA: Willie Crowther, Gardiner Perry, 1958

A wandering line past grassy ledges and (usually) wasp nests. Begin 100 feet right of **Asphodel** under the right edge of the **Beatle Brow Bulge** roof. Climb up to and around right of the roof to a left-facing corner. Follow this to a belay on the right. Climb up far left past two corners, then on to the GT ledge. Conclude this extravaganza by moving left and climbing an inside right-facing corner.

202 Seldom Mustard, Never Relish 5.10 G

FA: Steve and Corey Jones, 1976

Corey was a Mohonk Preserve ranger in the 1970s; Steve made the first .5 sized Friend-type devices used in the Gunks. Wander up the face between **Blueberry Ledges** and **Beginner's Delight** to the GT ledge. On the last pitch, swing over the hang ten feet left of **Beginner's Delight** and near a bush (crux).

203 Beginner's Delight 5.3 PG ★★★

FA: Hans Kraus, Roger and Del Wolcott, 1948

A great climb, but be careful protecting the second on the traverse. Also be aware that this route is sustained for its grade. Start 125 feet right of **Asphodel** below a big left-facing corner system. Scramble up right to the base of the corner system and a ledge, then up the corner to a belay (75 feet). Continue up the corner 40 feet, then traverse left about 40 feet and weave on up to a belay on the GT ledge below a beautiful left-facing corner capped by a roof (120 feet). The final pitch is great, and climbs the corner above, bypassing the first roof on the right. Continue up to another corner capped by a roof, and pass this on the left. From here, it's a short hop to the trees.

204 Octoberfest 5.8+ R

FA: Alan Long, Al Rubin, Paul Ledoux, October, 1979

An impressive line up a corner system on the arête right of **Beginner's Delight**. Ledoux, an active member of the Boston AMC,

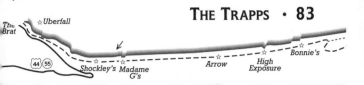

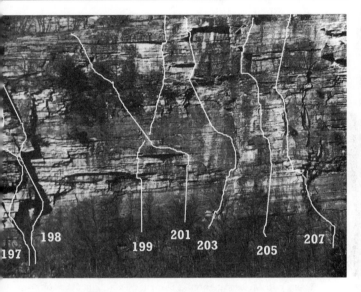

197	**Credibility Gap 5.6**	203	**Beginner's Delight 5.3**
198	**Asphodel 5.5**	205	**Snooky's Return 5.8–**
199	**Beatle Brow Bulge 5.9+**	207	**Minty 5.3**
201	**Blueberry Ledges 5.4+**		

died roughly ten years later in a climbing accident in the Needles of South Dakota. Bring small TCUs for the second pitch. Climb the face 30 feet right of **Beginner's Delight** past some trees (V1), to a belay at the base of the huge corner (5.7). Climb up the arête/corner past a ceiling (5.8 R), and on to the GT ledge. Climb the left edge of the **Minty** overhang to the top (5.7).

V1 Climb the crack and face just right of **Beginner's Delight**.

205 Snooky's Return 5.8– G ★
FA: Jim McCarthy, Dave Craft, Spring, 1958
Named for Oscar "Snooky" Dorfman. A very good first pitch of face climbing at its grade. Saunter up a vertical seam 45 feet right of

Beginner's (V1), past a dead pine (many people rappel from here), to a belay above. Climb a left-facing corner, move left, then wander up the steep face above to the GT ledge. Up a corner on the left, past a roof on the right, and on to the trail down.

V1 Snooky's Departure 5.7+ R FA: Unknown, 1960s. Up small right-facing corners (crux) and the face above to join **Snooky's Return** at the pine.

206 Friends and Lovers 5.9 R ★
FA: Ron Sacks, Anne Dubats, Mike Sawicky, Rick Cronk, 1978
A bit scary on the first pitch. Waltz up a thin, vertical crack 20 feet right of **Snooky's Return** to a ledge. Make a weird move off the ledge (crux), then up white rock to a belay (110 feet). Move far left to **Beginner's Delight**, and up the huge corner, until you can exit right, and on up to the GT ledge. Finish up the left-facing corner to the left of **Snooky's**.

NOTE: When walking along the carriage road from the Uberfall area, the first pine tree you will come to is the **Minty** Tree. Follow the path up from the tree to approach the climbs in this area.

207 Minty 5.3 G ★★
FA: Fritz Wiessner, Minty Warren, Betty Woolsey, 1941
A very popular beginner route. Starting 50 feet right of **Snooky's**, romp up a series of right-facing corners that diagonal up left past a horizontal pine tree, to the GT ledge (5.3, 150 feet). Above, climb a corner (V1), then go right over a roof to the top.

V1 Minty Overhang 5.5 G FA: Unknown, 1940s. A very good overhang problem that climbs the roof left of the final corner.

208 Bag's End 5.8+ PG
FA: Ivan Rezucha, Annie O'Neill, May, 1982
The first pitch up the face between **Minty** and **Tipsy Trees** (5.5) had been done earlier. After belaying at a pine at the top of the first pitch, climb past a small ceiling, then left around a bigger ceiling. Continue on past a short left-facing corner to cross **The Womb Step**, then on to the GT ledge. Swing around right, out of an obvious corner, and up through a notch in a huge block, to the top.

209 Tipsy Trees 5.3 G
FA: Gardiner and Mary Perry, 1958
Begin 65 feet right of **Snooky's Return** above a pile of rocks. Tiptoe up easy rock to a belay on a ledge at a pine (90 feet). From the left

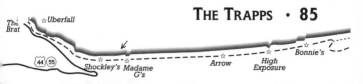

The Brat
☆Uberfall
44 55
☆Shockley's
Madame G's
Arrow
High Exposure
Bonnie's

220

209

207 210 211 214 215 217 219

207	Minty 5.3	215	Southern Pillar 5.2
209	Tipsy Trees 5.3	217	Madame Grunnebaum's
210	The Womb Step 5.7+		Wulst 5.6
211	Hawk 5.5	219	G Forces 5.10
214	Reach of Faith 5.10	220	Mr. P's Wurst 5.7+

edge of the ledge, clamber to an inside corner. At the top of the corner, climb the face on the right, then weave on up to the GT ledge (5.3). Up the face and corner above, then up right to the top.

210 The Womb Step 5.7+ PG
FA: Jim McCarthy, Bob Larsen, 1954
Named for the intimidating crux move on the second pitch. Up a four-inch-wide crack 35 feet right of **Tipsy Trees** to a belay at a

Guides' Wall

ledge below a right-facing corner. Up the corner, and out left across the face (crux, V1, V2) to join **Tipsy Trees**, which is followed to the top.

V1 Womb For Went 5.9 PG FA: Unknown, 1970s. Just before the crux, climb over an orange overhang, and up to another roof. Over this at a crack, then on past another ceiling to the woods.

V2 Womb with a View 5.8 Traverse left to the left edge of the ceiling, then climb straight up. Hand traverse right a bit then up and left, reaching the GT ledge just right of the large, left facing corner that **Bag's End** swings right around. The rock is a bit funky reaching the GT ledge.

211 Hawk 5.5 PG ★
FA: Willie Crowther, Gardiner and Mary Perry, 1958
An exposed, and exciting climb that is not for the inexperienced climber. Jam up a nice finger crack 150 feet left of **Southern Pillar**, and 55 feet right of **Tipsy Trees** to a belay under a big left-facing corner. Climb up and right around two corners (exposed crux), then on to the GT ledge. Follow the big left-facing corner above to the top.

212 Chimango 5.9+ PG
FRA: Ivan Rezucha, Bill Ravitch, June, 1980
The first pitch was added at a later date. Wander up the face left of **Hawk**, to the **Hawk** belay. Climb the corner above the belay, step right at the top, and up left past another ceiling at a weakness. Power by yet another roof to a belay off to the right at a tree on the GT ledge. Over a roof behind the tree (V1) to the shrubs.

V1 It is also possible to climb the roof left of the belay, at weaknesses.

213 Peregrine 5.8 PG
FA: Ivan Rezucha, Bill Ravitch, June, 1980
Difficult to protect. Fly up a small left-facing corner 25 feet right of **Hawk** to a ledge and belay. Over the roofs above into a left-facing corner, then swing right around the corner above **Hawk**, and weave past two ceilings to a tree. Move left and over another roof to the GT ledge. Follow a crack past a small roof 20 feet left of **Hawk** to the summit.

214 Reach of Faith 5.10 G
FA: Ivan Rezucha, May, 1980
From the start of **Southern Pillar**, climb straight up the face to a belay level with **Hawk** and **Chimango**. Wander up the face above,

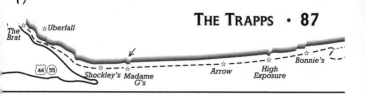

passing a hang at a notch below a tree, and on to the GT ledge. Out the overhangs above at a diagonal flake (crux, TCUs, V1), then on to the trees.

V1 Move left under the roof then climb the left-facing corner through the overhang; 5.9+.

215 Southern Pillar 5.2 G ★
FA: Hans Kraus, Roger Wolcott, Del Wilde, 1941
Popular, but not as nice as **Northern Pillar**. Start on the left side of the Madame G's Buttress, 40 feet right of **Hawk** and 100 feet left of **Northern Pillar**. Clamber up right at a chimney/flake along a series of left-facing corners to a belay under the obvious left-facing corner system (60 feet). Wander up the main corner system past a huge block any way of your choosing, to the GT ledge (130 feet). (It is possible to split this pitch by belaying at the block.) Scramble off to the right (V1).

V1 Direct Finish 5.7 PG FA: Unknown, pre-1964. Climb the corner above the ledge past a pointy overhang. Good moves.

216 Columbia 5.9– G
FA: Roy Kligfield, Dave Ingalls, Jim Driscoll, 1969. FFA: Joe Kelsey, 1969
Some good climbing on this one, especially if you climb the variation on the second pitch. Climb a leaning crack 15 feet right of **Southern Pillar** past a bulge (5.7+), to a spacious belay. Up the pink, left facing corner (crux, V1), then easily on up the right wall to the top.

V1 5.9+ FA: Unknown, 1970s. After the short crux corner, traverse out right, and climb past a small triangular roof to easier ceilings and the top.

217 Madame Grunnebaum's Wulst 5.6 G ★★★
FA: Hans Kraus, Harry Snyder, 1943
Not to be missed. Start below a steep, yellow and orange buttress that has a gully/chimney on its right side. Climb easily off some boulders 55 feet right of **Southern Pillar** to a belay on a platform below a yellow left-facing corner, at the base of the steep, orange buttress. Up the corner (5.6), move right, then weave past overhangs to a semi-hanging belay in the middle of the wall. Up over a bulge with a thin crack, then drift on to a handcrack, which will deposit you on top and at the end of a great route.

Guides' Wall

218 Madame Grunnebaum's Sorrow 5.8– PG

FA: Jim McCarthy, 1958

Originally top-roped, then led at a later date. From the top of the yellow crux corner on **Madame G's**, traverse far right to the right arête of the buttress, then around the corner to the **Le Teton** and **Northern Pillar** belay. Up a few body lengths, then back out left on the overhanging jugs above **Le Teton** (crux) to the nose, and on to the woods.

219 G Forces 5.10 PG ★

FA: Tad Welch, Todd Swain, October, 1985

The directissima of the Madame G's Buttress. Stroll up to the platform as for **Madame G's**, then over the first roof at a small left-facing corner (scary, V1). Move left and up a thin seam (crux) to the **Madame G's** belay. Continue straight over a bulge, then over the center of the big roof above (wild 5.9, Tri-cams), and up the tricky face to the top.

V1 5.10 G FA: Chuck Boyd, Terry Grainger, October, 1985. Climb the left-facing corner just right of **Madame G's** (5.8), then right, and up to the belay. Move right, then up an overhanging left-facing corner (5.10, contrived) to join **G Forces** at the final roof.

220 Mr. P's Wurst 5.7+ PG13 ★★

FA: Rich Perch, Ivan Rezucha, February, 1981

A good link-up of old and new climbing. Start ten feet left of the **Le Teton** gully. Climb straight up the face past a cleft to a ledge, then continue up the face to another ledge. Climb a groove near the right edge of the **Madame G's** face, exiting left at its top to a belay near **Madame G's** (5.6 R/X). Climb up and a bit right on steep rock (crossing **Madame G's Sorrow**) past some old pins to a trapezoidal roof. Move left and climb the ceiling a few feet left of a left-facing corner. Angle right towards the arête (where **Le Teton** comes in from the right). Climb left through a ceiling and up past blocks to the top (5.7+ PG).

221 Northern Pillar 5.2 G ★★

FA: Hans Kraus, Susanne Simon, 1941

The first recorded rock climb on the Trapps. Still considered a classic. From the base of the gully on the right side of the Madame G's

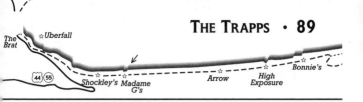

Buttress, angle up right (V1) to a belay on a ledge (60 feet). From here, scamper up left to a belay at a great ledge in the corner, then on up the huge corner (crux, V2), to the summit.

V1 Fingerlocks or Cedar Box 5.5 G ★ FA: Unknown. Climb the nice fingercrack 30 feet right of the gully, to connect with the belay.

V2 Cemetery Wall 5.8 G FA: Art Gran, circa 1958. Strenuous and a little loose. Power up the overhanging crack left of the final corner, to the pine tree.

NOTE: This is the leftmost climb on a small section of cliff known as Guides' Wall. It is possible to rappel off the pine, then downclimb **Northern Pillar** (or rappel from various trees) as a descent route.

222 Le Teton 5.9+ G ★★
FA: Jim McCarthy, Stan Gross, Spring 1955. FFA: Art Gran, Lito Tejada-Flores, 1965
An impressive climb, and a pumper to protect. Either climb the gully on the right side of the Madame G's Buttress, or scramble up **Northern Pillar** to the second belay below a beautiful thin crack on a white face. Climb the crack (crux), then move left to the arête, and up the overhanging jugs to the top. It is possible to belay out on the arête, as for **Mr. P's**, to split the crack and jug bashing into two short pitches.

223 Hyjek's Horror 5.8– PG ★
FA: Mike Hyjek, John Lomont, 1963
A very popular first pitch of face climbing. Many other lines have been climbed on either side of this route. Wander up smooth, white rock 65 feet right of the **Le Teton** gully and 20 feet left of the **Twin Oaks** crack past a small hang at 20 feet, to lower angled rock, and a ledge above (5.7+, 60 feet). Rappel, or climb straight up the face to the top, passing roofs on the right.

224 Twin Oaks 5.3 PG ★
FA: Gardiner and Mary Perry, 1957
Struggle up the wide left-leaning crack 20 feet right of **Hyjek's** to the belay ledge (5.3). Angle up left almost to the **Northern Pillar** belay (5.3). Climb up past a left-facing corner, then pass a roof on the right to the top (5.3).

Guides' Wall

225 Triple Bulges 5.5 G
FA: John Lomont, Francis Coffin, 1959
Starting at the top of the **Twin Oaks** crack, weave straight up above to a large overhang, which is climbed at the middle (crux), then scramble to the woods.

226 Delusions of Grandeur 5.9+ PG
FA: Chris Monz, Mike Sawicky, 1983
The last route on the Guides' Wall. Probably harder if you are short. From the base of the leaning **Twin Oaks** crack, climb directly over the roof above (crux; #1 RPs at lip) to a belay and the ledge. Move left, and climb the face between **Twin Oaks** and **Triple Bulges** (5.7).

227 Willie's Weep 5.2 G
FA: George and Herbert Evans, Robert Graef, 1953
Climb a small right-facing corner 40 feet right of **Twin Oaks**, to a ledge. Traverse way left to a belay on the Guides' Wall ledge, then move up and right past a small left-facing corner to another belay. Pitch three climbs a right-facing corner past an overhang to the bushes.

228 Don't Shoot 5.6 G
FA: Dave Ingalls, Vin Hoeman, Fall, 1965
Should've been named Don't Climb! Clamber up left-facing flakes 55 feet right of **Twin Oaks**, to a belay on the left at a pine. Continue up to a hang, move left until it can be climbed at a small corner, then walk left to a belay as for **Willie's Weep** at a tree. Climb a shallow dihedral to the top.

229 Lat-on the Season 5.7 PG
FA: Art Gran, 1964
Perhaps named for Layton Kor, who was visiting the area. Up the face at a thin seam 70 feet right of **Twin Oaks**, then wander first left, then right, to reach the belay, which is on a small ledge in the center of a long overhang. Climb the first hang via a vertical seam, then continue over another ceiling at a left-facing corner (V1), then diagonal left to easier ground.

V1 Traverse far left then up past a block to the woods (as for **Gleet Street**); 5.6.

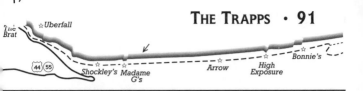

221	**Northern Pillar 5.2**	**229**	**Lat-on the Season 5.7**
221v	**Fingerlocks or Cedar Box 5.5**	**231**	**Funny Face 5.5–**
222	**Le Teton 5.9+**	**232**	**Son of Bitchy Virgin 5.6**
223	**Hyjek's Horror 5.8–**	**234**	**Bitchy Virgin 5.6**
224	**Twin Oaks 5.3**	**236v**	**Dat-Mantle 5.10**
227	**Willie's Weep 5.2**	**236**	**Dis-Mantle 5.10**
228	**Don't Shoot 5.6**	**236v**	**Kernmantle 5.8**

230 Gleet Street 5.8 R

FA: Keith Mercer, Jeff Street, 1986

Rope up at a slab, directly below a seam that runs through an overhang. This is just left of the **Funny Face** corner. Climb along the seam to a pine, then move left and go up to another ledge. Angle right past a right facing corner, then angle left to a small ledge below the center of a long ceiling. Belay on this ledge as for **Lat-On the Season** (5.8 R). Climb a crack, then through a ceiling at a cleft. Continue past a tree to a right facing corner capped by a ceiling. Exit left at the ceiling, then angle left to a belay ledge with blocks (as for **Lat-On the Season**; 5.6). Move right on a ledge then climb a ceiling at left facing flakes (5.5).

231 Funny Face 5.5– PG
FA: Jim McCarthy, Tim Mutch, Spring, 1954
Start 80 feet right of **Twin Oaks** and 50 feet left of the **Dis-Mantle** block below a ceiling and a small left-facing corner. Sneak around the low ceiling on its right, then angle right to an inside left-facing corner. Up the corner to its top, and belay higher on a ledge. Follow loose corners on the left to the GT ledge, and then another corner (V1) to the trees.

V1 Climb out left from the final corner below a roof, then on to the top; 5.5.

232 Son of Bitchy Virgin 5.6 PG
FA: Jim McCarthy, John Reppy, 1967
Historically a scary route, now protected with Tri-cams and TCUs. Climb a right-facing corner 25 feet left of the **Dis-Mantle** block (V1), escape around to the left of a roof, and on up the blank face to a belay as for **Bitchy Virgin**. Climb straight up the face above (Tri-cams) to the GT ledge, then on to the trail.

V1 Climb the roof to the left at a notch; 5.6.

233 Immaculate Conception 5.6 PG
FRA: Todd Swain, John Thackray, September, 1986
Climb the bulging wall and arête between the first pitches of **Bitchy Virgin** and **Son of BV** to a belay even with the big roof on the right (5.6 G). Continue up the face above as for the two routes (Tri-cams helpful).

234 Bitchy Virgin 5.6 PG
FA: Hans Kraus, Bonnie Prudden, 1954
The second pitch is now best protected with Tri-cams. Up the large right-facing corner in the back left side of the detached **Dis-Mantle** block. Move left at its top and belay. Wander up and slightly right (Tri-cams) passing loose blocks, to the GT ledge, then on to the top.

235 Unnamed 5.2 PG
FA: Fritz Wiessner, Betty Woolsey, Mary Cecil, 1942
Climb up from the recess on the left side of the **Dis-Mantle** block (V1), to the top of the pillar and a belay. From here, climb up right to a left-facing corner, and up this to the GT ledge. The final pitch scrambles to the top.

V1 Lemon Squeezer 5.2 PG FA: Unknown, 1940s. Slither up the chimney on the right side of the block to the top.

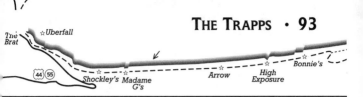

236 Dis-Mantle 5.10 PG ★

FA: Joe Strutt, Roy Kligfield, Jack Hunt, 1973

All three first pitches on this huge, detached block are worth doing.
Descend via rappel, or by downclimbing **Unnamed**. This climb is
much harder now that the "gearstick" knob has broken off. Starting
by a huge oak tree (V1, 2), climb the front face of the block to an
overlap. Over this (5.10), then over the bigger roof above (5.8), and
on to the top of the block. If you decide to continue upwards, go up
left through the middle of a roof (5.7 R), and then on to the shrubs.

V1 Dat-Mantle 5.10 PG ★ FA: Rich Perch, Kevin Bein, Barbara
Devine, Rich Ross, 1976. Climb up the left front of the block, and
over the roof (crux) to the pillar's top.

V2 Kernmantle 5.8 PG FA: Rich Ross, Dave Sweet, May, 1976. A
little bit tricky to protect. Climb the right front of the block, passing
a ceiling (5.7) to the big overhang. Move around right, then step
back left (crux) above the roof.

237 High Times 5.9 PG ★

FA: Rich Ross, Mike Sawicky, June, 1976

If the fixed pin fails on the face under the roof, the climb is R/X. Not
the route to push your limits on. Climb the tricky face 15 feet right
of the **Dis-Mantle** block (5.9) to the roof. Move right, and through
the hang at a corner, to a belay above at a pine. Rappel, or climb up
and around right at a left-facing corner, then up between **Raunchy**
and **Stop the Presses**.

238 Stop the Presses Mr. Williams 5.8+ PG

FA: Roman Laba, Roy Kligfield, 1972

Even with a name like this, the route didn't make it into the 1972
guide! A worthwhile boulder problem crux. Climb a face 20 feet
right of the **Dis-Mantle** block to a left-facing corner. Over the bulge
above the corner (crux) to a ledge with a big pine on the right.
Rappel, or move left and climb the face up to and over a bulge, then
left past a roof at a corner to the summit.

239 Osteo-path 5.8 PG

FRA: Todd Swain, John Thackray, September, 1986

Start on the left edge of the ledge ten feet left of **Raunchy**. Climb
over the small ceiling at a thin seam (often wet under the ceiling),
then up and right along the seam to a white bulge. Over this (crack

235	Unnamed 5.2		245	HELP! 5.11+
236	Dis-Mantle 5.10		246	V-3 5.7
237	High Times 5.9		246v	Galactic Hitchikers 5.9+
240	Raunchy 5.8–		247	City Streets 5.10–
241	Wild Horses 5.9		248	Country Roads 5.10
244	Badfinger 5.9+		250	Commando Rave 5.9

widens—old variation to **Stop the Presses**) and up to the pine tree to a belay. Climb up to the left-leaning corner above (**Raunchy**, **Wild Horses**, etc. break out right through this), and follow it to the top.

240 Raunchy 5.8– PG ★
FA: Jim McCarthy, Bill Goldner, Fall, 1963
The next three climbs all have attractive first pitches, and an easy rappel to get off. Begin 35 feet right of the **Dis-Mantle** block at a short slab below a ledge ten feet up. Climb up a thin, right-facing seam (hard), pass a ledge, then up a shallow right-facing corner (crux), which leads to the pine tree. If your goal is the summit, climb the face past a roof at a left-facing corner, and on to the top.

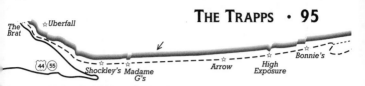

241 Wild Horses 5.9 PG13 ★
FA: Dick Williams, Roy Kligfield, Al Rubin, Ivan Rezucha, 1975
Gallop up the face right of **Raunchy** past the ledge to a vertical crack, which ends (crux). Continue up the face above to a tree on a ledge. Climb up right to the top of a left-facing corner, swing around right and up the steep face (5.8), then up to the descent trail.

V1 The face just left of the first pitch has been top-roped at 5.9+.

242 Gory Thumb 5.8+ G
FA: Jim McCarthy, Dave Bernays, Spring, 1954. FFA: Art Gran, pre-1964
Start just right of the last two routes at a short right-facing corner below a ledge ten feet up. Climb the corner, then up a vertical crack on a white face (crux), and on to the pine tree. Either rappel, or clamber up left past a bolt, then move far right past a left-facing corner to a belay under a hang. Climb the hang, and saunter on to the summit.

243 Everybody Needs Thumbody 5.9+ PG
FRA: Ivan Rezucha and others, November, 1985
Climb the arête and ramps angling right to the right of the start of **Gory Thumb**. Pull past a ceiling (crux), then up the right-hand seam on the white face above (5.8+, done previously) to a belay. Climb the face above to the top, or rappel from trees on the ledge.

244 Badfinger 5.9+ G
FA: Ivan Rezucha, Don Lauber, October, 1982
Climb the obvious right-facing corner 60 feet right of the **Dis-Mantle** block, to a point ten feet below the roof (V1, 2). Move right, and climb the roof at a flake. Traverse far left to the pine tree and rappel, or follow **Sword of Damocles** to the top.

V1 Sword of Damocles 5.9+ PG FA: Stan Hayes, 1983. Climb the corner to the roof, escape left (crux) to a belay, then up the face between **Gory Thumb**, and **HELP!**

V2 Sort of Damocles 5.7+ G FRA: Todd Swain, Andy Schenkel, 1984. Partway up the corner, climb the handcrack on the left wall to the belay.

245 HELP! 5.11+ PG ★
FA: Dick Williams, Joe Kelsey, 1965. FFA: John Stannard, John Bragg 1973
A long reach on the crux. Climb up the face right of **Badfinger** to the right edge of a huge block under the roof (5.9), then over the roof at the left edge of the block (crux, V1) to scary climbing, and the belay. Rappel, or climb left around a roof, and then up and left avoiding a roof on the right, to the woods.

V1 PLEH! 5.12– PG FA: Jim Damon, Mick Avery, 1984. Climb over the crux roof at the right side of the block.

246 V-3 5.7 G ★
FA: Hans Kraus, Ken Prestrud, Bonnie Prudden, 1954
The first pitch is very good, the second pitch very easy. If it weren't for Kraus' accent, this would probably be named We Three! Climb through the overhangs 140 feet right of the **Dis-Mantle** block, at a very obvious crack system/ V slot (V1), then up a 5.1 face pitch to the top (V2).

V1 Galactic Hitchhikers 5.9+ PG ★ FA: Todd Swain, Tad Welch, Dave and Marie Saball, Brad White, Dick Peterson, October, 1985. Climb the face right of **V-3** to a corner, swing right to a stance (crux), then up the arête (5.9), past an alcove, and roof (5.9) to the easy face above.

V2 V-3 Direct 5.7 G ★ FA: Unknown, 1960s. Climb the final roof direct, instead of escaping around right. Makes a good finish to the climb.

247 City Streets 5.10– G ★
FA: Ivan Rezucha, Joe Bridges, Rich Goldstone, 1976
Climb up the face 20 feet right of **V-3** into an obvious, left-facing corner formed by a block in the big roof. Rappel from the same anchor as **Country Roads** once you're above the roof.

248 Country Roads 5.10 PG ★★
FA: Unknown, circa 1964. FFA: John Stannard, Pat Milligan, 1971
Climb a thin crack 30 feet right of **V-3** to a ledge below the right side of a block in the big roofs above. Move right then up through the hangs into the right-facing corner (crux). Climb up this, then exit left to the belay at a tree. Rappel, or climb the very easy face to the top.

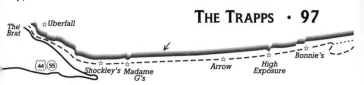

249 Metropolis 5.11 PG ★
FA: Russ Raffa, Ivan Rezucha, June, 1981
Once you've traveled the **Country Roads**, and **City Streets**, you're
ready to enter the **Metropolis**. Difficult to protect. Climb the face up
to the roof right of **Country Roads** then, from where **Country Roads**
starts the ceiling, traverse right through a roof at a left-facing corner
(possible to belay here), and then through the next hang left of a
thin seam. Continue on up the easy face above to the bushes.

250 Commando Rave 5.9 PG ★★
FA: Jim McCarthy, John Hudson, Spring 1963
A 5.9 that could take the wind out of your sails. Start as for **Country
Roads**, and from the ledge traverse far right, exiting around the
right edge of the roof (crux) to easier climbing. Rappel, or continue
to the summit.

251 Un-Appealing Ceiling 5.9+ R
FA: Bill Goldner, Pete Ramins, 1963. FFA: Doug Tompkins,
Jim McCarthy, 1963
Often wet, always scary. Tompkins and his former wife founded the
now famous Esprit clothing line. Start 115 feet right of **V-3** near the
right edge of the huge roof. Climb a right-facing corner past a
small roof to a large roof. Traverse up and left (scary crux), and over
the hang, to a belay. Rappel, or clamber up easy rock to the top.

252 Balrog 5.10 PG ★★
FA: Jim McCarthy, Rich Goldstone, 1967
A short crux but a real monster. Start 140 feet right of **V-3** and just
down left of a boulder pile. Climb a slab, then power up a right-
facing corner, and around left to a thin crack. Up the crack and into
an overhanging right-facing corner below a ceiling (crux). Traverse
left and up to a belay. Rappel, or join any of the neighboring climbs
to the brush.

V1 Balrog Escape (Bridge of Khaza-dum) 5.9 PG FA: Frank
Zahar, Tom Egan, 1976. Traverse out left above **Un-Appealing
Ceiling**, just before the crux of **Balrog**.

253 Bullfrog 5.12– R ★
FA: Felix Modugno, Jim Damon, May, 1984
A riveting climb. Start as for **Balrog**, but climb up right into an arching orange corner, until you can hand traverse left to another short corner. Up this (scary crux), then out left to easy ground. Rappel, or hop up the lily-pad-like handholds to the pond.

254 Sheep Thrills (aka Blind Alley) 5.9– PG13
FA: Ivan and Paul Rezucha, October, 1979
Climb straight up orange rock (crux) from the start of **Dry Heaves**, then follow the right-facing corner system to exit over the roof at **Alley Oop**. Rappel, or climb a flake system to the woods (5.6).

255 Dry Heaves 5.8 PG
FA: Mark Robinson, Sandy Stewart, Grant Calder, 1976
Starting just left of the top of the boulder pile, climb a right-facing corner then undercling a flake out right (crux). Follow flakes up and left to the right-facing corner. Swing around the corner at a notch below **Alley Oop** to the belay. Rappel, or jugbash to the shrubs.

256 Alley Oop 5.7 PG
FA: Jim McCarthy, Hans Kraus, Stan Gross, 1956. FFA: Art Gran, pre-1964
The boulder problem start was originally overcome by a three man shoulder stand! From the top of the boulder pile, climb thin face (crux) to a series of flakes leading left to the roof. Exit left over the roof at a short right-facing corner, to the belay. Either abseil, or bludgeon your way to the conclusion.

257 Cheap Thrills 5.10+ PG ★
FA: Kevin Bein, Roy Kligfield, 1972
A wee bit scary getting to the crux roof. Good climbing if you are solid on 5.10. Climb up the face 30 feet right of **Alley Oop** (V1) following thin cracks and flakes, to eventually climb the hang at a right-facing corner (crux). Descend, or ascend from there.

V1 Most people start up **Alley Oop** then move right, avoiding the first bit of dirty rock on the regular route.

258 Deep Chills 5.11 R
FA: Russ Raffa, Bob D'Antonio, Russ Clune, Hugh Herr, October, 1982
Exciting. Climb the face about ten feet right of **Cheap Thrills** to a

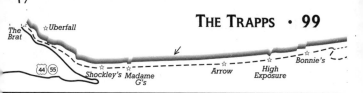

small roof. Over this (if you're tall, it's easier to the left), then up right to climb the main ceiling left of a flake.

NOTE: As with all of the climbs right to **Wise Crack**, it is best to rappel after P1.

259 Cakewalk 5.7 G ★
FA: Jim McCarthy, Hans Kraus, 1956
A popular first pitch, and rightly so. Thirty-five feet right of the boulder pile and 20 feet up is a prominent pine. Wander up the face left of the huge pine tree, to connect with a right-facing corner. Up the corner (watch for wasps), swing around left, and belay (5.7). Rappel, or wander to the finish.

260 Nurdland 5.10 R
FA: Mike Sawicky, January, 1981
Stumble straight up from the pine tree mentioned in **Cakewalk** past a bulge, to touch **Turdland** near the roof. Angle left, and up between **Cakewalk** and **Turdland**.

261 Turdland 5.9+ PG ★★
FA: Jim McCarthy, Jack Hansen, Spring, 1959. FFA: Dick Williams, 1966
If you don't use your feet, you might get pooped. From the pine tree mentioned in **Cakewalk**, waltz up right to a bolt, then back up left (5.7 R, V1) to a tiny corner, leading to a ceiling. Traverse right under the ceiling (crux, V2), then on up to a belay.

V1 Climb straight up (better protected).

V2 Original aid line 5.10+ G FFA: Dick Williams, 1966. Climb straight up above the right-facing corner past a bolt. Silly but safe.

262 Triangle 5.9– G ★
FA: Hans Kraus, Bonnie Prudden, Ken Prestrud 1954. FFA: Art Gran, Al DeMaria, 1960
Climb either of the cracks that form a detached block just right of **Turdland** to a ceiling (V1). Climb past the hang (crux), following a crack, to a belay above. Traverse right to **Never Never Land**, and rappel.

V1 5.9+ PG FRA: Ivan Rezucha, Annie O'Neill, May, 1981. Good climbing on this one. Climb up the center of the detached **Triangle** block (scary 5.8), then move left of the **Triangle** ceiling (crux) to join **Turdland**.

263 Never More 5.10 R
FA: Russ Clune, Rich Ross, August, 1982

From part way up the right **Triangle** crack, step right onto the face, and up to a vertical crack. Move up and left to a big horizontal (crux, V1), then right on the small ledge to a flake. Straight over this to the belay.

V1 Never Better 5.9+ PG FA: Russ Raffa, Fall, 1982. Top-roped, then led. After the crux on **Never More**, move left, and up a yellow streak to the belay. You'll have to climb 5.10 to reach this 5.9+ variation.

264 Never Say Never 5.10– R ★
FA: Dick Williams, Jim McCarthy, 1971

Great face climbing, but quite scary. Climb up right to a seam 15 feet left of **Never Never Land**. Up the seam (crux) and steep face to a large horizontal. Step right and up to a belay.

NOTE: Approach the next section from the carriage road via a stone stairway, just before a view towards New Paltz.

265 Never Never Land 5.10– PG ★★★
FA: Dave Craft, Jim McCarthy, Art Gran, 1959. FFA: Jim McCarthy, Dave Craft, Dick Williams, George Hurley, 1964

The best route in this area of the cliff. When it was first done, there were three bolts on the climb. Starting at the low point along the cliff and 25 feet right of **Triangle**, dance up the wonderful face and thin vertical seam past a bolt (crux), to a couple of scary moves, and then easier climbing slightly right to the belay ledge.

266 J'Accuse 5.10 PG
FA: Patrick Cordier (FR), Jim McCarthy, 1971. FFA: Scott Stewart, Rich Romano, 1973

Harder than 5.10 if you are short—even with the new bolt. The controversial bolt was placed standing on a pin, then led from the ground. Climb a difficult bulge 15 feet uphill of **Never Never Land** (crux, V1), to a thin seam and a bolt. Keep going straight up then go left on ledges to the **Never Never Land** anchor.

V1 Traverse in from the right then up past the bolt.

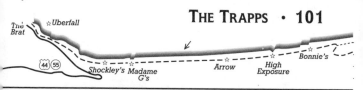

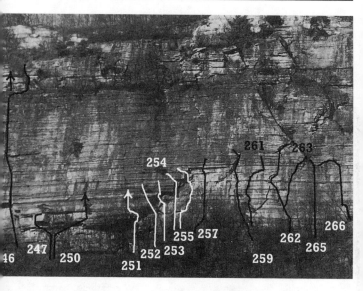

246	**V-3 5.7**	257	**Cheap Thrills 5.10+**
247	**City Streets 5.10–**	259	**Cakewalk 5.7**
250	**Commando Rave 5.9**	261	**Turdland 5.9+**
251	**Un-Appealing Ceiling 5.9+**	262	**Triangle 5.9–**
252	**Balrog 5.10**	263	**Never More 5.10**
253	**Bullfrog 5.12–**	265	**Never Never Land 5.10–**
254	**Sheep Thrills 5.9–**	266	**J'Accuse 5.10**
255	**Dry Heaves 5.8**		

267 Welcome to My Nightmare 5.10– X

FA (TR): Ivan Rezucha. FA (lead): Todd Swain, Randy Schenkel, August, 1986

Not only is it scary, but Swain was stung by wasps in the bushes at the big horizontal on the FA! Start just left of **Absurdland** and move up left to a stance. Climb up and very slightly right (crux) passing a large horizontal (bushes on either side) to the belay ledge.

268 Absurdland 5.8+ G/PG ★★
FA: Jim McCarthy, George Bloom, 1960
Short, but well worth doing. A tricky start has caused many ankle injuries. Climb the obvious vertical fingercrack 35 feet right and uphill of **Never Never Land** to a horizontal. Continue straight up to a large pine tree and rap off.

269 Blunderbus 5.9 R
FA: Mike Sawicky, Gene Smith, February, 1981
Another climb named for the bus that went over the hairpin turn! Good face climbing if cleaned. Step up onto the face right of **Absurdland** (crux), follow holds out right, then straight up (scary) keeping left of **Wise Crack**.

270 Wise Crack 5.6 G ★
FA: Art Gran, Pete Vlachos, 1965
A delightful pitch of crack climbing. Begin 70 feet right of **Never Never Land** and downhill and right of **Absurdland**. Jam up the steep crack to a belay. Rappel with two ropes, or climb straight up past a roof on the right to the trees (5.5).

271 Wiseland 5.9+ R
FA: Dick Williams, Dave Craft, 1989
Climb the face between **Wise Crack** and **Wonderland,** starting at a clump of three trees. Rappel from a pine tree.

272 Wonderland 5.8– PG ★
FA: Art Gran, Eric Stern, 1959
Very nice face climbing. The bolt was placed on a later ascent. Climb out right onto a white face below **Wise Crack** to a bolt (V1), and past this (crux) to a roof. Weave left around the roof, then on up to the belay. Either rappel, or climb up easy rock behind a pine tree to the GT ledge. The last pitch climbs the roof at a break on the left, then up a corner to the top.

V1 Climb straight up to the bolt; 5.9 R.

273 Faithless Journey 5.8 PG
FA: Joe Bridges, Paul Trapani, August, 1982
The crux roof on the third pitch is worth doing, as is the crux of **Bombs Away Dream Baby**. Follow cracks and flakes just left of **Middle Earth** to a ledge below the obvious roof system (this pitch is a bit dicey). Pitch three climbs the roof at a small right-facing corner and horn, then goes straight on to the top.

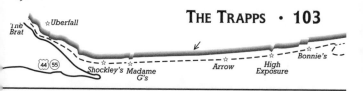

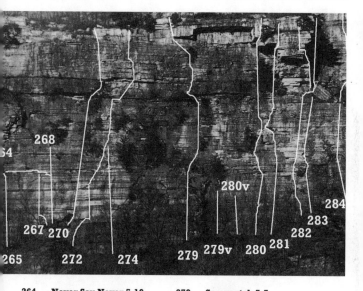

264	Never Say Never 5.10–	279	Snowpatch 5.5
265	Never Never Land 5.10–	279v	Pigpen 5.6+
267	Welcome to	280v	Sente 5.8+
	My Nightmare 5.10–	281	On Any Monday 5.11–
268	Absurdland 5.8+	282	Snake 5.7–
270	Wise Crack 5.6	283	Talus of Powder 5.8
272	Wonderland 5.8–	284	Steep Hikin' 5.7
274	Middle Earth 5.6+		

274 Middle Earth 5.6+ PG ★★

FA: Joe Kelsey, Roman Laba, 1967

A popular, moderate climb. Climb a fingercrack up a lower angled section of rock 60 feet right and downhill of **Wise Crack** to a belay ledge. Climb the same second pitch as **Wonderland**. Climb up a right-facing corner to the roof (V1), move left, and climb the hang. Angle right to a right-facing corner, and the top.

V1 Rhun 5.7 G FA: Unknown, late 1960s. A rather contrived variation, but good climbing. Climb the face right of **Middle Earth**

to the roof, then traverse far left (past where **Middle Earth** goes over the roof), and around a corner to a ledge. Diagonal up right to reach the trees.

275 Bombs Away Dream Baby 5.8+ G ★

FA: Ray Dobkin, Stan Hayes, October, 1980

A worthwhile crux pitch, through the same roofs as the previous climbs. Starting just right of **Middle Earth**, angle right to a tree, then straight up past a corner and crack (passing a bush), to a belay at trees. Scramble up to a belay below the roof, then up the face, and over the roof at a small right-facing corner and a vertical crack. Follow flakes, and a crack to the summit.

276 Journey's End 5.10– G

FA: Ivan Rezucha, Annie O'Neill, October, 1985

Climb the face left of **Red's Ruin** past bushes, then up a small left-facing corner to a ledge. Angle right to a belay (5.8+). Climb past a pine and hollow flakes to a ledge, then angle right to a ledge and belay. Step off a block and over a roof (5.8+), then up to a belay on low angled rock below the huge ceilings. Diagonal left to a corner under the left edge of the huge roof, then step up onto the big block, and around left (tricky to protect), then up the face (crux) to the top.

277 Red's Ruin 5.2 G

FA: Unknown, pre-1964

Dirty and best forgotten. Wade up a crack 60 feet right of **Middle Earth**, to many dirty ledges, and a belay. Continue on up through more dirt, to the GT ledge, then climb a left-facing corner to the top.

278 Pigeon and Smegma Garden Class 4

FA: Pigeon Hans Kraus, Roger Wolcott, 1948. FA: Smegma Garden Gerd Thuestad (Norway, of **Dirty Gerdie** fame), 1966

Both are dirty scrambles that lead up left from the left edge of the **Thin Slabs** area.

279 Snowpatch 5.5 G

FA: Art Gran, Dick Williams, 1970

Named for a peak in the Canadian Rockies, as was **Pigeon**. Start at the left edge of the **Thin Slabs** area. Climb a right-facing corner (V1) past some trees, to another corner and a belay on the GT ledge. Climb up to an overhang, and move left to a belay, at the top of a left-facing corner. The last pitch is airy, and pretty good. Up to

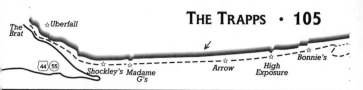

the left edge of the huge roof, and around this (crux) on the left, then wander back right to the top.

V1 Pigpen 5.6+ R FA: Unknown, 1970s. Climb over scary grass ledges right of the first corner, to join the pitch at the trees.

280 Thin Slabs 5.7– PG
FA: Art Gran, John Wharton, Bob Chambers, 1956

A great first pitch, and it also has two very popular first pitch variations. Gran's first, first ascent in the Gunks. In the center of the slab 35 feet right of **Snowpatch**, smear up the face (V1-3) along a seam, then past a bolt (crux) to a ledge. Walk off right, or up the face, avoid a roof on the right, and continue on to the GT ledge. Climb up a left-facing corner to the conclusion.

V1 Sente 5.8+ PG ★ FA: Willie Crowther, pre-1964. The bolts were supposedly placed on rappel. Wander up the face to the left, past three bolts to the ledge.

V2 Yenta 5.10 (TR) Climb the face between **Sente** and the regular **Thin Slabs** route.

V3 5.7– ★ Jam up the nice fingercrack right of the normal line.

281 On Any Monday 5.11– PG ★
FA: (complete) Dick Williams, Joe Bridges, 1971; P3 Art Gran, 1956. FFA, P3: John Turner, pre-1964

A very popular first pitch and a spectacular finish. The crux hold broke as Bridges was following, making this a more difficult route. Harder if you are short. Tiptoe up a thin seam 30 feet right of **Thin Slabs**, past a bulge (crux) to the ledge. Walk off right, or continue up the face above avoiding a roof on the left, to the GT ledge. The last pitch was climbed earlier and is known as Thin Slabs Direct. Up a corner on the left side of a huge prow, then after taking a deep breath, traverse out right to the front of the prow and on to the top (5.7+).

282 Snake 5.7– G
FA: Hans Kraus, Susanne Simon, 1944

For herptiles only. Begin 40 feet right of **Thin Slabs** at a right facing corner. Climb up a right-facing corner and the steep face on the left to a bushy crack (V1), and then on to the GT ledge. Slither up the disgusting corner above to the grass.

V1 Just Like Bayards 5.8 G FA: Joe Bridges, Dick Williams, 1987. From the **Snake** crack move out left and climb a difficult looking fingercrack through an overhanging bulge.

283 Talus of Powder 5.8 PG
FA: (complete) Rich Perch, Russ Clune, October, 1981. FA P2: Ivan Rezucha, Annie O'Neill, Summer, 1981
A pun on a famous Yosemite route name. Scamper up the dirty face between **Snake** and **Red Pillar** to the GT ledge. From here, climb the loose, mirror image of **On Any Monday's** last pitch (crux).

284 Steep Hikin' 5.7 R
FA: Todd Swain, Andy and Randy Schenkel, October, 1985
Climb the front of **Red Pillar** to its top (5.6 R), then up the face to the GT ledge. Climb the face between **Deep Lichen** and **Red Pillar** to a thin crack (5.7 PG) and the top.

285 Red's Arête 5.9 PG
FA: Ivan Rezucha, Annie O'Neill, October, 1991
Climb the right arête of the **Red Pillar** block to its top. From the right end of the ledge, climb up and past two tiny left-facing corners (crux). Climb past a tiny overhang to the GT ledge. Angle right, staying right of **Steep Hikin',** to the arête formed by the **Red Pillar** corner. Up the clean white face just left of the arête, then finish on the crux of **Red Pillar** (5.7 PG).

286 Red Pillar 5.4 G ★
FA: Unknown, pre-1964
Start 110 feet right of Thin Slabs and climb the right side of a large pillar leaning against the main cliff, 110 feet right of **Thin Slabs**, then on up the face to the GT ledge (5.4). From here, climb a right-facing corner to a roof, then around left, and up (crux) to the woods.

287 Deep Lichen 5.10– R ★
FA: Dick Williams, Roy Kligfield, Kevin Bein, 1975
Good climbing but both pitches are serious. Start as for **Red Pillar**, and after 15 feet, climb out right up cleaned rock to the highest portion of the GT ledge (5.10–; #1.5 Friend on left at crux). Scamper straight up the face just right of the **Snake** corner, passing a scoop (5.8+ R) to easier climbing.

288 Hawkeye 5.9+ PG
FA: Dick Williams, Joe Bridges, Dave Craft, 1988
Begin on the GT ledge between **Red Pillar** and **Three Doves**. Climb the face past a grassy ledge to the right side of a huge

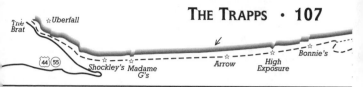

The Brat

☆ Uberfall

44 55

☆ Shockley's ☆ Madame G's

↓

☆ Arrow

☆ High Exposure

Bonnie's

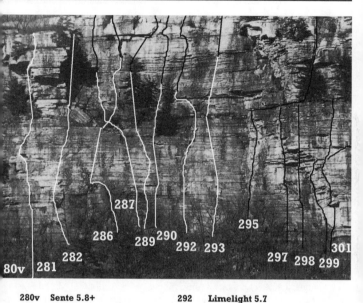

280v	Sente 5.8+	292	Limelight 5.7
281	On Any Monday 5.11–	293	Arrow 5.8
282	Snake 5.7–	295	Easy Verschneidung 5.2+
286	Red Pillar 5.4	297	Nurse's Aid 5.10
287	Deep Lichen 5.10–	298	Supper's Ready 5.12–
289	Three Doves 5.9–	299	Hans' Puss 5.7
290	Annie Oh! 5.8	301	The Feast of Fools 5.10

block. Climb up right past an overhang to a belay at a pine tree on
Three Doves (5.6). Go up left to a pine, then up the face past a
short crack to finish at a gap in the ceiling that is just left of the
Three Doves finish (done previously).

289 Three Doves 5.9– PG ★★★
FA: Dave Ingalls, Al Rubin, Richie Petrowich, 1968
A classic, as are many of the routes on this wall. Fly up a flake lean-
ing against the main crag 15 feet right of **Red Pillar**, then up the

face above, until you are forced left around a hang, and on to the GT ledge. Starting off a big rock, follow a right-facing corner to a thin seam on the left. Up the seam (crux) to an overhang, move right, then up a crack to the shrubs.

290 Annie Oh! 5.8 PG ★★

FA: Ivan Rezucha, Annie O'Neill, Rod Schwarz, Maury Jaffe, January, 1980

The second pitch is great! Climb the face ten feet right of the **Three Doves** flake to a left-facing corner, capped by a small ceiling. Swing over the hang, then up right to a seam and the GT ledge (5.8). Wander up the delightful face between **Three Doves** and **Limelight,** discovering all sorts of great moves enroute. Finish via a groove (crux) just right of **Three Doves**.

291 Road Less Traveled 5.9+ PG

FA: P1 Dick Williams, Joe Bridges, Dave Craft, 1988; P2 Ivan Rezucha, Keith Buesing, December, 1991.

Begin 15 feet right of **Three Doves**. Climb the face right of **Annie Oh!,** angling right to the clean face that is right of **Annie Oh's** thin crack. Climb the clean face and crack above (an old **Limelight** variation) to a belay on top of some blocks as for **Annie Oh!** (5.8+ PG). Climb up right along a crack, then up the steep face about ten feet left of the **Limelight** crux (5.9). Step right to a shallow, left-facing corner (#0 TCU) and do a weird move back left and up. Continue up to meet **Limelight** at the end of its traverse. Step left, then up to the top (5.9+).

292 Limelight 5.7 G ★★★

FA: Dick Williams, Art Gran, 1965

Everyone should want to be in the **Limelight**. Starting 50 feet right of **Red Pillar**, dance up the face to obvious right-facing flakes (5.5 PG, V1), and the GT ledge. From here (V2), parade up a shallow depression past a ceiling, up a groove to a roof, then traverse left (crux), until a crack leads to the finish.

V1 Climb the face left of the flakes over a roof, then on up a crack to the GT ledge.

V2 Scimitar 5.7 PG FA: Unknown, circa 1976. Climb the scary face just right of **Limelight**, following a thin seam (small wires helpful).

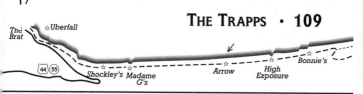

The Brat · ☆Uberfall · (44)(55) · Shockley's · Madame G's · ☆ Arrow · ☆ High Exposure · Bonnie's

NOTE: When walking from the Uberfall on the carriage road, the following section of cliff is easily found by a clean, white talus slope on the left and the first good view of the Wallkill Valley on the right.

293 Arrow 5.8 G ★★★
FA: Willie Crowther, Gardiner Perry, 1960
This classic route had the bolts on the second pitch placed on rappel prior to the first ascent. Excellent low-angle face climbing. Shoot straight up the face about 20 feet right of **Limelight** to the GT ledge, then on over a roof (5.7) to beautiful white rock, two bolts, and the final crux move.

294 Quiver 5.9 PG
FA: Ivan Rezucha, Annie O'Neill, December, 1984
Climb the face midway between **Arrow** and **Easy V**. When the rock becomes steeper and blanker, move left a few feet (V1) and climb just right of the lichen. Angle right, then go straight up to the GT ledge at a tree (5.8 PG). Walk left from the tree a few feet, then climb the overhang and angle left to the right edge of the **Arrow** notch (V2). Climb through the ceiling at the **Arrow** notch and belay on the lower angled rock above. Follow **Arrow**, then climb a thin crack to the left.

V1 The original route moved right into the **Easy V** corner, then went up avoiding the blank section which has been top-roped.

V2 It is possible to climb the ceiling left of the **Arrow** notch with some long reaches; 5.10+ PG13.

295 Easy Verschneidung (aka Easy V) 5.2+ G ★
FA: Fritz Wiessner, Hans Kraus, 1944
Quite the exciting 5.2. The second pitch has been likened to coming out of the womb. Climb the huge left-facing corner 100 feet right of **Red Pillar** to the GT ledge (5.2). Move right 'til below a chimney/notch. Up these weaknesses (crux) to the trail.

296 Cold Turkeys 5.9– PG
FA: Ivan Rezucha, Uwe Bischoff (Ger) March, 1980
Climb the arête just right of **Easy V** past old pins, and orange rock to ceilings. Power over these (some loose rock, V1), moving left at a fracture, then up to the GT ledge (5.9–). Continue through a roof capping a short left-facing corner to join **Arrow** to the summit.

V1 5.9 PG FRA: Ivan Rezucha, Annie O'Neill October, 1993. Traverse up and right around the ceiling.

297 Nurse's Aid 5.10 PG13 ★

FRA: Rich Romano, Russ Raffa, 1977

You may need the aid of a nurse if you come off below the crux. Wander up the face 45 feet right of **Easy V** to a couple scary moves (5.9+) over orange rock to the roof. Move left, pump the hang (crux), then up the deceptively hard flake/corner on the right, to the GT ledge. From the welcome rest, follow left-facing crack/corners up the wall right of **Proctoscope** to a roof. Traverse right (5.9+), and on to the shrubs.

NOTE: It is possible to rappel off a pine tree near the finish of this climb back to the GT ledge with one rope (exciting).

298 Supper's Ready 5.12– PG ★★

FA: Jim Damon, Felix Modugno, July, 1984

A climb for epic-cureans. Start as for **Hans' Puss** and climb directly up the corner, and over multiple roofs to the GT ledge (5.12-). Scramble up to a higher ledge and climb a right facing corner. Move left and climb the roofs above (5.12-).

299 Hans' Puss 5.7 PG ★

FA: Hans Kraus, Bonnie Prudden, 1951

Wanders a bit, but worthwhile climbing. Take the line of least resistance up the huge, left-facing corner 75 feet right of **Easy V**, then traverse out right (5.7) to a belay on the arête. Diagonal far right and up to an overhang (5.7), which is climbed to the GT ledge. Scramble up the big right-facing corner to the top.

300 Fast Food 5.10+ PG

FA: Ivan Rezucha, Keith Buesing, May, 1992

The first pitch was climbed six months earlier. Climb the face ten feet left of **Feast of Fools** past a flake. Pass the large, triangular roof at its left edge (#2/2.5 Friends above roof). Climb a tiny, left facing corner to the next roof, move left five feet, then climb the roof (5.10+; wires and TCU below). Above the roof, step up and left to a ledge on **Hans' Puss**. Climb another overhang to another ledge (V1), then downclimb to the **Hans' Puss** belay (5.10+ PG). Climb up and left to a ceiling. Traverse left, keeping about six feet above the lip of the giant **Supper's Ready** roof, to a thin vertical crack. Climb the bulge (5.10+; G), and continue straight up to the GT ledge. Walk left about ten feet to the outside corner, which is climbed past a

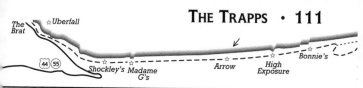

block. Angle left over an overhang (unlikely) to a ceiling, then traverse right to the nose. Climb straight up to the top (5.9 PG13).

V1 Avoid the last overhang by traversing straight right to the **Hans' Puss** belay.

301 The Feast of Fools 5.10 PG ★★

FA: Russ Raffa, Mark Robinson, 1977

Quite popular. Bring a #4 Friend for the first pitch. Climb up right from the start of **Hans' Puss** to a corner system near the nose. Over a big roof (5.10–) into an awkward dihedral (5.10), then step right at its top to the **Hans' Puss** belay. Climb to a short left-facing corner. Up this (crux) and up to the GT ledge. Climb a crack, move left, then right through a notch in a roof to easier climbing.

302 Too Old to Know Better 5.8+ R

FA: Jeff Lea, Al Rubin, 1987

Scary but good. Start 35 feet right of **Hans' Puss** and climb a wide crack to an optional belay stance at the top of the block. Climb the thin crack and face above, moving towards the left arête (5.8+ R), then to the communal belay above. From the belay, climb past the right side of a hang right of the **Feast of Fools** crux (5.8) to the GT ledge.

303 Proctoscope 5.9+ PG ★

FA: (complete) Rich Goldstone, Dick DuMais, Raymond Schrag, 1969. FA P1: Jim McCarthy, 1962

Good face climbing on the first pitch and a usually wet corner on the last. Jam up a wide crack 45 feet right of **Hans' Puss** to a ledge, then up a thin seam, moving left (crux) at its top, to a belay. Diagonal up left past a small overhang, then up a corner and face to the GT ledge. Most people end the route here, but if you're a hero, climb the huge left-facing corner to the top (ending just right of **Arrow**).

304 Snagglepuss 5.8 PG

FA: Todd Swain, Val Risner, November, 1982

Climb the left corner ten feet right of **Proctoscope** to a ledge, then up the right hand thin seam, passing a bulge (crux) when the crack ends, to a belay under a roof. Over the roof near a right-facing corner (5.7) to join **Hans' Puss** to the GT ledge.

305 Procter-Silex 5.9+ PG
FA: Joe Bridges, Jason Kahn, October, 1987
This route will keep you perking. Begin right of **Snagglepuss** at a left-facing corner with a crack. Climb the crack, then straight up the face above to the widest part of the overhang. Pull the hang at a shallow right-facing corner (5.9+). Continue up and slightly right (scary 5.6), then up a bulging orange face (5.9) to the GT ledge.

306 Silhouette 5.7 PG ★★
FA: Art Gran, Dick Williams, 1965
Two beautiful pitches of climbing. Starting at the base of the **Andrew** corner, climb up left to a stance 30 feet up, then traverse left and up past a bulge (crux) to easier face climbing that leads to a roof. Avoid the roof on the right (V1), then back left to a belay at a vertical crack system. Up the crack (5.6+) to the GT ledge (this pitch can be combined with P1). From boulders, angle left around the left edge of a ceiling to the brush.

V1 Climb the roof direct; 5.8+.

307 Man's Quest for Flight 5.11– PG ★★
FA: P1 Jim Munson, Morris Hershoff, Hardie Truesdale, 1983;
P2 John Stannard, John Bragg, 1973
The last pitch was originally a direct finish to **Silhouette** and is well protected. Starting at the base of the **Andrew** corner, climb up, then left onto the arête, which is followed to the GT ledge (5.9). Start as for **Traverse of the Clods** (V1), but continue straight up from the start of the traverse (5.11–) to a large roof. Traverse out left over a small ceiling at a thin crack then into a corner (crux) to a large roof. Pull through to the summit and the descent trail.

V1 FRA Ivan Rezucha, Mike Schneider, May, 1992. From the point where this route and **Traverse** diverge, move right then up, passing the small ceiling as for **Traverse**. Where **Traverse** begins its long traverse to the right, climb straight up to the giant roof. Traverse left (PG) to join **Man's Quest** above the crux; 5.8.

308 Skeletal Remains 5.11+ X
FA: Jeff Gruenberg, November, 1984
One of the most serious pieces of climbing at the Gunks—your teeth will be chattering and your knees knocking! From the GT ledge, climb up to a right-facing corner down left of **Twilight Zone**, and exit left at its top. Climb straight up crossing **Traverse of the Clods**, past the right side of a huge roof to the woods.

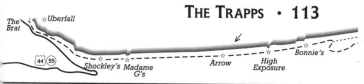

293	**Arrow** 5.8	304	**Snagglepuss** 5.8
296	**Cold Turkeys** 5.9–	306	**Silhouette** 5.7
297	**Nurse's Aid** 5.10	308	**Skeletal Remains** 5.11
298	**Supper's Ready** 5.12–	312	**Andrew** 5.4+
299	**Hans' Puss** 5.7	310	**The Zone** 5.13–
303	**Proctoscope** 5.9+	314	**Android** 5.10–

309 Traverse of the Clods 5.8 PG ★

FA: Ivan Rezucha, Paul Potters, 1976

Some exposed and exciting climbing on this one. Use common
sense in route finding and in protecting the second. Climb the face
right of the final **Silhouette** corner, until it is possible to traverse far
out right to the belay on **Twilight Zone** (5.7+). Over the roof above,
then head out right again (exposed) around the corner to finish at
an obvious handcrack.

310 The Zone 5.13– R

FA: P1 Jeff Gruenberg, Jack Meleski, Spring, 1986; P2 Jack Meleski, Jeff Gruenberg, Fall, 1986

While this route's crux is on **Twilight Zone**, the majority of the climb is an independent line. A tremendous amount of work went into this including "improving" holds and the placement of a bolt. Starting on the GT ledge, climb the arête and face left of **Twilight Zone** (5.10, Friend placement), then angle far left (5.11– X) to an old fixed peg. Move back right and up to the bolt (5.11 X, hard clip), then up difficult rock to the **Twilight Zone** traverse line (5.12 PG, people normally aid out **Twilight Zone** and set up a top rope for the previous section). Move left and pull the huge roof at the left-facing corner (5.13– G). The second pitch is called The French Connection (aka Jackhammered). From the belay, traverse straight right to the "Sandbar," then over the roof at a fingerlock (crux, fingerlock chiseled out to "improve" it) to the top (5.12+ G).

311 Twilight Zone 5.6 A2 G ★★

FA: Art Gran, Phil Jacobus, Fall, 1963

This hasn't gone free yet, despite many efforts. A wild but easy aid climb. Well worth the effort involved. Bring lots of runners and a small selection of wires. Climb up an obvious corner (5.6) off the GT ledge to the left of P2 of **Andrew**, then aid out left under a roof (V1). Follow your nose over the first roof, then up left to the communal hanging belay. Climb a corner above to an overhang, then right to the top (5.9, or A1).

V1 The Best Things in Life Aren't Free 5.9 A4 R ★ FA: Mike Sawicky, Chris Monz, May, 1984. Part way out the **Twilight Zone** traverse, a horn will mark the thin crack that is followed out the roof (A4), to a small right-facing corner at the lip. Follow another crack through a roof, then free climb a crack up right (5.9) to the finish. Bring RURPs, bashies, hooks, KBs, etc.

312 Andrew 5.4+ PG ★

FA: Hans Kraus, Fritz Wiessner, Bonnie Prudden, 1947

A popular climb up an impressive section of rock. Intimidating and pigeon populated. This climb was featured on the cover of *Climbing* magazine (#68, October, 1981). Starting 100 feet right of **Hans'**

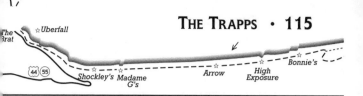

Puss, climb the face just right of a huge right-facing corner to a belay on the GT ledge. Diagonal up right from the base of another huge right-facing corner to the top, in one long pitch, or two short ones (**Twilight Zone** and other routes go up and left from here; V1, 2).

V1 Continue up the obvious, right-facing corner to an overhang. Traverse right to rejoin the regular route; 5.4.

V2 Moby Dick 5.8 PG FA: Unknown, 1960s. You'll have a whale of a time on this one! Climb up the corner as for **Twilight Zone**, then into a flaring chimney. Struggle up this to a roof, and escape left to the top.

313 Goldner's Grunge Class 4
FA: Bill Goldner, Sonja and Lotte Jensen, Al DeMaria, 1960
Scramble up the gullies right of the first pitch of **Andrew** to the GT ledge, then free climb **Twilight Zone** to the top.

314 Android 5.10– PG
FA: P1 Todd Swain (solo), June, 1985; P2-4 Ivan Rezucha, June, 1980
Climb a thin seam 80 feet right of **Andrew** and ten feet left of **Three Vultures** to the GT ledge (5.10–, boulder problem start). Starting midway between **Andrew** and **Three Vultures**, climb a flake off the GT ledge to a groove. Exit right around roofs (5.8), and up right (scary) to a belay under ceilings, and about 20 feet left of **Three Vultures**. Traverse left to a block, which is mantled, then diagonal right past ledges to the belay under a triangular ceiling (#1.5 and 2 Friends). Swing over the roof on its right (5.9+), then up a groove and face on the left to the conclusion.

315 Amber Waves of Pain 5.9 G
FA: Stephen Lewanick, Mark Goldman, September, 1987
The initial attempt was ended when a hold broke and the leader sprained his ankle. The route was then completed after cleaning on a top rope. Start on the GT ledge just left of the **Three Vultures** pedestal. Climb the face to a ceiling, move left and up past a nose. Work up and right across the face to right-facing corners. Climb through a ceiling above at a notch (crux, #2 Friend), then up through a second notch to the trees.

316 Three Vultures 5.9 G

FA: Willie Crowther, Bill Homeyer, Mike Levin, 1961
Follow a crack 105 feet right of **Andrew** past a difficult boulder
problem (5.9) to easier climbing and the GT ledge. Up to the summit of a pillar (V1, 2), then up a wide crack (V3) until one can traverse right, and on up easier rock to the top (5.8).

V1 5.10 PG John Myers, Mike Freeman, 1980. Climb the overhang
left of the crack to join **V3** to the top.

V2 5.10 PG FA: Rich Romano, late 1970s. Move out right from the
arch then angle left across the wall to the top.

V3 5.10 PG FA: Rich Perch, John Bragg, late 1970s. From the top of
the crack, climb a roof to the foot of an arch. Swing out left, then on
to the top.

317 Face to Face 5.10 PG ★★

FA, P1: Alan Long, Roy Kligfield, John Kingston, Al Rubin, 1977. FA,
P2: Bob Richardson, Ivan Rezucha, 1975. FA (final traverse): John
Stannard, 1970s
Climb up into a depression 100 feet right of **Andrew**, then out left
past a bulge (5.7). Continue up easier climbing, moving back right
on white rock to the GT ledge. Starting on the left, clamber up a
huge left-facing corner, hand traverse right around the roof (5.9)
and belay. Pull over a ceiling to a thin crack, up this (5.10), then
angle right to a nose. Angle back left across a steep face (5.9,
exposed) to the top.

318 No Glow 5.9– G ★

FA: Jim McCarthy, Tim Mutch, 1954. FFA: Art Gran, Lito Tejada-
Flores, 1965
Clean white rock, exhilarating moves and airy situations—don't miss
the second pitch. Start 115 feet right of **Andrew** and just right of a
groove. Climb the face past a slab, and continue around the right
side of a ceiling to a corner, then to the GT ledge (140 feet). Climb
up the face just right of an arch, passing flakes to a white ceiling.
Pull over this at a notch (crux), and up the pretty white face to the
top.

319 Shell Shock 5.10+ PG

FA: Russ Clune, Dan McMillan, August, 1982
Wander up the face between **No Glow** and **Keep On** climbing the
center of a roof that is just below the GT ledge (5.9). Near the left

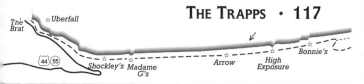

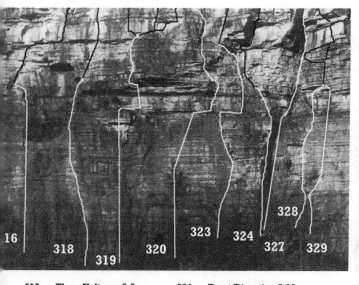

316	**Three Vultures 5.9**	324	**Erect Direction 5.10**
318	**No Glow 5.9–**	327	**Updraft 5.5**
319	**Shell Shock 5.10+**	328	**Cascading Crystal**
320	**Keep On Struttin' 5.9+**		**Kaleidoscope 5.7+**
323	**Moonlight 5.6**	329	**CCK Direct 5.9**

side of roofs, climb up a short face, and over the ceiling to a right-facing corner. Traverse left, then up to join **Keep on Struttin'** to the finish.

320 Keep On Struttin' 5.9+ PG ★

FA: Dave Loeks, Walter Baumann, 1973

Exciting, and if the bolt fails, fatal. Named in memory of climber Joe Strutt. Starting 30 feet left of **Moonlight**, bop on up to the GT ledge passing a pine at mid-height, then walk right about 30 feet. Follow a thin crack up and over a small roof (5.9), then up left to the bolt. Up a few more feet until a traverse left leads past a roof at a notch (5.9). Move up to a corner to belay. Climb a little further up the right-facing

Updraft Area

corner until a traverse left leads to a large hourglass flake. Up the flake (V1), and past the roof on the left to the top.

V1 5.9+ PG FA: Ivan Rezucha, Don Lauber, Annie O'Neill, October, 1984. Follow a thin seam right of the flake, then step right, and over the hang to the trees. A very nice finish.

321 Wop Stop 5.11– PG
FA: Russ Raffa, Rich Romano, April, 1982
An indistinct pitch can be done from the ground, but the best climbing is off the GT ledge. Ascend the face between **Keep On Struttin'** and **Step Lively**, starting at a thin vertical seam. From the GT ledge, climb the face and right-facing corners 20 feet left of **Keep on Struttin'**, then through the roofs (crux, fixed pin). Climb the ceilings above to the path.

322 Step Lively 5.9+ PG
FA: Ivan Rezucha, Annie O'Neill, November, 1984
The second pitch is slightly contrived, but very exposed. Climb the face 15 feet left of **Moonlight**, past a small overhang on the right, then up past a white bulge to the GT ledge. Follow **Moonlight** to the traverse, then angle up left over a ceiling to the second inside corner (crux). Left around the arête, then back right above the roof to the summit crack.

323 Moonlight 5.6 PG ★
FA: Bill Ryan, Willie Crowther, Fall, 1960
Best done during daylight hours so that you can relish the view from the exposed crux. A bolt at the crux was chopped soon after the first ascent. Begin 55 feet left of the huge **Updraft** corner. Zoom up an obvious left-facing flake (5.6, V1) to the GT ledge. Walk right 40 feet, then climb to a right-facing corner. Traverse left around the nose (crux), and up past a pine to the end.

V1 Move right below the flake, and up the easy face; 5.4.

324 Erect Direction 5.10 PG ★★★
FA: Bill Goldner, Dennis Mehmet, 1966. FFA: John Stannard, John Bragg, 1973
One of the best 5.10s at the Gunks. If the second falls off the last pitch, an epic may ensue. Fasten your seat belts for this one! Climb a handcrack just left of **Updraft** to the GT ledge (5.8, V1). From here, climb up the **Moonlight** corner, and over the hang (crux) directly above. Crabcrawl right, and layback desperately to a hanging belay.

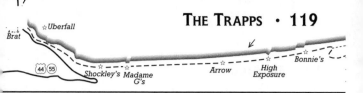

Traverse left a few feet, reach over the roof above (V2), then wildly hand traverse right to the center of the roof. Up the overhanging, awkward corner to the top (5.9+).

V1 5.8 PG FA: Ivan Rezucha, Annie O'Neill, October, 1992. From the base of the crack, angle left around the nose, then climb the face near the arête (a bit runout). When the lichen gets thick, move a bit left and up a thin crack in a clean streak (crux), then on to the GT ledge.

V2 Traverse left to the nose, reach up, then hand traverse back right to the center of the roof. Better protected.

325 Point Blank 5.12 R ★★
FA: Russ Raffa, November, 1981
May be easier if you are short. Start on the GT ledge as for **Erect Direction**. Move out right from the initial corner on **Erect Direction** (V1) through a notch in the roof (crux) to a slab. Climb up the right side of the slab, then right around the nose, and on to the trees.

V1 Vanishing Point 5.12 R ★ FA: Jeff Gruenberg, Russ Clune, Hugh Herr, Mike Freeman, Jack Meleski, June, 1983. The obvious line. Easier if you are tall. Instead of climbing out right through the notch on **Point Blank**, reach left out of the notch, up a slab, then continue up through more ceilings above the slab at small corners.

326 Crack'n Up 5.11+ PG13 ★
FA: John Bragg, Mark Robinson, Bob Murray, 1978
An impressive line up the overhanging wall left of **Updraft**. Difficult to protect and named for the gear used to protect the first ascent. Starting a short way up P2 of **Updraft**, traverse out left to a thin vertical crack and follow this into a sentry box and exit up (crux) and left to a good horizontal. Continue on to the woods. It is possible to split this into two pitches, by escaping right to **Updraft** below the crux.

NOTE: This climb is just above and right of the large boulder overhanging the carriage road (the Andrew Boulder).

327 Updraft 5.5 PG ★
FA: Fritz Weissner, Hans Kraus, 1944
In the 1964 Gran guide this was listed as a possible descent route! Climb the huge, right-facing corner 300 feet right of **Andrew** to the GT ledge. Continue up to the chimney above (crux) to the conclusion.

Updraft Area

---

328 Cascading Crystal
Kaleidoscope (CCK) 5.7+ PG ★★★

FA: Dick Williams, Dick DuMais, 1968

The last pitch is out of this world—not to be missed. Wander up the face 20 feet right of **Updraft**, passing bulges, a left-facing corner and a vertical crack to the GT ledge. Climb up to a roof, and pass it on the right (5.7 PG) of a slit. Angle left to belay on **Updraft**. Traverse out right on a beautiful white face, and up a crack (5.7+ G), until it's possible to escape right (V1) to the top.

V1 Just before reaching the end of the rightwards traverse, angle back up left through the ceiling; 5.10.

329 CCK Direct 5.9 PG ★★★

FA: Unknown, 1970s

A link-up of previous climbed sections. It's actually better than the regular route if you are solid in the grade. Double ropes helpful on the final pitch. Climb up the center of a slab just right of **Diana** to a ledge with boulders. Continue straight up, then left a bit to finish the pitch on thin flakes 15 feet right of **CCK**. Climb left-facing flakes off the GT ledge (above where **Diana** reaches the ledge), then right slightly to pull a ceiling just left of **Diana Direct** (crux). Angle left, then straight up a shallow corner through small ceilings to the base of the crux crack/flake on **CCK** (5.7+, It is possible to move left to the **Updraft** belay here). Follow the normal route to the top of the crux crack, climb a hang, then left through a bigger roof (5.8+, V1). Exposed, and a super finish.

V1 CCK Super Direct 5.11+ FA: (lead) Dave Luhan, 1991. Climb to the final ceiling, then angle out right (a crucial TCU eliminates a good fingerhold) to the top.

330 Diana 5.8 PG

FA: Art Gran, Pete Vlacho, 1964

Wanders a bit, but interesting. Starting at boulders 55 feet right of **Updraft**, weave up the face to the GT ledge. After walking right about 40 feet (V1), climb back up left, and around a roof on the right, following the line of least resistance (5.8, V2) to the left edge of the summit roofs. Either belay, or go on to the top.

V1 Diana Direct 5.7 Climb straight up to join **Diana** midway through the pitch; 5.7.

V2 Wicked Diana 5.9 R FA: Jim Kolocotronis, Lincoln Stoller, April, 1973. As grim for the second as for the leader. Where **Diana** starts

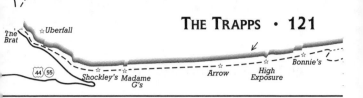

The Brat · ☆Uberfall · 44 · 55 · Shockley's · Madame G's · Arrow · High Exposure · Bonnie's

moving left, climb up to roofs, and traverse left, staying tight under the hangs to eventually rejoin **Diana** (V3). This climb had an obscure first pitch up to the GT ledge.

V3 Dastardly Diana 5.9 R/X FA: Todd Swain, Bob Kamps, 1987
Instead of rejoining **Diana**, angle back right to the top.

331 Ken's Blind Hole 5.6 PG
FA: Ken Prestrud, Hans Kraus, 1948. FFA: Jim McCarthy, 1961
Saunter up the face starting at a groove 85 feet right of **Updraft** to a large boulder on the GT ledge. From the boulder, climb up right to a dihedral, up this, then exit right, to the top (5.6).

NOTE: Beware of wasps on all of the first pitches in this area.

332 Unholy Wick 5.7 G
FA: Dick Williams, Bill Goldner, 1965
The last pitch is interesting and on pretty good rock. Climb a right-facing corner capped by a roof 125 feet right of **Updraft**, up past a block on the left, then back right to a belay (85 feet). Diagonal right up to a roof, which is climbed on the right, to the GT ledge. Start up **Ken's Blind Hole**, but continue straight up, exiting left out of a white alcove (crux), then over left past a block (V1) to an obvious dihedral leading to the summit.

V1 Bowtie Ceiling 5.9 PG FA: Hardie Truesdale, Beau Haworth, 1979. Climb through the middle of a bowtie shaped ceiling above the block at a crack.

333 Lost and Found 5.8 PG
FRA: P1 Ivan Rezucha, Annie O'Neill, 1984. FRA, P2: Todd Swain, Dave Levenstein, August, 1985
Start left of the **Last Will Be First**. Follow right-leaning thin cracks to the right side of a ceiling (5.8). Continue up the face to a left-facing corner (left of **Last Will Be First**) and the GT ledge. Climb the face just left of a left-facing corner to the ceiling. Reach over this (5.8–), then straight up to the left side of a block under the roof. Swing around right (V1) to the woods.

V1 Old Dog's New Tricks 5.11 PG FA: Dick Williams, Joe Bridges, 1989. Pre-protected on rappel before the FA. Probably quite a bit harder to lead on sight. From the final block on **Lost and Found** traverse out left along an obvious horizontal, then up the white face above along a cleaned crack.

High Exposure Buttress Area

334 The Last Will Be First 5.6 PG
FA: Ants Leemets, Elmer Skahan, 1965
That's assuming the first are willing to be last. Begin 200 feet right of **Updraft** below a tree 15 feet off the ground. March past the tree to vertical seams, then climb a left-facing corner. Exit right, then on to the GT ledge (long pitch). Scamper up left past the left edge of a roof, then follow **Ken's Blind Hole** to the top.

335 Strolling on Jupiter 5.10+ PG
FA: Sam Slater, Rich Strang, Mark Borque, Bruce Thompson, 1983
You might get to see the Red Spot if you come off the last pitch. Begin 230 feet right of **Updraft** and 85 feet left of **High Exposure**. Climb a shallow left-facing corner capped by a roof, then up to a ceiling at a short right-facing corner. Angle left then up the crest of a rounded white buttress. P2 follows flakes leading left to the GT ledge (5.10). P3 starts 15 feet left of **Jim's Gem**, and climbs diagonally left to the left edge of the hang, then back right through the final roof to the top (5.10+, scary).

NOTE: The pine tree at the lip of the final roof makes a good rappel point to return to the GT ledge.

336 Exit Stage Left 5.9 PG
FA: Hardie Truesdale, Morris Hershoff, Dave Feinberg, 1979
Snagglepuss' favorite phrase. The last pitch is quite good, the first wasp infested. Ramble up a right-facing corner, 65 feet left of **High E**, then up right to a roof with a flake underneath. Move right through the hang, and on to the GT ledge (long pitch). Follow **Modern Times** to the roofs, and climb them directly, exiting as the name implies, to the top (5.9 G).

NOTE: When walking from the Uberfall, the triangular-shaped High Exposure Buttress (High E Buttress) is easily found 200 feet beyond the Andrew Boulder.

337 Jim's Gem 5.8 PG
FA: Jim McCarthy, Stan Gross, 1954. FFA: Art Gran, pre-1964
Jog up a left facing dihedral 55 feet left of **High E**, moving right to a ceiling. Wander right up a groove, then left to the GT ledge. Climb a left-facing dihedral to the huge roof (V1), traverse right to the arête (crux), and on to the top.

V1 Gem's Gym 5.9 R FA: Rich Romano, Rod Schwarz, 1981. Really scary, and a wee bit loose. Climb the mirror image to the right of the last pitch.

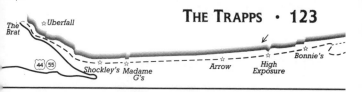

330	Diana 5.8	337	Jim's Gem 5.8
330v2	Wicked Diana 5.9	338	Modern Times 5.8+
330v3	Dastardly Diana 5.9	339	Psychedelic 5.8
331	Ken's Blind Hole 5.6	340	High Exposure 5.6
332	Unholy Wick 5.7	342	Directissima 5.9
333	Lost and Found 5.8	344	Doubleissima 5.10
334	The Last Will Be First 5.6	346v2	First Trapps Chimney 5.6

338 Modern Times 5.8+ G ★★

FA: Dick Williams, Dave Craft, Brian Carey, 1964

The last pitch is not to be missed. Strenuous and exposed. Climb a corner 30 feet left of **High E** to a roof, move left and belay (75 feet). Wander right, then left, and up left past a roof to the GT ledge (can be done in one pitch). Climb up to a huge flake system, and follow this to the roofs. Swing over the roofs on the right (crux), move up and hand traverse right (exciting isn't the word; V1) to a pine. Crawl to the top.

V1 Direct Finish 5.9+ FA: Mike (you know who you are), 1990. Instead of traversing, pull the roof and climb straight up past a pocket.

High Exposure Buttress Area

339 Psychedelic 5.8 PG

FA: Yvon Chouinard, Dick Williams, 1965

The first pitch of **Psychedelic** climbs the obvious left-facing corner on the left of the High E Buttress to the GT ledge (5.5). From here, climb over a roof in a corner (5.8), traverse far out right along horizontals (#3 Friend helpful), and then up to the top. Make sure to protect the second.

340 High Exposure 5.6 G ★★★

FA: Hans Kraus, Fritz Wiessner, 1941

Without a doubt, Kraus' finest route at the Gunks. The most popular and classic 5.6 route in the area. Climb up **Psychedelic** about 50 feet (5.5), then diagonal right and up the face to a fantastic belay ledge (it's also possible to follow **Psychedelic** to the GT ledge). This is it—climb the face left of the nose to the roof, then swing around the roof on the right (crux, beware of rope drag). Angle back left up the exposed face to the top.

341 Beyond Good and Evil 5.11 R

FA (complete): Dan McMillan, Russ Clune, Hugh Herr, Morris Hershoff, October, 1982. FA (last pitch): Henry Barber, 1978

Starting 20 feet up **High Exposure**, traverse right past **Wagissima** to the arête. Move up the edge, then back left past a ceiling to the easy face just right of the **Psychedelic** corner, and the GT ledge (5.10+, scary). Climb a face and overhang above a tree (5.11 G), then follow seams left of **Enduro Man** (5.11) through another roof to join **Psychedelic**.

342 Directissima 5.9 G ★★

FA: Hans Kraus, Stan Gross, 1956. FFA: Jim McCarthy, 1963

Great climbing at its grade. Starting at **Psychedelic**, follow a ramp out right (5.8, V1, 2), then up a corner to a belay at a small ledge on the right. Hand traverse back left almost to the nose, then up (crux) to a small belay ledge. Follow the arête to the GT ledge. Finish on **High E** (5.6), or **Directissima** (5.8).

V1 Wagissima 5.12– R FA: Sam Slater, Harry Brielman, Bruce Thompson, Tony Trocchi, 1983. Named for an '80s version of the Vulgarians—The Wags, who were from the Boston/Connecticut area. Start on **Directissima**, and climb straight up the face along a thin crack, keeping left of the arête.

V2 5.10 G Climb the **Directissima** ramp around and into the corner. Reach left over an overhang and climb a thin crack and the face

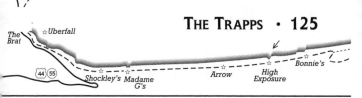

to the left to rejoin **Directissima** near the end of the P2 hand traverse.

343 Enduro Man 5.11 R ★★★

FA: (complete) John Bragg, Doug Strickholm, October, 1980. FA, P1: John Bragg, Russ Raffa, 1979. FRA, P2: Kevin Bein, Vern Clevinger, 1977 (known as Ridicullissima). FA, P3: John Bragg, Bob Murray, Mark Robinson, 1977

This sustained and scary climb was named for Bragg and his efforts to complete the route. Climb a lovely seam 15 feet right of **Psychedelic** to the first **Directissima** belay (5.11 R; V1). Climb vertical seams above the left edge of the belay ledge, and left of **Directissima**, past a roof. Climb up, then move around the arête, and up to the GT ledge (5.10+ PG). From the left side of the triangular **High E** belay ledge, climb up and left to a very loose block, pull a ceiling to a horizontal (5.11 PG), then traverse left under a ceiling to its left edge (V2). Climb straight up to join the finish of **Psychedelic**.

V1 5.11(TR) Climb the arête between the initial **Enduro Man** seam and the **Doubleissima** crack.

V2 Ignorance 5.11 PG ★★ FA: Colin Lantz, et al, 1985. The first ascent party thought they were still on **Enduro Man**! Most people will be happy just finishing the regular route. Immediately after the crux, diagonal back out right (5.11) to the nose, and up this to the summit.

344 Doubleissima (aka Directississima) 5.10 G ★★★

FA: Jim McCarthy, Hans Kraus, John Rupley, 1957. FFA: (no hanging belay) John Stannard, Howie Davis, 1967

The straighter the line the better? In this case, yes. All three pitches are worth doing. This route had all of its moves free-climbed earlier than 1967, but a hanging belay was used under the second pitch roof to reduce the pump factor. Climb a vertical crack system on the right side of the High E Buttress to the **Directissima** belay (5.8). Follow the fingery seam directly above (crux, V1), until a traverse right leads to a notch in the roof. Over the roof (5.9+), and on to the GT ledge. Climb the left hand crack to the top (5.8).

V1 Tripleissima 5.11– R FA: Jeff Gruenberg, Russ Clune, April, 1984. Start as for the second pitch of **Enduro Man**, then follow a seam and flakes up right over a roof, and on to the GT ledge.

High Exposure Buttress Area

345 Lakatakissima 5.10 R/X
FA: Jack Meleski, Todd Ritter, circa 1980
So named for the first ascentionists desire to squeeze yet another route onto the High E buttress (lack of tact). Scramble up **First Trapps Chimney** to a belay at a tree. Up a crack on the left until you can move left to a broken area. Climb back right below a roof, over this a few feet right of the **Doubleissima** roof (crux), then up to the GT ledge. Climb the right hand crack on the wall above (5.6, done previously).

346 First Trapps Chimney 5.3 G
FA: Unknown, 1940s
Wade up the first dirty chimney right of the High E Buttress to the trees.

V1 Climb the crack, and corner just right of the start, joining the regular route higher (nicer); 5.6.

V2 Climb a shallow dihedral 15 feet right of V1 to a crack and face; 5.6.

347 Second Trapps Chimney 5.4 G
FA: Unknown, 1940s
Climb the second chimney right of the High E Buttress, in two or three pitches.

NOTE: Many people rappel the Second Trapps Chimney to descend from the climbs on the High Exposure buttress.

348 Buckets Above 5.9 G
FA: Rick Cronk, Peter Behme, September, 1980
Far better than the neighboring routes. Cronk wrote the first ice climbing guidebook to this portion of New York. Start 20 feet right of **Second Chimney** at a yellow corner. Climb past a low roof in the corner (crux) to a belay. Jam a loose crack above to another belay, then up a corner to a roof. Move right on the face, and continue to the weeds.

349 Third Trapps Chimney 5.3 G
FA: Unknown, 1940s
The furthest right of the vegetated chimney systems.

350 Obstacle Delusion 5.8+ PG ★
FA: Dave Loeks, Claude Suhl, 1973
Begin 100 feet right of **High E** and left of a big flake. Climb the face left of the flake past a ledge, to orange rock and a belay under a

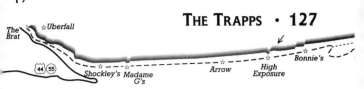

double hang (60 feet). Climb the hang (crux), then move right and up a left-facing corner to a steep face. Up left on this to a triangular ledge, then move up to a bigger belay ledge (5.8+, V1). Scramble on to the bushes.

V1 OD Direct 5.10 G FA: John Stannard, 1970s. Climb the final roof at a thin crack.

351 Insuhlation 5.9+ G ★
FA: Dave Loeks, Claude Suhl, 1973
Strenuous and interesting. Climb the flake just right of **Obstacle Delusion**, then up right to the highest ledge. Angle slightly right (V1), then up a steep, left-facing groove passing ceilings and a steep face (crux) to the summit.

V1 FA: Ivan Rezucha, early 1980s. From the ledge climb to a short, shallow, right-facing corner then up the very steep and somewhat runout face to the top.

352 Alpine Diversions 5.8 G
FA: Todd Swain, John Thackray, November, 1981
Climb thin cracks just right of **Insuhlation** to a pine (5.7+), then up right to the base of an obvious yellow corner. Up this, past a roof into a second corner. At its top, pull over a grungy roof or escape right (5.8).

353 50-50 5.5 PG
FA: Hans Kraus, Bonnie Prudden, 1949
Begin 135 feet right of **High E** and just left of a low roof. Climb a clean face following a crack, to a right-facing corner. Climb over the bulge above (crux), moving left to a ledge (possible belay, and rappel here), then back right to a chimney and a pine tree. Climb the munge to the conclusion.

354 60-40 5.8– PG
FA: Todd Swain, Andy Schenkel, December, 1984
Start on **Missing**, move left, and climb the arête right of **50-50** along a thin seam (5.8). Either rappel, or wade up the dirty corner above.

355 Missing, But Not Lost 5.4 G
FA: Unknown, 1960s
Worth missing. Climb the right-facing corner 30 feet left of **Ants' Line** to the ledge (crux). Rappel, or follow **60-40** to the top.

346	**First Trapps Chimney 5.3**	354	**60-40 5.8–**
347	**Second Trapps Chimney 5.4**	355	**Missing, but Not Lost 5.4**
348	**Buckets Above 5.9**	357	**Sleepwalk 5.7–**
349	**Third Trapps Chimney 5.3**	359	**Ants' Line 5.9**
350	**Obstacle Delusion 5.8+**	362	**Bonnie's Roof 5.8+**
351	**Insuhlation 5.9+**	364	**Ursula 5.5**
352	**Alpine Diversions 5.8**	366	**Groovy 5.8+**
353	**50-50 5.5**	368	**In the Groove 5.6**

356 Lichen 40 Winks 5.8 PG

FA: Dick Williams, Joe Bridges, Dave Craft, Fall, 1988
Start just left of an overhang that is left of the nose 20 feet left of
Ants' Line. Climb up past bushes and a ceiling to the **Sleepwalk**
traverse line. Ascend the face between **Missing** and **Sleepwalk** to
the communal belay (5.8 PG). Move right above a roof (crossing
Ants' Line), and up an obvious steep face and crack to the summit
(5.8 G).

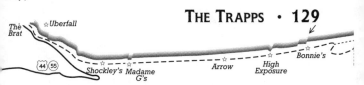

The Brat ☆Uberfall

44 55 Shockley's Madame G's Arrow High Exposure Bonnie's

357 Sleepwalk 5.7– PG
FA: John Waterman, Al Rubin, 1970
Starting on the face left of **Ants' Line** (V1), follow a crack up and left to the arête. Move around the arête, then climb the face and arête to the finish.

V1 5.8 PG FA: Joe Bridges, Dave Craft, Dick Williams, 1988. Start under the overhang to the left of the regular start and climb up to the first horizontal crack. Follow this left around the nose, then move up to join the regular route.

358 Ent's Line 5.11– PG
FA: John Bragg, Bob Murray, Mark Robinson, 1979
Climb the cracks up the steep wall left of the **Ants' Line** dihedral to a big horizontal, then traverse right and up flakes (V1, 2) to the **Ants' Line** crux.

V1 5.11+ (TR) FA: Kevin Bein, 1987. Continue straight up.

V2 It is also possible to traverse right towards **Ants' Line**, up, then back out left above the **Ants' Line** crux (contrived); 5.11.

359 Ants' Line 5.9 G ★★
FA: Ants Leemets. FFA: Dave and Jim Erickson, 1968
Thoughtful and stimulating—bring your technique. Climb the obvious dihedral 200 feet right of **High E**, passing a roof enroute (crux).

360 Condemned Man 5.12– X
FA: Hugh Herr, Jack Meleski, October, 1981
Watch out! Climb the nose right of **Ants' Line**, starting on the left. Climb past a roof to the right, then left around the arête again to an orange face, and a ceiling above.

361 The Throne 5.12– PG ★
FA: Art Gran, Ants Leemets, Spring, 1963. FFA: John Stannard, Steve Wunsch, 1973
A high altitude boulder problem that is height related. Climb up the left wall of the **Bonnie's Roof** corner, following thin cracks past a bulge (crux), to a stance in the corner. Traverse left to the arête, and up that to the woods.

362 Bonnie's Roof 5.8+ G ★★★
FA: Bonnie Prudden, Hans Kraus, 1952. FFA: Dick Williams, Jim McCarthy, 1961
A classic climb up an impressive corner. The direct variation on the last pitch is fantastic. Starting on a ledge 20 feet up and 25 feet right of **Ants' Line**, climb the huge corner past a ceiling (crux) to a belay under the giant roof (V1, V2). Traverse out left to the arête (5.7, wild), then up to the trail.

V1 BR Direct 5.9+ G ★★★ FA: Ivan Rezucha, Jeff Pofit, 1975. Climb the ceiling up and right from the belay in the corner, then out left beneath a large roof.

V2 Undercling the roof out left above the normal traverse line; 5.8+.

363 Knockout Drops 5.11 R
FA: Mark Robinson, Bob Murray, John Bragg, 1978
Climb the orange face just right of **Bonnie's Roof**, following seams and flakes past an overhang, to a belay on **Bonnie's**. Move back out right and up more difficult rock to another communal belay. Finish on **Bonnie's Roof Direct**.

364 Ursula 5.5 PG ★
FA: John Wharton, F and B Adams, Al Alvarez, 1958
Climb the corner system 25 feet right of the **Bonnie's Roof** corner (crux), then up right to a belay ledge (75 feet). Rappel, or climb the face up left to the summit (5.4).

365 Nose Drops 5.9+ PG
FA: Russ Clune, Rich Gottlieb, Bill Ravitch, September, 1982
After a difficult boulder problem up a corner just right of **Ursula** (crux, V1), climb up to a sentry box, exit right (5.9, V2), and up to the belay. Rappel, or move left, then straight up to the top (5.6).

V1 Climb the nose on the outside of the corner; 5.9.

V2 Climb an orange groove past creaky flakes to a ceiling. Go straight right to the belay.

NOTE: The next few climbs all have good first pitches and a communal belay and rappel.

366 Groovy 5.8+ G ★
FA: Jim McCarthy, Bob and Jane Culp, Fall, 1963
Climb the very nice left-facing corner 25 feet right of **Ursula** up to a roof. Traverse left (crux) to easy ground, and the belay.

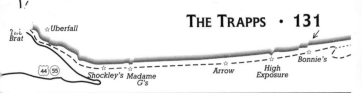

Brat
2 mi.

☆ Uberfall

44 55

Shockley's   Madame   Arrow   High   Bonnie's
              G's   Exposure

367 Space Invaders 5.10+ PG
FA: Felix Modugno, Rich Strang, John Goobic, April, 1981
Start at the left edge of a pinnacle 50 feet right of **Bonnie's Roof**.
Climb the arête just right of **Groovy**, then up a crack past a bulge
(crux), to easier climbing up left and the belay. There is a toprope
route between **Groovy** and **Space Invaders**. No more is known.

368 In the Groove 5.6 G
FA: Art Gran, Al De Maria, Jim Mays, Spring, 1963
At the right edge of a pinnacle 50 feet right of **Groovy**, climb a
crack, flake and left-facing corner to a belay. Continue up another
corner to the top.

369 In the Silly 5.3 G
FA: Art Reidel, Greg Lee, 1972
Start as for **In the Groove**. Prance up a ramp to a left-facing corner,
and belay above (20 feet left of **Silly Chimney**). Walk and roll up the
easy face to the trees.

370 Slipping Into Incipiency 5.10 R
FA: Jason Stern, Alex Gordon, 1987
Begin just right of **In the Groove** and climb the face to a ceiling.
Move right and go up to the belay ledge (5.10 PG). Follow a thin
crack up an orange face to a ceiling. Pull this, then scamper to the
top (5.10 R).

371 Make that Move, or Six Foot Groove 5.9 PG
FRA: Todd Swain, Ivan Rezucha, October, 1987
Start 20 feet right of **In the Groove**. Up a crack and left-facing yellow flakes to a shallow left-facing corner (crux) and a large horizontal (#4 Friend). Continue up the face to a belay and the summit.

372 Silly Chimney 5.1 G
FA: Hans Kraus, 1941
Climb up or down the obvious chimney 90 feet right of **Bonnie's Roof**.

373 No Man's Land 5.11 PG ★★
FA: Dick Williams, Art Gran, 1964. FFA: John Stannard, Ajax Greene, 1973
Many people start at the first platform on **Silly Chimney**. From the
ground, climb a groove to a roof 30 feet right of the chimney, moving left to belay on the platform. Move right and up a right-facing
corner through overhangs (crux, difficult pro), then right and up a
groove to a belay in a dihedral (fixed anchors). Move up and right
to a large flake, then up right again to a belay under the huge roof.
Escape out right to the top.

The Yellow Wall

364	Ursula 5.5	374	Tiers of Fears 5.12
366	Groovy 5.8+	375	The Yellow Wall 5.11
367	Space Invaders 5.10+	376	Scary Area 5.12–
368	In the Groove 5.6	377	Airy Aria 5.8
369	In the Silly 5.3	378	Carbs and Caffeine 5.11–
372	Silly Chimney 5.1	379	Lots of Malarkey 5.7
373	No Man's Land 5.11	380	Wasp Stop 5.12–

NOTE: This section of cliff is known as The Yellow Wall, and harbors some excellent climbing. It even stays dry in the rain! Watch out for wasps in the warm months.

374 Tiers of Fears 5.12 PG ★
FA: (complete) Russ Raffa, Russ Clune, May 1983; P2: Steve Wunsch, John Bragg, 1973
Wild. Climb the all too obvious face and corner system right of **No Man's Land**, moving up right to a big, pointed flake. Climb the ceilings left of **Yellow Wall**, and then up to that belay. From the belay, step over left, then straight up to join **No Man's Land** (5.10 R).

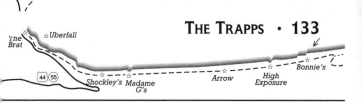

The Brat • ☆Uberfall ... 44 55 ... ☆ ... ☆ Shockley's Madame G's • ☆ Arrow • ☆ High Exposure • Bonnie's

375 The Yellow Wall 5.11 PG ★★★

FA: Dick Williams, Ants Leemets, 1966. FFA: (complete) John Bragg, Russ Raffa, 1977 FFA, P2: Steve Wunsch, John Bragg, 1973
Probably the best outing in the Gunks. The climb was originally freed using the second pitch of what is now **Tiers of Fears**. Start 75 feet right of **Silly Chimney**, atop a big boulder pile under the center of the wall. Scoot part way up a corner above boulders until it is possible to step out left, and up the face to a belay (5.8, V1). Weave up to a bolt directly overhead, then move right (5.9) to another bolt. Up to the "Mummy" roof, and over this (5.11) to a small belay. Crank through the roof above at a notch (5.11), then out right (tricky face climbing) and up through more hangs to the top.

V1 The blank face between the first pitch of **The Yellow Wall** and **Scary Area** has been top-roped at 5.12.

376 Scary Area 5.12– R ★

FA, P1: Roy Kligfield, Dave Ingalls, 1970s. FFA: John Bragg, Mark Robinson, 1979
Many people have taken the whipper on the first pitch, and many more have backed off before taking flight. Starting ten feet right of **The Yellow Wall**, climb up along a shallow corner past three bolts to a belay below a corner at a left-facing flake (5.11 R, V1). Climb a groove above the flake, then left to a notch, where a hand traverse right leads to a stance. Climb up and right past another notch (crux) to a belay out around the corner. Shuffle easily to the top.

V1 Darey Area 5.12– (TR) FA: Todd Swain, Paul Pomeroy, Marty Trumbull, 1986. Climb the face between **Scary Area** and **Airy Aria** to the **Scary Area** belay. A second "pitch" of top-roping was done later (5.12–).

377 Airy Aria 5.8 G ★★

FA: Hans Kraus, Ken Prestrud, 1956. FFA: Jim McCarthy, 1960
The first pitch is very popular. Start at the right edge of the big boulder pile and struggle up the orange, right-leaning corner (crux) to a belay. Move out right to corners leading past a notch in the ceilings, and belay on the right. Scamper up on easy rock to the trees.

The Yellow Wall

378 Carbs and Caffeine 5.11– PG ★★

FFA: (complete) Mark Robinson, Kevin Bein, April 1979. FA, P2:
Dave Loeks 1970s. FFA, P2: John Bragg, Ivan Rezucha, 1975
Named for Robinson's diet of Friehoffer's chocolate chip cookies
and Mountain Dew. The first pitch is often done by itself, and marks
the right edge of The Yellow Wall. Climb the thin seam five feet right
of **Airy Aria** to the communal belay (5.9–). Climb the corner above,
past a roof to another corner, then out left past a bolt up onto a slab.
Move right to another bolt and up a groove to a belay on the right
underneath the large roof (5.10). Step back left to the notch/corner
in the roof, then out this (crux) to easier ground.

379 Lots of Malarkey 5.7 PG

FA: Dick Williams, Roy Kligfield, 1973
Clamber 20 feet up a crack on the nose just right of **Carbs and
Caffeine**, then out right along a horizontal to a stance on a grassy
ledge. Climb the arête, taking care to protect the second, to a belay.
Wander up then traverse right to the nose and up to join **Airy Aria**
at the second belay. Continue straight up, then out left above the
huge **Yellow Wall** ceilings, to the GT ledge and the woods. The last
pitch is terrible, so you may want to finish on **Airy Aria**.

380 Wasp Stop 5.12– G

FA: Dave Ingalls, Roy Kligfield, 1968. FFA: John Stannard, 1975
The crux is short, but very hard. Most people rappel off after the
crux, and even more lower off before it! Start 50 feet right of **Airy
Aria** and climb a thin crack past a bulge (crux) to roofs, which are
passed to the left, and on to the belay. Rappel, or move around a
ceiling on the left, then back right to a groove, and the GT ledge.
Climb straight up through overhangs to the top (5.9).

381 The Sting 5.11+ PG ★★

FA: Russ Clune, Dan McMillan, Russ Raffa, January, 1983
A classic in its grade. Climb the white face right of **Wasp Stop** past
numerous chalked horizontals to a rappel anchor in a large horizontal. Either rappel, or traverse right, then back left, and up the easier
face to the GT ledge.

V1 5.11+ PG FA: Russ Raffa, Lynn Hill, Eric Keto, Paul Niland, Mark
Robinson, October, 1984. From the final horizontal, move left and up
flakes just right of **Wasp Stop**, then left onto **Wasp Stop**, until a traverse

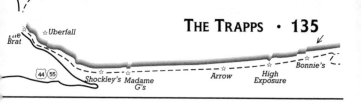

back right leads through the roofs. Join the regular line above to the GT ledge.

382 Lisa 5.9+ PG
FA: Ants Leemets, Jim Andress, Spring, 1963. FFA: Ants Leemets, 1964
Certainly not the 5.8 it was once rated. Prior to 1985, you could step off a block into the middle of the initial corner. Climb a shallow left-facing corner (crux, V1, 2, 3) 80 feet right of **Airy Aria** to ceilings, then up right to the belay. Rappel, or up obvious cracks and a corner to the GT ledge. Climb a right-facing corner to the conclusion.

V1 ASIL 5.9 G FA: Russ Raffa, Dan McMillan, Mike Freeman, 1983. Climb the shallow, right-facing corner just right of **Lisa**.

V2 Leonardo 5.11 PG FA: Jason Stern, Don from Santa Cruz, July, 1988. Climb the difficult face between **ASIL** and **Mona** to the **Lisa** belay.

V3 Mona 5.9 G FA: Russ Raffa, Laura Chaiten, 1982. Climb the corner 15 feet right of **Lisa** to the roof, then up left (V4) to join **Lisa** at the belay.

V4 Exit out right to join **Full Face**.

383 Full Face 5.8 PG
FA: Art Gran, Ants Leemets, Fall, 1962
If it were clean, it could be a pretty good climb. 45 feet right and uphill from **Lisa**, climb past a small pink corner to a ledge. Push on up the lichen covered face to the GT ledge. Climb a right-facing corner in the roof, then exit left to easier climbing, and a shower (5.8).

384 Long Distance of the Lonely Runner 5.10 G
FA: Dick Williams, Dick DuMais, 1968. FFA: Henry Barber, John Stannard, 1973
Climb a dirty corner ten feet right of **Full Face** and 60 feet left of **Ventre de Boeuf**, to a ledge. Up a groove on the right to the GT ledge. Climb a left-facing corner to a roof (V1), and around it on the right to the top (5.10). Many people approach the crux pitch via **48** or **Lisa**.

V1 Foops Trapp 5.11 G FA: Henry Barber, John Stannard, 1974. Climb the crack in the overhang to the left.

385 48 5.2 G
FA: Hans Kraus, Bonnie Prudden, 1948
Starting just right of **Long Distance**, wade up the arête and face right of a chimney, then enter the chimney, and swim up that to the GT ledge. Stomp up a corner to the top.

386 Roast Boeuf (aka Vader) 5.10+ R
FA, P1: Ivan and Paul Rezucha, 1976. FA, P2: John Stannard, Rich Romano, 1970s
The first pitch is popular and well protected by fixed pins placed on a later ascent. Climb the corner left of **Ventre de Boeuf** to a roof, then left, and back right to the top of the block (5.10+). Climb up the center of the orange face (V1) then move left to climb ceilings to the GT ledge (5.10+ R).

V1 Climb the better protected corner on the left; 5.8.

387 Ventre de Boeuf 5.9+ PG
FA: Jim McCarthy, Claude Lavalle, Jim Andress, 1958. FFA: Gary Brown, John Stannard. 1968
IF it's dry, and IF you've done all of the other moderate routes in the Gunks, this is actually pretty wild. Start below the overhanging chimney/corner 60 feet right of **48**. Make some tricky face moves just right of the offwidth (crux, V1) to gain the crack. Squirm and chimney up to the roof, then move out (V2) around the lip to a belay ledge. Scamper to the top, or rappel.

V1 Climb the offwidth direct (#4 Friend or larger needed); 5.10+.

V2 If you are short and skinny, you can do a bit of spelunking up inside the chimney and avoid going out the roof.

388 Uphill All the Way
(aka The Man Who Fell to Earth) 5.12– PG ★
FA: Dennis Mehmet, Bill Goldner, 1965. FFA: Hugh Herr, December, 1981
People were falling all over each other to do this as an aid climb, and it's not much different now that it's free. Climb a corner just right of **Ventre de Boeuf** to a bulge and traverse right (5.11+), then up into the arch. Over the arch (5.12–) to the slab, and an anchor. Rappel, or traverse right and down (5.11+, scary), then up to a belay. Diagonal up left around some roofs, then back right to the GT ledge, and on to the bushes (5.9).

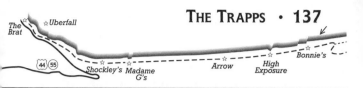

380	Wasp Stop 5.12–	389	Where Fools
381	The Sting 5.11+		Rush In 5.10+
382	Lisa 5.9+	391	Lito and the Swan 5.9
383	Full Face 5.8	394	Broken Hammer 5.5
384v	Foops Trapp 5.11	395	The Zig Zag Face 5.7–
384	Long Distance of	396	49 5.2
	The Lonely Runner 5.10	397	Forces of Nature 5.11
385	48 5.2	398	Who Knows? 5.10–
386	Roast Boeuf 5.10+	399	The Nose 5.8+
387	Ventre de Boeuf 5.9+	401	Fillipina 5.9–
388	Uphill All the Way 5.12–	402	Boulder-Ville 5.10+

389 Where Fools Rush In 5.10+ R
FA: John Bragg, Bob D'Antonio, 1978
D'Antonio, originally from Philadelphia, was widely known for his spectacular falls and his "go for it" approach to climbing—hence the nicknames "Bullet Bob," and "the Philadelphia Flyer." He is still putting up hard routes around the country today. Start at **Double Crack** and traverse left to the nose. Move up the arête, moving side to side (rather than up and down) for two pitches to the top.

390 Double Crack 5.8 G ★★
FA: Jim McCarthy, Hans Kraus, 1955. FFA: Jim Geiser, Jim McCarthy, 1958
Steep and continuous, a classic 5.8 pitch. Follow the left hand crack system on the wall 60 feet right of **Ventre de Boeuf**.

391 Lito and the Swan 5.9 PG
FA: Jim McCarthy, Lito Tejada-Flores, 1965
Named for the spectacular swan dive taken by McCarthy on the first ascent. TCUs helpful. Climb the green and red crack system on the center of the wall, finishing up on the chimney above.

392 Ivan and the Saum 5.9 PG
FA: Ivan Rezucha, Dick Saum, 1976
Romp up a crack system to a tree, then up steep rock behind the tree to a belay stance. Step left, then back right and up steep rock to a stance (keeping right of the red rock on **Lito**). Continue up to a belay on the GT ledge at a pine. Follow the crack above past a ledge to the weeds.

393 High Jinx 5.9+ G
FA: Ivan Rezucha, Annie O'Neill, November, 1985
Scramble up **Broken Hammer** to the first ledge on the left, then climb a crack right of a tree to an overhang. Climb the overhang on the left, move right, then over the next roof near the corner (no cheating). Up the steep face along cracks and flakes to a belay on **Broken Hammer**. Rappel, or continue straight up from the alcove to the woods.

394 Broken Hammer 5.5 PG
FA: Hans Kraus, Ruth Tallan, 1952
The hammer was probably broken while trying to beat the bushes into submission on the first ascent! An ice hammer is occasionally useful during cold and wet winters. Bushwhack up the dirty corner system 105 feet right of **Ventre de Boeuf**.

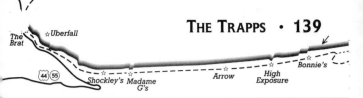

395 The Zig Zag Face 5.7– R
FA: Art Gran, Dick Williams, 1970
Not as good as **The Zig Zag Man**. Starting at **Broken Hammer**, move
out right to a crack, then wander up the face past a notch in a roof to
the belay. Avoid the hangs above on the right, then climb around the
next set on the left and on to the GT ledge. Zip to the top.

396 49 5.2 G
FA: Hans Kraus, Bonnie Prudden, 1949
Better than **Broken Hammer** (but what does that tell you?). Clamber
up a left-facing corner 20 feet right of **Broken Hammer**, then up
right to a belay. Wander easily to the summit.

397 Forces of Nature 5.11 PG
FA: Mike Robin, Mike Law (Australian), August, 1983
This short, hard crux was attempted previously by other parties.
Climb the thin crack just right of **49** (crux, tricky protection), continue up the face, then over a roof at a crack to a belay. Move left
around the roofs as for **The Nose**, then over the double overhang at
a corner, and on to the woods (5.11–).

398 Who Knows? 5.10– PG
FA: Unknown, circa 1979
Climb a shallow corner 20 feet left of **The Nose** to the left edge of
the ceiling (crux), then up the scary face to join **The Nose** at the
belay.

399 The Nose 5.8+ PG
FA: Charlie Porter, Roy Kligfield, 1969. FFA: Gary Brown, John
Stannard, 1969
Porter was training for his later ascents of El Cap. Originally rated
5.7 A2, then freed at 5.7 (!?). Legend has it that Kligfield told Stannard
about his new aid route and challenged Stannard to free it. Stannard
did, and rated it 5.7 to frost Kligfield! Bring large nuts, or Friends for
the traverse. Starting 65 feet right and downhill of **49**, climb an obvious corner past a roof to a horizontal (V1). Hand traverse left to the
arête, then up the face (crux) to easier climbing, and the belay.
Around the roofs above on the left, then up to the shrubs.

V1 Lord Knows 5.11 G FA: Al Diamond, Scott Franklin, Jordan Mills,
August, 1985. Up **The Nose** to the first horizontal, traverse left under
the roof to a crack, and out this (crux), to the next horizontal.

400 Lady's Lament 5.10– PG
FA: Ivan Rezucha, Don Lauber, September, 1981
Saunter up the crack system just right of **The Nose** to a right-facing corner, and a ceiling. Traverse left under the roof (scary crux), then up easier rock to the GT ledge. Hop to the top.

401 Fillipina 5.9– PG
FA: Jim McCarthy, Stan Gross, 1954. FFA: Howie Davis, Pat Crowther, 1968
A fun crux. It's possible to link up P1 of **The Nose** and P2 of **Fillipina** and hit both cruxes. Climb a corner about 25 feet right of **The Nose**, then left, and up another right-facing corner to a belay on the arête to the left. Step right and climb the roof at a pair of cracks (5.9– G), then on to the GT ledge and the finish.

402 Boulder-Ville 5.10+ R
FA: John Bragg, Russ Raffa, 1978
Climb a lovely crack/groove just right of **Fillipina**, then move up a seam in the middle of the face to the belay (5.10– R, 70 feet). Wander up to large ceilings, left over these (crux) to the GT ledge and an easy conclusion.

403 Bold-Ville 5.8 G ★★
FA: Art Gran, Rittner Walling, 1959
A superb first pitch of crack climbing. Start right of **Boulder-Ville**, following the arching corner to its end, then up to a ledge (5.8). Up and left across the face to a right-facing corner, left around this and on to the GT ledge. Scramble to the shrubs.

404 The Scummer 5.10 X
FA: Mike Freeman, Vadim Marcovallo, July, 1987
Climb the green slab between **Bold-Ville** and **Four Seasons**, joining **Bold-Ville** at the top of the arch.

405 Four Seasons (aka Winterlude) 5.10 PG
FA: Ivan Rezucha, Josh Korman (Can), November, 1985
Difficult to protect on the first pitch. Climb up past a ceiling just right of **Bold-Ville**, then step right, and up the face just left of **The Winter** arête (V1) to the **Bold-Ville** arch. Out left through the arch to a belay on the left (5.10). Step back right, then angle right to join **The**

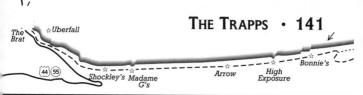

The Brat ☆Uberfall

(44)(55) ☆ Shockley's ☆ Madame G's ☆ Arrow ☆ High Exposure Bonnie's

Spring to its crux roof. Traverse straight right, then over the roof. Move right again to a right-facing corner below a ceiling, and over this (5.9+, as for **The Fall**) to easier rock. Walk off left, and rappel **Broken Hammer**.

V1 Continue up the arête; 5.11.

406 The Winter 5.10+ PG ★★
FA, P1: John Bragg, Steve Wunsch, Fall 1974. FA, P2: Rich Perch, John Bragg, 1978

The best line climbs the second pitch of **The Spring**. Start 12 feet left of **The Spring** at a small right-facing corner plastered with chalk. Climb the corner (V1) to a ledge. Finish on **The Spring** (5.10), or move right, and climb the corner above the first pitch of **The Spring** (5.10−) to end on **Shit Creek**.

V1 From the base of the corner, move out right and climb the face; 5.10− R.

407 The Fall 5.11 R
FA P1: Henry Barber, Ric Hatch, 1974. FA P2: John Stannard, 1975

A difficult and scary first pitch. Layback up the flake just left of **The Spring** (crux, V1) to the ledge, then through multiple hangs at a notch (V2) to join **Shit Creek**.

V1 The Summer 5.11 ★★ (TR), 1980s. Easily top-roped after doing one of the other climbs. Worthwhile. Climb the steep face between **The Spring** and **The Fall** (where else?).

V2 Climb to the right of the notch; 5.10.

408 The Spring 5.10 PG ★★★
FA: Bill Ryan, Willie Crowther, Phil Nelson, 1962. FFA: John Reppy, Sam Streibert, 1960s

A classic first pitch. By doing the second pitch of **The Winter**, the entire climb is 5.10−. Stem up the left-facing corner 55 feet right of **Bold-Ville**, moving right and up to a ledge (5.9, V1). Belay on the left. Climb up to a large roof which is passed at an obvious right-facing corner (wild crux) to the GT ledge. Scramble to the top.

V1 Manly Yes, But I Like It Too 5.10 R FA: Scott Franklin, Jordan Mills, August, 1985. Climb the arête and face just right of P1. If you climb directly up the arête it's harder.

409 Oblique Twique 5.8+ G

FA: Ken Prestrud, Hans Kraus, Bonnie Prudden, Lucien Warner, 1949. FFA: Unknown, pre-1964

The first pitch is worthwhile, the rest an expedition. Climb the crack/chimney 15 feet right of **The Spring** to a ledge (5.8+, V1). Climb right and up to a long ledge, then up right to another ledge. Continue up right, passing corners, ledges and overhangs to a huge boulder. Climb the left-hand corner and crack above to the summit.

V1 Climb the shallow right-facing corner just to the right of the chimney; 5.9.

410 Tweak or Freak 5.10 PG

FA: Ivan Rezucha, Don Lauber, September, 1984

Start just right of **Oblique Twique** and climb straight up the face. Where it steepens, angle right over the bulge (almost touching **Shit Creek**, V1) and then back left to a belay ledge (5.9 R). Move left and climb the right-facing corner past a roof. Climb straight up to a belay on the **Shit Creek** block (5.10 PG). From the block, traverse right through a ceiling, then up to the top.

V1 5.10+ R FA: Todd Swain, Brett Wolf, 1985. Top-roped then led. Continue straight up the steep face along a seam.

411 Shit Creek 5.7 PG

FA: Bill Goldner, Bill Yates, Spring, 1961

Despite the name, some good climbing. Paddle up left along a groove 50 feet right of **The Spring** to a roof, move around right (5.7), then up past a loose overhang to an airy belay at a block on the left (100 feet). Move left through a notch (5.6, exposed), then up left on easy rock to a pretty, white crack (crux) that leads to the top.

412 Unslung Heroes 5.10– R

FA, P1: Mark Robinson, Bob D'Antonio, Bill Ravitch, Sandy Stewart, 1979. FA, P2: John Bragg, Ivan Rezucha, 1975

Thin climbing, thin protection. Climb a seam 15 feet right of **Shit Creek** and at the top of a hill to a ledge (5.10–). Move slightly right and climb up the orange dihedral past roofs to join **Blistered Toe** (5.10–, V1).

V1 Climb the steep, thin crack straight up (5.10+ R). This may be the original second pitch led by Bragg.

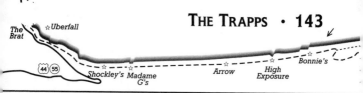

The Brat ☆Uberfall

44 55 ☆ Shockley's ☆ Madame G's ☆ Arrow ☆ High Exposure Bonnie's

413 Los Tres Cabrones 5.9 PG
FA: P1 Ivan Rezucha, Annie O'Neill, September, 1983; P2 and 3 Dick Williams, Jim McCarthy, Jose Anglada, 1963
Translation: The Three Bastards. Climb up the arête just left of **Blistered Toe** to a thin crack and a right-facing corner that leads to a belay ledge. Continue up a corner to a roof, then left to another corner and ceiling. Climb the hang on the right and on to the GT ledge. Angle up right through a ceiling at a notch (5.9), then easily to the trail.

414 Blistered Toe 5.8 PG
FA: Jim McCarthy, John Wharton, 1958
Climb flakes 40 feet right of the **Shit Creek** (V1), until a short traverse right leads to a crack. Climb the crack to its top, traverse left and belay. Diagonal up right across the face to a corner, then left at its top, avoiding a ceiling to reach the GT ledge. Move left, and romp to the top.

V1 Climb a short corner just right of the regular start; 5.9.

415 Torture Garden 5.8 PG
FA: Howie Davis, Willie Crowther, 1968
Start up **Blistered Toe**, but traverse further right (V1), to another crack system. Jam the crack to a ledge (5.8). Continue straight up, passing a ceiling on its right. Climb up past a tree on a ledge, then up along right-facing flakes to the left edge of a ceiling. Angle right to join **New Frontier**.

V1 The short, overhanging crack directly below the main crack system apparently hasn't gone free yet.

416 Last Frontier 5.10– G
FA: Dick Williams, John Hudson, Jim McCarthy, Fall, 1963. FFA: Rick Horn, 1964
A popular and strenuous first pitch. Climb the overhanging chimney/crack 45 feet right of **Blistered Toe** to a ledge. Rappel, or continue up the corner to a ledge. From the GT ledge, climb right around ceilings, and on to the finish.

417 Climb and Punishment 5.11 G ★
FA: John Stannard, 1970s
Climb the deceptive crack/corner 30 feet right of the **Last Frontier** to a stance. Either wander to the top, or traverse left and rappel.

418 Yellow Crack 5.12 R ★

FA: Art Gran, Jorge Pons, Fall, 1963. FFA: Lynn Hill, Russ Raffa, November, 1984

Given the difficulty and danger, Hill's on-sight FFA has to rank as one of the great leads in Gunks history. Climb straight up the yellow corner that is 45 feet right of **Last Frontier**, then move right to the belay (5.12 R). Follow a crack to the highest ledge, then up to the roof, and a belay. Climb the roof above on the right, and on to the GT ledge. Climb a crack and the face to the top.

V1 The original free line 5.11 R ★ FA: Henry Barber, Paul Rezucha, John Stannard, John Bragg, 1973. Climb the corner to a point about eight feet below a ceiling, then move right and go up flakes that form a small hang. Above this, step back left into the corner, which is followed up and right to a belay.

419 Bragg-Hatch 5.10+ PG

FA: John Bragg, Ric Hatch, 1975

Climb the left-facing corner system just left of **Kligfield's Follies**, then right around a hang into a left-facing corner and a belay below another roof. Climb the roof, then move far left to a tree, and the rappel.

420 Kligfield's Follies 5.11+ PG ★★★

FA: Roy Kligfield, Robert Krumme, 1971. FFA: John Stannard, 1973

A very popular route to attempt—perhaps better spelled Kligfield's Fallies! Climb up thin cracks and the face on the left to an obvious right-leaning arch 95 feet right of **Last Frontier** (V1). Undercling out this to an overhang (crux, pro difficult to place) and the belay. Diagonal left past blocks to a roof with a crack (5.10), then on up to another belay. Continue up right towards the arête, then right around this, and on past a ledge to the woods.

421 Cluney's Jollies 5.12 R

FA: Russ Clune, November, 1984.

A serious lead that was top-roped prior to being led. You'll find a #2.5 Friend and double ropes helpful. Begin 25 feet to the right of **Kligfield's** and down left from the **Simple Suff** corner. Climb a shallow, right-facing corner to its top then weave up the steep, pink face keeping left of **Simple Suff**'s left arête. Hopefully you'll make it to the safety of the **Kligfield's Follies**' belay.

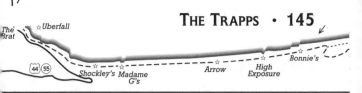

403	**Bold-Ville 5.8**		415	**Torture Garden 5.8**
405	**Four Seasons 5.10**		416	**Last Frontier 5.10–**
406	**The Winter 5.10+**		418	**Yellow Crack 5.12**
408	**The Spring 5.10**		419	**Bragg-Hatch 5.10+**
409	**Oblique Twique 5.8+**		420	**Kligfield's Follies 5.11+**
411	**Shit Creek 5.7**		422	**Simple Suff 5.10–**
414	**Blistered Toe 5.8**			

422 Simple Suff 5.10– G ★★★

FA: Ants Leemets, Olaf Sööt, 1962. FFA: Bob Anderson, Henry Barber, 1972

A classic first pitch. Stem up the overhanging dihedral 125 feet right of **Last Frontier** (crux) to slings (V1, 2). Rappel, or clamber to

The Slime Wall

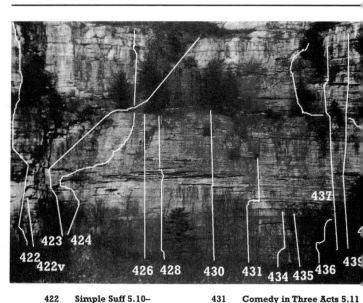

422	Simple Suff 5.10–	431	Comedy in Three Acts 5.11
422v	Techo-Suff 5.12–	434	Frustration Syndrome 5.10
423	Blue Stink 5.3	435	The Stand 5.11–
424	Hookey 5.6	436	Coprophagia 5.10
426	Falled on Account	437	WASP 5.9–
	of Strain 5.10	439	Expedition to Nowhere 5.10
428	April Showers 5.11	440	Sticky Gate 5.4
430	Called on Account		
	of Rain 5.11+		

the GT ledge, then up the white nose to the top (5.8).

V1 Direct Start 5.10 PG13 FA: Unknown. Start down and left of the **Simple Suff** corner. Angle up right along a curving crack, then up to the ledge at the base of the main corner.

V2 Techo-Suff 5.12– (TR) Russ Clune, 1985. Climb the overhanging thin cracks and face just right of **Simple Suff**.

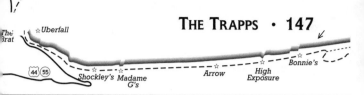

The
Brat

☆Uberfall

44 55 ☆ Shockley's ☆ Madame ☆ Arrow ☆ High ☆ Bonnie's
              G's   Exposure

423 Blue Stink 5.3 PG

FA: Hans Kraus, Bonnie Prudden, Ken Prestrud, 1947

Starting 20 feet right of **Simple Suff**, surge up the easy, broken corner to a stance on the left (50 feet). Move out right on the face, then up to the GT ledge. Hike right 30 feet (V1), then up the white face to the trees.

V1 From a block, climb a flake, then move right to a groove and on to the summit; 5.5.

424 Hookey 5.6 PG

FA: Nick Pott, Steve Jervis, 1971

A wandering line. Jervis did this first ascent 19 years after he started climbing! He still climbs regularly. Climb up the right side of a small pillar 75 feet right of **Simple Suff** to a belay on the left (V1, 2). Move over the roof at a right-facing corner (crux), then traverse far right just above the roof, until easy climbing leads to the GT ledge. Amble on to the shrubs.

V1 Hookey Direct 5.9 PG FA: Ivan Rezucha, Don Lauber, August, 1984. Climb straight above the pillar on **Hookey**, then move right, and through the roof at a left-facing corner to rejoin the regular route.

V2 Yesterday (aka Why Bother?) 5.9+ PG FA: Russ Clune, Hugh Herr, November, 1982. A bit tricky to protect. Climb a difficult and dirty face right of **Hookey**, then through a roof at a left-facing, orange corner 20 feet right of **Hookey Direct**. Move left to join **Hookey Direct** at the final roof.

425 Tomorrow and Tomorrow and Tomorrow 5.11 R

FA: Dick Williams, Jim McCarthy, 1966. FFA: John Stannard, John Bragg, 1973

Scamper up to the right edge of an small overhang 90 feet right of **Simple Suff**, then move left to a vertical grassy seam (dicey pro), which is followed to the belay (40 feet). Climb up the easier face to the ceiling, and over this (5.10), and on to the top.

NOTE: Tommorow and Tomorrow marks the left-hand edge of The Slime Wall, home of many excellent face climbs.

The Slime Wall

426 Falled on Account of Strain 5.10 PG ★
FA: Russ Raffa, Eliot Williams, 1977
One of the easier cruxes on this wall. Starting 100 feet right of
Simple Suff and 20 feet left of **April Showers**, climb a thin crack
and the face above (5.9+) to a belay. Climb a corner to the huge
roofs and angle right through these at a tiny right-facing corner to
easy ground (5.10).

427 Wet Dreams 5.12- R
FA: Russ Clune, Jeff Gruenberg, Dan McMillan, Mike Freeman, Russ
Raffa, November, 1982
Climb a thin crack and face left of the start of **April Showers** (crux)
to the ceiling 15 feet up. Move slightly right then over the small ceil-
ing to rejoin **April Showers** above (5.10). Climb the last pitch of
Golden Showers over the big roofs above.

428 April Showers 5.11 PG ★
FA: Ants Leemets, Dick Williams, Jim McCarthy, 1966. FFA: John
Stannard, John Bragg, 1973
The bolt above the crux was placed on a later aid ascent. Start 120
feet right of **Simple Suff** below a small ceiling 15 feet up, and near a
tree and blocks. A difficult boulder problem off the ground (crux)
leads to the low ceiling. Move left and up past a bolt (5.10, V1), then
up to the belay. Rappel, or climb the massive roof above at its
widest point (slightly loose 5.11, V2) to easier rock.

V1 5.11+ R FA: Dave Karl, Dave Luhan, 1988. Start just right of the
regular route and climb up past the low ceiling, staying about ten
feet left of **Golden Showers** to the belay.

V2 5.11 FA: John Stannard, John Bragg, 1973. Move out right
through the roof.

429 Golden Showers 5.11 PG ★
FA: Russ Raffa, Eliot Williams, May, 1982
Great face climbing with hard moves and tricky pro. Technique up
the thin crack just right of **April Showers**, then up the right-slanting
seam (crux) to a belay. Climb the roof above at a loose, left-facing
flake (5.10).

430 Called on Account of Rain 5.11+ R
FA: Ants Leemets, Elmer Skahan, 1963. FFA: John Stannard, John
Bragg, 1973
Certainly not the 5.10 it used to be, now that the crux hold is missing.

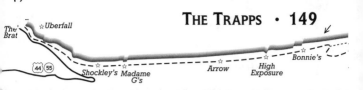

Not only is it hard, the protection is a bit manky. Follow a thin crack up the face 40 feet right of **April Showers** (crux) past a left-facing corner to a ledge. Up to the roofs, and over these at a crack (5.9) to easier climbing, and the woods.

431 Comedy in Three Acts 5.11 PG ★★

FA: Dick Williams, Jim McCarthy, Ants Leemets, Fall, 1963. FFA: John Stannard, Gary Brown, 1968

A popular pitch, with a short technical crux. Start 70 feet right of **April Showers** below a thin, vertical crack. Climb over a ceiling, then up a vertical crack through a bulge (5.11) to a belay. Rappel, or continue up past more 5.11 climbing to trees and the top.

432 Drop Zone 5.12– R

FA: Russ Clune, Russ Raffa, July, 1982

Follow a seam and shallow left-facing corner 15 feet right of **Comedy** to easier climbing. Hard to protect.

433 Pressure Drop 5.11+ R

FA: John Bragg, Don Hamilton, 1980

Climb the face 30 feet right of **Comedy** and behind a large oak tree to the ceiling. Move right and climb over this at a small left-facing corner (crux, V1) to easier climbing.

V1 Direct Finish 5.11+ R FA: Rich Gottlieb, Felix Modugno, November, 1989. Top-roped, then led. Continue straight up a difficult thin seam (RP behind loose flake).

434 Frustration Syndrome 5.10 G ★★

FA: Dick Williams, Jim McCarthy, 1964

A great first pitch. Starting 45 feet right of **Comedy**, climb up 15 feet and traverse right to an obvious left-facing corner capped by a ceiling. Climb up the corner (crux) to a belay. Rappel, or climb easily to the top.

435 The Stand 5.11– PG ★

FA: Russ Raffa, Rich Goldstone, March, 1981

You need to be limber for this one! Climb a crack to the short left-facing corner just right of **Frustration Syndrome**, then do "the Stand" (crux). Step left (#4 HB nut helpful), then up to easier rock.

Sleepy Hollow

---

436 Coprophagia 5.10– PG
FA: Dick DuMais, Rick Wheeler, 1969. FFA: John Stannard, Henry Barber, 1973
A rather wandering line. If you climb it just right, it may be 5.9. Climb up to a right-facing corner 20 feet right of **Frustration** (V1), then move left and up to an overlap. Traverse back right to a vertical crack, and up this to a belay. Rappel, or climb easier rock to the top.

V1 5.11 (TR) FA: Todd Swain, 1986. The face between this route and **WASP** has been top-roped starting off a ledge near a tree.

437 Wasp 5.9– G ★★
FA: Jim Andress, John Hudson, Dave Craft, Pete Geiser, 1961
A popular first pitch. When combined with P2 of **Expedition to Nowhere**, a great climb. Climb the obvious vertical crack and small corners 40 feet right of **Frustration** (crux) to easier climbing and the GT ledge (long pitch). Climb a right-facing corner, then a left-facing corner through the roof to the woods (or climb P2 of **Expedition to Nowhere**).

438 Back to the Future (aka AP) 5.10 G
FA: Todd Swain, Dick Williams, Bob Elsinger, 1986. Climb the face between **WASP**, and **Expedition**, past a difficult mantle (crux, .5 Tri-cam). Continue straight up, then join either route.

439 Expedition to Nowhere 5.10– R
FA P1: Russ Clune, Bill Ravitch, 1983. FA P2: Dick Williams, Jim McCarthy, 1960s
A necky first pitch. The crux is well protected with a .5 Tri-cam, but the 5.9 above isn't. Climb the vertical seam 15 feet right of **WASP** (crux), then up the face to the GT ledge. Follow the old variation Stubai to You (5.8+) over the roof above at a clean, left-facing corner to the top.

440 Sticky Gate 5.4 G
FA: Hans Kraus, Dick Hirschland, 1949
From the top of the boulder pile right of The Slime Wall, climb up and left to the GT ledge. Walk 60 feet left along the ledge to a low angled face, which is climbed past a roof on the right to the top.

441 Mud, Sweat, and Tears 5.9+ PG
FA: Dick Williams, Jim McCarthy, Winter, 1964. FFA: Henry Barber, John Stannard, 1973

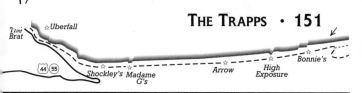

This climb almost saw the demise of Williams and McCarthy on the first ascent when McCarthy slipped on an icy hold. Climb a right-facing corner just right of the **Sticky Gate** boulder pile to another corner, and the GT ledge (beware of loose boulders). Climb the overhang above at a notch (crux, V1, 2), then traverse far right around the roofs (V3) and belay. Climb up to a belay at a pine, then straight to the top.

V1 M, S, and T Redirect 5.9 PG FA: Doug Strickholm, Rich Romano, 1980. Climb straight up above the crux to a right-facing corner in a roof, then move up and left to the conclusion.

V2 M, S, and T Direct 5.10 FA: Unknown, late 1970s. Angle up right about 15 feet past an overhang near a nose, then back left under a roof. Out right below another roof to easier climbing and the top.

V3 Climb up and left to the edge of the roofs, then angle left to the woods.

442 Withering Heights 5.11 PG
FA: Ivan and Paul Rezucha, 1978 FFA (TR) Paul Rezucha, 1978 FFA: Ed Webster, Russ Raffa, 1979
The only route in the 1980 guide to be listed as having poor pro, pro diff, and loose rock! Not as bad as all that, despite the fact that Ivan broke his wrist during a fall on the FA. Climb the center of three corners 130 feet right of the **Sticky Gate** boulder pile, until it is possible to step out left and climb the face to a ledge. Move right and pump the hang, then move left to a roof (5.9 R). Traverse right ten feet through the biggest roofs (crux), to easier climbing up right to a small belay stance. Scamper to the top.

443 Moondance 5.7– G
FA: Todd Swain (solo), November, 1982
Climb a short arête left of **Sundance** to a ledge. Climb the roof just left of **Sundance** (contrived, V1), then angle left to a left-facing corner, and a roof. Over this (crux, V2), and up a nose to the summit.

V1 Start to the right, climb up to the roof, then traverse back left to join the regular route; 5.3.

V2 Move left and up to the top; 5.6.

444 Sundance 5.6 G ★
FA: Jim McCarthy, John Rupley, Spring, 1954
Well worth the walk. Climb up an easy face about 200 feet right of the **Sticky Gate** boulder pile to the GT ledge. Climb a small roof, and then up to a corner leaning right. Move around left (crux), and up to the woods.

445 Ghostdance 5.7 PG
FA: Mike Steele (solo), September, 1984
Pull over an overhang right off the ground (5.7, V1), then float up the center of the face right of **Sundance**.

V1 If you avoid the initial overhang on the right, the entire climb is 5.5.

446 Raindance 5.5 G
FA: Todd Swain (solo), November, 1982
Climb up the obvious left-facing corner 50 feet right of **Sundance** to the GT ledge, then up the face directly above (crux), moving left at mid-height.

447 Contradance 5.6 PG
FA: Todd Swain (solo), November, 1982
Climb straight up the clean, white rock 100 feet right of **Raindance**, and about midway up **Roger's Escape Hatch**.

448 Roger's Escape Hatch Class 4
An easy way up or down this section of the cliff. It is usually marked on top by a cairn at the north end of the summit slabs, and is about 300 feet right of the **Sticky Gate** boulder pile, on the bottom.

449 Casa Emilio 5.2 G ★
FA: Bonnie Prudden, Norton Smithe, 1953
Worth the walk for both the climbing and solitude. From the top of a huge block to the right of **Roger's Escape Hatch** (V1), move out left and up the easy face to a belay even with the large roofs to the right. Climb the pretty, white face above to the top (crux).

V1 Climb the right-facing corner to the ledge; 5.5.

NOTE: The next three routes are on the front of the huge, detached block that **Casa Emilio** starts atop.

450 Creaky Joints and Trigger Points 5.10 PG
FA: Dick Williams, Joe Bridges, 1988
Begin in the middle of the face at a boulder that rests against the face. Climb a crack to an alcove, then angle right along a crack to a

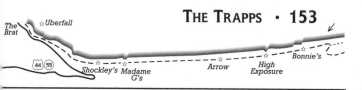

The Brat   ☆Uberfall   (44)(55)   Shockley's   Madame G's   ☆Arrow   ☆High Exposure   Bonnie's

440	Sticky Gate 5.4	445	Ghostdance 5.7
441	Mud, Sweat and Tears 5.9+	446	Raindance 5.5
442	Withering Heights 5.11	448	Roger's Escape Hatch
443	Moondance 5.7–		Class 4
444	Sundance 5.6	447	Contradance 5.6

left-facing corner. Climb a right-facing corner above, then move right and over an overhang to the top of the pillar (5.10). Climb the first pitch of **Casa Emilio** (5.0), then move right and climb the face between **Casa Emilio** and **Casablanca** (5.5).

451 The Devil Made Me Do It 5.9 R
FA: Dick Williams, Joe Bridges, 1988
A popular saying by 1970s comedian, Flip Wilson, although in this case it refers to the route being pre-protected on rappel. Rope up near the right edge of the block at an obvious crack. Climb the crack a few moves, then angle left and up to a short corner capped by a ceiling. Pull this, go up, then angle right past a pine to a larger tree near the top of the block. Rappel.

Sleepy Hollow

452 You Bet Your Bippie
(aka Almost Pure and Simple) 5.8 G
FA: Todd Swain (solo), November, 1982
Originally thought to be too insignificant—but hey, that was during the 1980s! Start as for **The Devil Made Me Do It**, near the right edge of the block. Climb the obvious zigzag crack up and right past one overhang to another. Pass this on the right, then traverse left under yet another to join **The Devil** to the rappel tree.

453 Strings Attached 5.12 (TR)
FA: Jeff Morris, Jim Damon, 1987
Climb the overhanging wall around the corner and right of **Casa Emilio**.

454 Casablanca 5.8 G ★
FA: Dick Williams, Roy Kligfield, 1973
A wild crux roof. Wander up the face 30 feet right of the **Casa Emilio** corner (5.6+) to the roof, and over this at a flake, to a belay tree. Rappel, traverse left to finish up **Casa Emilio**, or follow obvious weaknesses above to the top (5.6).

455 Emilio 5.7+ PG
FA: Hans Kraus, Fritz Wiessner, 1941. FFA: John Turner, 1955
A historic route, as this was the first artificial climb (a shoulder stand) in the Trapps. Named for famed alpine climber Emilio Comici. Diagonal right up the face 40 feet downhill of **Casa Emilio** passing a flake and an alcove to the GT ledge. Climb up left through the ceilings (crux), then back right following weaknesses to avoid a roof near the top on the right.

456 Casanova 5.8 PG
FA: Mike and John Steele, April, 1985
Starting 80 feet downhill of **Emilio**, climb the face past an overhang, and right of a small corner (5.8) to the GT ledge. Swing over the roof right of **Emilio** (5.8, V1), then move way out left (V2) and up the dirty face to the woods.

V1 Instead of traversing and then pulling the overhang, climb straight over the roof to another ceiling. Hand traverse left to rejoin the regular route; 5.9- PG.

V2 5.8 G FA: Ivan Rezucha, Annie O'Neill, May, 1980. It is possible to stay right of **Emilio**, then move left and climb past the left side of the roof near the top of **Emilio**. This is a much nicer finish.

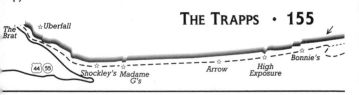

445	Ghostdance 5.7	447	Contradance 5.6
446	Raindance 5.5	449	Casa Emilio 5.2
448	Roger's Escape Hatch Class 4	453	Strings Attached 5.12

457 Independent Hangover 5.10+ R

FA: Dick Williams, Ants Leemets, 1965. FFA: Henry Barber, John Bragg, 1973

Bring a #3.5 and 4 Friend. Wander up the face 115 feet right of **Casa Emilio**, starting at a short groove and passing a couple bulges enroute to the GT ledge. Climb up left through the roof at a corner (crux, slightly loose), and then on up to a belay above. Follow a corner above to a huge boulder and then around to the right to the shrubs.

Sleepy Hollow

---

458 Yo Mama 5.10 G ★
FA: Ivan Rezucha, Chris Monz, October, 1985
Extra Friends helpful. Climb the face 15 feet right of **Independent Hangover** past an unlikely white bulge (5.8) to the GT ledge and a belay at a long block. Walk right, then out left on a flake left of the pine tree (crux) to a belay. Climb easier rock to the huge block then exit left to the top.

459 Worp Factor 1 5.11 PG13
FA: Dick Williams, Dick DuMais, 1968. FFA: John Stannard, Henry Barber, 1973
Part of the pro for the crux is a 26 year-old, ¼" bolt driven up into the roof! Bring double ropes and a double set of TCUs. Just left of a boulder pile 55 feet right of **Independent Hangover**, clamber up the face to a right-facing corner. Up a ramp above and around a roof on the right to the GT ledge. Jump for the lip of the roof about six feet right of the bolt, then after some hard moves on the face above, continue to the woods.

460 Interstellar Overdrive 5.8 PG
FA: P1 and P2 Todd Swain, Corky Woodring, October, 1981; P3 Mike Steele, 1984
Start 50 feet left of **Emilietta** below a huge, left-facing flake. Climb up to the top of the flake, then slightly right to climb a roof at a V-notch (5.8). Move past another roof and on to the GT ledge. Escape right until the roof can be pulled, then move out left to the trees (5.6).

461 Emilietta 5.3 G
FA: Hans Kraus, Bonnie Prudden, 1952
The first pitch isn't too bad. Climb the face and huge left-facing corner about 170 feet right of **Independent Hangover** to the GT ledge (5.3). Either rappel off the tree, or move right, then wander up the dirty face to the summit (5.3).

NOTE: The next few routes have first pitches that stay dry in the rain. Hike straight up from where the carriage road makes the turn at Sleepy Hollow to approach this area.

462 Counter Strike 5.9 PG
FA: Todd Swain, Corky Woodring, October, 1981
An exciting crux roof. Climb a shallow left-facing corner and the face just right of **Emilietta** to a belay under the roof (5.7 R). Climb out the big roof above along a wide horizontal (multiple #4 Friends helpful) then up the easier face to the ledge. Walk left and rappel down **Emilietta**.

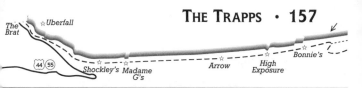

449	Casa Emilio 5.2	459	Worp Factor 1 5.11
454	Casablanca 5.8	460	Interstellar Overdrive 5.8
455	Emilio 5.7+	461	Emilietta 5.3
457	Independent Hangover	462	Counter Strike 5.9
	5.10+	465	Sudden Death 5.8
458	Yo Mama 5.10	464	Trigger Point 5.6

463 Sudden Death 5.8 R/X ★

FA: Todd Swain, Corky Woodring, Derek Price (UK), October, 1981
Good climbing, but the name says it all. **Trigger Point** may be combined with this second pitch to make a safer outing. Stroll up a corner just right of **Counter Strike** to a ledge, then straight up the steep, orange face to the **Counter Strike** belay (5.7 X). Move out left on blocks, then back up right past a pin (5.8 PG13) to the arête, and the ledge above. Rappel down P1 of **Emillietta**.

Sleepy Hollow

464 Trigger Point 5.6 G ★
FRA: Todd Swain, Derek Price (UK), Corky Woodring, October, 1981
A worthwhile pitch. Climb up the obvious orange flake and crack
system under the center of the massive roof (V1, 2) to a belay.
Either rappel, or traverse out right to join **Krazy Krack**.

V1 5.7 R FA: John Thackray, Todd Swain, November, 1982. From the
top of the flake, climb straight up the face, left of the crack.

V2 Trigger Happy 5.7 PG FA: Todd Swain, Val Risner, November,
1982. Climb straight up through the V-notches 20 feet right of
Trigger Point to the belay.

465 Krazy Krack 5.6 G
FA: Todd Swain, Corky Woodring, October, 1981
Climb a crack system up left to the right edge of the **Trigger Point**
roof, and a belay. Continue up left following cracks (crux) to the GT
ledge. Rappel, or climb a right-facing flake, then join **Crack of
Despondency**.

466 Crack of Despondency 5.4 G
FA: Dick DuMais, Steve Scofield, Keith LaBudde, 1972
Climb the crack system 20 feet left of **Pfui Teufel** to the GT ledge
(crux), then up right past an overhang to another ledge, and finally
up the face above to the top.

467 Pfui Teufel 5.3 G
FA: Marguerite Baumann, Bill Kemsley, 1958
Kemsley was the founder of *Backpacker* magazine. Climb the very
vegetated left-facing corner 50 feet right of **Trigger Point** to the GT
ledge, then back right around the roof, and up left to the forest.

468 Four Foot Face 5.3 G
FA: George Evans, John Rupley, 1953
Start as for **Pfui Teufel**, then angle up right to a belay on a ledge
(5.3, 50 feet). Climb up a corner, then step out right and up the face
to the top (5.3).

NOTE: In the woods of Sleepy Hollow there are two huge blocks
detached from the main cliff. Thom's Thumb is the left (south) spire,
and was named for Thom Scheuer, Mohonk Preserve Ranger.

The Brat · ☆Uberfall · 44 55 · Shockley's · Madame G's · Arrow · High Exposure · Bonnie's

469 Thom's Thumb, Left Hand 5.4 PG
FA: Derek Price (UK), Todd Swain, October, 1981
This route climbs the left (south) edge of the left pinnacle. Climb the outer arête 30 feet from the base of **Pfui Teufel** to the top of the spire (5.4 PG), then up a vertical crack system to a corner, which is climbed up and left (5.4), to the top.

470 Future Shock 5.12– R
FA: Darrow Kirkpatrick, Frank Minunni, September, 1986
Top-roped then led after a bolt and other gear was placed on rappel. On the front of Thom's Thumb, climb a deceptive face past a bolt to a very shallow right-facing corner/flake. Angle slightly left to the summit (V1).

V1 Direct Finish 5.12 (TR) FA: Frank Minunni, September, 1986.
Continue straight up from the flake to the top.

471 Meat Byproducts 5.10+ R
FA: Frank Minunni, Ken Driese September, 1987
Attempted earlier by another party. Start at the base of **All Thumbs** and angle up left on a ramp to its end. Make scary and difficult moves up the steep face above to the top. Another route may have been done in this area.

472 The Numbers Racket 5.12 (TR)
FA: Frank Minunni, Kevin Bein, September, 1987
Start at the bottom of the ramp mentioned in the previous route, and climb straight up the face, keeping left of **All Thumbs**.

473 All Thumbs (aka Art's Route) 5.9 G
FA: Art Gran, 1960s
Climb the nice, right-leaning crack on the front face of Thom's Thumb to an overhang. Climb the V-notch (crux, V1) to the top of the spire.

V1 Thumbs Up 5.8 PG FA: Todd Swain, Deane Morrison, October, 1981. Escape out right under the roof, then up the arête to the top.

474 Renaissance 5.12 R ★
FA: Darrow Kirkpatrick, Frank Minunni, September, 1986
A scary lead—use caution. Fixed gear placed on aid, some may now be missing. Climb the steep, clean face right of **All Thumbs** up a thin crack and past a roof.

Sleepy Hollow

475 Modern Love 5.12+ (TR)
FA: Dave Lanman, Summer, 1988
Climb the steep face 15 feet right of the vertical crack on
Renaissance to the big roof (left-facing corner above). Straight over
the roof above using a desperate layback hold, then up the face to
the top.

476 Thom's Thumb, Right Hand 5.10– PG
FA: Todd Swain, Tad Welch, October, 1984
Climb the prow on the right (north) side of the pinnacle using a
flake system and the arête.

477 Ranger's Revenge 5.5 PG
FA: Todd Swain, Thom Scheuer, September, 1981
This route starts off the top of the spire and climbs the dirty face
directly above the left chockstone passing a bulge with a fixed piton
(crux) to the top.

478 True Brit 5.7 G
FA: Todd Swain, Rick Ayres (UK), August, 1981
Scramble up the back side of Thom's Thumb, then climb the dirty
face straight up from the right-hand chockstone, passing a notch in
a roof (crux) to the woods.

479 The Circumcisor 5.12 PG13
FA: Russ Clune, Al Diamond, Summer, 1986
Steep and difficult climbing, but not as popular as **Bone Hard**.
Climb the smooth face on the main cliff right of the Thom's Thumb
pinnacle past numerous horizontals and fixed pegs. Rappel from
fixed gear at an obvious horizontal.

480 Bone Hard 5.12 PG ★★
FA: Al Diamond, Russ Clune, Summer, 1986
An excellent climb that is often top-roped by soloing out right from
the start of **True Brit**. Climb the right-hand of the two routes on the
main wall between the two pinnacles.

481 Death's Head Mask 5.12+ R
FA: (TR) Lynn Hill, August, 1988. FA: (lead) Jason Stern, August, 1988
A very serious lead. Climb the steep wall and fingercrack right of
Bone Hard and just behind the left (south) edge of the Dick's Prick
Pinnacle.

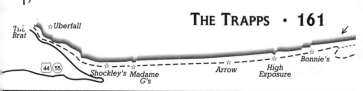

482 Girls Just Wanna Have Fun 5.12+ PG13
FA: Lynn Hill, 1988
This route was first attempted by others. Eventually it was top-roped, gear was placed on rappel, then led. Climb the weaknesses up the overhanging wall just left of **10,000 Restless Virgins**. Sharp holds on the upper section—many people tape up. Check the anchor carefully—the block may come loose one of these days!

483 10,000 Restless Virgins 5.10+ PG ★★
FA: Sam Slater, Mike Freeman, 1983
Climb the appealing flake system on the main wall directly behind **Dick's Prick** over the roof, then up the steep face above. Rap from the Dick's Prick Pinnacle rappel station.

NOTE: The next eight routes are on the right-hand of the two free-standing pinnacles in Sleepy Hollow. This spire was named for the late Dick Hirschland.

484 Dick's Prick (aka Richard's Spire) 5.6+ PG ★
FA: Hans Kraus, Dick Hirschland, Bonnie Prudden, 1954
About 100 feet right of Thom's Thumb is another pinnacle. This is the original line up this spire, and climbs the right (north) front face to the top. Descend via rappel.

485 Foreign Lesion 5.10 (TR)
FA: Todd Swain, Claire Mearns, November, 1985
Start below **Dick's Prick** and traverse out left to a shallow corner, then up this (crux). Climb up and left to the top of the pillar.

486 Rise to the Occasion 5.11 R ★
FA (TR): Don Hamilton, 1977 FA (lead): Todd Swain, July, 1987
A serious lead that was top-roped and had gear placed on rappel prior to being led. Climb the rappel line of the Dick's Prick Pinnacle. Crux is the first twenty feet, 5.10 or so above.

487 Circumcision 5.7 PG
FA: Dave Ingalls, Sean Hayes, 1963 FFA: Art Gran, 1963
Starting at a corner on the southeast (front left) side, traverse out right on a horizontal (crux) to a vertical crack and up to the summit.

488 Penal Colony 5.7 PG
FA: Todd Swain, John Thackray, November, 1982
Climb straight up from the start of **Circumcision** over two ceilings (crux at first ceiling) to slabs and the top.

Sleepy Hollow

489 V.D. 5.10 PG
FA: Sean Hayes, Joe Kelsey, Dave Ingalls, 1963 FFA: Layton Kor, 1965
If this route got sun, it could be catching. Climb the crack system on the back of **Dick's Prick**. Often wet and slimy.

490 Penis Colada 5.9 X
FA: Todd Swain, October, 1981
Climb the northwest corner of the spire to a horizontal, then up right past a very small pine to the top. It's essential to be tall on this one.

491 Chirpies 5.10+ R
FA: (TR) Todd Swain, November, 1985 FA: Todd Swain (solo), August, 1986
A canarial disease that can lead to hospitalization. Climb the narrow north face (towards **Wegetables**) without using the tree. Crux is the first 15 feet.

492 The Lone Ranger 5.3 G
FRA: Todd Swain (solo), August, 1981
Climb up the center of the slab 75 feet right of **Dick's Prick**.

493 After the Prick 5.4 PG
FA: Bill Goldner, Wally Schamest, Dick DuMais, 1966
Climb a short way up the huge, left-facing corner just right of **Lone Ranger** (crux), then move out right to the arête, and up this to the top.

494 The Deadline 5.9 R
FA: Todd Swain, Andy and Randy Schenkel, June, 1985
Climb the overhanging face right of **After the Prick** to a ledge (5.6, done previously), then continue straight up the overhanging wall to the top. Small Tri-cams helpful.

495 Wegetables 5.10– PG ★★
FA: Steve Wunsch, Kevin Bein Fall, 1974; Variations 2-4 Rich Romano, John Bragg, 1980
A climb that grows on you. The first climb to be done at the Gunks with Friends. If it were at the Uberfall, it would be the most climbed route in New York. 35 feet right (downhill) of **After the Prick**, climb up to a crack splitting a triple-tiered roof and follow this to a ledge (5.10-, V1). Walk off left, or climb up and left (V2-4) to a left-facing corner, which is followed through the ceiling above (5.9 PG).

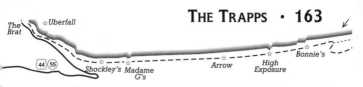

461	**Emilietta 5.3**	480	**Bone Hard 5.12**
463	**Sudden Death 5.8**	483	**10,000 Restless Virgins 5.10+**
464	**Trigger Point 5.6**	492	**The Lone Ranger 5.3**
465	**Krazy Krack 5.6**	493	**After the Prick 5.4**
466	**Crack of Despondency 5.4**	494	**The Deadline 5.9**
468	**Four Foot Face 5.3**	495	**Wegetables 5.10–**

V1 Shut Up and Eat Your Greens 5.12- (TR) FA: Colin Lantz, 1986. Climb the large roof left of the first pitch on **Wegetables**.

V2 Climb to the roof above the ledge then move right to a pointed flake. Traverse out the flake, then up to a birch tree. Either lower from here, or go up and left past a ceiling to the summit (5.10+).

V3 Climb to a right facing corner, then straight up the face above (5.9 PG).

V4 Move right on the ledge about 25 feet (roughly above **Hawaii Five-Ten**) and climb the obvious crack in the roof above; 5.11+.

Sleepy Hollow

496 Tennish Anyone? 5.10 PG ★
FA: Ivan Rezucha, Don Lauber, November, 1981
Although there is no move harder than 5.9, this is a pumper to lead without falling. Climb the crack system above a tree 15 feet right of **Wegetables** to a horn under the roof. Climb over the roof to a flake, then finger traverse right to a very small corner, which is followed up to the belay ledge. Move right, and climb the big roof at a giant flake (5.10–, done previously as part of **Wegetables**), then over the next roof on the left to the trees.

497 Hawaii Five-Ten 5.10 PG
FA: Todd Swain, Brad White, Andy Schenkel, Dave and Marie Saball, Dick Peterson, August, 1986
Climb the short fingercrack ten feet right of **Tennish Anyone**, then up to the top of a flake (.5 Tri-cams here). Angle up right towards the right edge of the bulging wall above (crux), then up the wide crack to the belay.

498 Foot Loose 5.8 PG
FA: Ivan Rezucha, Don Lauber, Annie O'Neill, October, 1981
Start 25 feet left of the huge, left-facing corner that is right of **Tennish Anyone**. Climb a dirty vertical crack to a belay. Move right to the corner, and traverse out right around the arête, then up the face to the pine tree. Continue to the top, or rappel with two ropes.

499 The Boron Destroyer 5.10 PG
FA: (TR) Todd Swain, Andy Schenkel, August, 1986. FA: (lead) Todd Swain, Randy Schenkel, August, 1986
Named for a squash racquet seen on the NYC subway. Climb the thin seam eight feet left of **Fancy Free** past a fixed peg (shaky). Continue up easier rock above to a belay at bushes in the corner (fixed slings here to rappel from). Traverse out right to the nose along a big horizontal, then up the dirty face to the top (or rappel from the **Fancy Free** pine tree, 5.6).

500 Fancy Free 5.8+ PG
FA: Ivan Rezucha, Annie O'Neill, October, 1981
Starting off a block, climb the obvious left-facing corner system until just below a roof. Traverse out right along a thin horizontal seam (crux, V1) to a ledge, and a belay at blocks. Climb up, go

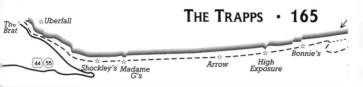

right around a ceiling, then left to a lone pine and belay. Climb to the top, or rappel with two ropes.

V1 Continue up and left around the roof, then traverse out right along a big horizontal (as for **The Boron Destroyer**) to the same belay. This makes the climb 5.6.

501 Alligator Alley 5.9 PG
FA: Ivan Rezucha, Annie O'Neill, October, 1991
Begin on the block as for **Fancy Free**. Step off the block onto the clean, white arête. Climb the arête, stepping right above an overhang to a thin, vertical crack. Follow the arête above (as for **Fancy Free**), continuing straight up past an overhang at a notch that is right of center. Climb straight up to rejoin **Fancy Free** at the pine tree. Rappel or continue up to the large ledge above.

502 The Headless Horseman 5.10 G
FA: Mike Steele, Bill Ravitch, 1986
Start atop the same block as **Fancy Free**, and just to the right. Step onto the face to a stance just right of an overhang. Gallop up the thin vertical crack (crux) up to overhangs and a corner, then right around the corner to a small ledge and tree. Rappel.

503 Crustacean Syndrome 5.8 PG
FA: Ivan Rezucha, Annie O'Neill, December, 1981
One of the best puns in the Gunks. A bit tricky to protect. Starting in a pit 30 feet right of **Fancy Free**, climb up a shallow corner to the roof, then escape out left to the face. Follow a left-facing corner, then out right to the nose and a belay. Climb up the face and cracks to the top.

504 Slime World 5.12 PG
FA: Mark Robinson, John Bragg, Sandy Stewart, September, 1978
A wild roof problem in the heart of Sleepy Hollow. Wait until a dry spell before trying this one. Climb the enormous roof 75 feet right of **Wegetables** at a crack and left-facing corner, then up the easier face on the right to the top. Difficult to protect.

505 Swamp Gas 5.10+ PG
FA: Mark Robinson, Sandy Stewart, September, 1978
Climb into a left-facing corner 75 feet right of **Slime World**, then make a 30-40 foot traverse left under the big roof to eventually link up with **Slime World**. Many small wires, TCUs and Friends helpful.

Sleepy Hollow

506 A Long Walk For Man 5.4 G
FA: Robert Fenichel, Ken Marts, 1973
Clamber up a large, left-arching corner further into the swamp.
Naturalists have theorized that Sleepy Hollow is the northern-most
possible habitat for alligators. Believe it or not.

NOTE: The area beyond this point has been closed to climbing to
preserve the natural vegetation, habitat and alligators.

The
Brat   ☆Uberfall

(44)(55)   ☆   ☆
           Shockley's Madame
                    G's

                              ☆   ☆
                            Arrow   High
                                     Exposure

                                              ☆- - - - -
                                                    Bonnie

John Thackray on first ascent of *Penal Colony* 5.7 R

Randy Schenkel on *Farewell to Arms* **5.8**

The Near Trapps

The Near Trapps is the second most popular cliff in the Gunks. Ranging in size from 50-170 feet in height, it is about 0.75 miles long and home to over 200 routes and variations. The north (right) end of the crag is the most popular, while the south (left) end has good rock and is usually less crowded. The middle of the Near Trapps (climbs left of **Grease Gun Groove** and right of **Ground Control**) has lots of loose, dirty rock. Use caution and the guide-book recommendations in this section.

To approach The Near Trapps, refer to the map on page 20, and look for a trail leading south towards the cliff from Route 44-55, starting about 100 yards downhill from Trapps Bridge. The trail runs along the entire base of the cliff and naturally, all climbs are described from right to left. The cliff-base topos beginning on page 172 describe in sections of two-page widths the cliff from right to left. Descend climbs right of **White Pillar** by walking north along the Millbrook Ridge Trail (blue blazes) back to the right end of the crag. For climbs left of **White Pillar**, walk south along the cliff top and descend down the gully between The Near Trapps and Bayards cliff.

1   Easy Rider 5.9 G ★★

FA: Joe Kelsey, Roman Laba, 1969. FFA: Unknown, 1970s. FRA: P7-11
Todd Swain and partner, 1981

A partial traverse of The Near Trapps. A worthwhile expedition that is
mainly 5.7 to 5.8 climbing and stays dry during light rain.

P1   Climb the first pitch of **Outer Space** to the belay (5.8-).

P2   Move over to **Le Plié** and reverse its rightward traverse to join
       Broken Sling. Climb a notch on **Broken Sling** and belay (5.8).

P3   Move straight left to join **Disneyland** under the roofs and con-
       tinue left to a belay under the **Swing Time** roof.

P4   Move left above the crux of **Te Dum**, then up and left to pass
       Inverted Layback just above the crux. Belay on the large
       Layback ledge (5.7+).

P5   Traverse left to under the final **Grand Central** roof (as for the
       old variation Portland), then step down and past a difficult sec-
       tion (feet below the slab in a hidden horizontal) to a belay on
       Alphonse (5.9).

P6   Move left to **Yellow Belly**, then down and across to join **Yellow
       Ridge** on the traverse on pitch two.

P7   Continue left around the nose of **Yellow Ridge** (original ascent
       finished up that route) to the **Baskerville Terrace** traverse and
       reverse **Baskerville** to the pitch two belay (5.6).

P8   Down climb **Baskerville** to the belay on pitch one (5.5).

P9   Climb up the corner, then out left past **Requiem** and **Fat City
       Direct** to a belay on **Fat City** (5.8).

P10   Continue across exposed climbing to the second belay on
       Gelsa (5.7).

P11   Finish on **Gelsa** (5.4).

2   Wichita 5.3 G

FA: Unknown, circa 1960

Begin a little left of the extreme right edge of the cliff at a crack with
a tree eight feet up. Climb the vegetated right crackline past a flake.
Step left to pass a ceiling, then finish on a slab. Watch for wasps!

3   St. Louis 5.5 G

FA: Unknown, circa 1960

Climb the dirty crack system on the face ten feet left of **Wichita** with
a left-facing corner at the base. Make a hard move off the ground then
angle a bit left to finish up a right facing, left leaning, flared corner.

4 Independence 5.2 G

FA: Unknown, circa 1960

Start at a left-leaning corner 18 feet left of the previous route, and just right of cleaner rock with a huge overhang above. Climb right-facing corners past bushes to a clean, open book. Exit via the right wall.

5 Kansas City 5.12 G ★★★

FA: Dick Williams, Dave Craft, 1962. FFA: John Bragg, 1973

A classic roof climb. It's actually easier barefoot! Climb easily up steep rock below a massive roof at the right (north) end of The Near Trapps to a belay (5.4, V1). Continue out the crack in the roof to the top.

V1 Topeka 5.10 PG FA: Unknown, circa 1960. From the belay, traverse out right around the corner then up over a ceiling to the trees.

6 Outer Space 5.8– PG ★

FA: Art Gran, Jim Geiser, Spring, 1959

Easier than it looks. Directly under the **Kansas City** roof/crack, climb up the middle of the slab to a bulge (V1), then up and left (crux) to a notch with a block jammed in above. Up into this notch, then left again to a belay at the edge of the roof. Climb up right to the woods.

V1 Weave up to the **Kansas City** block, starting between **Outer Space** and **Kansas City**; 5.7 PG.

7 Le Plié 5.7– PG

FA: Art Gran, Roman Sadowy, 1957. FFA: Unknown, pre-1964

One of the many climbs that are harder for tall people. Move up the left side of the slab to a big block wedged in the roof. Climb over this (crux) to a cramped leftwards traverse and eventual belay. Clamber up left to a roof, then back right to the top.

8 Infinite Space (aka Hyperspace) 5.12– PG

FA: Rich Romano, 1981

From the crux block on **Le Plié**, move up right to below the notch on **Outer Space**. Hand traverse left about 20 feet, then out the roof at thin cracks (crux).

9 Outer Space Direct 5.10 PG

FA: Unknown, 1960s

A link up of old variations. Start as for **Crass**, then climb up right to the block on **Le Plié**. Diagonal right to the notch on **Outer Space** (as for **Infinite Space**), and belay. Follow the weaknesses above past a jammed block (crux), then move right to the summit.

10 Crass 5.10 PG
FA: Ivan Rezucha, Kevin Bein, 1977
A linkup of old and new climbing. Start 20 feet left of **Le Plié** and
climb over the roof above a short dihedral (5.9, V1), then move up
left below a triangular ceiling (crux) to a belay. Follow **Le Plié**
around the ceiling (V2), then back right and over a roof at a small
flake (5.8) to the top.

V1 Traverse left around the initial roof, then out the right-facing
overhanging corner above; 5.9.

V2 Direct Finish 5.11– R FA: Rich Gottlieb, Tom Spiegler,
November, 1989. Top-roped then led. Climb the roof direct.

11 Iron Cross 5.12+ PG
FA: John Bragg, Fall, 1978
Climb the roofs six feet right of **Criss**, to eventually join **Crass** near
the top. Being tall (and very strong) is extremely helpful.

12 Criss 5.11 PG ★★
FA: John Stannard, Willie Crowther, 1967
A short and popular crux that is right off the ground. Struggle up
the overhanging, right-facing corner, ten feet right of **Criss Cross**
and 45 feet left of **Le Plié**. Follow cracks and a left-facing corner to

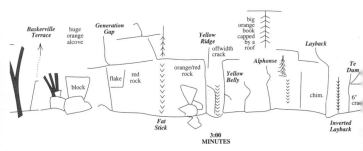

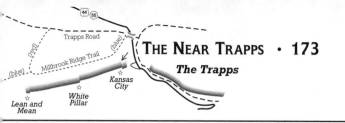

The Trapps

the **Le Plié** belay (5.11 G). Climb the roof directly above (5.11 PG) (crossing **Le Plié**) to the top.

13 Criss Cross 5.10 PG ★★★

FA: P1 Jim Andress, Doug Tompkins, 1959. FFA: P1 Jim McCarthy, Jim Geiser, 1961. FA: (complete) Pete Ramins, John Stannard, 1971
The first pitch is even more popular than **Criss**, but most people avoid the scary second pitch. On the first ascent the climb angled off right above the crux roof (now the finish of **Crass**). Starting 55 feet left of **Le Plié**, climb a right-facing corner with a fingercrack in it past two roofs (crux) to a belay above. Climb the face above keeping right of a corner, to the final roof (5.8+ R). Out right on the block/roof (5.9+) to the top.

14 Between the Lines 5.11 R

FA: John Burns, Gordon MacLeod (both UK), 1973. FFA: unknown, 1970s
One of the biggest sandbags in the 1980 guide. Climb a thin, left-facing corner 20 feet right of **Criss Cross** (V1), then right and over the roof. Move over left to a belay on **Broken Sling** (5.11 R). Continue

**This map describes approaches to
Routes 5 to 39 (right to left)**

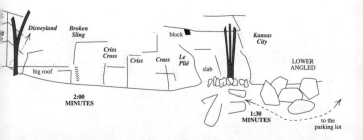

left around the nose, then climb a crack in a roof to join **Disneyland** near the top (5.11–).

V1 Sling Line 5.11 (TR) FA: Unknown, 1980s. Climb the face between **Broken Sling** and **Between the Lines**.

15 Broken Sling 5.8+ PG ★★★

FA: John Turner, Craig Merrihue, Harry King, 1956. FFA: Jim McCarthy, 1962

A classic and hard 5.8. Attempted earlier by Doug Kerr. Start at a right-facing corner at the right edge of a huge roof and 25 feet left of **Criss Cross**. Boulder up the corner (crux) to an overhang, step left (V1) then up and right along cracks to a belay in an alcove. Angle right from the alcove (5.7, V1, 2) past a roof, up, then back left through a notch (5.8) to the shrubs.

V1 Continue straight up the crack past the overhang to rejoin the regular route; 5.8.

V2 Broken Sling Direct 5.9+ PG FA: Unknown, 1970s. From the belay, climb straight up the flared crack, then left and up to the top.

V3 Original aid line 5.10 G FFA: Kevin Bein, 1970. Climb up from the belay and traverse right directly under the overhang to rejoin the regular route.

**This map describes approaches to
Routes 40 to 73 (right to left)**

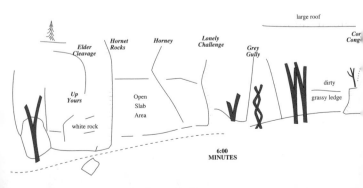

5 **Kansas City** 5.12	**12** **Criss** 5.11
6 **Outer Space** 5.8–	**13** **Criss Cross** 5.10
7 **Le Plié** 5.7–	**15** **Broken Sling** 5.8+
9 **Outer Space Direct** 5.10	**17** **Disneyland** 5.6–

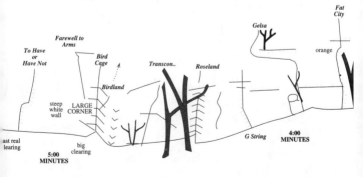

12	Criss 5.11	19	Swing Time 5.11
13	Criss Cross 5.10	21	Te Dum 5.7+
15	Broken Sling 5.8+	22	Linverted Layback 5.9
17	Disneyland 5.6–	24	Layback 5.5
17v2	Disney Point 5.10		

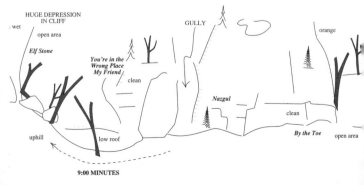

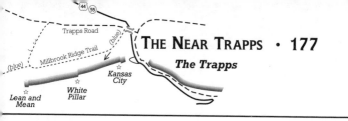

The Trapps

16 Squat Thrust 5.12– PG ★

FA: Russ Clune, Jeff Morris, 1986

Climb the initial **Broken Sling** corner, angle up left on the face, then climb the obvious, overhanging right-facing corner (5.10+ R) past a small overhang. Move right underneath another overhang, then climb a thin crack to the top.

17 Disneyland 5.6– PG ★★★

FA: Dave Craft, Pete Geiser, 1959

Walt would be proud of this one. A true Gunks classic in its grade. Begin 20 feet left of **Broken Sling** at the back of a wide dihedral that is just left of a huge roof. Traverse up and out right on an orange face to an awkward mantle (crux, V1) and a cramped belay. Climb the dihedral on the left above, to a large roof. Move right (V2) and over the ceiling to the summit.

V1 Instead of mantling on the ledge, continue traversing right around the nose, then up a thin crack (old pin) to the belay.

V2 Disney Point 5.10 PG ★★ FA: Kevin Bein, Fall, 1978. Move out left from the top of the corner along a big, triangular flake. Up left from the point of this to the top.

This map describes approaches to Routes 90 to 79 (right to left)

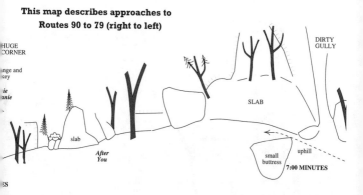

18 Sling Time 5.11+ PG ★★
FA: Dick Williams, Jim McCarthy, 1964. FFA: John Stannard, 1968
Hard! Climb the roof just left of **Disneyland** past fixed slings and
then immediately traverse right (crux) and up to a belay. Clamber
up the face above, and over the ceilings at a notch, to easier climbing above (5.7).

19 Swing Time 5.11 PG ★
FA: Ants Leemets, Elmer Skahan, 1964. FFA: John Stannard, 1968
Easier than the previous route, but still hard. Pull over the roof just
left of **Sling Time** (5.10 PG13), then up left along a small corner to
a belay under a double overhang. Climb up left over the first roof,
then back right past the second to the trees (5.11 PG).

20 Leftovers 5.7 PG
FA: Russ Clune, Rosie Andrews, 1981
An overlooked, moderate route in the most popular section of the
Nears—amazing! Rope up at a left-facing corner ten feet left of
Swing Time. Stem up the corner, then move right, then back left
past a crack to the **Te Dum** belay stance (5.7). Angle right under a
ceiling to join **Te Dum** and **Swing Time**. Traverse left (V1, 2) then up
the center of the face to the left side of the **Swing Time** roof. Turn
the roof on the left into a left facing corner, then up to a ceiling.
Finish on **Inverted Layback** (5.7).

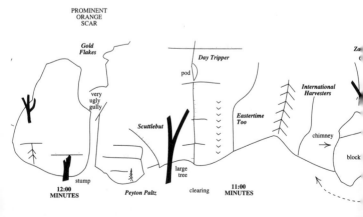

V1 5.10 G FA: Ivan Rezucha, June, 1992. Traverse right below the ceiling and above another ceiling then up to the top.

V2 5.9 G FA: Ivan Rezucha, June, 1992. Traverse left, reach over the ceiling, then hand traverse back right to join **V1**.

21   Te Dum 5.7+ G ★
FA: Hans Kraus, Roger Wolcott, 1949. FFA: Art Gran, 1960s
Worthwhile. Forty feet left of **Swing Time**, climb an obvious crack/flake system on the right wall of a dihedral to a roof (V1, 2). Move right around the nose, then up into a hanging corner (crux) to a belay stance (120 feet). Climb up right from here to the trail (5.4).

V1 Climb up the left side of the corner, then move right about 40 feet up to join the regular line.

V2 Where the regular route traverses right below a wide section of crack, continue up to a block. Either angle left to the large ledge on **Layback** (5.6), or move up, then go left to the **Layback** ledge (5.6+).

22   Inverted Layback 5.9 PG ★
FA: Dave Craft, Pete Geiser, 1959
Exciting and harder if you're tall. Jam up the obvious crack system on the left wall of a dihedral, 45 feet left of **Swing Time** (V1). Undercling out right on a flake (crux) to a small belay stance. Move right to clear the roof and on to the top (5.8+).

V1 Climb the crack right of the normal line to the roof; 5.6+.

**This map describes approaches to
Routes 110 to 91 (right to left)**

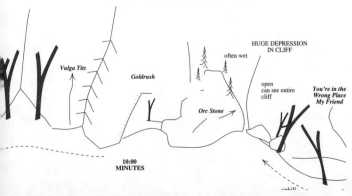

21 **Te Dum** 5.7+	28 **Alphonse** 5.8
22 **Inverted Layback** 5.9	32 **Yellow Belly** 5.8+
24 **Layback** 5.5	33 **Yellow Ridge** 5.7–
25 **Grand Central** 5.9–	35 **Fat Stick Direct** 5.10

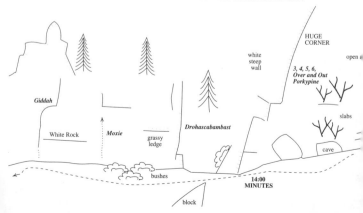

23 Burning Babies 5.11 PG

FA: Mike Law (Australian), Russ Clune, 1983

Climb the arête right of **Layback** to the **Layback** belay (5.11). P2 climbs the ceilings left of the **Layback** second pitch roofs.

24 Layback 5.5 PG ★★

FA: Fritz Wiessner, George Temple, 1941

A classic. Start 60 feet left of **Swing Time** at a left-facing chimney/corner. Power up the chimney/corner to a spacious belay (5.5), then up right around ceilings to the weeds (exposed 5.3).

25 Grand Central 5.9– PG ★★★

FA: Bonnie Prudden, Hans Kraus, Dick Hirschland, 1947. FFA: Jim McCarthy, 1963

A great route. Climb a nice dihedral 25 feet left of **Layback** to a roof (V1), move left and up to a belay (5.6). Move right around the nose and up the steep face (crux) to a belay below an overhang. Climb the roof (5.8+, harder if you are short) to the top.

V1 Climb the small corner just left of the dihedral to the roof; 5.6.

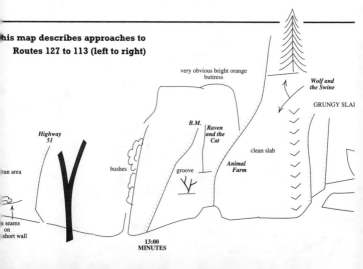

his map describes approaches to
Routes 127 to 113 (left to right)

26 Penn Station 5.10 PG
FA: P1 John Stannard, Rich Goldstone, Steve Wunsch, Fall, 1981; P2 Ivan Rezucha, Mike Sawicky, March, 1981
A bit hard to figure out. Climb the small nose just right of **Grand Central** to the roof, then move out right below the roof (crux) and up the face to join **Grand Central** at the second belay. Move down and right, then climb the roof up left above the **Layback** belay ledge.

27 Hot Clime 5.9+ G
FA: Todd Swain, Andy Schenkel, August, 1986
A linkup of previously climbed sections with a name that reflects August in the Gunks. Start 15 feet right of **Alphonse** and climb a left-facing corner past a pine tree. Traverse left to a belay (5.9). Follow the **Alphonse** corner to the big roof (V1), then reverse the **Easy Rider** traverse (crux). Climb right-facing corners and overlaps on the right to a belay on **Grand Central**. Move out left around the ceiling (5.9–, exposed) to the top.

V1 5.9/5.10 (TR) FA: Ivan Rezucha, circa 1980. Climb the steep, wasp infested face directly above the belay and just left of the nose.

28 Alphonse 5.8 G ★
FA: Ken Prestrud, Lucien Warner, 1948. FFA: John Turner, 1950s
Popular. Begin 55 feet left of **Layback** below a large, obvious dihedral.

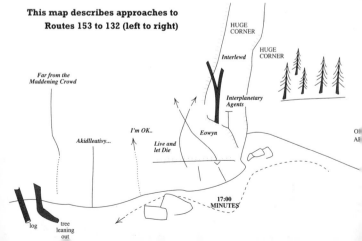

This map describes approaches to Routes 153 to 132 (left to right)

HUGE CORNER

Interlewd

HUGE CORNER

Far from the Maddening Crowd

Interplanetary Agents

Akidlleativy...

I'm OK..

Eowyn

Live and let Die

O A

17:00 MINUTES

log

tree leaning out

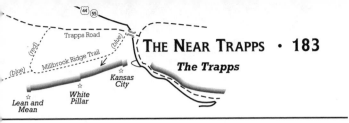

Climb the face just left of a left-facing corner to a belay ledge (5.6). Stem up a clean corner to a roof, traverse left and belay (5.6). Angle right past a notch in a roof (crux) to the summit.

29 Sissy Boys 5.10+ R

FA: P1 Ivan Rezucha, Annie O'Neill, 1983; P2 Jason Kahn, Eugene Pulumbo, 1986; P3 Todd Swain, John Thackray, Fall, 1984

Climb the face and thin crack left of the first pitch of **Alphonse** to a tree (5.8+ PG). Move right and climb a thin crack through a ceiling, then up the face above, keeping left of a water streak. Belay on the **Alphonse** belay ledge (5.10 + R). Follow **Alphonse** through the notch in the ceiling, then angle out left on a slab to climb a roof (5.10 PG) to the trail.

30 No Slings Attached 5.10 R

FA: (complete) John Bragg, Mark Robinson, Russ Raffa, 1977; P1 and P2 Rich Perch, Mark Robinson, 1977

Maybe not quite as scary as people think, but then again…. Starting on the nose left of **Alphonse**, boulder out right from a small sentry box (5.10–), then up the arête to a belay. Climb left of the nose to a roof, then move around right and up to the **Alphonse** belay (5.10). Climb steep rock just left of **Alphonse** (crux, a wee bit contrived), then left and over another roof to the trees.

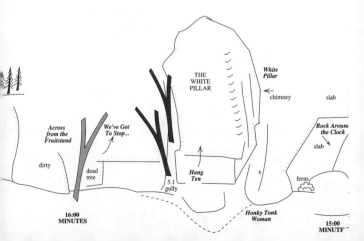

31   Bongos and Beached Whales   5.10 R

FA: Russ Clune, Pete Black (UK), May, 1983

This route's last pitch was originally described as what is now **Sissy Boys**' last pitch. Climb the face just right of the **Yellow Belly** corner along a thin crack to a belay ledge (5.9 R). Up an orange face to a roof, that is climbed on the left, then angle right past more over-hangs to the **Alphonse** belay (5.10 PG). Move left on the ledge to the left side of a ceiling, climb this, then continue to the top (5.9).

32   Yellow Belly   5.8+ PG ★

FA: Jim McCarthy, Bob Larsen, Ken Prestrud 1957

The climb that firmly established 5.8 in the Gunks. Scamper up a clean dihedral ten feet right of **Yellow Ridge** to a ceiling (V1), and climb straight over this to a belay stance on the top of a pillar (5.8+). Climb the corner above (V2, 3) moving right to an alcove in the ceilings. Exit left from the alcove (5.8+, exposed), then up a left facing corner to easier climbing.

V1   Underbelly   5.11– PG   FA: Rich Gottlieb, Teri Condon, 1986. Begin left of the regular route and climb a short dihedral to an

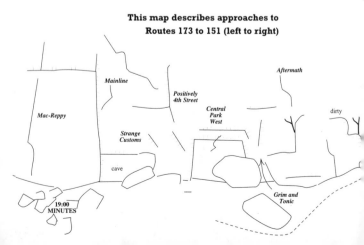

This map describes approaches to
Routes 173 to 151 (left to right)

Aftermath

Mainline

Positively 4th Street

Central Park West

dirty

Mac-Reppy

Strange Customs

cave

19:00 MINUTES

Grim and Tonic

28	Alphonse 5.8	
32	Yellow Belly 5.8+	
33	Yellow Ridge 5.7–	
35	Fat Stick Direct 5.10	
36	Generation Gap 5.11	
37	The Hounds 5.10	
38	Requiem 5.12	
39	Baskerville Terrace 5.7+	
40v2	Fat City Direct 5.10+	
42	Gelsa 5.4	

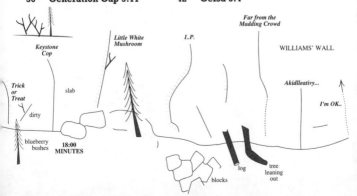

overhang. Move right to the nose, then up and left to join the route at the upper overhang.

V2 The original line moved left and climbed a crack past a tree to the alcove; 5.8.

V3 Climb the scary face on the right, traversing left to the alcove; 5.8.

33 Yellow Ridge 5.7– PG ★★★

FA: Fritz Wiessner, Edward and Ann Gross, 1944
Don't miss this one. Not suprisingly, the first ascent party did not climb the final overhangs—they traversed left to **Baskerville Terrace**. Start at boulders 100 feet left of **Layback** and below an

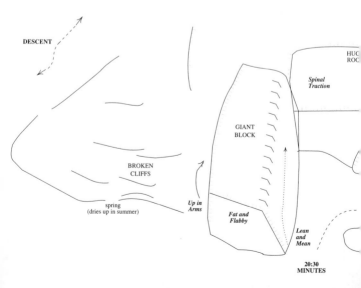

This map describes approaches to
Routes 187 to 174 (left to right)

DESCENT

HUC
ROC

Spinal
Traction

GIANT
BLOCK

BROKEN
CLIFFS

Up in
Arms

spring
(dries up in summer)

Fat and
Flabby

Lean
and
Mean

20:30
MINUTES

obvious offwidth crack that is just left of a nose. Climb up left (V1) to the off width crack. Struggle up the crack (crux) to a belay ledge. Bridge up the corner, then a long traverse left leads to a belay below the final ceilings on a long ledge (5.5, V2). Move left to the arête, and up this (exposed 5.6), moving right through the roofs at a notch.

V1 It is also possible to climb the arête directly below the offwidth (5.9), or the face and corner on the left (5.8).

V2 5.8+ PG FA: Ivan Rezucha, Annie O'Neill, July, 1983. From part-way out the second pitch, just where the route moves left, climb straight up and over a ceiling, then move a bit right and up to the trees.

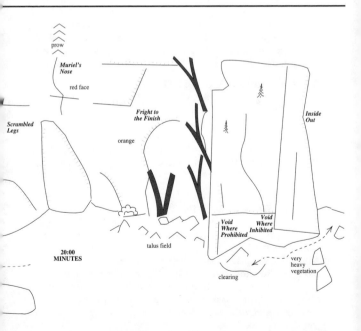

34 Fat Stick 5.8 G
FA: Jim McCarthy, Hans Kraus, 1957

The first pitch is worthwhile, the rest an expedition. Climb an obvious prow left of **Yellow Ridge** past a notch in the huge ceiling (crux). Traverse far left to a belay in a corner (above the crux of **Generation Gap**). Move up the corner (V1), then angle up left to a belay below the right end of huge ceilings (as for **Baskerville Terrace**). Follow **Baskerville Terrace** to the top.

V1 Climb the corner to a roof, then go right to **Yellow Ridge** at either of two levels—a much better alternative.

35 Fat Stick Direct 5.10 PG ★★
FA: John Stannard, G. Livingston, 1968

Climb **Fat Stick** through the crux notch (5.8). Before the first belay, climb straight over the next roof at a left-facing corner (5.10 G). At the top of the corner, move out right and up to the second belay on **Yellow Ridge** (the long, narrow ledge). Climb the shallow left-facing corner above the belay, then move right (5.9 PG) and over the ceilings to the top.

36 Generation Gap 5.11 G
FA: Jim McCarthy, Dick Williams, 1968. FFA: John Stannard, Howie Davis, 1969

Failure is common on this one unless you have the Beta. Rumor has it that McCarthy knew this would go free on the first ascent— hence the name? Start 30 feet left of the **Fat Stick** pillar and climb the roof at a corner (crux) to a belay (most people rappel from here). Up the corner above, to eventually move right and join **Yellow Ridge** on the final arête.

37 The Hounds 5.10 PG
FA: P1 (initial corner) Ivan Rezucha, Rich Perch, February, 1981; P1 (crux) Todd Swain, Mark Wallace, October, 1986; P3 Brett Wolf, Dave Cason, May, 1982

A linkup of variations that will have you yelping. From the top of the block that **Requiem** starts on, climb a right-leaning corner to a roof (5.8+). Step left and climb straight up the steep, streaked wall (pins, crux) to a belay on **Baskerville Terrace**. Halfway along the final traverse of **Baskerville**, climb the creaky roofs, then up a cleaned streak to the trail (5.9–).

Dana Bartlett on *The Hounds*, 5.10

38 Requiem 5.12 PG ★★

FA: see below for details

A difficult and involved route. Bring a #4 Friend for the last pitch
and some talent for the crux. This climb may be harder since the
crux hold broke. P1 starts atop stacked blocks and climbs the face
just right of **Baskerville Terrace**, staying left of a thin seam to a
ledge (5.10 R) (FA: Russ Raffa, Russ Clune, May, 1981). P2 jams out
the obvious hand crack above (5.10+), then traverses left slightly,
and over a bulge (crux), to easier rock, and a belay on the left as for
Fat City (FA: Ivan Rezucha, Howard Doyle May, 1981. FFA: Russ
Clune, Russ Raffa, August, 1982). P3 moves back right about 30 feet,
then climbs the left-facing notch (right of the **Fat City** crux), and
continues up right to easier climbing, and the top (FA: Russ Raffa,
Ivan Rezucha, May, 1981).

39 Baskerville Terrace 5.7+ PG13 ★★

FA: John Wharton, Dave Isles, 1958. FFA: Jim McCarthy, 1961

This climb will have you howling. Start 75 feet left of the **Fat Stick**
pillar and just left of stacked boulders. Trot up to a shallow facing left
corner, then make a tricky face move above (crux) to reach a
ledge. Either belay there, or continue up cracks in an orange face

(5.5) to a belay out right on the arête. From the upper belay, climb up left to the big roofs, then traverse back right under the roof to a big corner, which is climbed to the top (5.5).

40 Fat City 5.10 PG ★★★

FA: Dick Williams, Dave Craft, 1966. FFA: John Stannard, Gary Brown, 1968

Excellent climbing. Once you clip the 24 year old crux pin, you'll be in **Fat City**! Climb up and over a roof in a left-facing corner, 25 feet left of **Baskerville Terrace** (5.9). Move left under a steep bulge (V1), then up easy rock to an exposed belay. From the belay, creep up to an obvious left-facing roof/corner and climb out the roof (crux—scary clipping the pin) to a belay 25 feet to the left on a small ledge. Scamper up to a big ledge, then diagonal left around the final ceilings to the summit.

V1 Fat City Direct 5.10+ G ★★ FA: John Bragg, John Stannard, 1970s. A great addition to **Fat City**. After the initial overhang, climb straight up the bulge/nose, then move left and up to the belay. Climb through the regular crux, then diagonal right to the top.

41 Land of the Giants 5.11 X

FA: Jeff Gruenberg, Scott Franklin, April, 1985

If you're capable of leading this, watch out for a guy with a slingshot named David. Climb up through the overhangs to cross **Fat City** near the end of its traverse. Continue up, climbing the right side of the roof above.

42 Gelsa 5.4 PG ★★★

FA: Fritz Wiessner, Beckett Howorth, George Temple, 1942

One of the best 5.4s in the Gunks. The third pitch is fantastic. From the top of a boulder pile 95 feet left of **Baskerville Terrace** and 75 feet right of **Roseland**, climb up a crack, then left below roofs to a good belay ledge (5.3). Climb up off the left end of the ledge to a horizontal (V1, 2) and follow this left to a nose, which is climbed to a great belay ledge at the base of an huge, overhanging corner (5.4). Climb the corner and face on the right to the trail (5.3).

V1 From the first belay, climb up to the horizontal, then straight up the slab (tricky 5.4+) to another, good horizontal. Traverse left to the belay in the corner.

V2 It is also possible to move right off the ledge then up to join **V1** on the leftwards traverse.

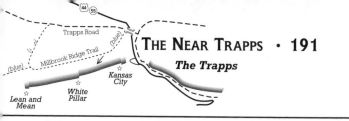

The Trapps

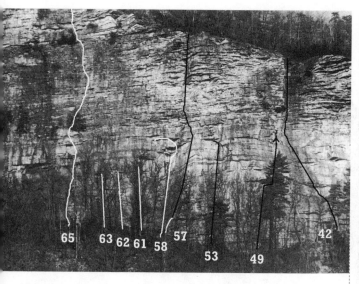

42	Gelsa 5.4
49	Roseland 5.9
53	Transcontinental Nailway 5.10
57	Birdland 5.8+
58	Bird Cage 5.10–

61	To Be, or Not To Be 5.11+
62	To Have or Have Not 5.12
63	Son of Stem 5.11
65	Grease Gun Groove 5.6

43 G String 5.10 R

FA: Jim Kolocotronis, Herb Laeger, 1973

Laeger lived in D.C. in the 1970s and put up many fine routes all along the East Coast. He now lives near the Needles of California and is still establishing hard routes. Starting 15 feet left of **Gelsa**, climb a crack/corner to a roof and move right five feet and up a slab to the **Gelsa** belay ledge (5.10 R). Move right from the belay and up a crack (V2 on **Gelsa**), moving right to the **Fat City** belay (5.6). Power straight up through ceilings past the bolt on **Fat City** to the top (5.9).

44 Pain Strain 5.11+ PG

FA: Russ Clune, Kevin Bein, Pete Black (UK), Barbara Devine, Russ Raffa, May, 1983

Difficult to protect. Climb the face and ceiling 30 feet left of **Gelsa** to the tree on the first ledge (5.11). Climb either second pitch variation of **Gelsa** to another belay (5.4). Power up the steep face out right of **Gelsa**'s last pitch to the woods (5.9 R).

45 Forbidden Zone 5.12 (TR)

FA: Russ Clune, 1986

Climb the face and thin seam between **Pain Strain** and **Eraserhead** to the first **Gelsa** belay ledge.

46 Eraserhead 5.12– R ★

FA: Russ Raffa, Russ Clune, May, 1983

Very good climbing but hard to protect. The crux hold has partially broken off, making this a bit harder then it was on the FA. Begin 40 feet left of **Gelsa** and climb the face between **Pain Strain** and **Shitface**, passing a small left-facing flake (crux) at 40 feet. Belay at the **Roseland** belay on the left. Climb up and left past a roof to the second **Roseland** belay. Climb up the arête left of the **Gelsa** corner (5.8).

47 Shitface 5.10 R ★★

FA: Jim McCarthy, Jim Andress circa 1963

Holds have broken off since the first ascent making this harder. Climb straight up the face 20 feet right of the **Roseland** corner to the belay on **Roseland**. This is typically top-roped after doing **Roseland**.

48 Revolving Eyeballs 5.10 R

FA: Russ Clune, December, 1983

Even if you don't come off, it's an appropriate name. Climb the rounded arête just right of **Roseland** along thin cracks to a stance at a bulge. Over the bulge to the **Roseland** traverse (crux), move left and up past a roof to the **Roseland** belay (the original **Roseland** aid line).

49 Roseland 5.9 G ★★★

FA: Jim McCarthy, Hans Kraus, 1958. FFA: Jim McCarthy, 1960

One of the best pitches in the Gunks. Climb a beautiful right-facing

corner 75 feet left of **Gelsa** past a ceiling to big ceilings. Traverse right (crux), then over a bulge to the belay (most people rappel from here). Move up, then left to a shallow corner and climb past this to a ledge (5.8). The final pitch diagonals right to the arête, and joins **Eraserhead** to the top.

50 Boogey Man 5.12– R ★★
FA: Jeff Gruenberg, Russ Clune, John Myers, September, 1983
Definitely a force to be reckoned with. TCUs and talent are essential. Climb the face just left of **Roseland** past an overhang and a green streak (crux), into a shallow left-facing corner under a roof. Move left around the ceiling, then up a left-facing corner (5.10, done previously) to join **Roseland**.

51 El Kabong 5.12 R
FA: (TR) Jeff Gruenberg, circa 1983; (lead) Gene Smith, Timmy Harter (Ger), Guenther Mann (Ger), July 1989
Originally done on a top-rope, this climb was then protected on rappel before being led. A sustained route. Start as for **El Camino**, but climb straight up the steep orange face into a hanging corner. Climb up and right, then join either **Boogey Man** or **El Camino** to the top.

52 El Camino 5.11– PG13
FA: Alex Lowe, Russ Clune, Dan McMillan, August, 1982
Not the fabled Golden Road, unless you are solid on 5.10+. Starting at **Roseland**, climb out left along a ramp and horizontals until you are just right of **Transcontinental**. Make a hard mantle move near the edge (crux), then climb the scary face up right to a small roof. Continue up right over a bulge to a belay at a tree. Pump through the ceilings above, to the top.

53 Transcontinental Nailway 5.10 PG ★★★
FA: Joe Fitschen, Art Gran, 1961. FFA: Jim McCarthy, 1965
Known as the Transcontinental Freeway for a short time after the FFA. McCarthy climbed V1 on the FFA; Rich Goldstone later climbed the scary 5.8 section. Lots of climbing on this one. Climb an awkward slab to a roof 40 feet left of **Roseland**, then over the roof (crux) and up a shallow corner (V1) to its top. Move right, then back left (scary 5.8), and up to a belay. Either traverse left and rappel from **Birdland**, or climb the face up right to a ledge (V2), then up

left past a few small ceilings to the summit. Some loose rock near the top.

V1 At the top of the corner, traverse left under roofs, then directly up to the belay; 5.9+. Watch for rope drag.

V2 5.10 R FA: John Bragg, Ajax Greene, 1970s. From the belay, climb an overhang into a groove and up this to the ledge. Climb past ceilings above to the path.

54 Road Warrior 5.11+ R
FA: Russ Raffa, 1983
This route and the next are usually top-roped. Climb the first bit of **Transcontinental**, then move left at the roof and climb the face past an inside corner left of **Transcontinental**'s **V1** to rejoin **Transcontinental** at the belay. Rappel, or climb the second pitch variation of **Transcontinental**.

55 Slammin' the Salmon 5.12
FA: (TR) Russ Clune, 1986; (lead) Gene Smith, June, 1989
Top-roped, then protected on rappel with natural gear. Pins were later placed on rappel, which were soon stripped from the route. Climb the very steep face between **Road Warrior** and **Bird Brain**, crossing **Bird Brain** to finish on the orange streak right of **Birdland**.

56 Bird Brain 5.11+ R ★
FA: (TR) Steve Wunsch, 1974; (toproped then led) Russ Raffa, Russ Clune, January, 1983
Scary and difficult to protect. Starting 20 feet right of **Birdland**, weave up the overhanging face and traverse right towards a thin crack, which is followed to the **Birdland** belay. Rappel, or follow any of the other climbs to the shrubs.

57 Birdland 5.8+ G ★★★
FA: Jim McCarthy, John Rupley, Jim Andress, 1958
A classic face climb. Most people rap off after the first pitch, but the second pitch is well worth doing. Starting 45 feet left of **Roseland** at a dihedral, move out right and climb the lovely face following fixed pegs to an exposed belay station on the nose (5.8+). Climb over a bulge and up to a left-facing corner, which is exited right to reach the top (5.8, V1).

V1 The original line climbed diagonally left above the bulge on P2.

58 Bird Cage 5.10– PG ★★

FA: (P1 corner) Jim McCarthy, John Rupley, Jim Andress, 1958; (complete) Dick Williams, Steve Arsenault, Wilbur Cain, 1971.FFA: (P1 corner) Yvon Chouinard, pre-1964; (complete): Henry Barber, Bob Anderson, 1972

A worthwhile climb that can, with enough gear, be done in one pitch. Climb the dihedral just left of the **Birdland** face to the roof (5.9, possible belay here), then move right and over the roof (crux, V1, 2) to a cramped stance. Move left to the belay and rappel (V3). Should you really want to reach the summit, climb left to a roof, then up right to the finish (5.7).

V1 Traverse right ten feet below the roof to the **Birdland** belay.

V2 Go up and right, then down climb to the **Birdland** belay and rappel.

V3 Go right and up to join **Birdland** on pitch two.

59 Farewell to Arms 5.8 PG ★

FA: Jim McCarthy, Al DeMaria 1960

Not as bad as it sounds; well worth doing. Starting ten feet up the **Bird Cage** dihedral, traverse out left (V1, 2), then up an obvious corner past a roof to a belay (5.8). Rappel, or climb up left, then back right to the trail.

V1 Climb the left-leaning fracture to join **Farewell to Arms** on its initial traverse; 5.10.

V2 Farewell to Fingers 5.12– R ★ FA: Unknown, pre-1964. FFA: Rich Goldstone, Dick Williams, 1970. Since the time of the FFA, the bolt and some holds have broken off. Climb the face directly up to the corner on the first pitch.

60 The Boy From Above 5.11+ (TR)

FA: Dave Lanman, Summer, 1987.

From the top of **Farewell to Fingers,** move up left (staying below **Farewell to Arms**) on difficult climbing to the green face. Climb the steep face just right of **To Be** near the arête to the communal belay.

61 To Be, Or Not To Be 5.11+ R ★

FA: (TR) Russ Clune, July, 1983; (lead): Russ Raffa, Russ Clune, Lynn Hill, July, 1983

To lead or top-rope, that is the question. Should you be one of the few to answer the former, bring small wires and #2.5 and 4 Friends. Begin thy journey midway between **Farewell to Fingers** and **To Have or Have Not**. Ascendeth thine face to a thin crack, then move thyself left with difficulty past a tiny corner. Venture up right onto yonder steep face to a bulge. Escape to the left then up to thy belay or go straight up (a wee bit harder; 5.12–).

62   To Have or Have Not 5.12 R ★★★

FA: Pete Carman, Jim McCarthy, 1966. FFA: John Stannard, 1973
Still hard and often top-roped. On the FFA, the crux nut was placed with a coathanger from below. If you come off while leading this, the bell will toll for you! Climb a short, green, left-facing corner 55 feet left of **Bird Cage**, then move right and up another incipient corner (crux) to the belay. Rappel, or climb straight to the top.

63   Son of Stem 5.11 R

FA: Mike Robin, Stokie Baker, Bruce Breslau, July, 1983
Start at a left-facing corner 60 feet left of **Birdcage**. Follow the corner to a ceiling, then over this (crux, #1RP) and up the face above, angling right to the **To Have or Have Not** belay. Rappel, or climb the face left of **To Have**.

64   Solyent Green 5.11 R

FA: Mike Robin, Stokie Baker, Ed Fripps, July, 1983
Bring extra RP nuts and an appreciation of science fiction for this one. Starting at a loose flake just right of **Grease Gun Groove**, climb the steep face to a ledge (5.11). Move up the easier rock, keeping right of **Grease Gun**, to the path.

65   Grease Gun Groove 5.6 G ★

FA: Gary Hemming, Art Gran, Roger Chorley, 1958
Worthwhile climbing. Originally done in the rain, hence the name. Boulder into a clean, left-facing corner 85 feet left of **Bird Cage**, then up, exiting right at a roof (V1) to another corner, and up this to a belay on the right (5.6, pine tree). Scamper to a roof and move left, then up past ledges to the top.

V1 Climb straight up, then traverse over to the pine tree; 5.5.

NOTE: This route marks the end of the popular section of The Near Trapps. Anyone climbing beyond here should pay heed to comments in the descriptions.

66 Tulip Mussel Garden 5.10+ G

FA: Dick Williams, 1989

Rope up ten feet left of the **Grease Gun Groove** corner below a low
ceiling. Climb past the ceiling (5.8+) to a second ceiling. Move left
and climb past a short right-facing corner to some loose looking
blocks. Surmount these and climb the face to an obvious pine tree.
Rappel.

67 Corporate Conglomerate 5.10– PG

FA: Ivan Rezucha, Don Lauber, November, 1981

Starting 50 feet left of **Grease Gun**, climb past a ledge and flake left
of a roof, then move left and up a crack to a tree. Belay up right, at
another tree. Wade up classic Near Trapps terrain until below a roof,
then move left to belay as for **Grey Gully**. Diagonal right, and climb
the roof at a left-facing notch.

68 Grey Gully 5.7 PG

FA: Hans and Madi Kraus, 1959

The next few climbs are best forgotten. Climb the right-hand, left-
facing corner 105 feet left of **Grease Gun**, moving out right and up
to a belay. Skip up another corner on the left, then on up to another
ledge. Walk right to the right end of a roof and belay just above.
Move left from the belay to a corner and exit out right and on to the
top.

69 Lonely Challenge 5.5 PG

FA: Art Gran, Joe Kelsey, 1965

The challenge may be finding someone with whom to do the route!
Climb the left-facing corner that is 25 feet left of **Grey Gully** to a
tree (70 ft, 5.5). Continue up the corner, to eventually join **Grey
Gully** to the top.

70 Horney 5.7 PG

FA: Art Gran, Pete Vlachos, 1965

Abstinence is advised. Starting in the center of the slab left of **Grey
Gully**, climb the left side of a pillar, then move up right around ceil-
ings to a belay at a pine. Up a corner/crack above, past roofs to join
Grey Gully near the top.

71 Hornet Rocks 5.5 PG
FA: Norton Smithe, Cecil Grace, Steve Jervis, 1953
Smithe manufactured one of the first angle pitons used at the Gunks.
They were made out of soft iron, and a few are still in place today!
From the center of the slab as for **Horney** (V1), diagonal left to the
huge, right-facing corner and up this to a belay on the left. Follow
another corner up left to the GT ledge. Wander to the left edge of
the ceilings, up a corner on the left then follow clean white rock to
the top (5.5).

V1 Bee Bite 5.7 G FA: Unknown, pre-1964. Climb the corner
direct.

72 Elder Cleavage 5.10 PG ★★★
FA: Ivan Rezucha, November, 1980
The best route in this section of the cliff, with every pitch being
worthwhile. Start atop a small boulder 40 feet right of **Loose Goose**
and 150 feet left of **Grease Gun Groove**. Hand traverse left along
the first horizontal to a corner (V1, V2) and up this to a belay on the
slab above (5.9–). Climb the left-arching flake and the roof above, to
a belay as for **Loose Goose** (5.10). Move left and climb the obvious
handcrack to the GT ledge (5.8+, done previously). Walk right and
climb straight up the face right of **Hornet Rocks**, then swing out the
wild, left-facing corner in the huge ceilings (5.10–).

V1 Carlos Buhler's Day Off 5.12– (TR) FA: Mike Dimitri, 1986.
Start atop the small boulder and climb thin seams and a flake
straight up. Move left to the first belay.

V2 Avoid the initial hand traverse by climbing straight up to the
corner from the ground; 5.10+.

73 Up Yours 5.7 G ★
FA: John Weichsel, Bill Goldner, Fall, 1961
Originally called You're Up. Saunter up S-cracks ten feet right of
Loose Goose to the slab. Cross **Elder Cleavage** and stem up a cor-
ner system to a belay (5.7). Rappel, or wade to the GT ledge and
finish on **Hornet Rocks**.

74 Loose Goose 5.5 G
FA: Fritz Wiessner, Beckett Howorth, Hans Kraus, 1942
Really not very loose, and it's actually an okay route. Climb up right

Trapps Road

Millbrook Ridge Trail

(red)

(blue)

(blue)

Kansas City

White Pillar

Lean and Mean

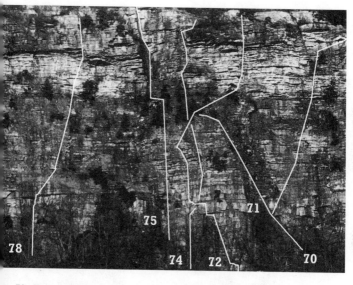

70 Horney 5.7	**74** Loose Goose 5.5
71 Hornet Rocks 5.5	**75** SwissAir 5.9
72 Elder Cleavage 5.10	**78** Vultures Know 5.10

along corners and cracks, 190 feet left of **Grease Gun** and directly below an obvious crack (P3 of **Elder Cleavage**) to a nice belay at the base of a left-leaning corner. Climb the corner to the GT ledge (5.4) and finish on **Hornet Rocks**.

75 SwissAir 5.9 PG

FA: Todd Swain, Kurt Graf (Swiss), Max Strumia, September, 1981
Despite the fact that this route was extensively cleaned on the FA, it never became popular. It's now filthy again, though the last pitch is still worth doing (and can be approached via rappel). Scramble up to a right-arching flake 30 feet left of **Loose Goose**, and up this to a ledge (5.7+). Straight up the dirty face to the highest belay ledge (5.5). Climb the big dihedral to the top (5.9).

76 Ain't Dis Yab Yum? 5.5 PG
FA: Ted Dillard, Eric Lucas, 1973
The first ascent party was lost and you probably will be, too.
Starting 60 feet left of **Loose Goose**, climb a crack in a slab
between two huge blocks to a pine. Move right, and climb a corner
to another tree. Wander up dirty rock to the GT ledge, then angle
right to the summit.

77 Where the Wild Things Are 5.10+ PG
FA: Mike Steele, Nick Miskowski, Bill Ravitch, 1985
Start 20 feet left of **Ain't Dis**, at a small slab leading up to an overhang. Up the slab, hand traverse left at the second horizontal (to
miss the overhang), then up and right on a steep face to a tree and
ledge (5.9). Climb straight up to the GT ledge (5.5). Walk right 25
feet, and get atop a block. Climb up and right to surmount the crux
hang, then left ten feet on a slab above to belay. Swing around left
and up the face to the pines (5.5)

78 Vultures Know 5.10 R
FA: Don Perry, Maury Jaffe, 1979
Climb a dirty, left-facing corner 15 feet right of **After You** to a ledge,
then move far right and belay. Up a right-facing corner to the GT
ledge and another belay, then up and over the ceilings at a prominent left-facing corner (crux).

79 After You 5.7 PG
FA: Bill Goldner, Muriel Mayo, Fall, 1962
A climb for myrmidons. Friction up a white slab 160 feet left of
Loose Goose and just right of a pine tree on the cliff to a belay
niche under a ceiling. Escape right around the roof then up a corner on the right to the GT ledge and a belay. Up a right-facing corner to a roof, then over this on the left, to lower angled rock and the
top.

80 Yum Yum Yab Yum 5.3 G ★
FA: Art Gran, Al DeMaria, 1960
One of the better, easy climbs in the middle of The Near Trapps.
With more traffic, this could be a great route. The name is a take-off
on Himalayan mountain names, and supposedly means "delicious
love." Starting as for **After You**, climb up left to a corner (V1), then to
the same belay as for **After You**. Move down left, then up an obvious

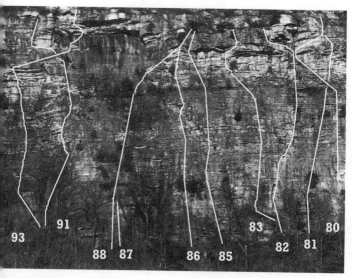

80 **Yum Yum Yab Yum 5.3**
81 **B. Warewolf 5.8+**
82 **Eenie Meenie 5.6**
83 **My-Knee-Moe 5.8+**
85 **By the Toe 5.9+**
86 **Nazgul 5.10–**

87 **Wrong Place, Right Time 5.10**
88 **You're in the Wrong Place, My Friend 5.6**
91 **Orc Stone 5.5**
93 **Lost World 5.11**

left-facing corner to the GT ledge. Scamper up a big right-facing corner (crux), and traverse right across an exposed slab, then up to the top.

V1 Climb the left-facing corner left of the normal start; 5.8.

81 B. Warewolf 5.8+ PG
FA: Todd Swain, Brett Wolf, September, 1981
A bit creepy, even with a full set of Friends. Start 25 feet left of **Yum Yum Yab Yum** at a tree and climb a left-facing corner and crack to a ledge. Climb straight up behind a tree (5.8) to a V-notch and through this to the GT ledge. From a bunch of oaks, ascend straight up and over a roof just right of a left-facing corner to join **Yum Yum**.

82 Eenie Meenie 5.6 PG
FA: Al DeMaria, Art Gran, Fall, 1959
Loose. Climb a large, orange right-facing corner, 50 feet left of
After You, until you can step left and belay. Up the face above to a
ceiling, which is passed on the right and on to the GT ledge. Up a
large corner, then traverse far left and on to the shrubs.

83 My-Knee-Moe 5.8+ G ★
FA: Dick Williams, Hilton Long, 1965
Two good pitches of climbing on this one. Follow **Eenie Meenie** for
20 feet, then traverse left on a tree ledge to a crack/seam system.
Up this (5.8+) to a belay at a tree. Jugbash straight up the face to the
GT ledge, then climb out right at a left-facing corner in the roof to
the top (5.7+).

84 Catch a Tiger 5.9+ PG
FA: Todd Swain, Donette Smith, Randy Schenkel, June, 1994
The last ceiling had been done previously as a variation to **By the
Toe**. Start at the right edge of a clean, bulging section of rock that is
40 feet left of the **Eenie Meenie** corner. Scramble up past a couple
of ledges then climb a thin crack left of an easy looking, vegetated
ramp that leads up and left to a prominent pine tree (5.7; V1, 2).
Keeping left of a giant, left-facing corner, climb up the face, passing
a prominent tree on its left, to the GT ledge. Climb the ceiling
between **My-Knee-Moe** and **By the Toe** at a crack (5.9+).

V1 Climb the easy looking, vegetated ramp to the pine; 5.4.

V2 The center of the bulging face between this route and **By the
Toe** has been top-roped; 5.11+.

85 By the Toe 5.9+ PG
FA: Dick Williams, Bill Goldner, 1965. FFA: John Stannard, 1973
The last pitch is worthwhile. Start 40 feet right of a cave at the base
of the cliff and 80 feet left of the **Eenie Meenie** corner. Climb the
obvious corner system with a bush 30 feet up. Bridge up a short,
right-facing corner to a roof, then around this on the left and up
right to a corner (V1) to belay (140 feet). Hike up easy rock to the
GT ledge. Climb up to a ceiling, hand traverse left to a notch and
through this (crux) to easier climbing.

V1 Climb a crack a bit left of the corner.

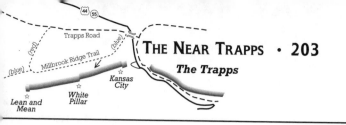

86 Nazgul 5.10– X

FA: Rich Goldstone, Dick Williams, 1971

Death is in store for those that meet the Nazgul unprepared. Begin at a point where the trail descends, 110 feet left of **Eenie Meenie**, at a small tree growing against the cliff and down and right from a gully. Float up a small, clean left-facing corner. At its top, move left and climb steep, white rock to a ledge (40 feet). Up the face left of a corner, then up the left-facing corner to the GT ledge. Starting on the left of a small prow, climb up right past a roof to another ceiling (crux). Hand traverse right, then up to the top.

87 Wrong Place, Right Time 5.10 PG13

FA: Todd Swain, Andy Schenkel, John Courtney, 1986

The next two routes start at the right edge of a large depression in the entire cliff, about 100 feet left of **Nazgul** and 65 feet right of **Elf Stone**, where the trail starts to rise. This is the cleanest little bit of cliff in this section. Starting on the slab just right of the corner on **You're in the Wrong Place, My Friend**, climb straight up to a small ledge at 20 feet. Step left and make a hard move up the yellow rock to a short, right-facing corner and a pine tree (5.10). Rappel, or climb the dirty face to the GT ledge (5.5). Move right 15 feet and climb an obvious crack formed by blocks to join **You're in the Wrong Place** to the trees (5.2).

88 You're in the Wrong Place, My Friend 5.6 PG

FA: Dick Williams, Dave Loeks, 1971

Amen. Begin as for **Wrong Place, Right Time**. Climb up to a nice looking right-facing corner, move left (V1), then weave up past cracks and corners to the highest ledge and a belay at a tree (5.6). Scramble up more dirt and loose rock to the GT ledge, then continue to a ledge with a tree and a block as for **Elf Stone**. Diagonal right to the top (5.2).

V1 5.8+ G FA: Todd Swain, Andy Schenkel, John Courtney, 1986. Climb directly up the nice looking corner to rejoin the regular route or rappel from the tree.

89 Tooth and Nail 5.10 PG
FA: Joe Rommel, Dave Lage, August, 1990
Start ten feet left of **You're in the Wrong Place** at the right-hand edge
of a large overhang where a notch breaks the roof. Pull a small,
blocky overhang about ten feet above the ground, then through a
cleft in a second overhang two feet higher. Continue up the slightly
overhanging notch (crux) to easier ground and the bottom of a short,
prominent corner facing right. Climb the corner and continue straight
up the crack above until it runs out at a pine tree (5.10 G). Move left
ten feet to a short left-facing corner, then up to a large vertical crack.
Climb the crack on its left side and continue up to narrow ledges
below the left edge of the giant overhang at the top (5.5). Traverse left
on ledges past the notch where the final pitch of **Orc Stone** goes,
then angle downward to a belay at a pine. Climb up a few feet to the
right of the tree, pull a tiny overhang and layback into a short, left-
facing corner. Go up the corner to its top and step around right to
easier ground. Follow the line of least resistance to the top (5.9+ PG).

90 Elf Stone 5.10 R ★
FA: Dick Williams, Dave Craft, 1966. FFA: Steve Wunsch, Dick
Williams, 1971
Since the tree on the wild last pitch died this climb is serious. At the
right edge of the large depression and the left edge of low overhangs, follow holds out right until below a notch in a ceiling (V1).
Over this and up to a belay. Continue up easy rock past the GT ledge,
to a belay under a huge, left-facing corner capped by a roof. Sneak
up the corner, then hand traverse right to the arête (crux) and up this
to the woods.

V1 5.7 G FA: Dave Lage, Joe Rommel, August, 1990. Begin to the
right of the normal start, under the overhang. Step right onto the face
then up a crack through a small overhang to join the regular route at
the notch in the overhang.

91 Orc Stone 5.5 PG
FA: Dick Williams, Dave Craft, 1966
Who likes Orcs? The site of a huge banner in 1980 that said "Mariott
Go Home!" in response to the proposed resort planned for Lake
Minnewaska. Trudge up a corner just left of **Elf Stone**, then angle
right to white rock and a left-facing corner. Climb this to a belay, then
up the dirty face to a corner on the right and another belay. Follow
this corner to its top, traverse left below roofs, then up to the weeds.

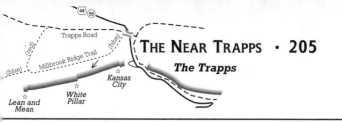

The Trapps

92 Cherry's Climb 5.5 PG

FA: Dick Williams, Cherry Merrit, 1971

Obscure and deservedly so. After the initial corner on **Orc Stone**, go up the face past a left-facing corner to a ledge. Belay to the right at a tree (5.5). Climb a left-facing corner above, cross **Lost World**, then go up left to the top (5.5).

93 Lost World 5.11 R

FA: Don Perry, 1978. FFA: Mark Robinson, Don Perry, 1978

Wild and scary. Wander up **Orc Stone** and **Cherry's Climb** to a belay off to the left under a orange roof. Climb back right and pull the hang at a vertical crack and small corner (5.10), then wade up to the GT ledge passing tons of loose rock, to a belay under the big ceiling. Climb straight up from some blocks to the roof, then climb the first hang at a right-facing corner. Move left until the ceiling can be climbed, then up past another roof to the top (5.11).

94 Fellatio 5.6 PG

FA: Mike and Sally Westmacott (UK), Paul Ramer, 1965

The climb everyone's talking about— a classic Vulgarian route name. Friction up a slab and curving crack 30 feet left of **Orc Stone** and right of a horizontal tree, to a belay ledge with two small trees. Zoom up to orange roofs and a ledge, then step left and up a white dihedral past a roof to a ledge. Scramble to the shrubs.

95 Gold Rush 5.9 G

FA: Dick Williams, Pete Geiser, Phil Jacobus, 1964. FFA: Bob Anderson, John Stannard, 1973

Start 65 feet left of **Orc Stone** and 40 feet left of a horizontal tree. Layback a right-leaning corner past a roof to a belay (70 feet). Ramble up the white rock above, then move left and climb a corner to the GT ledge. Head up right, then back left, to an obvious ceiling with a crack in it. Climb through the overhang and up a corner to the top (5.9).

96 Vulga-Tits 5.6 PG

FA: Gerd Thuestad (Nor), Kaye Arnott, Evy Goldstone, 1968

Climb the left face of a right-facing corner, 80 feet left of **Gold Rush** and just left of a triangular slope above the trail. Continue past ledges to the second pine tree and a belay. Move up to a notch in a roof, exit left, then up a steep face. Drift right to the top.

97 Three Generations 5.5 G
FA: Todd Swain, Ira Brant, Kurt Graf (Swiss), September, 1981
Ira Brant is the only person in the Gunks to own the land his first ascent is on. Climb the first right-facing corner left of **Vulga-Tits** up to steep rock, and flakes to a belay at a cedar tree (5.4). Climb the face just right of the huge, right-facing corner, then climb a bombay chimney (crux), to a corner on the right and the belay. Follow a right-facing corner to the trees.

98 Nowhereland 5.8– PG
FA: Mike Steele, Jon Graul, September, 1984
Starting at **Three Generations**, angle left to the corner and orange rock, then swing left on thin holds (5.8–), and up easier rock to a ledge. From the left end of the ledge, climb the face by a tree, then swing left again (5.8–) at right-facing flakes and up to the GT ledge. Move up to a roof, then up right past another roof to a chimney and the woods.

99 Zachariah 5.8 PG ★
FA: Dick Williams, Al DeMaria, 1971
Climb a chimney and the buttress 70 feet right of **Eastertime Too** to a ledge, then wander up to another ledge with trees. From here, weave up the face past a bulge, to a belay under a roof at a notch. Swing right through the notch (crux) then left and up the face to the GT ledge. Up some easy rock, then climb a nice crack through roofs to the top (5.7).

100 International Harvesters 5.9+ PG
FA: Todd Swain, Ed Grindley (UK), Mick Lovatt (UK), July, 1981
Good climbing, but still dirty. Grindley wrote the Ben Nevis (Scotland) ice climbing guide, and Lovatt was featured on the cover of Dave Jones' excellent book, *Rock Climbing in Britain*. Climb the thin, clean cracks on the buttress 50 feet right of **Eastertime Too** to a tree (5.8). Jam up the orange fingercrack above (5.9), then angle left to a ledge. Climb the big, left-facing corner through the roof (crux, #4 hex) and up to the GT ledge. Follow **Zachariah** to the finish (5.7).

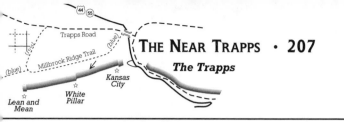

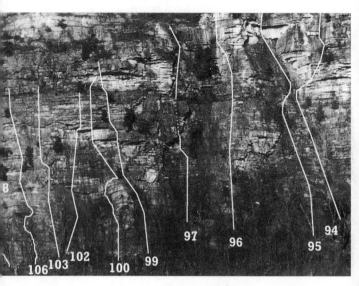

94 **Fellatio** 5.6	**100** **International Harvesters** 5.9+
95 **Gold Rush** 5.9	**102** **Good Friday Climb** 5.9+
96 **Vulga-Tits** 5.6	**103** **Eastertime Too** 5.8+
97 **Three Generations** 5.5	**106** **Day Tripper** 5.8–
99 **Zachariah** 5.8	**108** **Scuttlebutt** 5.5

101 Between a Rock and a Hard Place 5.8 R

FA: Mike Steele, John Graul, 1984

That's what it'll be if you come off while holding the loose block on the second pitch! Begin 20 feet left of **International Harvesters** at a wide crack leading to a dirty ledge. Climb to the ledge, then go up and left past another ledge and a ceiling to a belay at a cedar tree (5.8). Climb towards the left edge of the roof above, passing a precariously placed block. Continue up to a belay on the GT ledge (5.8), then scamper to the summit.

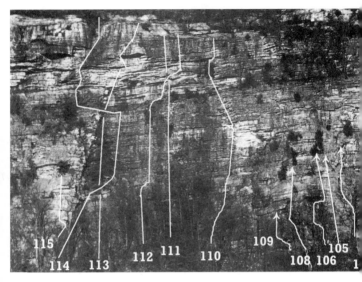

103 **Eastertime Too** 5.8+
105 **Boston Tree Party** 5.9+
106 **Day Tripper** 5.8–
108 **Scuttlebutt** 5.5
109 **Peyton Paltz** 5.9
110 **Gold Flakes** 5.7

111 **Energy Crunch** 5.8
112 **Deception** 5.7
113 **Wolf and the Swine** 5.9
114 **Animal Farm** 5.6
115 **Raven and the Cat** 5.11–

102 Good Friday Climb 5.9+ PG ★

FA: (complete) Dana Bartlett, Todd Swain, July, 1981; P1: Jim Munson, 1980

The first pitch of this route and **Boston Tree Party** can easily be top-roped after doing **Eastertime Too**. Climb the thin seam just right of **Eastertime Too** past a bulge, to a large ledge (5.9+). Pump through the ceiling at the left-hand corner by a laurel bush (5.9+) and up the face to the GT ledge. Follow **Zachariah** to the weeds (5.7).

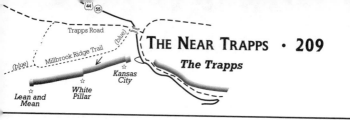

103 Eastertime Too 5.8+ G ★★

FA: Dick Williams, Jim McCarthy, John Hudson, 1966
Named for Hudson, who died later on Huascaran in Peru. Jam the wonderful hand- and fingercrack (crux), climb up a right-facing corner, then move left to a ledge. Rappel, or ruin a good experience by climbing yucky rock to the top.

104 Woolly Clam Taco 5.10 PG

FA: Gary Terpening, Joe Bridges, Fall, 1989
A #0 Alien will help protect the bottom of the route. Climb the face left of the **Eastertime Too** crack, then up the steep, narrow face just left of the right-facing corner on **Eastertime Too**, then up a thin, diagonal crack above.

105 Boston Tree Party 5.9+ R

FA: Todd Swain, Ed and Cynthia Grindley (UK), August, 1981
Climb the arête just left of **Eastertime Too**, then straight up the face past a thin vertical crack to a bulge and the belay (5.9+). Rappel, or climb up to the left edge of the ceilings, and angle right past a loose block to the GT ledge. Finish on **Zachariah**.

106 Day Tripper 5.8– G ★

FA: Dick Williams, Dave Craft, Larry Roberts, 1966
Starting 15 feet left of **Eastertime Too**, climb a yellow dihedral then step left past a ceiling (crux), into a chimney/groove, then exit right (V1) around the next roof and up to a tree. Rappel, or wander up the face past the left edge of an overhang, to a corner, and the top.

V1 5.11– G FA: Mick Avery, Mike Dimitri, July, 1984. Climb directly out the roof at the thin crack (watch for bats in the crack!). A long reach.

107 As the Cliff Turns 5.8 G

FA: Todd Swain, Kathy Beuttler, October, 1986
Climb the cleaned face and thin crack right of **Scuttlebutt**. Over the left end of the **Day Tripper** roof at a crack to the belay.

108 Scuttlebutt 5.5 G ★

FA: Dick Williams, Tom Bridges, 1973
Angle left up the face just left of **Day Tripper** to the nose, then up a clean slab to a belay at a tree (5.5). Rappel, or follow a crack and a corner to another ledge. Move up and left to another corner and climb the face left of this to the GT ledge. Climb up left past a ceiling to the shrubs.

109 Peyton Paltz 5.9 G

FA: Todd Swain, John Goobic, November, 1985

Completed on Goobic's birthday, which is a day before Swain's.
Climb out left through the low ceilings 15 feet left of **Day Tripper**,
then up the arête to join **Scuttlebutt** at the belay.

110 Gold Flakes 5.7 PG

FA: Dick Williams, Dave Craft, 1965

A large rockfall occurred here in 1987, making the route suspect.
Use caution in this area of the cliff. 120 feet left of **Day Tripper** and
130 feet right of an orange buttress, climb a slab to a ledge. Move
right and climb an orange corner to a roof (rockfall area), then move
left and up past another roof to the GT ledge. Follow a weakness up
past a tree, then move right under a ceiling and up easier rock to the
woods.

111 Energy Crunch 5.8 R

FA: Todd Swain, Brett Wolf, October, 1981

If you lose power at the crux, you could hear the sounds of bones
breaking. Start at the top of a hill 145 feet left of **Day Tripper**. Climb
the face and obvious left-facing flake system to the GT ledge (long
pitch). Follow **Deception** to a roof, then move left and over another
hang at a thin seam (crux). Angle left to the finish.

112 Deception 5.7 PG

FA: Dick Williams, Pete Geiser, 1964

When this line was originally spotted from the Brauhaus parking lot
(then known as Emil's—aka Slime), it looked like it would be more
difficult. Climb up a dihedral 170 feet left of **Day Tripper** and 80 feet
right of an orange buttress to a belay (5.2). Move right, and climb the
clean face just left of a flake system to the GT ledge (5.4), then climb
up right along a ramp to a roof and over this to the top (5.7).

113 Wolf and the Swine 5.9 PG

FA: Brett Wolf, Todd Swain, October, 1981

Climb directly up the face 30 feet right of **Animal Farm** to the pine
tree (5.8+), and belay. Daintily climb up the huge, loose corner to the
GT ledge (5.5). Climb a small, left-facing corner to a roof (touching
Cherokee), move right five feet, then climb an overhang with a thin
crack (crux) to another roof. Move slightly right to the big roof,
around this on the right and to the trees.

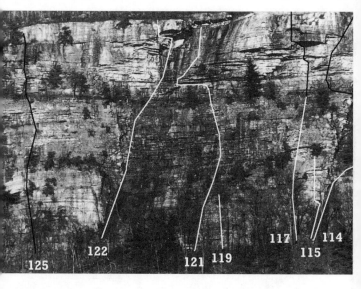

114 Animal Farm 5.6
115 Raven and the Cat 5.11–
117 BM 5.8
119 Eat Here and Get Gas 5.8

121 Highway 51 5.5
122 3, 4, 5, 6, Over and Out
 Porkypine 5.9
125 Drohascadamfubast 5.8+

114 Animal Farm 5.6 G

FA: Dick Williams, Brian Carey, 1964

Start at a right-facing corner on the right side of an orange buttress 200 feet left of **Day Tripper**. Gallop up the corner to a large pine tree (5.4). Climb the face right of the corner to the GT ledge, then walk left 40 feet until below a notch in a roof, and a tree (5.4). Clamber up to a roof, then angle up to a crack, which is followed to a large ceiling. Move right to a right-facing corner, then right again and up clean, white rock to the summit (5.6).

115 Raven and the Cat 5.11– PG13 ★
FA: Paul Craven (UK), Felix Modugno, 1984
An excellent pitch but a bit scary to lead. Previously attempted by another party in 1981. Starting on **Animal Farm**, move out left past a pin to a vertical seam. Up the seam past another pin (crux) to roofs and the ledge.

116 Cherokee 5.9 PG
FA: Ivan Rezucha, Uwe Bischoff (Ger), September, 1981
Some good climbing to be found. Climb the orange buttress near its left side (V1), following thin cracks to a roof which is passed on the left to a belay ledge (5.8). Step right and climb the face to the GT ledge, then walk right until above the large corner of **Wolf and the Swine**. Climb up to a roof, then move right and over a ceiling. Diagonal left to another roof, then traverse left across **Animal Farm**. Move left around a nose (above, and right of the **BM** crux traverse), then up to the trees (5.9).

117 BM 5.8 PG
FA: Dick Williams, Brian Carey, Jim McCarthy, 1964
Climb a right-facing corner on the left edge of the **Animal Farm** orange buttress past a notch to a belay. Waltz up the face left of a loose left-facing corner to the GT ledge. Climb up 20 feet, move left and through a roof to a corner (one can belay here). Hand traverse left (exposed crux), then up to the top.

118 Slab Shtick 5.8 PG
FA: Ivan Rezucha, Annie O'Neill, May, 1980
Climb the face 35 feet left of **BM** to a horizontal and a bush. Traverse left around a nose, then up the face until forced right to a corner/crack and up to a belay ledge. Weave up the face to the GT ledge, then move to a belay at trees on the left. Climb past a pointed flake/overhang on the left, then right to a rest. Hand traverse left around a ceiling, then angle right on slabs to finish between roofs and a crack.

119 Eat Here and Get Gas 5.8 G
FA: Todd Swain, Andy Schenkel, 1986
On the steep, clean wall 30 feet right of the start of **Highway 51**, climb a thin crack past a bulge (crux) to easier rock and the belay at a tree.

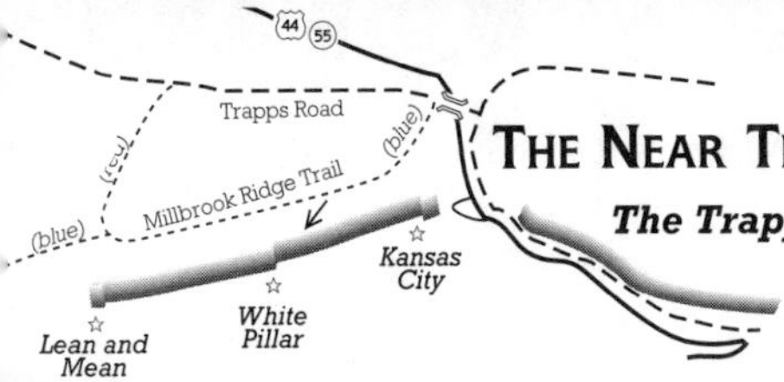
44
55
Trapps Road
(red)
(blue)
Millbrook Ridge Trail
(blue)
Kansas City
White Pillar
Lean and Mean

120 Pump Ethyl 5.11+ (TR)

FA: Todd Swain, 1987

The clean, thin seam 15 feet right of the start of **Highway 51** has also been climbed. There has been a fixed #1 RP in the seam since 1986—the leftovers of the initial lead attempt.

121 Highway 51 5.5 G

FA: Dick Williams, Claude Suhl, 1973

This is not the scenic route unless you are a botanist. Start 30 feet right of **Porkypine** and 130 feet left of **BM**. Motor up a face, drift right on a ramp and belay at a ledge (120 feet). Climb past a roof to a left-facing corner, then move right and up a crack to the GT ledge. Drive up to a right-facing corner on the left, then up to a large roof. Escape left, then on to the rest area.

122 3, 4, 5, 6, Over and Out Porkypine 5.9 PG

FA: Dick Williams, Brian Carey 1964. FFA: Henry Barber, John Stannard, Eric Marshall 1973

Originally rated 5.6 A2, the name gives the pitch ratings, the description, and tells about a visitor on the summit. Starting 160 feet left of **BM**, climb the face just right of a huge, right-facing corner to the GT ledge (5.4). Climb up to a roof, then angle right to a belay stance (30 feet). From the top of a flake, move over left under a roof then out through a notch (crux) to a last corner and the trees.

123 Mighty White of Us 5.11+ (TR)

FA: Frank Minnuni, Darrow Kirkpatrick, April, 1987

Start just left of **Porkypine** atop a sickle shaped flake, then climb up the pretty white face to the arête, which is followed to the top and a belay.

124 Bush League 5.8 G

FA: Ivan Rezucha, Annie O'Neill, May 1980

Climb the face 20 feet right of **Drohascadamfubast** and 65 feet left of **Porkypine** to a roof. Move right ten feet, then up right to a belay at a pine. Climb the laurel bush left of the belay (hence the name), then angle right past the lip of a roof to a groove and right to a ledge. Up past a roof above some flakes and on to the GT ledge. From here, climb up then right to clean rock. Angle left past ceilings (down and left of **Porkypine**) to the trees.

125 Drohascadamfubast 5.8+ PG
FA: Dick Williams, Claude Suhl, 1971
Not as dirty, rotten, hard, scary, etc. as once thought. It is possible to combine this with the last pitch of **Porkypine**. Climb a vegetated right-facing corner 85 feet left of **Porkypine** to a grassy ledge (V1), then move left to a crack/shallow corner in a white face. Up the crack, traverse left (crux) to a slab and up right along a seam (5.7) to a pine. Rappel, or wade up a left-facing corner, then climb the face on the right to a ledge. From here, step left, then up past a bulge and red rock to the GT ledge. Move left and up an obvious weakness, then move left again, and up past a broken section to a slab and a ledge. Climb a short dihedral to the woods.

V1 Direct Start 5.8 PG FA: Todd Swain, Dana Bartlett, 1985. Perhaps a better start than the dirty corner. Climb straight up the cleaned face to the vertical crack/corner, then follow the regular route.

126 Moxie 5.8+ PG ★
FA: Dick Williams, Bob Anderson, Steve Lessin, 1973
Rope up 140 feet left of **Porkypine** and 90 feet right of **White Pillar** below the biggest roof in the area. Climb up a face and obvious, white, left-facing corner that passes the left side of the roof to a ledge (5.8+). Rappel, or wander up to a ledge and belay 15 feet higher. Climb up to an orange slab, traverse left 15 feet to a right-facing corner. Move up the face just right of the corner to the GT ledge, and belay. Angle right along an obvious weakness, then right and up a dihedral to the top.

127 Giddah 5.6 G ★
FA: Dave Craft, Dick Williams, 1965
Climb up the face 20 feet left of **Moxie**, then layback a right-facing flake to a ledge (5.6). Rappel, or wander up the face to the GT ledge. Trot up past a dead cedar tree and a notch to a roof. Move left and up to the shrubs.

128 Rock Around the Clock 5.6 R
FA: Dave Loeks, Claude Suhl, 1973
Clean rock, scary climbing. Start 45 feet right of **White Pillar** below a clean slab. Bop up to a right-leaning crack/ramp and follow this to a small left-facing corner. Belay on the right in a corner. Angle left to an orange flake in a roof and over this to the GT ledge. Diagonal left around roofs to a right-facing corner, and up this, escaping left to the top.

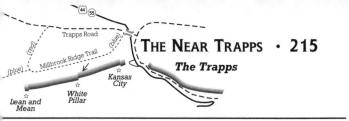

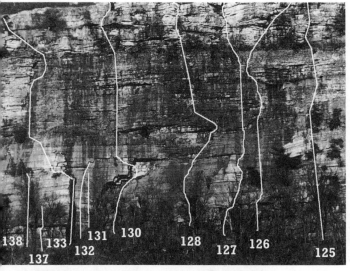

125 **Drohascadamfubast** 5.8+
126 **Moxie** 5.8+
127 **Giddah** 5.6
128 **Rock Around the Clock** 5.6
130 **Just Allow Me**
   One More Chance 5.6

131 **She's the Boss** 5.9+
132 **Honky Tonk Woman** 5.9
133 **White Pillar** 5.7–
137 **Hang Ten** 5.10–
138 **Tree Filled Chimney** 5.1

129 Flake, Rattle and Roll 5.6+ PG13

FA: Dick Williams, Dave Craft, Joe Bridges, 1988

Scary rock, scary climbing. Rope up 35 feet right of **White Pillar** at a 15 foot high vertical crack. Climb the crack and a right-facing corner above a ceiling, then angle right to a shallow dihedral. Go up flakes, then move left and up to a belay (5.6). Angle right to a ledge under the right edge of a ceiling. From the right edge of the ledge, angle back left, then up to the GT ledge. Walk left about 25 feet and belay at a pine (5.6+, PG13; loose rock). Climb up the face just right of the tree past a ceiling, then angle left to overhangs. Angle right around the overhangs to another belay at a pine (5.5; loose rock). Strut to the summit.

130 Just Allow Me One More Chance 5.6 PG
FA: Dick Williams, Cherry Merritt, Al DeMaria, 1971
Climb the easy face 25 feet right of **White Pillar** to a pine, then up
the huge right-facing corner to an obvious and exposed traverse
left to the arête. Up the easy face to a ledge, then move left and
belay. Climb the steep face past an overhang to a big, orange roof,
then left around this and over more ceilings to the GT ledge. Follow
a right-facing corner past a notch, then on to the weeds.

131 She's the Boss 5.9+ X
FA: (top-roped, then led) Todd Swain, Iza Trapani, June, 1985
A daring leap up an indistinct line. Climb a short nose just right of
Honky Tonk and left of a fern-covered ledge to a bulge, then right
up a short, orange dihedral to its top. Step left (crux) and up the
clean face to a horizontal tree, and the rappel.

132 Honky Tonk Woman 5.9 PG ★★
FA: Dick Williams, Dave Loeks, 1971
A classic first pitch that is well protected if you are good at placing
protection. Climb an obvious groove just right of the chimney on
White Pillar, past a bolt and a bulge (crux, small wires) to easier
rock and a belay at a big horizontal. Move left or right to rappel
from trees, or wander up to the GT ledge, then follow **White Pillar**
to the top.

133 White Pillar 5.7– PG ★
FA: Fritz Wiessner, Mary Miller, 1940
One of the historical classics. Struggle up the right-facing chimney
formed by a huge block leaning against the cliff (5.7–) and belay.
From the top of the block, traverse up and left to a tree and another
belay. Follow a loose right-facing corner to the GT ledge. Climb a
left-facing corner to the trees.

134 Harvest Moon 5.11– G ★★
FRA: Alex Lowe, Fall, 1980
Starting in the **White Pillar** chimney, step left and jam the beautiful
finger crack to the top of the block.

135 The Mincer 5.12 R ★
FA: Jim Damon, August, 1984
Starting on the ground, climb the thin overhanging cracks just left of
Harvest Moon. Difficult to protect.

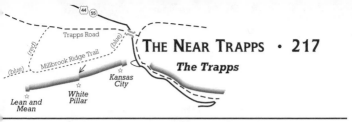

132 Honky Tonk Woman 5.9
135 The Mincer 5.12
137 Hang Ten 5.10–
142 We've Got to Stop
    Meeting Like This 5.8
143 Across from the
    Fruitstand 5.4
145 Roman's Climb Next to
    Across from the Fruitstand
    5.6
147 Interplanetary Agents 5.10
148 Interlewd 5.5
150 Live and Let Die 5.10–
151 I'm OK—You're OK 5.8+

136 Shootin' the Curl 5.10– PG

FA: Dick Williams, 1989

Tubular, man. Start just left of **The Mincer** and climb up to the left arête of the **White Pillar**. Pull the ceiling, then up a right-facing corner and the face above to the anchor.

137 Hang Ten 5.10– G ★

FA: Todd Swain, Andy and Randy Schenkel, October, 1985.

Bring TCUs. On the front of the **White Pillar**, climb up to a short, left-facing corner under a roof. Move right, then over the roof (crux) to easy rock.

138 Tree Filled Chimney 5.1 PG
FA: Unknown, circa 1950s
Climb the tree filled chimney that is 35 feet left of the **Shootin' the Curl** arête to the top of the **White Pillar**.

139 Boogey Bored 5.11 R
FA: Todd Swain, 1986
Sort of an extended boulder problem. Start 12 feet left of the **Tree Filled Chimney** and climb the short, difficult face to the low ceiling. Pull over this, then climb the face to the top of the **White Pillar**.

140 Far Trapps 5.4 PG
FA: Unknown, circa 1950s
Climb the clean, right-facing corner 30 feet left of the **Tree Filled Chimney** (V1), then continue up the face to the top of the **White Pillar**.

V1 The Far Side Trapps 5.10+ FA: Todd Swain, 1986. Boulder up the overhanging arête just left of the 5.4 corner.

141 Just For the Record 5.7+ PG
FA: Dick Williams, Joe Bridges, Dick DuMais, 1972
Rope up at the next right-facing corner, ten feet left of **Far Trapps**. Climb the corner, move left, then up past some pines to a belay under an overhang (130 ft, 5.5). Ascend orange rock, then wander up to a ceiling formed by a left-facing flake. Move left, climb the flake, then angle left through some ceilings to a ledge (5.6). Either escape off to the sides, or climb a bulge, a left-facing corner, and another ceiling to the summit (5.7+).

142 We've Got To Stop Meeting Like This 5.8 G
FA: Todd Swain, Iza Trapani, October, 1985
Pump a hang ten feet left of the **Just For** corner at a cleaned, white face (crux), then up the face past a small, bulging ceiling to a small pine (50 feet).

143 Across from the Fruitstand 5.4 PG
FA: Dave Craft, Jim Andress, 1958
Like the proverbial apple—don't pick this one. Begin 120 feet left of **White Pillar** and climb right-facing corners in a slab that is just left of a dead tree, then up the face to a clump of pine trees and a belay. Continue up steep rock to the base of a huge, detached summit block, which can be avoided, or climbed to its top (5.4).

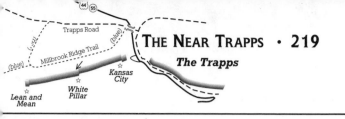

144 To Come or Become 5.5 G

FA: Dick Williams, Burt Angrist, 1987

Begin about 15 feet right of a giant right-facing corner (**Roman's Climb**). Friction up a slab to a left-facing corner, then move right and scamper up past a few ledges. Wander up the face to a ceiling with some left-facing flakes below it, then go up to a large block on a ledge. From atop the block's right side, continue to the woods.

145 Roman's Climb Next to Across From the Fruitstand 5.6 PG

FA: Roman Sadowy, circa 1965

Long lost and rightly so. Scamper up the face 150 feet left of **White Pillar**, then follow a huge right-facing, corner/gully system up right to the pine tree clump and a belay (80 feet). Traverse left on a ledge under a roof (V1), then up the vertical fault to a ledge (50 feet). From the belay, follow the fault to the top.

V1 5.8+ PG13 Climb up to a ceiling, move right ten feet (V2), then up past another ceiling to a ledge with an oak tree. Rappel.

V2 5.4 PG Continue right for another ten feet or so, then up to the ledge. This avoids the 5.8 ceiling of **V1**.

146 Parsifal and Potato Chips 5.7 PG13

FA: Dick Williams, Ed and Karen Clark, 1987

Follow **Roman's Climb** to the huge ledge, then move right ten feet to an obvious left-facing corner. Stem up the corner, move right, then up past two ledges. Weave up the face above to another ledge with an oak tree (the same ledge that the variations to **Roman's** end on). Weave up the next face to a pine, then bushwhack up right to a rappel tree.

147 Interplanetary Agents 5.10 PG

FA: Todd Swain, Iza Trapani, November, 1985

A scary lead completed on Swain's birthday that climbs the clean arête just right of **Interlewd**. Ascend the face to a shallow dihedral, and up this to a ceiling. Pull the ceiling to a pocket, angle slightly left (crux, bashie for pro), then back right to the nose. Climb directly up the arête (5.6 X) to fixed anchors. Rappel, or climb loose rock to the top. Bring small Tri-cams to 1.5 and a #1.5 Friend.

The Williams' Wall

---

148 Interlewd 5.5 G
FA: Dick Williams, Burt Angrist, Kaye Arnott, 1967
A raunchy respite. Climb the fairly clean, orange, right-facing corner 220 feet left of **White Pillar** and just left of another huge corner (**Roman's**) past an overhang, then exit out left, or up right and on to the trees.

149 Eowyn 5.4 G ★
FA: Dick Williams, Cherry Merritt, Herb Cahn, 1971
Named for Williams' dog, who in turn was named for a J.R.R. Tolkien character. This section of the cliff is known as The Williams' Wall and has many worthwhile face climbs of a moderate standard. Downhill 60 feet and left from **Interlewd** is a nice, clean section of cliff with a long low roof. Follow a crack through the low roof (5.3) at the right end of this section, then diagonal left to a pine tree belay. Climb a right-facing corner above (5.4), then move left and up to roofs. Escape right and up, then angle right to a ledge. Move left and up past a notch to the shrubs.

150 Live and Let Die 5.10– PG ★
FA: Dave Saball, Todd Swain, October, 1985
Wings might be helpful on the runout section. Climb straight up the face and over the roof at a flake ten feet left of **Eowyn** (crux, V1, 2) to a ledge. Climb the white face right of **Eowyn**'s corner (5.7 X) to the arête, which is followed to the top. Rappel with two ropes, or walk off the south (left) end of the cliff between The Bayards and Near Trapps.

V1 5.11 (TR) FRA: Andy Tuthill, 1985. Climb over the roof to the left aiming for an obvious jug.

V2 5.9+ (TR) FRA: John Thackray, Tad Welch, 1985. Climb the face and small flakes around the left edge of the long, low roof.

151 I'm OK—You're OK 5.8+ PG ★
FA: Dick Williams, Roy Kligfield, 1975
Excellent face climbing on P1, but a little tricky to protect. Dance up the face just left of the low roof along angling cracks, then follow the right hand vertical seam (5.8 G) to a pine tree belay. Climb the bulge above in the center (5.8+ PG), then angle right to the summit.

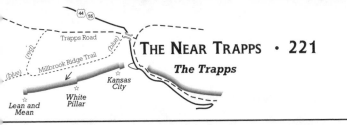

147 Interplanetary Agents 5.10
149 Eowyn 5.4
151 I'm OK—You're OK 5.8+
152 Akidlleativytoowouln'tyou? 5.5
153 Far From the Madding Crowd 5.8
154 Punch and Judy 5.5
155 LP 5.8
156 Little White Mushroom 5.3
157 Gil-Galad 5.7
158 Keystone Cop 5.7

152 Akidlleativytoowouldn'tyou? 5.5 PG

FA: Dick Williams, Dave Loeks, 1971

Plenty of grass for goats. Climb a dirty fingercrack 60 feet left of
Eowyn, then up the face passing a yellow bulge on the right to a
horizontal. Traverse right to a flake/corner, and up this to a belay on
the left at a tree (5.5, 80 feet). Angle left up the face past a notch in a
roof. Move right to a vertical weakness, which is followed to the
bushes.

The Williams' Wall

153 Far From the Madding Crowd 5.8 PG ★
FA: Roy Kligfield, Ivan Rezucha, 1975
Dance up the face 70 feet left of **Eowyn** past a block 15 feet up.
Climb a vertical crack, and small roof to a pine tree belay (5.8). Up
through roofs to finish by angling left, crossing **LP**.

154 Punch and Judy 5.5 PG
FA: Mike and Judy Yates, Al DeMaria, 1965
95 feet left of **Eowyn** and 30 feet right of **LP**, climb the face and vertical seam just right of a corner past a mantle move (crux) to easier
rock and a belay above a tree ledge but under a shallow dihedral
(100 feet). Up the dihedral, then move right under a corner (crossing **Akidll'** and **Far From the Madding Crowd**) and angle right to
the top.

155 LP 5.8 PG
FA: Dave Craft, Dick Williams, 1965
Rumor has it the initials stand for Lonely Penis! This climb marks the
left edge of the Williams' Wall and has a difficult boulder problem
start. Try repeatedly (!) to climb straight up to a large, white, right-
facing flake 125 feet left of **Eowyn** and 15 feet off the ground. When
you finally reach it (V1), follow a shallow corner to a belay ledge
(125 feet). Angle right (or left) past a tree and ceilings to the woods
(5.7, loose).

V1 If you get tired, it's possible to climb a ramp on the right to
reach the flake; 5.6.

156 Little White Mushroom 5.3 G
FA: Art Gran, Toni Wilson, Dottie Baker, 1970
Climb the right hand, right-facing corner (crux) 35 feet left of **LP** to
a belay at a pine (75 feet). Climb up, then follow an easy ramp up
left to the trees.

157 Gil-Galad 5.7 G
FA: Joe Kelsey, Roman Laba, 1967
Another climb that was lost for a while. Climb the flakes up a white
face 45 feet left of **LP**, then straight up the face to a pine tree belay.
Push on to the ceilings above, then move left onto a large block.
Steep climbing (crux) leads to low-angle climbing and an escape
right around the summit roof.

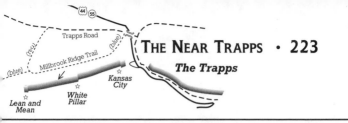

Trapps Road

Millbrook Ridge Trail

(red)

(blue)

(blue)

Kansas City

White Pillar

Lean and Mean

66 165 162 160 158 157 156 155 154

154 Punch and Judy 5.5
155 LP 5.8
156 Little White Mushroom 5.3
157 Gil-Galad 5.7
158 Keystone Cop 5.7

160 Trick or Treat 5.7
162 Roman's Climb Next to
  Keystone Cop 5.5
165 Grim and Tonic 5.8+
166 Central Park West 5.10

159 Keystone Cop 5.7 PG

FA: Dick Williams, Dave Craft, 1965

Thirty years after the first ascent, the loose death block is still there. Maybe it's not so loose? Up a dirty vertical crack and left-facing flakes 60 feet left of **LP**, past a roof to lower-angled rock. Belay at a tree under a right-facing corner. Up the corner, then right and up to a huge block glued to the ceiling. Tiptoe left and up to the trees.

159 De Colores 5.6 PG
FA: Dick Williams, Burt Angrist, 1987
Rope up just right of a heavily vegetated left-facing corner that is 30 feet left of **Keystone Cop** and 20 feet right of an obvious right-facing corner (**Roman's**). Climb the face to a pine tree, then move left and up to a ledge below a ceiling. Move left to belay (5.6). Pull the ceiling then angle right along a fault to a block. Angle left, then up to the woods (5.6).

160 Trick or Treat 5.7 PG
FA: Dick Williams, Tom Bridges, 1973
Sweet or sour? Climb the face 100 feet left of **LP** and just left of a left-facing corner to an arch. Follow the left-facing arch nearly 60 feet, then move right and up to a belay (85 feet, 5.5). Jam up a crack in orange rock, then angle right to ceilings which are climbed directly to a tree and the finish (5.7).

161 DSB 5.8+ PG
FA: Dick Williams, Joe Bridges, October, 1987
This route's name is closely related to **LP**! Rope up at a vegetated gully with a right-facing flake. From the top of the flake, move left, then go up past a small ceiling. Angle right to join **Trick or Treat**, which is followed to the belay (5.6). Climb straight up past two ceilings to the right edge of a pointed block which is five feet right of **Roman's** corner. Move right and climb through a cleft to the trees. Walk off left (south) or rappel from a suitable tree.

162 Roman's Climb Next to Keystone Cop 5.5 PG
FA: Roman Sadowy, 1965
He had quite a way with route names, eh? Wade up a gully/corner 115 feet left of **LP** to a huge right-facing corner which is followed to a belay under large, blocky ceilings. Wander through the loose hangs to the top.

163 Aftermath 5.5– G
FA: Dick Williams, Dick DuMais, Dave Craft, 1972
Climb flake/cracks on a small arête 20 feet left of **Roman's** and 130 feet right of **Main Line** to a ledge. Step left, then up a clean face to a belay at a tree (5.3). Follow the right-leaning right-facing corner directly above the pine to the top (5.5–).

164 Omega 12 Clausthaler 5.7 X
FA: Dick Williams, Joe Bridges, Dave Craft, 1988
Start 25 feet left of **Aftermath** below a grassy ledge. Climb past a tree to a left-facing corner. Climb the face above past the right edge of a ceiling to the obvious **Aftermath** crack. Step right and climb the scary face to a cedar tree (5.7 X). Move left, then climb to a right leaning, right facing corner (**Aftermath**). Go up, then traverse right about 15 feet before climbing through ceilings to the trail (5.6).

165 Grim and Tonic 5.8+ PG13 ★
FA: Ivan Rezucha, Annie O'Neill, April, 1980
Good climbing on this one. Climb up to a clean thin crack which is 30 feet left of **Aftermath** and behind a tree with a double trunk, then follow this almost to the roof (crux, V1). Traverse left around the roof, then up the lower-angled face (5.6 R) to a belay even with the **Aftermath** tree. Move right and rappel, or climb straight up past a roof to join **Positively** to the top.

V1 Computer Blue 5.11 G FA: Felix Modugno, September, 1984. Climb the roof directly above the crack, then up the face to the **Aftermath** belay.

166 Central Park West (aka Shirley Tumble) 5.10 PG
FA: Todd Swain, John Thackray, 1986
Start atop a boulder ten feet right of **Positively** and pull the overhang (crux) to a wide horizontal. Continue straight up the face to a belay just right of an obvious right-facing corner (belay as for **Positively**). Move left (V1) and swing onto the arête (5.7) then up to the top.

V1 Direct Finish 5.9 PG FA: Ivan Rezucha, Bill Ravitch, October, 1991. Climb up and right (as for **Positively**) then through a series of overhangs on somewhat suspect rock to finish through a notch.

167 Positively 4th Street 5.6 G
FA: Dick Williams, Dave Craft, 1965
Stem up an obvious, right-facing corner 70 feet left of **Aftermath** to a ceiling. Step right (V1), then up the face (crux) to a belay under a right-facing corner. Follow the corner up and right to the woods.

V1 Move left at the ceiling, then up to the belay. This makes the climb 5.4.

168 Ground Control 5.9+ PG13 ★★
FA: Paul Clark, Lotus Steele, Laura Chaiten, Ivan Rezucha, August, 1979

Excellent climbing and a little intimidating. Start ten feet left of **Positively** and just right of a cave at the base of the cliff. Climb the clean face to the roof (5.7 R), then traverse left around the ceiling (V1) and up right to belay as for **Main Line** (5.8). Cross **Main Line** and traverse left through a roof above the belay (crux), then straight up the face passing more roofs to the woods.

V1 GC Direct 5.10 PG FA: Felix Modugno, Paul "Base" Boissonneault, October, 1984. Climb directly over the roof then up the face to the belay. A long reach.

169 Strange Customs 5.11 PG
FA: Ed Webster, Todd Swain, August, 1987. FFA: Todd Swain, Paul Trapani, August, 1987

The crux pin and bashie were placed on aid during the bolting ban, hence the name. Climb the overhanging face between **Ground Control** and **The Main Line** past three pins (crux), then up the slab above to a left-facing corner. Swing around right (pin), then up the slab to the belay ledge.

170 The Main Line 5.8 G ★★
FA: Dick Williams, Dave Craft, Claude Suhl, 1965

Shoot up the face and the obvious left-facing corner 60 feet right of a huge detached block until just below a roof. Exit right, then up to the belay under a notch in the roof above (5.8–). Climb up right through the notch, then weave through steep rock to the trees (5.8).

171 High Anxiety 5.9 R
FA: (lower face) Paul Rezucha and others, circa 1980; (final face) Ivan Rezucha, October, 1981; (complete): Todd Swain, Randy and Andy Schenkel, Fall, 1986

The contrived nature of this route is silly enough to please Mel Brooks. Climb the center of the face between **Main Line** and **Mac-Reppy** to the roof (5.8– R). Move right and pull over the roof at a flake just left of **Main Line** (contrived 5.9), then move back left to a belay on the upper face. Angle up into the **Mac-Reppy** corner then out right on the face to the trees (5.7).

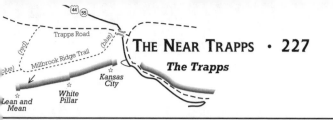

Trapps Road

44 55

(red)

(blue)

Millbrook Ridge Trail

(blue)

Lean and Mean

White Pillar

Kansas City

175 174 172 170 169 168 167 166 165

165	**Grim and Tonic 5.8+**	
166	**Central Park West 5.10**	
167	**Positively 4th Street 5.6**	
168	**Ground Control 5.9+**	
169	**Strange Customs 5.11**	
170	**The Main Line 5.8**	
172	**Mac-Reppy 5.11**	
174	**5.8**	
175	**Void Where Inhibited 5.11**	
176	**Void Where Prohibited 5.11**	

172 Mac-Reppy 5.11 G ★★

FA: Jim McCarthy, John Reppy, 1965

Much harder than 5.8 since the crux hold broke off in the spring of 1987—being tall really helps now. Starting just right of a huge block, climb a corner and obvious crack past a roof (5.11) to lower-angled rock. Climb the intimidating corner through the ceilings above (5.8).

173 Inside-Out 5.6 PG
FA: Dave Craft, Dick Williams, John Weischel, 1965
Different. Chimney up the back of the huge block (V1) to daylight and the belay. Climb up the face on the right to a notch and through this to the trees (5.6).

V1 5.7 PG FA: Jim Kolocotronis, H. Goldstein, 1973. Another route done by Kolocotronis, known to many at the time as "Fifi the Greek" for his ever present Fifi Hook attached to his harness. Climb the right-facing corner formed by the block.

174 5.8 G
FA: Ivan Rezucha, Annie O'Neill, October, 1981
Climb the vertical crack on the right side of the block (left of the **Inside-Out** chimney) to the belay.

175 Void Where Inhibited 5.11 G ★★
FA: Rich Romano, 1977
Climb the left-facing corner on the front of the **Inside-Out** block (crux). Jam the wonderful finger crack to the top of the block.

176 Void Where Prohibited 5.11 G ★★
FA: P1 Rich Romano, 1975; P2 Ivan Rezucha, 1975
The easiest looking 5.11 in the Gunks. On the front of the **Inside-Out** block, climb the left-hand inside corner (crux, V1) and the thin crack to the top of the block. From the top of the block, climb up left to a roof, then out right and on to the finish (5.8).

V1 Climb the chimney formed by the left side of the block; 5.0.

177 Fright to the Finish 5.10– R
FA Ivan Rezucha, Harvey Arnold, July, 1980
Good climbing, but the name says it all. Double ropes and a full set of Friends help. Saunter up a low angled, orange arch that is 45 feet left of the huge **Inside-Out** block, to a ledge under the roof. Traverse left, move up at a streaked face, then move back right around an arête to a corner (V1). Up the shallow right-facing corner (crux) to a belay on a ledge below a roof. Pull the roof above at a left-facing corner (5.7+).

V1 Climb the clean arête to the belay ledge; 5.9 R.

171 High Anxiety 5.9
172 Mac-Reppy 5.11
173 Inside-Out 5.6
175 Void Where Inhibited 5.11
176 Void Where Prohibited 5.11
177 Fright to the Finish 5.10–
178 Muriel's Nose 5.10

179 Hold the Mayo 5.9
180 Scrambled Legs 5.10+
181 Spinal Traction 5.6 A3
182 Dark Side of the Moon 5.12
183 Lean and Mean 5.8
184 Fat and Flabby 5.11–

178 Muriel's Nose 5.10 PG13 ★★★

FA: Bill Goldner, Ants Leemets, 1966. FFA: John Bragg, Rick Hatch, 1975

A classic route. Named for Vulgarian climber Muriel Mayo, who caught Dick Williams' first leader fall. The crux is well protected but the easier climbing above isn't. Scramble up to the top of a huge flake 60 feet left of the **Inside-Out** block, then pump an awkward roof to a bigger roof split by a thin crack. Follow the crack past the roof (crux), then up the scary orange face to a ledge on the right side of the prow. Diagonal up left to the top of the prow (5.8).

179 Hold the Mayo 5.9 G ★

FA: Todd Swain, Sue Rogers, September, 1985

Named in honor of those who may have held Muriel's leader falls.
Follow **Muriel's Nose** 'til below the crux roof, then traverse left to
low-angled rock. Follow an orange corner to a roof, then swing right
and up the left side of the prow to the top.

180 Scrambled Legs 5.10+ G

FA: Ivan Rezucha, October, 1981

Wild but dirty. Climb a flake up to the right edge of the **Spinal
Traction** roof, then out left along another flake (crux) to easier rock
and the woods.

181 Spinal Traction 5.6 A3 PG ★

FA: Ivan Rezucha (roped solo), 1978

Someday this will go free. For now, people are happy to succeed on
aid! Climb a right-facing corner 160 feet left of the **Inside-Out**
block and at the left edge of a big roof to the ceiling. Aid out the
right angling crack to the lip and the top.

182 Dark Side of the Moon 5.12 PG ★

FA: Felix Modugno, Kevin Bein, November, 1984

Starting on **Spinal Traction**, move left into an orange corner, then
follow a crack past two very impressive roofs to the woods.

183 Lean and Mean 5.8 PG ★

FA: Ivan Rezucha, November, 1980

A little bit scary on P1, but a good route nonetheless. Starting 40
feet downhill from the start of **Spinal Traction**, tiptoe up the face just
right of an arête (5.8 PG) to easier climbing and the top of the
block. Climb the overhanging right-facing corner to the summit
(5.8, V1).

V1 Climb a corner on the main wall behind the block, then move
left to join the regular route at the final corner; 5.8.

184 Fat and Flabby 5.11– G

FA: Todd Swain, Iza Trapani, July, 1985

The protection is tricky to place, and if it fails, you'll be hurting.
Harder if you're short. On the front of the **Lean and Mean** block,
climb up to a thin seam, then directly up this (contrived crux, V1) to

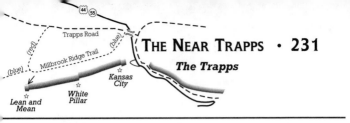
a roof. Reach over the roof in the left center (5.9+), and up easy rock to the top of the block.

V1 By avoiding the crux seam to the right, the climb is 5.9+.

185 Short and Sassy 5.5 G
FA: Todd Swain (solo), October, 1985
Climb the clean, zig zag crack left of **Fat and Flabby**.

186 Up in Arms 5.9 G
FA: Frank Valendo, Maury Jaffe, June, 1981
Interesting and strenuous. Friends are very helpful. Climb the over-hanging cracks on the left side of the **Lean and Mean** block (5.9), then stem up a shallow right-facing corner on the main cliff to the top (5.8).

Smede's Cove
This is the historical name given to the area between The Near Trapps and The Bayards. It was purchased by the Mohonk Preserve in 1993, thanks to the help of the climber's advocacy group, The Access Fund.

Brad White on the second pitch of *The Time Eraser* 5.10–

Millbrook

Millbrook Mountain is the largest cliff in the Gunks and also the most serious on which to climb. Millbrook has a large ledge system splitting the cliff at about one-third height. The rock below the ledge is generally very loose and dirty, hence only routes on the upper section of the cliff are described. The upper section ranges in height from 130 to 200 feet with over 110 routes and variations.

The cliff itself is owned by the landowners in the valley below, while the summit is shared by the Mohonk Preserve and the Palisades Interstate Park Commission (PIPC). The land along the cliff top to the right (north) of **Westward Ha!** is owned by the Mohonk Preserve, while the land left (south) is owned by the PIPC. The issue of land ownership is important at Millbrook, because the PIPC (Minnewaska State Park) does not allow rock climbing. In the past there have been confrontations between the state park rangers and climbers on what was actually Preserve land! The best solution is to keep a low profile when climbing at "The Bank."

Extreme caution should be used when climbing at Millbrook. It is unlike any other crag at the Gunks in that the routes often have no obvious lines and protection is frequently nonexistent. Loose rock will be encountered on all routes, and normally the first 20 to 30 feet

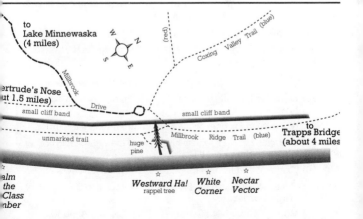

off the main ledge has no protection. Millbrook is not the place to push your limits—a quick rescue is not likely.

The best approach to Millbrook is via the Coxing Valley Trail (blue blazes) from Trapps Carriage Road, or the Millbrook Ridge Trail (blue blazes) from Trapps Bridge. Either route is about a 4 mile hike each way. The normal approach to the climbing is by rappelling down **Westward Ha!** (150-foot rappel — see the Millbrook map for details). It is also possible to scramble down to the traverse ledge at either side of the cliff. The routes are described from the base of **Westward Ha!** First the routes on the right (north) side of the cliff are described, starting at **Westward Ha!** and moving to the right edge of the cliff. Next, the routes on the left (south) side of the cliff are described, starting at **Westward Ha!** and working left to the left-most end of the cliff.

1   The Marching Morons 5.9 A0 PG13 ★

FA: Ivan Rezucha, Paul Potters, 1977

A right-to-left girdle of Millbrook. Continuous and of good quality between **New Frontier** and **Never Again**. The first ascent took 1 1/2 days and 20 pitches. The following are ''check points'' along the way, not pitches:

1) Climb up left above the **Brown Bomber** roofs.

2) From halfway up the crag, traverse to the **Strange City** corner, and move left beneath the hangs.

3) Climb down **Artistry in Rhythm** to a ledge.

4) Traverse straight left, reversing the **Swinging Cunt** traverse.

5) Cross **Sweet Meat** at the belay.

6) Climb down, then over to the **Directpissima** pine tree.

7) Rappel to near the traverse ledge, then over to the **New Frontier** corner.

8) Follow **New Frontier** to the base of an overhanging corner.

9) Crabcrawl straight left until just before the right-facing corner at the top of **High Plains Drifter**.

10) Climb up and left to a triangular block (ant's nest here on FA).

11) Continue left above the **Sudden Impact** roofs to the last bit of **White Corner**.

12) Move down slightly, then straight left below **Big Band Era**.

☆
**Realm of the
Fifth Class
Climber**

☆
Westward Ha!

☆
**Nectar
Vector**

13) Climb to the final right-facing corner on **The High Traverse** (the FA party bivouacked here).

14) Climb down the corner, then left to a belay on **Westward Ha!** (below the blank face).

15) Continue straight left beneath ceilings, crossing **Promise of Things to Come**.

16) Gradually angle up left to cross **Remembrance** in the final corner.

17) Continue angling slightly up left to cross **Never Again** near the top.

18) Angle slightly down (obvious ledges).

19) Cross **Fifth Class Climber** where it moves left.

20) Keep moving left at this level until boredom forces you up **Old Route** to the finish (obvious ledge systems).

2   Westward Ha! 5.7 PG ★★★
FA: Jim McCarthy, Harry Daley, Hans Kraus, 1962
A classic route that provides a good introduction to Millbrook climbing. Sustained. The climb ascends near the line of the approach rappel. Start directly below an obvious left-facing corner. Angle up right to a small pine at 40 feet, then continue up the face and corner to a ceiling. Move right and up to a belay at a tree at the top of the corner. Climb a blank looking face to a corner and follow it to the top.

3   Rags to Rich's 5.10 PG13
FA: Rich Romano, Dick Williams, 1987
Start about 25 feet right of **Westward Ha!** at a block and forked pine tree. Climb just left of a steep, left-facing corner, then angle right to a weakness in the ceiling above. Climb a short, right-facing corner, go up and right, then up to the **Westward Ha!** belay ledge (5.9). Move right under an overhang, then pull this to a short, right-facing corner (crux). Weave up the face above, then angle right to finish on **Cruise Control** (5.10).

4   Cruise Control 5.9– PG ★★★
FA: Rich Romano, Beau Haworth, Spring, 1978
After dealing with a short section of loose rock at the bottom, the rest is a cruise on good rock. Start 30 feet right of **Westward Ha!** aiming for a series of shallow left-facing corners and thin cracks

leading to a ceiling (crux). At the ceiling move up right to a belay in a right-facing corner (**The High Traverse**). Climb up the corner ten feet, then easily out left below a yellow roof (V1) to a clean face with a thin, vertical crack. Over the ceiling along the crack, then right and up past another hang along a second crack to the top.

V1 5.10 PG FA: Ivan Rezucha, Todd Swain, 1986. Climb straight over the roof and up the face to a loose flake. Move right to join the regular route at the next hang, or left to join **Rags to Rich's** (this was an aborted FA attempt on that route's crux ceiling).

5   The High Traverse 5.5 PG ★
FA: Fritz Wiessner, Percy Olton, 1937
A historical classic. Climb a right-facing corner 100 feet right of **Westward Ha!** to the base of a bigger right-facing corner and a belay at a large tree (5.3). Traverse left around the nose (V1, 2), then angle left up to a belay at a ledge (70 feet; 5.5). Continue up a dirty right-facing corner to the weeds (5.3).

V1 Recollection 5.8 G FA: Hans Kraus, Jim McCarthy. FFA: Dick Williams, John Weichsel, 1965. Continue up the corner (crux), then exit left to join the normal route to the bushes.

V2 Direct Finish 5.8+ R FA: Bob Hostetter, Todd Swain, September, 1986. At the top of the **Recollection** corner, continue straight up the steep face on pockets to the top.

6   Rib Cracker 5.8+ PG
FA: Jim McCarthy, Hans Kraus, Werner Bishof, 1961. FFA: John Stannard, 1968
A vague line up interesting rock. Start at the top of the first corner on **The High Traverse**. Move right under a ceiling, then up corners and the face above to a belay (110 feet). Power up over a ceiling on its left edge, up the face to another ceiling, then over this at a corner. Follow the corner above to the trees.

7   The Last Waltz 5.11 R
FA: Jeff Gruenberg, Jack Meleski, Spring, 1982
Start right of **The High Traverse** on the main ledge system. Climb up the face along an incipient crack system to a belay at 80 feet (5.10+ R). Continue up through an overhanging bulge (difficult pro) to a belay under the final roofs (5.11 PG). Climb the final roof at a small right-facing corner (5.11 PG).

Realm of the
Fifth Class
Climber

Westward Ha!

Nectar
Vector

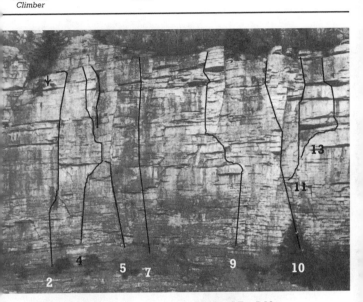

2	Westward Ha! 5.7	9	Big Band Era 5.10+
4	Cruise Control 5.9–	10	White Corner 5.9
5	The High Traverse 5.5	11	White Rose 5.11–
7	The Last Waltz 5.11	13	Sudden Impact 5.12

8   Conflict of Interest 5.9+ R
FA: Rich Romano, George Willig, 1977
This route was done the same year as Willig's famous ascent of the
World Trade Center (May 26, 1977). Follow **Rib Cracker** to the right
edge of the first ceiling, then angle right to a right-facing corner at
the right edge of another ceiling. Move right again and belay in a
right-facing corner (5.9+ R). Traverse right under yet another ceiling (crossing **Big Band Era**) to a huge left-facing corner. Stem up
this to the woods (5.8).

9   Big Band Era 5.10+ PG13 ★★
FA: Rich Romano, Chuck Calef, November, 1979
Some call this the Talus Field That Time Forgot. Use extreme caution
on the first pitch. Climb a red right-facing corner 30 feet left of

White Corner and 70 feet right of The High Traverse to another small right-facing corner. Exit left and up a large right-facing flake, then left again to a right-facing corner. Climb up the corners past ceilings, moving left under the final hang to the bottom of a huge right-facing corner and a belay (5.9 X). Move left and over a ceiling along a handcrack (5.10), then up the face 30 feet to a shallow right-facing corner. Move left and up to a roof, move right and over this to a huge roof. Escape left to a left-facing corner (V1), and then to the top (5.10+ PG).

V1 The King of Swing 5.11 G ★★ FA: Chuck Calef, Rich Romano, Summer, 1980. Climb the huge roof at a thin crack.

10   White Corner 5.9 R ★★

FA: Jim McCarthy, Phil Jacobus, 1959. FFA: John Stannard, 1968
Once you overcome the loose unprotected section at the bottom, this is a super climb. Weave up the steep loose rock 100 feet right of The High Traverse and 200 feet left of New Frontier to the base of a huge right-facing corner. Angle left to a belay at the base of another huge right-facing corner (5.8 R, 100 feet). Stem up the corner 20 feet (V1), passing a ceiling, then exit left (V2, 3) and up the face to the top.

V1 White Knuckles 5.11 FA: Rich Gottlieb, 1990s. Step left from the belay and climb the outside edge of The White Corner, connecting with V3 to the top.

V2 Continue further up the corner to a roof, exit left and up through a notch (5.10+) to easier climbing and the top. This is the logical line.

V3 After exiting the corner, climb up the arête to the top; 5.9+.

11   White Rose 5.11– PG ★★

FA: Rich Romano, Fred Yaculic, 1977
Follow White Corner up to the base of the first huge right-facing corner (5.8 R, White Corner moves left here, V1). Climb straight up the corner to a belay at the top under a roof (5.9). Traverse out left to the arête, then up right into a hanging corner (crux). Climb the dihedral, then move left over a ceiling to the trees.

V1 Climb a flake out right, then go up past a ceiling with a pointed overhang to join High Plains Drifter or Sudden Impact; 5.10 PG.

Realm of the
Fifth Class
Climber

Westward Ha!

Nectar
Vector

9v2 5.10+

11 White Rose 5.11–

12 High Plains Drifter 5.10–

13 Sudden Impact 5.12

15 Schlemeil 5.10

16 Square Meal 5.11–

12 High Plains Drifter 5.10– PG ★★

FA: Rich Romano, Chuck Calef, May, 1981

Interesting and involved. Bring double ropes and lots of slings.
Scramble up left on ledges 100 feet right of **White Corner** and 120
feet left of **New Frontier** (V1) to a block and a wide crack. Angle right
up a slab and a right-facing corner (5.9). Angle left to a ceiling with a
small right-facing corner. Swing over the hang (crux) and belay
under the roof above. Move far right, then up the face and a vertical
crack (5.9+) to its top. Angle right to a sloping ledge and a belay at
the base of a gully. From the left end of the ledge, climb a corner to its
top, hand traverse left, then up the face past a ceiling to the trail.

V1 5.8+ FRA: Todd Swain, Bob Hostetter, September, 1986. Start as
for **White Rose** but climb straight up past a crack/corner in an overhang. Angle right to the belay.

13 Sudden Impact 5.12 R ★

FA: Jeff Gruenberg, Russ Clune, Clint Eastwood, May, 1984

Follow **High Plains Drifter** or **White Rose** to the first belay in the **White Rose** corner. Traverse right under the overhang for 20 feet to where it tapers. Pull the small roof and run for your life to a small right-facing corner (25-foot runout). Continue up to another roof/dihedral, then move left and belay (5.12 R). Pop through the final roof to the summit (5.11+).

14 Band of Renown 5.10+ PG

FA: Rich Romano, Russ Clune, November, 1981

Starting 40 feet right of **High Plains Drifter**, climb the face past a small ceiling, then move right to a shallow right-facing corner which is followed to its top. Step left, climb a flake up right, then move back left past a ceiling to flakes and a belay at a pine (5.10+). Move right, follow a seam and the face above (keeping right of **Schlemiel**) past a notch in a roof, then angle left to the top (5.10).

15 Schlemiel 5.10 PG ★

FA: Jim McCarthy, Burt Angrist, 1968. FFA: Rich Romano, Dave Feinberg, Fall, 1977

Starting 60 feet right of **High Plains Drifter** at a tree, climb the face past a ceiling at 20 feet, then climb a right-facing flake/corner. Swing left (5.10 PG) and up to an overhang. Up a series of right-facing corners to a belay ledge. Hike left and follow the obvious left-leaning corner to the top (5.7).

16 Square Meal 5.11– PG ★★

FA: Chuck Calef, Rich Romano, Summer, 1979

Follow **Schlemiel** to the first belay. Move straight right from the belay and pull past one ceiling (5.10) to another. Move right (crux) to an optional belay stance in a right-facing corner. Climb past a bulge (5.10) to the obvious left-facing corner. Follow this for about 40 feet, then traverse out right along a horizontal to the arête (V1), and up this to the top (exposed).

V1 Climb the huge corner to the trees; 5.6.

17 Nectar Vector 5.12 R ★★★

FA: (complete) Jeff Gruenberg, Jack Meleski, Summer, 1984; P1 John Myers, Rich Romano; P2 John Myers, Mike Freeman, July, 1981

A modern classic and a sweet line. This part of Millbrook is reputed to have the longest unbroken vertical section of cliff in the East.

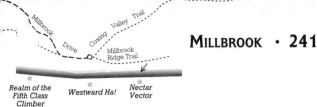
☆ *Realm of the Fifth Class Climber*   ☆ *Westward Ha!*   ☆ *Nectar Vector*

Climb the face 90 feet right of **High Plains Drifter** to a belay in an obvious dihedral starting 60 feet up (V1). From the top of the dihedral, climb a steep right-facing flake, then the overhang above at a small right-facing corner. Step right, and pull the hang to the **Square Meal** belay below the obvious left-facing corner (5.11+). Angle right across the face to a small corner system, exiting left at its top into a niche under a huge roof. Move out left past a bulge (crux), then climb up left to the prow, eventually testing the "pancake" before pulling over the top.

V1 5.9 R FA: Jeff Gruenberg, John Myers, 1981. Climb the face between **Nectar Vector** and **New Frontier** to the first **Nectar Vector** belay.

18 New Frontier 5.11– PG ★★★
FA: Jim McCarthy, Ants Leemets, 1962. FFA: Gary Brown, John Stannard, 1969

An ancient classic. If you come off on this one, it could well be a break-through climb. Starting 100 feet left of **Sweet Meat** and 120 feet right of **High Plains Drifter**, climb the face and a vertical seam, moving left to a right-facing corner. Move left at the top of the corner (V1, 2) to a stance (possible belay). Continue straight left to a belay in a right-leaning corner (scary, long pitch). Climb the corner, then a crack above to a ceiling. Pull through the ceiling on the left, then past a notch to the top (crux pitch—the crux can be protected off to the left with a small unit straight up in the ceiling).

V1 Gottlieb's Variation 5.10+ R FRA: Rich Gottlieb, 1980s
Makes the climb even better (and more scary). At a clump of vegetation in the corner, move out left around the corner and follow ramps up left to the big right-facing corner below the crux.

V2 5.9 PG FA: Bill Ravitch, Jeff Pofit, Ivan Rezucha, June, 1993. Traverse left (first down, then left, then up and left) below the regular traverse but above the **Gottlieb's Variation**.

19 Back to the Land Movement 5.11 PG
FA: Rich Romano, Chuck Calef, Malcom Howells (UK), Fall, 1979

Start at the stance on the P1 of **New Frontier**. Step right from the stance to a left-facing flake. Climb the flake to a ceiling, pump this, then up a pretty white face to another ceiling. Move left, climb an orange face to a ceiling, swing over this at a crack, then up an obvious left-facing corner to a roof. Traverse right under the roof, then up a chimney to the top (long pitch).

20 Manifest Destiny 5.12 R ★★★

FA: P1 and P2 Rich Romano, Jim Munson, July 1982; P3: Jack
Meleski, Jeff Gruenberg, 1983

The best 5.12 in the Gunks, according to Gruenberg. Starting 20
feet right of **New Frontier**, climb up past an overhanging right-facing
corner to a slanting belay ledge (5.10– R). Move left 20 feet, climb a
left-facing corner, then past a bulge to another left-facing corner.
Angle left up the face to a ceiling, swing over this to a scoop and up
to a bigger ceiling. Climb through the ceiling at a crack on the right
to a hanging belay, or move left to a better stance (5.11+ R). Power
through the huge roof directly above (5.12 G, V1).

V1 The original line traversed left to join **Back to the Land
Movement**; 5.11.

21 Land Grab 5.11 X

FA: Rich Romano, Jim Munson, 1982

Both this climb and **Directpissima** were explored in 1979 by Mike
Burlingame and Don Perry. Their controversial mixed route was entitled The Meat Cleaver, after a large flake on the first pitch. Start 50
feet right of **New Frontier**, below a long overhang 100 feet up, and
just left of an obvious pine tree above the ceiling. Climb up, then left
20 feet around ceilings (V1). Angle right, stem up a corner/flake facing left, then move right past a ceiling to a face. Climb the hang
above at a thin vertical crack and belay at the pine (5.11). Climb a
left-facing corner above, then angle left over a ceiling to a roof.
Escape right to a right-facing corner, move up this, then left to a right-
facing crack/corner in a ceiling. Surge past two ceilings, then move
right and climb another. Follow weaknesses to the trees (5.11 X).

V1 Direct Start 5.11 X FA: Jeff Gruenberg, Harrison Decker, 1980s.
Climb straight up past the ceilings to the belay.

22 Directpissima 5.11– PG13 ★★

FA: Rich Romano, Francis Gledhill, Fred Yaculic, November, 1981

Weave up the face 20 feet right of **Land Grab** and below the right
end of a long ceiling, past loose blocks to a left-facing corner.
Traverse left 10 feet, climb a ceiling, then angle left to the right edge
of the long ceiling. Pump the hang at its smallest point using a right-
facing flake, then move left to a belay at the pine (5.11–). Step right
(crossing **Land Grab**) and climb the face to ceilings. Move right,
climb a right-facing corner past ceilings to its top, then climb cracks
past more overhangs to another right-facing corner. Stem up this to
the woods (5.9).

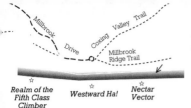

Realm of the
Fifth Class
Climber

Westward Ha!

Nectar
Vector

17	Nectar Vector 5.12	21v1	Land Grab Direct 5.11
18	New Frontier 5.11–	24	Time Being 5.10
19	Back To the Land	25	Mission Improbable 5.10
	Movement 5.11	26	Sweet Meat 5.9–
20	Manifest Destiny 5.12	28	Swinging Cunt 5.8
21	Land Grab 5.11	29	Hang 'em High 5.11

23 In Search of Lost Time 5.11 R ★

FA: Rich Romano, Albert Pisaneschi, 1986

Rope up about 15 feet left of **Time Being**. Climb past a shallow left-facing corner and an overhang to another, shallow, left facing corner/groove. Belay on a ledge to the left, below a corner (5.11). Stem up the right facing corner to a ceiling. Move left, then climb to another ceiling. Move left again, then up to a right-facing corner. Go right, climb a ceiling to a small left-facing corner, then angle right to a belay (as for **Time Being**; 5.11). Move left and climb a right-facing corner to the weeds (as for **Time Being**; 5.10).

24 Time Being 5.10 R
FA: Rich Romano, Hardie Truesdale, 1980
While in the middle of a long runout on the first ascent, Romano was asked by Truesdale how he was doing. Romano replied "Okay. . . for the time being." Start 25 feet left of **Sweet Meat** and just right of a left facing corner. Climb up to a left-facing groove, move right, then back left to a ceiling with a notch in it. Climb past this, then right to a belay ledge (long pitch, 5.9 R). Move left into a corner and follow thin cracks past two ceilings, step left under the third ceiling (**Mission Improbable** traverses right from here) and climb this at another crack. Move up to a roof, step left and climb this at a small flake. Step right and climb a left-facing corner to a belay at its top (5.10). Move left and climb a right-facing corner to the weeds (5.10).

25 Mission Improbable 5.10 PG
FA: Rich Romano, Dave Feinberg, 1977
You may wish you had Jim, Barney and their bag of tricks with you at the crux. Start atop the **Sweet Meat** pillar. Move out left, climb a ceiling in the center, then move left 15 feet at the next ceiling. Climb the ceiling to a flake, up this, then step left to a belay ledge on **Time Being** (5.8). Follow **Time Being** to the second ceiling, traverse right and up, and belay in a right-facing corner (5.10). Climb a ceiling and follow the corner to the summit.

26 Sweet Meat 5.9– PG ★
FA: Art Gran, Bill Yates, 1960 FFA: John Stannard, G. Livingston, 1968
Ramble up the left side of a broken pillar 100 feet left of **Swinging Cunt** and 100 feet right of **New Frontier** to a belay at its top. Climb straight up to a ceiling, escape left, then up (crux) to a belay. Angle right around ceilings, then back left to a belay at a pine. Angle right from the right end of the belay ledge, then diagonal left around ceilings to the trees.

27 Super Sunday 5.10 PG
FA: Rich Romano, Chuck Calef, January, 1981
A fine alternative to watching football. Climb the first pitch of **Swinging Cunt**. Follow this to a point halfway along the traverse, then climb a right-facing corner past ceilings and a huge flake to a belay ledge. Walk right 15 feet, climb the face to a crack, and follow this over the right side of a roof. Finish up a right-facing corner.

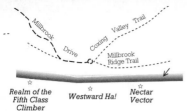

Realm of the
Fifth Class
Climber

Westward Ha!

Nectar
Vector

28 Swinging Cunt 5.8 PG ★

FA: Bill Goldner, Paul Karmas, Gerd Thuestad (Nor), 1962 FFA: John
Stannard, Don Morton, 1968

A climb named in true Vulgarian tradition. Clamber up the right
side of the **Sweet Meat** pillar starting 100 feet to the right and belay
on top. Climb up off the right side of the pillar (V1) past a black
ceiling to bigger overhangs. Traverse right to a belay at a left-facing
corner (5.8). Follow the corner systems above, moving right near
the top (5.7).

V1 Singing C 5.9+ R FRA: Todd Swain, Derek Price (UK),
October, 1981. Angle right from the top of the pillar, then up to connect at the belay.

29 Hang 'em High 5.11 PG13 ★

FA: Rich Romano, Russ Clune August, 1980

Begin at an oak tree that is 50 feet left of **Bank Manager**. Climb the
face to the right of a birch, then go up left-facing flakes to an overhang. Move right 15 feet, go up ten feet, then go back left 15 feet to
a right-facing corner. Ascend the corner, pass a flake on its left,
then belay on a ledge above (5.9). Climb straight up from the right
end of the ledge along a black streak, past several roofs to a notch
(V1) and the top (5.11).

V1 By escaping left below the final tier, the climb is 5.10. The final
tier was added in 1983.

30 Bank Manager 5.10 PG

FA: Greg Collum, Morris Hershoff, Rich Pleiss, 1979

Named for Rich Romano, the "manager" of "Millbank." Legend has
it that Romano was apprehended by the state park rangers on his
way to climb on Millbrook (which the PIPC rangers consider illegal
to climb on). Romano was able to convince them he was looking for
Millbank Mountain. Rather than give the confused park visitor a tick-
et, they simply told him that climbing wasn't allowed in the park!
Wander up broken rock 50 feet right of **Swinging C** to a large pine.
Angle up right, then straight up the face to the left hand pine on a
belay ledge (5.10). Step left, climb a shallow left-facing corner (5.8,
V1), then exit right onto the face and up to the trees.

V1 The CEO 5.10+ PG FA: Todd Swain, Bob Hostetter,
September, 1986. A direct finish to **Bank Manager**. Climb up left
into another left-facing corner, then out right and over a roof (crux)
to the top.

31   Artistry in Rhythm 5.10– PG13
FA: Rich Romano, Rich Ross, April 1981
Start at a lone pine 70 feet right of **Swinging C**. Wander up the face
just right of **Bank Manager** (5.10–), then move left to flake/overhang
facing right. Up this, then left and up to a belay on a ledge at a
prominent pine. Angle right to a left-facing corner which is followed
to the top (5.7).

32   The Tempest 5.10 R
FA: Rich Romano, Fred Yaculic, Alan Kousmanoff, 1984
Follow **Artistry** up the face to a bush below the overhang, then go
up and left to a ceiling. Follow **Artistry** over the ceiling, then climb
up to a shallow left-facing corner which is followed to its top. Angle
right to the ledge with pine trees and belay (5.10 R). Start to the
right of some bushes, climb to a ledge, then finish through layered
overhangs (5.9).

33   Side Pocket 5.9+ PG ★
FA: Rich Romano, Vincent Valente, Spring, 1980
Starting 110 feet right of **Swinging C**, climb small left-facing corners (V1) to the right edge of a long ceiling 80 feet up. Climb the
ceiling on the right, move right, then angle left to a belay ledge with
a tree. From a block left of the tree, climb a ramp to a ledge, and
belay at the base of an obvious left-facing corner. Stem up the corner, move out right to the arête (crux) and finish on easier rock.

V1   Writhe to the Occasion 5.7+ FA: Ivan Rezucha, Annie O'Neill,
1980. Climb the obvious (and easier) left-facing corner to the middle of the ceiling. Traverse right to join the regular route. Beware of
rope drag.

34   Leap Frog 5.10– PG
FA: Rich Romano, Doug Strickholm, April, 1981
Bring lots of TCUs, Tri-cams, etc. Start 150 feet right of **Swinging C**
and 60 feet left of **Strange City**, directly below the left edge of the
Danger UXB ceiling. Weave up to the left end of the ceiling (5.8 X),
pass this on the left (crux), then up the left side of a detached flake.
Climb up and slightly left above the flake past a ceiling with a small
left-facing corner. Move right and up a groove (5.7 R) to a belay
ledge. Climb past a ceiling (easy), keeping just left of **Strange City**.

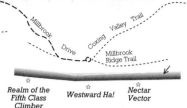

☆	☆ ☆
Realm of the Fifth Class Climber	Westward Ha! Nectar Vector

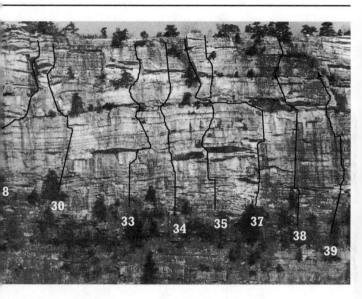

28	Swinging Cunt 5.8	35	Danger UXB 5.10
30	Bank Manager 5.10	37	Strange City 5.7
33	Side Pocket 5.9+	38	Brown Bomber 5.10
34	Leap Frog 5.10–	39	Sing, Sing, Sing 5.10

35   Danger UXB 5.10 PG13

FA: Rich Romano, Rich Ross, April, 1981

The UXB stands for UneXploded Bomb after a popular British TV show about a WWII police bomb squad. A wild route. Wander up the face 30 feet right of **Leap Frog** to an obvious right-facing corner through the middle of the overhang (5.8 PG13). Pull up into the corner (crux), then hand traverse out left to a belay 25 feet above the ceiling. Climb straight up past a small left-facing corner (15 feet right of the final **Strange City** corner) and swing right around an overhang and up to the top.

38	Brown Bomber 5.10	42	Insallah 5.9+
39	Sing, Sing, Sing 5.10	43	Garden of Allah 5.10
41	Three Buzzards 5.4		

36 Explosive Bolts 5.11 PG13

FA: Jim Munson, Albert Pisaneschi, May, 1986

Climb **Strange City** for 30 feet, then go left under a ceiling and around a nose. Climb a thin crack, then a right-facing corner that leads up left. Belay on the **Strange City** traverse line (5.11). Climb the ceiling above, left of the **Strange City** 5.7+ finish (5.10).

37 Strange City 5.7 PG ★

FA: Jim McCarthy, Hans Kraus, Stan Gross, 1955. FFA: John Stannard, G Livingston, 1968

Difficult to protect on the first pitch. Climb a huge right-facing corner 100 feet left of **Three Buzzards** and 30 feet right of **Danger UXB**

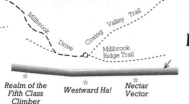

☆
Realm of the Fifth Class Climber

☆
Westward Ha!

☆
Nectar Vector

to a roof. Exit left to a belay ledge (5.7). Traverse left to a huge left-facing corner (V1) and follow this to the trees (5.5).

V1 5.7+ PG FA: Ivan Rezucha, Annie O'Neill, November, 1985.
Halfway across the traverse, climb a handcrack (crux), then follow obvious cracks slightly right to a shallow corner and the top.

38 Brown Bomber 5.10 R ★★
FA: Rich Romano, Rich Ross, April 1981
Previously attempted by Joe Louis who was turned back at the crux by his inability to crimp edges in his boxing gloves. Starting 30 feet right of **Strange City** climb up past a small pine, then over a small ceiling directly above. Continue up along shallow corners and cracks, then a steep face to a belay on the right under a double overhang with a right-facing corner (5.9 R). Climb up into the corner, then out left (5.10 G) past the hang to the woods.

39 Sing, Sing, Sing 5.10 PG
FA: Rich Romano, August, 1981
Starting 55 feet right of **Strange City**, climb up to a short left-facing corner at 50 feet. From the top of the corner, angle left over a ceiling, then up 30 feet to a ledge. Walk left 15 feet to a right facing corner and flake 15 feet below a roof belay under the middle of the roof (5.9 PG). Through the ceilings above by hand traversing right to the arête (wild crux) and up easier rock to the shrubs.

40 Nothing To Write Home About 5.8 PG
FA: Hardie Truesdale, Beau Haworth, 1978
Better than being on a deserted island—they usually don't have any climbing! Difficult to protect. From a cluster of trees 75 feet right of **Strange City**, climb up along an obvious crack past a ceiling. Angle left along flakes above, then on to a ledge below a right-facing corner. Climb the corner and munge to the top.

41 Three Buzzards 5.4 G
FA: Hans Kraus, Ken Prestrud, Bonnie Prudden, Dick Hirschland, 1949
A clue about the route name—look at the first ascent party. Fly up a right-facing corner and chimney 100 feet right of **Strange City** to a belay ledge. Follow a corner/crack system up right past a ceiling to the woods.

42 Insallah 5.9+ PG

FA: Rich Romano, Mike Ward 1977

Mike Ward's only new route at the Gunks—he's now putting them up at Red Rocks, Nevada. Climb the face 65 feet right of **Three Buzzards** (V1), past a hang to a left-facing corner capped by a roof. Escape left (possible belay here) and follow more corners to a ledge (100 feet, 5.9). Jam up a crack to the huge summit block, traverse right under the block, then follow another crack through hangs (crux) to the woods.

V1 Follow **Garden of Allah** to the ceiling, then traverse left to join the regular route.

43 Garden of Allah 5.10 PG

FA: Jim McCarthy, Hans Kraus, John Rupley, 1958. FFA: John Stannard, 1968

If this were heaven, it'd have quality stars. Starting about 15 feet right of **Insallah**, stem up a left-facing corner to ceilings. Move right and up a right-facing corner (5.10, V1) to a hang. Exit left (5.10) to a belay stance with a pine. Climb the face above, keeping left of a corner system to roofs. Swing over these on the right, then to the top.

V1 Climb a right-facing corner to the left of the normal corner, rejoining the route at the belay ledge; 5.10.

44 Pelvic Thrust 5.9+ PG

FA: Rich Pleiss, Greg Collum, Morris Hershoff, 1980

Shades of Elvis! Start 100 feet right of **Garden of Allah**, directly below a huge left-facing corner at the top of the cliff, and at the right edge of the terrace. Climb the face past a bulge, then up past a pine tree to a belay at the base of the corner. Follow the corner past a ceiling to the top (5.9+).

NOTE: The following routes lie to the south (left) of the rappel route down **Westward Ha!**

45 Under the Wire 5.11– PG

FA: Rich Gottlieb, Russ Clune, Howard Doyle, August 13 (Friday), 1982

This route climbs the face a little left of the rappel line (V1). Start 55 feet left of **Westward Ha!** at a grassy ledge with a small oak tree that is 30 feet from pine trees on either side. Climb the face past a ceiling, move right and up a crack/flake, then up a right-leaning cor-

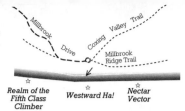

☆
Realm of the
Fifth Class
Climber

☆
Westward Ha!

☆
Nectar
Vector

ner above. Move left at the corner's top, climb a flake to a ceiling, undercling right, then pull the ceiling in the middle to a belay (140 feet). Move right under an overhang, over this at a crack, then up the face to another belay on a ledge. Move left and climb a right-facing corner and an overhang to the weeds.

V1 The Rappel Line 5.11 (TR) ★ FA: Jeff Gruenberg, 1987. Climb directly up the rappel line on beautiful white rock.

46   The Enthizer 5.12– (TR)
FA: Jeff Gruenberg, Jack Meleski, John Myers, Mike Freeman, 1980s
This route climbs basically straight up the cliff, starting on **The Time Eraser** and climbing left of **Wire Wizard**. The crux is at about two-thirds height. No more is known.

47   Wire Wizard 5.8 R
FA: Morris Hershoff, Lindi McIlwaine, 1977
Start 75 feet left of **Westward Ha!** on a ledge with a pitch pine and 15 feet right of a gold streak leading to a ceiling. Climb to a belay ledge along a fault (large block, 5.8 R). Traverse right from the belay to a shallow corner system that leads to a ceiling. Climb the corner (V1, 5.7+ R) and the ceiling above at a notch (5.8), then up to a belay ledge (tree). Continue up the dirty corner to the top (30 feet).

V1 Move left and up a right-facing flake, then back right under the ceiling to rejoin the route (less scary).

48   The Time Eraser 5.10– PG ★★★
FA: Rich Romano, Morris Hershoff, Spring, 1980
Named for a popular Italian seafood restaurant in New Paltz. The best route in its grade at Millbrook. Climb up **Wire Wizard** a short way (5.8 R), then diagonal far left to the left edge of a long ceiling. Face climb up along a thin crack just left of a gold streak (5.10– G) to a belay at a small tree and block (long pitch). Angle right along obvious flakes and corners to the top (5.8).

49   Promise of Things to Come 5.11– R
FA: Dave Ingalls, Roy Kligfield, 1968. FFA: Henry Barber, John Stannard, 1973
Start 130 feet left of **Westward Ha!** at the first prominent left-facing, slightly left-leaning corner system. Climb hard and scary rock past a ceiling (crux) to the obvious, left-facing corner system and eventually a belay ledge. Jam up a crack to ceilings, then angle left to the trees (5.8).

The Planetary Wall

50 The Good, the Bad and the Ugly 5.10 R

FA: Rich Romano, Francis Gledhill, 1981

A route name similar to **3,4,5,6, Over and Out, Porkypine**. Begin under a left-facing corner system 90 feet left of the obvious corner system on **Promise** and 60 feet right of the **Remembrance** corner. Climb past a tree to an overhang, move right, then go up a steep face past another overhang to a shallow left-facing corner. Belay above on a ledge (5.10 R). Climb a left-facing corner to the top (5.8).

51 Remembrance of Things Past 5.10 PG

FA: Jim McCarthy, Ants Leemets, 1962. FFA: John Stannard, 1968

Start 150 feet left of **Promise** at an obvious right-facing corner system,

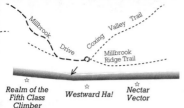

Realm of the
Fifth Class
Climber ☆

Westward Ha! ☆

Nectar
Vector ☆

and a small pine tree on the uppermost traverse ledge. Climb loose rock (5.6 X) up to the huge right-leaning corner and climb this (crux) to a belay under some ceilings. Escape out right around the roof (V1, 2), then bridge up a corner to the woods.

V1 The Future is Now 5.10– PG FA: Rich Romano, Chuck Calef, May, 1981. Continue straight up the corner from the belay to a roof. Move right across a steep face to the arête (crux), and up this to the top.

V2 I'd Walk a Mile To Not Be Senile 5.9 R FA: Todd Swain, Bob Hostetter, September, 1986. Instead of moving right to the arête, escape out left to join **Orbit of Jupiter** for the final 5.9 R slab.

52 Rings of Saturn 5.11 X ★
FA: (toproped then led) Jeff Gruenberg, John Myers, Mike Freeman, 1982
You'll see stars if you come off this one! This section of the cliff is known as the Planetary Wall and is characterized by being steep and clean with ceilings about 70 feet up. Climb the face 30 feet left of **Remembrance**, then up a shallow left-facing corner to its top. Move up right to a hollow flake, then angle back left (5.11) to the left edge of a ceiling. The crux is 20 feet above, passing a small ceiling at a scooped bulge (about 60 feet up and 20 feet left of **Remembrance**—fixed #1 stopper). Steep but straightforward climbing above leads to the safety of your spaceship.

53 Orbit of Jupiter 5.9+ R
FA: Rich Romano, Alex Lowe, October, 1981
Make sure you're tied into your Van Allen Belt! Wander up the face about 35 feet left of **Remembrance** with no pro or obvious line (5.8 X), eventually passing the ceiling on the left (crux). From a belay ledge above, follow small corners past a ceiling on its right to a steep, gray slab. Slither up the slab (5.9 R, 1.5 Tri-cam or #2 Friend) to the summit.

54 Asteroid Belt 5.10 X
FA: Rich Romano, Chuck Calef, Rich Ross, Fred Yaculic, April, 1981
Bring your deflector shields. If you come off, you'll make a crater! Begin 50 feet left of **Remembrance** at a pine tree below an obvious left-facing corner in a ceiling that is about 70 feet up. Climb the face past the left edge of a horizontal band of brown rock, then angle slightly left to a small left-facing corner. Move right from the corner

The Planetary Wall

under a ceiling, then over this to a steep face (V1) and a ledge below a roof (**Orbit of Jupiter** belays here). Move left to a left-facing corner and up this to a belay on the right (5.10 X). Climb the corners above (as for **Search**) to the shrubs.

V1 5.10+ PG Just before reaching the **Orbit of Jupiter** belay ledge, move left about ten feet and climb a left-facing corner to rejoin the regular route.

55 Search For Tomorrow 5.10 PG13
FA: Rich Romano, Rod Schwarz, 1978. FFA: Chuck Boyd, John MacLean, 1979
Start 40 feet left of **Asteroid Belt** below the right edge of a huge ceiling 50 feet up. Climb up to the right-facing corner with a birch tree, swing left towards the left-facing corner, then immediately angle right (V1) across the face to a right-facing corner above the right edge of a ceiling. Move left from the top of the corner to a low angled corner slanting right and belay. Climb the obvious corners to the summit.

V1 Diaper Man 5.10 PG13 FA: Chuck Calef, Rich Romano, Rich Ross, April, 1981. Climb the left-facing corner above the ceiling to another ceiling. Climb this on the right, then up the face to rejoin **Search For Tomorrow** at the belay.

56 Paral-Lax 5.11+ PG
FA: Russ Raffa, October, 1984
Begin 20 feet left of **Search For Tomorrow**, below a right-angling fissure in a huge ceiling 50 feet up. Climb up the face past a small bush, then up left to a belay on **Cuckoo Man**, to the left of the huge roof (5.8 R; 70 feet). Traverse right 15 feet, then pull the roof at diagonal slashes (crux) to easier ground. Rappel, or wander up the face to the summit.

57 Cuckoo Man 5.10 PG ★★
FA: Rich Romano, Chuck Calef, April, 1981
A good route but not for chickens. Rope up 50 feet left of **Search For Tomorrow** and 40 feet right of the rightmost of two right-facing corners (**Never Again**) at a birch tree on the traverse ledge. Climb past a low ceiling, then wander up the face following right-facing corners to a ledge below the left edge of the huge roof (5.8 R; possible belay here as for **Paral-Lax**). Climb a small left-facing corner

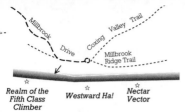

☆
Realm of the Fifth Class Climber

☆
Westward Ha!

☆
Nectar Vector

through the left edge of the roof (crux), then weave up to a crack which is followed to a belay at a block (130 feet). Step right and up a short steep face (5.8), then follow a right-facing corner (as for **Again and Again**) to a belay ledge (90 feet). Continue straight up to a roof, traverse right to the arête (5.10), then swing over the roof to the top (60 feet).

58 Again and Again 5.7 PG13 ★★

FA: Art Gran, Jim Geiser, 1958.

A good introduction to the terrors of Millbrook. Fairly safe but very exciting. Climb the first pitch of **Never Again** (5.7; 100 feet). Traverse far right to the right end of the big ceilings and a belay perch (5.7, spooky). Stem up the right-facing corner above (5.7), then angle right (**Cuckoo Man** climbs straight up) past the right edge of a ceiling to the woods.

59 Never Again 5.11 PG13

FA: Hans Kraus, Bonnie Prudden, 1951 FFA: John Stannard, 1968

An amazing collection of rusty pins and loose rock at the crux! Start 180 feet left of **Remembrance** at the rightmost of two right-facing corners. The main right-facing corner is 50 feet further left and marks the right edge of a large roof that is 40 feet up. Climb a broken right-facing corner, then angle left to the huge corner (possible belay here). Climb the easy face right of the corner to a belay (100 feet; **Again and Again** traverses right from here). Pull over the huge hang (crux) to a large ledge. Clamber up the corner to the weeds.

60 Happiness is a 110° Wall 5.12 G ★★★

FA: Art Gran, Jim McCarthy. FFA: Mark Robinson, Mike Sawicky, 1979

Difficult to protect. Climb straight up the obvious right-leaning corner 50 feet left of **Never Again** to a communal belay ledge (5.10; 60 feet). Move out left to the arête, then climb the face and a thin crack just right of the arête (crux) to a stance on the arête (short pitch). Move right and up the crack/corner past a ledge to the top (5.10+).

61 Agent Orange 5.11 X

FA: Rich Romano, Francis Gledhill, Fred Yaculic, November, 1981

Dangerous to your health. Start 15 feet left of **Happiness** at an oak tree and hemlock on the traverse ledge. Climb through the narrowest part of low ceilings, then pass another ceiling by moving slightly left. Step right above the ceiling and climb to a belay ledge (5.10 X). Pull a hang above at a thin crack, drift up left, then up a shallow, right-facing corner. Move right under a bush-filled horizontal to a crack, and jam this to a belay ledge (5.11 R). Stem up the right-facing corner to the trees (5.5).

62 Birth of the Blues 5.11 R
FA: Rich Romano, Russ Raffa, June, 1982
Most of the last two pitches had been done earlier as variations to **Bank Shot**. Start 50 feet right of **Happiness** (as for **Bank Shot**). Angle up right across golden rock, then back up and left to a small right-facing corner in a ceiling that is four feet left of a seam splitting the ceiling. Power over the hang at the corner, then follow this and a thin crack to the belay ledge (5.11 R). Walk to the right end of the ledge and climb corners and a crack to another belay ledge (5.9). Walk left 50 feet and climb a groove to a roof, jam over this at a crack, then up to the top (5.10).

63 Bank Shot 5.11 PG ★★
FA: Rich Romano, Doug Bower, Spring, 1980
Begin 50 feet left of **Happiness** at the next oak and hemlock on the traverse ledge and below a shallow right-facing corner leading to a ceiling 40 feet up. Climb the face and corner to the ceiling, move right and pull the ceiling at a right-facing corner. Above, pull the first hang on the left, then move right and up a corner through the next ceiling. Climb a crack, then a right-leaning flake to a belay ledge (5.10). Climb the right-arching corner above (crux) to a ledge, then up a left-leaning corner past the right side of a large roof to the summit.

64 Blue Streak 5.9+ X
FA: Rich Romano, Hardie Truesdale, February, 1980
This climb may have you swearing. Start 100 feet left of **Happiness** and 50 feet left of **Bank Shot** on the left side of a narrow section of the traverse ledge. Climb left-facing flakes that are just right of a large brown spot past a ceiling to a left-facing corner. Move left below an overhang, over this into a left-facing corner, then up the face to a belay at a pine (5.9). Climb up along a crack in an orange face to a niche. Exit left, weave up the face, then up a right-facing corner to its top. Move right, and up a bomb bay chimney/crack to the woods (5.9+).

Realm of the Fifth Class Climber   Westward Ha!   Nectar Vector

52	Rings of Saturn 5.11	60	Happiness is a 110° Wall 5.12
56	Para-Lax 5.11+		
57	Cuckoo Man 5.10	63	Bank Shot 5.11
59	Never Again 5.11		

65 Little Brown Jug 5.11 PG13

FA: Rich Romano, Russ Clune, May, 1981

Start 30 feet left of **Blue Streak** at a pine tree on the traverse ledge and 45 feet right of a prominent right-facing corner (**Fifth Class Climber**). Climb steep flakes just left of a vertical seam to a bigger flake. Undercling/layback up right, then up to a ledge. Move right and climb the left-leaning corner and face above to a belay ledge (5.10–). Chug past a strange bulge along thin cracks, then up right on a slab to a ceiling. Swing over this into a left-facing corner, then on to the trees (5.11).

60 Bank Shot 5.11	**68** Mood Indigo 5.9+
66 Realm of the	**69** Bankrupt 5.8+
Fifth Class Climber 5.9	**71** Golden Years 5.7+

66 Realm of the Fifth Class Climber 5.9 G ★

FA: Dick Williams, Art Gran, Jim McCarthy, Hans Kraus, 1964

Talk about an All-Star team on the first ascent! Rope up 180 feet left of **Happiness** at an obvious right-facing corner with a bush on its left side about 40 feet up. Stem and layback up the corner (V1), passing a ceiling on the right (crux) to a belay ledge (100 feet). Climb an easy corner to a ledge, then up a short layback flake to the top (5.8).

V1 Diagonal right from a ledge at 40 feet to a left-facing corner. Avoid the ceiling at the top of the corner, then up the face and right-facing corner to the top.

☆
Realm of the
Fifth Class
Climber

☆
Westward Ha!

☆
Nectar
Vector

67 Delta Waves 5.10+ PG

FA: (complete) Rich Romano, Chuck Calef, May, 1981; P3 Rich
Romano, Jim Munson, 1980

Start 30 feet left of **Fifth Class Climber**, below an obvious left-facing
corner in a ceiling 45 feet up. Climb the ceiling at the corner, then
up left along a flake to its top. Continue angling left, jam over a ceiling at a crack, then up a right-facing corner to a belay at a pine
(5.10). Weave up left to another belay on a long ledge (5.8). Climb a
crack left of red rock past ceilings, then climb a right-facing corner
to the woods (5.10).

68 Mood Indigo 5.9+ PG

FA: Rich Romano, Morris Hershoff, May, 1981

Begin 60 feet left of **Fifth Class Climber** at a right-facing corner
that leads to a ceiling. There is a bush in the corner and a pine tree
on the traverse ledge. Ascend the face and right-facing corner past
an overhang. Continue up the face and a left-facing corner past
another ceiling to a belay on the right (5.9). Wander up right along
broken rock, passing a long ledge to a belay below a right-facing
corner on another ledge (5.9). Climb the low-angle corner, move
out left, then up steep white rock and a left-facing corner to the
woods (5.9+).

69 Bankrupt 5.8+ R

FA: Todd Swain, Kathy Beuttler, October, 1986

Go for broke on this one. Start 20 feet right of an obvious right-facing
corner (**Old Route**) and ten feet left of an oak bush that is above a
pine tree. Climb straight up the face along an intermittent, vertical
seam, passing a bulge at about 70 feet (crux). Belay above amidst
loose blocks and ten feet left of a heavily forested corner (this belay
is on the traverse line of **Golden Years**). Either climb the dirty corner or finish to the right up **Golden Years** (5.7+).

70 Old Route 5.5 G ★

FA: Fritz Wiessner, John and Peggy Navas, Spring, 1935

The first recorded technical climb at the Gunks—a historical classic.
Begin 180 feet left of **Fifth Class Climber** at an obvious, broken
right-facing corner with a large pine tree on its left edge about 100
feet up. Climb the corner to a long ledge on the left, then walk to
the left end of this ledge and belay (5.5).Climb the face above, finishing at an obvious notch left of a large red section (5.5).

69 Bankrupt 5.8+	**71 Golden Years 5.7+**
70 Old Route 5.5	**72 Apollo Theatre 5.9**

71 Golden Years 5.7+ PG

FA: Jim Knowlton, John Goobic, Mark Squibb, Spring, 1985

The first ascent party got off-route while trying to do a 50th anniversary climb of the **Old Route**. Follow **Old Route** up the obvious corner to the long ledge. Instead of exiting left on the ledge, continue straight up the corner system past two overhangs (5.7+) to an obvious traverse line leading right. Move way right to a tree at the base of a mungy dihedral. Climb the dihedral (loose), then move out right and up clean, white rock (5.7+, spooky) to the top.

72 Apollo Theater 5.9 PG

FA: Rich Romano, Francis Gledhill, December, 1981

Begin 75 feet left of **Old Route** at an obvious right-facing corner that is just left of a vegetated 30-foot-high left-facing corner. Climb up, then left to reach the right facing corner, which is followed to a belay at a pine (5.8). Stem up a right-facing corner above, moving

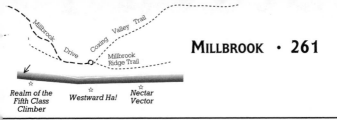

Realm of the
Fifth Class
Climber

☆ Westward Ha!

☆ Nectar
Vector

---

right through ceilings to another ledge. Starting in the middle of the
ledge, climb a right-facing corner to a hang, move right to the
arête, then up this to the trees (5.9).

73 Prelude 5.9 PG

FA: Rich Romano, George Peterson, 1981

Rope up 60 feet left of **Apollo Theater** at a right-facing corner
capped by a roof. Stem up the corner to the roof, move right to a
bush, then go up another right facing corner to a belay ledge with a
pine (5.9). Continue up the corner to a vegetated corner. Move left
and climb easier rock up and left to the summit (5.8).

74 Fugue 5.9 PG

FA: Rich Romano, George Peterson, 1981

Begin 95 feet left of **Apollo Theater** at a block sitting on the highest
traverse ledge. Power past two overhangs at the easiest point to a
large ledge on the left. From the middle of the ledge, climb a crack
past some bushes and a slot to a white dihedral. Climb the dihedral
past a bulge and a ceiling, then angle up left to a ledge with pine
trees (5.9). From the right edge of the ledge, climb a short nose to
the top (5.8).

75 Let Go My Allegro 5.9 PG

FA: Todd Swain, Donette Smith, May, 1994

If it the FA party had been all male, the route name would've been A
Fugue Good Men. Begin 185 feet left of the **Old Route** at a large
oak tree on the lower traverse ledge and below a right-facing corner leading to a outcrop 70 feet up. Climb the corner for 15 feet to a
ceiling, then angle up and right past ledges to a short, shallow left-
facing corner. Climb this to a small ceiling with two blocks underneath. Traverse left through a bulge to a small slab (crossing
Allegro), then straight up a thin crack through a bulge. Continue up
and slightly left past slabby ledges to belay on the highest ledge at
a pine (5.9; belay as for **Allegro** and **Better Late**). Climb the broken
right-facing corner above to the first ledge (as for **Better**), then go
up and right to the top (5.6).

76 Allegro 5.10 PG

FA: Rich Romano, George Peterson, 1981

Rope up at an obvious corner as for the last route. Climb straight up
the right-facing corner to a belay at a cave-like feature on a ledge

just right of the jutting outcrop (5.8). Climb up and slightly right to a shallow, broken, right facing corner (crossing **Let Go My**) which is followed to its top. Angle up left past bushes to the highest of two ledges and belay (5.9; belay as for **Fugue**, **Let Go My**, etc.). From the middle of the ledge, climb the steep, short headwall past some right-facing flakes to the summit (5.10).

77 Better Late Than Never 5.8 PG

FA: Fred Polvere, Leif Savery, 1986

Start as for the last two routes, at an obvious right-facing corner. Climb the corner past a ceiling to a belay under the outcrop (5.8, 70 feet). Move left six feet, then up a shallow crack. Angle left past overhangs until a large roof forces you back right and up to another belay ledge with a pine tree (5.8, 90 feet). Scamper up and left along the right-facing corner/gully to the top (5.3).

78 Top Brass 5.9 PG

FA: The Bank Manager, Albert Pisaneschi, 1987

Rope up 60 feet left of the **Better Late** corner at a clump of pines that are just right of a left-facing corner. Climb up to an obvious ledge, then move right and belay. Climb to a shallow left-facing corner, then angle up left to another. Follow this up right to a ledge, move right, then angle back left to another ledge (possible belay here; 5.8 R). Climb the face and yet another left-facing corner to a ceiling. Move right, then on to the trees (130 feet, 5.9).

79 Face-Off 5.11 R

FA: Rich Romano, Albert Pisaneschi, 1987

Climb the face and left-facing corner that is just left of **Top Brass** to the same belay ledge. Climb a left-facing corner, move left and climb to a ceiling. Move left, climb another left facing corner, then move right and follow a thin crack and face to the left edge of a ceiling. Angle left to the right edge of an overhang. Move right, climb a right-facing corner, move left, then up past a ceiling. Angle left through a cleft in an overhang to the top and salvation (130 feet, 5.11).

80 M32L 5.8 PG

FA: Rich Romano, Russ Clune, 1981

Climb either the first pitch of **Face-Off** or **Top Brass** to the ledge. Climb an obvious left-facing corner system to an alcove, then angle left through a ceiling to the woods (5.8).

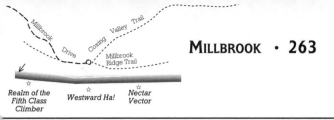

☆
Realm of the Fifth Class Climber

☆
Westward Ha!

☆
Nectar Vector

81 Saucony 5.9 PG
FA: Rich Romano, Russ Clune, 1981

One of Romano's regular outings entails climbing at least one 5.10 route on each of the four main Gunks cliffs in a day. Whether he runs between them in Nikes or Sauconys is unknown! Climb either the first pitch of **Face-Off** or **Top Brass** to the ledge. Start near the left end of the ledge about 20 feet left of **M32L** and 30 feet right of a huge flake. Follow a crack system past the left side of an overhang to a left-facing corner, then up the face to the trail.

82 Rubble Without a Cause 5.14+ X
FA: John Tompkins, Claude Suhl, April 1st, 1972

A climb well ahead of its time. Bring snow pickets, deadmen and make sure your life insurance policy is paid in case they don't hold! Begin exactly 216.374 feet from the left end of the cliff at a four-inch-high blade of grass that vibrates at 60 cycles per minute in a ten knot breeze. Angle up left across vertical gravel to a mossy chimney filled with precariously stacked house-sized boulders. Pussyfoot up this to a ledge stacked with KMart-sized loose blocks, then dyno right to a belay tree (it used to be the only solid thing on the climb, but it died due to the 1981 gypsy moth infestation). Crawl on your belly in a horizontal chimney to a notch. Tunnel through the dirt that usually clogs the notch, then prance up the overhanging face above past multiple grass bog mantles (tied off grass clumps for pro) to the summit (98.625 feet, 5.14c).

NOTE: The next three routes are probably best approached via rappel or the left (south) end of the cliff.

83 Raging Bull 5.10 PG
FA: Rich Romano, Dick Williams, 1987

Romano led the FAs of **Presto** and this route in sneakers—any idea what brand they may have been? Rope up 45 feet left of an obvious, large left-facing corner. Follow a thin seam past the left edge of a ceiling, eventually moving left to a left-facing corner. Climb the corner and a cleft in the ceiling above, then head right at the next roof. Go up, angle right past another ceiling, then go up and left to the top.

84 Presto 5.10 PG
FA: Rich Romano, Dick Williams, 1987

Start 80 feet left of the obvious, large left-facing corner below a right-facing corner capped by a roof. Work up and right to the corner which is followed to the roof (50 feet). Move left, then up to the top.

85 Air for a G-String 5.6 PG

FA: Dick Williams, Joe Bridges, 1987

Begin 100 feet left of the obvious, large left-facing corner at another obvious corner. This climb begins about 20 feet left of **Presto**. Climb the corner to a roof, move left ten feet, then climb up and right past a ledge to the woods.

Realm of the
Fifth Class
Climber

Westward Ha!

Nectar
Vector

Nectar Vector, 5.12. Photo by Michael S. Miller

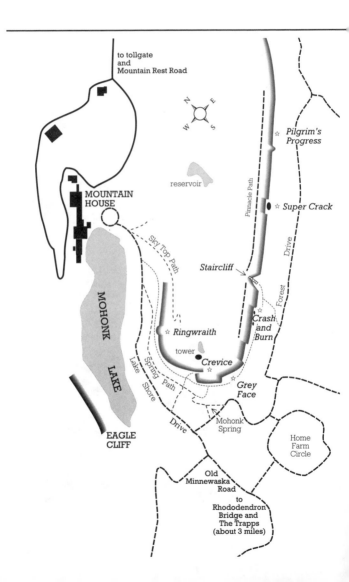

Sky Top

With its striking profile and tower, Sky Top is, to many, symbolic of the Gunks. Located on Mohonk Mountain House land three miles north of the Trapps, Sky Top boasts over 400 routes and variations ranging in height from 50-150 feet. It is imperative that you read the section in the introduction on the Mountain House rules. Climbing at Sky Top is a very special privilege that could be revoked at any time. The cliff is divided into three sections: Left (west) of **The Crevice**, Right (east) of **The Crevice**, and Right (east) of Staircliff. **The Crevice** is a huge fissure/chimney with a series of wooden ladders in it. The very popular Labyrinth Path winds along the bottom of Sky Top left and finishes up **The Crevice**, bringing lots of crowds and noise. A marked trail continues along the base of the cliff to **Staircliff** (a wooden stairway running up the cliff). For climbs to the right of **Staircliff**, an unmarked trail runs along the foot of the crag. There are also numerous descent chimneys and rappel routes along the cliff (see text and cliff photos).

To approach Sky Top from the Trapps, follow either Undercliff Road or Overcliff Road to Rhododendron Bridge. Cross the bridge and turn left on Old Minnewaska Road. A long, steep hill will soon be encountered (if you don't reach an obvious hill within 100 yards of the intersection, you've gone the wrong way). Follow Old Minnewaska Road past two intersections until a field is on your right (Home Farm Circle). Continue on Old Minnewaska Road another 200 yards until you reach Mohonk Spring (potable water here in the spring and early summer). From here the cliff and **The Crevice** will be visible—follow the red-marked trail through the talus to the cliff base.

1   The Longest Day 5.10– PG ★

FA: Ken Nichols, Mike Heinz, June. 1975. Final pitches: Ken Nichols, Todd Swain, June, 1988

A partial left to right girdle of Sky Top that now ends at Staircliff. The original climb took 1½ days and 15 pitches to complete. The longer route was done in 9 hours of climbing. Start at a birch clump left of **Rain of Watermelons**.

P1   Follow a horizontal right across the **Ringwraith** wall and around the nose to **Strawberry Yogurt**. Continue up right along **Pineapple** to a belay at the nose (on Arrivato).

P2   Move right, then up a corner to the **Petie** belay tree. Continue straight right past the first belay on **Lakeview**, to a belay at the base of the vertical cracks on **Lakeview's** second pitch.

P3   Move down and right to join the second pitch of **Beardlings**. Angle up right along the arête, then hand traverse down into a corner. Move down to cross **Mary**, then straight across to the first belay on **Intimidation**.

P4   Climb down a bit, then hand traverse straight right across the first pitch of **Sound and Fury** to a ledge on **Dirty**. Follow **Pete's Meat** to the arête, then up slightly to a belay on **Foops**.

P5   Continue straight right, step across **The Crevice**, then follow a ledge on **Little Face** to the nose. Traverse right to the second belay on **Crack of Bizarre Delights**.

P6   Climb down a flake from the belay, traverse right to the chockstone on **Giant Chockstone**, then climb down this. Move right past a nose and corner to a huge flake. Belay in an alcove just right of the flake.

P7   Move down slightly, then right to the **Lip Service** arête. Continue right to a belay on **Grey Face**.

P8   Traverse right to the **Hidden Piton** buttress, and reverse the crux **Hidden Piton** hand traverse. Belay just down and left.

P9   Continue right, crossing **This Petty Pace** above the crux to a belay on **Intermediate**.

P10   Climb up **Intermediate** (V1), then climb down **Minne Belle**

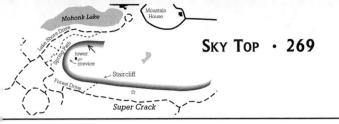

behind a chockstone to a ledge. Walk right to a belay on the nose.

V1 Traverse straight right just under the ceiling on **Trinity** to **Minne Belle** (5.10–). Continue across exposed rock to a belay on the arête of **True Grip**.

P11 Hand traverse strenuously right to **Up Against the Wall**, then past an arête to a belay at a flake on **Mellow Yellow**.

P12 Continue right across dirty rock to a belay just short of the **Tunnel**'s exit.

P13 Follow **The Bull and the Virgin** to a ledge, then move right to a belay under the crux roof of **True Gunk**.

P14 From the right end of the ledge, climb down to a smaller ledge, then out right along the ledge to a left-facing corner. Hand traverse right to the exposed ledge just before the crux of **Hardware Route**. Belay at the second belay on **Hardware Route**.

P15 Down climb **Hardware Route** 20 feet, then right to a ledge with a tree. Angle right to a cramped belay on the arête.

P16 Move down (V2), and wildly traverse between roofs to **Jekyll and Hyde**. Down climb diagonally right (5.10–) across **Talus Food** and over to a belay on **Half Assid**.

V2 The original route angled up right above the main roofs and finished on **Comfortably Numb**.

P17 Move straight right, then down to the narrow ledge on **Crash and Burn**. Follow this right to the dirty corner. Continue right to belay on the **Pussy Foot'n** ledge.

P18 Scamper right to **Staircliff**.

2 Nut Goblin 5.8 G

FA: Dave Loeks, Joe Bridges, 1971

This short route is located on the south face of a boulder that is along the Labyrinth Trail, 50 feet below the intersection with the Skytop Trail. The boulder is roughly 200 feet left of **Neat Exit**. Climb the obvious finger crack to the summit.

3　Neat Exit　5.6 G
FA: Dick Williams, Pete Burnes, 1974
At the left (west) end of Sky Top, just where the cliff goes into the woods, climb a crack to a hang, move left and up to another crack, traverse right from its top, and up through a chimney (crux, V1) to the trail.

V1　Climb out right below a ceiling instead of climbing the chimney.

4　The Fish That Saved Pittsburgh　5.9+ PG
FA: Ivan Rezucha, Doug Fosdick, 1975
A bit hard to figure out, but interesting. Starting 20 feet right of **Neat Exit**, at a dihedral with a roof split by a crack above, climb the initial corner to a roof. Traverse left around a nose, then climb towards the **Neat Exit** chimney. Move back right under ceilings to a belay on **Hand Job**. Traverse left between roofs down left from the **Hand Job** crux roof, then up easy rock to the woods.

5　Hand Job　5.10 PG
FA: Dave Loeks, Jon Ross, 1974
Strenuous. Climb the same dihedral as for **Fish**, then exit right at the roof, and up the right hand crack to the roof. Out the roof at the obvious left hand crack (crux) to the trees.

6　Hand Jam　5.0 G
FA: Unknown, pre-1986
Climb the lower angled hand crack 20 feet right of **Hand Job** (V1).
V1　Start up the corner, then join the hand crack to the top.

7　Patti Cake　5.6 G
FA: Joe Bridges, Patti Gorman, 1983
Climb a gully/chimney 40 feet right of **Hand Job** to a stance, then angle left up to the top of a crack. Climb past a tree, then traverse right 15 feet around an arête to a right facing corner. Climb the low angled corner past a ceiling to the trees.

8　Bulta's Horse's Bloody Elbow　5.6 G
FA: Ken Paduch, Gwen McLaren, August, 1980
Jam up a corner 30 feet left of **Finger Lickin'** to a ledge, step left, and up another corner. Step left again to a hemlock, then straight up to the top.

Mohonk Lake

Mountain House

Lake Shore Drive

Spring path

tower
crevice

Staircliff

Forest Drive

☆

Super Crack

5   Hand Job 5.10
6   Hand Jam 5.0
12 Finger Lickin' Good 5.6
15 Ring Ding 5.10
16 Ringwraith 5.10–
17 Reign of Terror 5.11

19 Strawberry Yogurt 5.8+
22 Pineapple 5.8+
23 Arrivato 5.6–
27 Ladyslipper 5.7
30 Petie's Spare Rib 5.4

9   Handyman Special 5.8 G

FA: Ivan Rezucha, May, 1981

Follow a crack system 20 feet left of **Finger Lickin'**, and above some birch trees past roofs to the trail.

10   Shock the Monkey 5.12– PG

FA: (TR) Scott Franklin, 1985; (lead) Keith Lenard, Todd Mazzola, 1986 (Lenard is currently Access Fund Executive Director.) Toproped and protected prior to being led. This route climbs thin seams past two ceilings and a fixed peg just right of **Handyman Special**.

11 Knickerbocker Rock 5.5 G
FA: Dick Williams, Dave Loeks, 1974
Climb the corner system immediately left of the **Finger Lickin'** arête.

12 Finger Lickin' Good 5.6 PG
FA: Dave Loeks, Patty Mattesson, 1971
An unusual climb up the front of a prominent rib 100 feet right of the forest. The crux is down low (V1), and a bit tricky.

V1 Scramble up the talus right of the rib, then traverse out left to the front, and follow the normal route up left past roofs to the top; 5.1.

13 Big K 5.5 G
FA: Peter Darmi, Ralph Peri, June, 1980
Not to be confused with **Circle K**. Struggle up the off width/corner just right of **Finger Lickin'** to a roof, then move right, and up to the summit.

14 Rain of Watermelons 5.10 PG
FA: Mike Freeman, John Myers, Mike Sawicky, 1983
A bit hard to protect—bring small Tri-cams. Climb the left arête of the **Ringwraith** block to the top. Crux is near the top on the left of the arête (V1, 2).

V1 Finish directly up the arête; 5.10+.

V2 Escape left into the corner, then up to the top; 5.8.

15 Ring Ding 5.10 PG ★
FA: John Stannard, 1970s
As good as the snacks it's named for. Climb the thin, overhanging cracks just left of **Ringwraith**.

16 Ringwraith 5.10– G ★★
FA: Roman Laba, Joe Kelsey, 1966
A climb ahead of its time. Even if you are from Middle Earth, you'll like this one. Jam over a roof, then up the steep crack 50 feet right of **Finger Lickin'** to the top. The face between **Ringwraith** and **Reign of Terror** was top-roped prior to 1990. No more is known.

17 Reign of Terror 5.11 G ★★
FA: Henry Barber, Ric Hatch, Ajax Greene, 1974
A fine example of Barber's ability. A bit harder since a key block fell off. Climb the roof (5.11), and crack system (crux) right of **Ringwraith** to the top of the buttress.

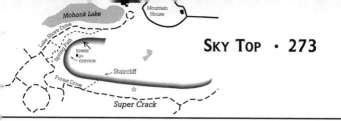

Super Crack

---

18 Mechanical Boy 5.11– PG ★
FA: Hugh Herr, Morris Hershoff, August, 1982
Difficult to protect. Climb the roof at the very bottom of the **Ringwraith** buttress to a ledge (5.10), then up the right arête of the buttress, moving left, then back right on the edge above.

19 Strawberry Yogurt 5.8+ PG ★
FA: Roman Laba, Wally Shamest, 1967
Certainly not the 5.6 it was once rated. Right and uphill from **Ringwraith**, climb a thin crack in a corner past a hang (crux) to a ledge. Traverse left and up the steep crack to the gazebo.

20 Inflatable Girl 5.9+ PG
FA: Rich Ross, Marco Fedrizzi, August, 1985
A route that could deflate your ego. Climb the face just right of the crux of **Strawberry**, then climb straight up the overhanging wall right of the **Strawberry** crack (crux), escaping left along flakes to the top.

21 Giant Toads of Surinam 5.3 G
FA: Peter Darmi, Robert Schehr, August, 1980
Hop up the huge inside corner just right of **Strawberry**, finishing up a chimney.

22 Pineapple 5.8+ PG
FA: Dave Loeks, Dick DuMais, Dick Williams, 1973
The next few plant climbs, are pretty unredeeming. Climb the face 15 feet right of **Giant Toads**, keeping just right of overhangs (5.7), then move up left through more ceilings (crux) to the top.

23 Arrivato 5.6– G
FA: Hans Kraus, Bonnie Prudden, 1950
A bit loose. Scramble up to the top of boulders 40 feet right of **Mechanical Boy**, then climb the face just right of the arête, moving left at 15 feet, and up to ceilings. Climb up left to a crack, and the summit.

24 Artichoke 5.6– G
FA: Roy Kligfield, Roman Laba, 1972
Starting as for **Arrivato**, climb straight up the face along a shallow corner to the roofs, then up through a notch to the woods.

25 Avocado 5.4 G
FA: Roman Laba, Joe Kelsey, 1968
Downhill and right from the **Arrivato** boulders, climb the face up to
the same grass ledge as for the last two routes. Climb the face just
left of a pretty, right leaning corner (V1) past small roofs to the final
overhang. Climb the roof at a notch, or escape left .

V1 Obligato 5.5 G FA: Paul Sinacore, Harvey Arnold, June, 1980.
Climb the right leaning corner to a ledge, then up the face between
Avocado, and **Artichoke** past a ceiling. Angle left to the top.

26 Now and Then 5.7 PG
FA: Joe Bridges, Fritz Wiessner, Ed Clark, Faith Aubin, 1983
Wiessner was 83 when he completed this climb! Forty-eight years
earlier, he climbed **Gargoyle**, the first recorded route at Skytop.
Begin 15 feet left of the vegetated **Petie** corner at a short crack that
leads to a ledge. Climb the crack (V1), move left, then up a thin
seam to an overhang. Escape right, climb a corner, then climb the
next overhang on the right. Belay on a ledge above (5.7). Climb up
to an overhang, move right then left, cross **Petie**, then climb a low
angled corner to an overhang. Climb through a notch to the woods
(5.6+).

V1 5.9 PG FA: Joe Bridges, Burt Angrist, 1984. Climb a vertical
seam to the left of the regular start.

27 Ladyslipper 5.7 G
FA: Ivan Rezucha, Annie O'Neill, May, 1982
Starting behind some bushes just left of the **Petie** corner, climb up a
crack, and shallow corner (crux) to a tree. Climb the right-facing
corners above, moving right below the final ceiling to the shrubs.

28 Petie 5.2 G
FA: Hans Kraus, Bonnie Prudden, 1950
Bushwhack up the dihedral 20 feet left of **Petie's Spare Rib**. Halfway
up, traverse left, up a corner, then left across the face to the finish.

29 Pete's Pancreas 5.8 G
FA (TR): Joe Bridges, 1987. FA (lead): Joe Bridges, Dick Williams,
1987.
Climb the face between **Petie** and **Petie's Spare Rib**.

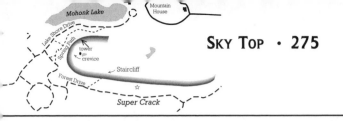

24	Artichoke 5.6–	36	Beardlings 5.9
25v	Obligato 5.5	37	Toit Slot 5.11+
28	Petie 5.2	38	The Mohonk Flake 5.7–
31	Juggernaut 5.10+	39	Krapp's Last Tape 5.10
32	The V 5.11–	41	Cretin Corner 5.6
34	Lakeview 5.4	42	Mary 5.2

30 Petie's Spare Rib 5.4 PG ★★★

FA: Doug Kerr, Norton Smithe, 1952

One of the Sky Top classics. 20 feet right of **Petie**, climb a short crack, move right around the prominent arête, then up the face to a roof. Step back left, then up the face left of the arête to the face above and the summit.

31 Juggernaut 5.10+ PG
FA: Rich Ross, Dave Karl, Marco Fedrizzi, August, 1985
Climb the steep face directly below the arête, and ten feet right of the **Spare Rib** start to a ledge (crux). Follow a vertical fault right of the arête, moving left after the third hang (5.10) to join **Spare Rib** near the top.

32 The V 5.11– PG13
FA: Chuck Calef, Rich Ross, 1978
Clamber up a dirty corner 20 feet right of **Petie's Spare Rib** to a belay, then climb the corner to the roof. Move right, and into the "V" (crux), then up left around the upper ceilings to the finish.

33 Turnip 5.4 G
FA: Dave Loeks, Dick Williams, 1973
A root. Climb the face just right of the dirty corner on **The V**, then up a crack on the arête to the ledge, and a belay. Traverse out right, then up into the chimney/corner, and the weeds.

34 Lakeview 5.4 G ★★★
FA: Fritz Wiessner, Lorens Logan, 1943
A superb climb—not to be missed. Climb a short crack 50 feet right of **Petie's Spare Rib**, and just right of a big pine to a ledge (crux). Up a right-facing corner to a belay ledge on the left. Traverse right along a horizontal, then up an obvious vertical crack to a small stance. Climb directly over the small roofs above (5.4).

35 Lost Souls 5.8– PG
FA: Jim Kolocotronis, Harvey Goldstein, 1973
If you are solid on 5.7, you'll enjoy this route. Climb a short corner just right of **Lakeview**, then straight up the face (tiny unit) right of the **Lakeview** corner, angling right (crux) to a roof. Over the roof at a crack to a belay on **Lakeview**. Climb up the face right of the **Lakeview** cracks (5.7) to the conclusion.

36 Beardlings 5.9 PG ★
FA: Dave Loeks, Karl Beard, 1971
Wild and exciting to lead, or follow. Double ropes are helpful. Struggle up an offwidth/corner 20 feet right of **Lakeview** to a ledge, then climb the small corner to the roof. Traverse right under the roof (crux, harder for tall people, V1) to the arête, and up this to a belay.

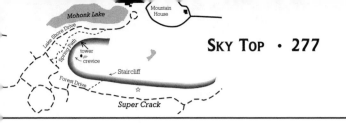

Up the arête above following a corner (5.7+), then angle right to an easy finish.

V1 Close Shave 5.10 PG FA: Mike Steele, 1985 Climb straight up the face to join **Lost Souls** at the next roof.

37 Toit Slot 5.11+ R
FA, P1: Rich Perch, Ivan Rezucha, 1975. FA, P2: Mark Robinson, Kevin Bein, 1978

The first pitch is popular, the second pitch contrived. Climb a very nice corner 35 feet right of **Lakeview** past a roof (5.10– G) to a belay. Climb the face just left of the big corner, then traverse out left under the huge roof (5.9+ R) to daylight. Step back right, and climb the roof at a hand crack (crux).

38 The Mohonk Flake 5.7– PG
FA: Unknown, pre-1964

The first 30 feet is good, then the climb deteriorates. From the top of a big boulder 45 feet right of **Lakeview**, climb a prominent flake to a ledge (crux), then up the corner above past a tree (possible rappel) to the top.

39 Krapp's Last Tape 5.10 G ★
FA: Henry Barber, Ric Hatch, 1974

Popular. Starting as for the **Mohonk Flake** (V1), climb out right along an arching crack (V2), then up a vertical crack to easy rock and a tree.

V1 Start in the pit and climb the vertical crack direct; 5.10+. This may have been the original line.

V2 Climb straight up the short vertical crack to join the **Mohonk Flake**.

40 Cretin's Last Crap 5.9+ X
FA: Sam Slater, Mike Heinz, 1981

Boulder up a short dihedral just left of **Cretin** corner, then over the roof (5.9–), and up the scary white face to the arête (crux) to join **Krapp's** at the tree.

41 Cretin Corner 5.6 G
FA: Dave Loeks (solo), June, 1974

This was never the 5.4 it was rated in the 1980 guide. Climb a small dihedral 20 feet right of **Krapp's** to a ledge, then angle right (V1) to the shrubs.

V1 5.7 PG FA: Ivan Rezucha, Larry Randall, Keith LaBudde, November, 1991. Start halfway up **Cretin Corner**, where the route angles right to bypass some overhangs. Angle left above the overhang and then climb the center of a narrow face that is just right of the final corner of **Mohonk Flake**.

42 Mary 5.2 G
FA: Mary Cecil, Fritz Wiessner, 1944
Ramble up the vegetated corner 40 feet right of **Krapp's Last Tape** to a ledge, then up the left face to the summit.

43 Tor and Feathered (aka Grin and Bear) 5.9 PG
FA: Rich Ross, Chuck Boyd, 1979 FA (final ceiling): Tor Raubenheimer, Joe Bridges, August, 1983
The first ascent party traversed off below the final ceiling, making the climb 5.8. Climb the low angled, broken rock just right of **Mary** to a belay at the left edge of the huge roofs. Pull over ceilings on the left to a ledge, then traverse right to a hand crack. Go up then left through the final ceiling.

44 Intimidation 5.6 PG ★
FA: Yvon Chouinard, Dick Williams, 1965
Climb the right-facing corner, and face 80 feet right of **Krapp's** to huge roofs, then traverse right and up to a belay at a small ledge. Traverse back left under the upper roof, then straight left between the massive hangs (crux) to easier climbing, and the top.

45 Blockparty 5.11– G ★
FA: Rich Ross, Rich Gottlieb, Marco Fedrizzi, Dave Karl, July, 1985
Climb straight up the face ten feet right of **Intimidation** past a ceiling (5.9 R) to the roofs. Angle left over a bulge to the **Intimidation** traverse line, then climb the white face above. Continue up a short, thin vertical crack (crux) through more ceilings to the woods.

46 It's Only the Beginning 5.9+ PG ★
FA: Hardie Truesdale, Dan Goodwin, Harvey Arnold, 1979
Very good climbing on P2. "Blueberry Dan" went on to climb the Sears Tower in Chicago in a Spiderman suit! Climb the face just right of **Blockparty**, passing the right edge of the low roof, then up

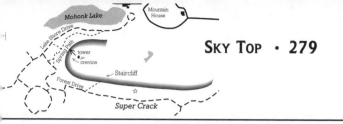

39 Krapp's Last Tape 5.10	**48 Cinnamon Girl 5.12**
40 Cretin's Last Crap 5.9+	**52 Open Cockpit 5.11+**
43 Tor and Feathered 5.9	**53 Sound and Fury 5.8**
44 Intimidation 5.6	**56 Amazon 5.11–**
46 It's Only the Beginning 5.9+	**58 Pete's Meat 5.7+**

to a belay as for **Intimidation** (5.8 PG). Move left, then up through the roofs at a right-facing corner past another roof, to the top (5.9).

47 Kashmir 5.8+ R
FA: Rich Ross, Marco Fedrizzi, Morris Hershoff, August, 1985
Dangerous climbing on the first pitch. Start just right of **It's Only the Beginning**. Angle right past a pointed block to the arête (crux) and a belay on **Hans' Yellow Face**. Climb straight up over the roofs above to a "beached whale" finish (5.8).

48 Cinnamon Girl 5.12 R ★★
FA: Hugh Herr, October, 1983
An impressive climb with a wild finish. Climb the thin corner just left of **Hans' Yellow Face**, then move left at the top (crux, V1), and up another corner to easier rock. Up, then traverse across **Poops**, to a belay on the arête (this was the old variation Overhanging Traverse). Hand traverse left along the lip to the point, then up left of **Poops** to the top.

V1 Moving right is easier, at 5.10.

49 Hans' Yellow Face 5.6– PG ★★
FA: Hans Kraus, Ken Prestrud, 1948
Climb up clean rock 30 feet left of **Open Cockpit,** and 130 feet right of **Krapp's** to a right-facing corner, exit out left to the nose, then up a crack to the belay. Climb up right around the hangs to the top (V1).

V1 Climb through the final overhang; 5.9.

50 Poops 5.6 A3 R
FA: Yvon Chouinard, Dick Williams, 1965
Hugh Herr came very close to freeing this, then the flakes in the roof broke... Climb a thin crack and corner six feet right of **Hans' Yellow Face** to a belay under the large roof. Aid out the thin seam to the lip, then up right (crossing **Cinnamon Girl**) to the top.

51 Mystery Woman 5.11– PG
FA: Steve Levin, Rich Ross, 1977
Dubbed "Misery Woman" after the painful crack at the start. Good climbing. Starting just right of **Poops**, climb a thin crack (crux) and the easier, but scary face above to a belay. Climb the nose right of **Poops**, then on up to the trees.

52 Open Cockpit 5.11+ PG ★★★
FA: Dave Loeks, Karl Beard, 1971. FFA: Steve Wunsch, 1973
Named for Beard's grandfather, a WWI flying ace. A classic climb that is well protected if you are solid in the grade. Often top-roped via **Sound and Fury**. Fly up the beautiful, vertical crack 20 feet right of **Hans' Yellow Face** and 110 feet left of **The Crevice** to a horizontal, then move right to belay on **Sound and Fury** (5.11+). Move back left and up past a ceiling at a notch to the summit. The striking arête to the left of the first pitch hasn't gone yet, despite many tries.

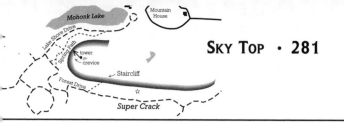

Mohonk Lake
Mountain House
Lake Shore Drive
Spring path
tower
crevice
Staircliff
Forest Drive
Super Crack

53 Sound and Fury 5.8 G ★★★

FA: Dick Williams, Jim McCarthy, 1963

Fantastic climbing. Follow a vertical crack system ten feet right of **Open Cockpit** to an obvious belay at 50 feet. (5.8). Move slightly left, and continue up the crack to an alcove, then left past ceilings to the top (5.7+).

54 Dirty Talk 5.8 PG

FA: Unknown, pre-1981

Scramble up the **Dirty** corner ten feet, climb up left, then past a roof. Jam up a crack system just right of **Sound and Fury**.

55 Dirty 5.2 G

FA: Hans Kraus, Roger Wolcott, Del Wilde, 1940

Scamper up a right-facing corner 95 feet left of **The Crevice** and just right of **Sound and Fury** to a birch, then move right and up to a ledge. Pitch two climbs up a corner and moves left, then right around a ceiling and up to the shrubs.

56 Amazon 5.11– PG

FA: Rich Romano, Rich Ross, May, 1979

Starting at **Dirty**, diagonal right easily, then to a belay at a tree in a dihedral. Climb the crack above, then right through a roof (crux, fixed pins) and up to the finish.

57 Footloose and Fancy Free 5.11 PG

FA: Hugh Herr, Russ Clune, August, 1982

Named after a climbing episode where Huey's artificial leg fell off! Originally titled Footless and Fancy Free. Start 20 feet left of **Pete's Meat** at a right leaning crack. Climb the crack and a left facing corner to right side of a bushy ledge. Angle up left, then climb the roof left of the **Amazon** crux at a flake.

58 Pete's Meat 5.7+ PG ★

FA: Pete Vlachos, Art Gran, 1965

A good crux. Climb the left side of an inverted V, 30 feet right of **Dirty** and 65 feet left of **The Crevice** past a roof (crux) to a corner and belay. Diagonal right around the arête and up a crack to the top (5.6).

59 Watermelons and White Sheets 5.12– PG

FA: Mike Freeman, Russ Clune, May, 1983

Climb a very thin crack just left of **Scare City** (crux), then around the nose and up to an exposed belay as for **Scare City**. Climb the ceiling left of **Scare City** at the lowest level and then on to the conclusion.

60 Scare City 5.10+ PG ★

FA: Dave Loeks, Dick Williams, 1974

A bit tricky to protect and scary even once you are clipped in. Climb the thin cracks five feet left of **Foops** to a horizontal, move left, then up the face to a better horizontal. Angle left to an exposed belay around nose (5.10+). Unprotected climbing off the belay leads to a roof, which is climbed near the right edge to the top (5.10).

61 Foops 5.11 G ★★★

FA: Jim McCarthy, John Rupley, 1955. FFA: John Stannard, 1967

Probably the most often sieged climb at the Gunks. Legend has it that John Salathé was rappelling in Yosemite and found his rope too short to reach a ledge. The disgruntled Salathé was heard to exclaim in a heavy Swiss accent "Foops (whoops), no more rope!" He then cut off the ends of his rope and prussiked back up to the anchor! *Life* magazine also featured McCarthy aiding out the roof in one of its issues. Climb a nice 5.9 crack system 40 feet right of **Pete's Meat** and 25 feet left of **The Crevice** to a huge roof. Swing out the roof (crux, V1, 2) and up to a belay, then follow a crack system to the top.

V1 Spoof (aka Too Pooped to Foop) 5.10+ G ★ FA: Kevin Bein, Steve Wunsch, 1974. Climb the crack/corner in the roof just right of **Foops**.

V2 Escape left under the roof to join **Pete's Meat** to the top (this makes a fine 5.9 route).

62 Emory Crack 5.7– G

FA: Hans Kraus, Bob Emory, 1941

Contrary to popular notion, the crack is not like sandpaper. Emory died during the D-Day invasion at Normandy in WWII. Struggle up a chimney/crack just right of **Foops**. Up to the huge roof and around it on the right to the top.

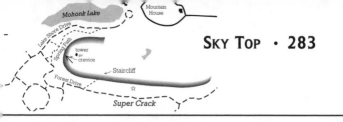

60 Scare City 5.10+	71 Positions 5.10+
61 Foops 5.11	72 No Exit 5.10+
62 Emory Crack 5.7–	73 Overhanging Overhang 5.5
63 Emory Buttress 5.12	75 Men-Who-Pause 5.10–
65 Minerva 5.5	76 Crack of
66 The Crevice	Bizarre Delights 5.11
70 Little Face 5.2+	79 Giant Chockstone 5.6

63   Emory Buttress 5.12 (TR)

FA: Mike Siacca, 1987

The small buttress to the right of **Emory Crack** makes a good top-rope route.

64   Gandydancer 5.5 G ★

FA: Dick DuMais, Bill Gilbert, 1972

Starting at a small right-facing corner, climb the crack system right of **Emory Crack** to the top.

65 Minerva 5.5 G

FA: Dick Williams, Yvon Chouinard, Pete Carman, 1965.
Climb the crack system just left of **The Crevice**, and 25 feet right of **Emory Crack**.

66 The Crevice (aka The Lemon Squeeze)

The Mohonk Mountain House requests climbers not to use the Crevice as a descent route as it interferes with their guests. Please comply so that Sky Top remains open to climbing.

67 Under Exposure One Stop 5.5 G

FA: Ralph Peri, Peter Darmi, August, 1980
Inside **The Crevice**, at the top of the second ladder, climb a crack on the main cliff. At the top, move right to the bridge.

68 The Darkroom 5.7 G

FRA: Todd Swain (solo), 1981
Starting in the same place as the last route, climb the overhanging crack on the other wall of **The Crevice**.

69 Lost in Space 5.7 R

FA (TR): Dick Williams, 1965. FA (lead): Unknown.
Climb straight up the face, keeping just right of **The Crevice**.

70 Little Face 5.2+ PG ★★★

FA: Fritz Wiessner, Ed Gross, 1944
A classic route that is exposed and clean. Starting at the bottom of **The Crevice**, move out right on the face, then up right to a ledge. Continue up the right side of the face above.

71 Positions 5.10+ X

FA: Jim Munson, Hugh Herr, Morris Hershoff, 1982
If you fall, you'll be in a bad position. Climb the left face of the arête between **Little Face** and **No Exit**.

72 No Exit 5.10+ G ★★★

FA: John Stannard, 1969
Unusual climbing for the Gunks—the crux involves crack climbing technique. Start 30 feet downhill and right of **The Crevice**, and climb the crack through a roof (crux). Continue up an overhanging crack past a hang, then angle right to a belay on **Overhanging Overhang**. Move back left and climb the steep face to the summit.

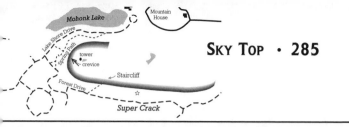

Mohonk Lake

Mountain House

Lake Shore Drive

Spring path

tower
crevice

Staircliff

Forest Drive

☆

Super Crack

52	**Open Cockpit** 5.11+	74	**Gargoyle** 5.5
53	**Sound and Fury** 5.8	78	**Wizard** 5.9
55	**Dirty** 5.2	79	**Giant Chockstone** 5.6
61	**Foops** 5.11	81	**Grandstand** 5.5
62	**Emory Crack** 5.7–	83	**The Move** 5.6
72	**No Exit** 5.10+	84	**MooseStash** 5.6

73 Overhanging Overhang 5.5 G ★

FA: Fritz Wiessner, Hans Kraus, Beckett Howorth, 1940

How true. From the top of boulders 15 feet right of **No Exit**, move left, and up a crack to its end. Move up left to a belay ledge (5.5). Join **No Exit** to the top.

74 Gargoyle 5.5 G ★
FA: Fritz Wiessner, John Navas, Percy Olton, 1935
The first recorded climb at Sky Top. Starting as for **Overhanging Overhang**, climb up right along the left side of a small buttress to a ledge. Follow a crack to a chimney and up this to a belay on the left (5.5). Step back (V1) right and climb the chimney to the top (5.5).

V1 From the belay, climb the face left of the chimney; 5.4.

75 Men-Who-Pause 5.10– PG
FA: Unknown, 1960s. FRFA: Joe Bridges, Bill Swan, 1983
Climb the front arête of the **Gargoyle** boulder to its top and belay. Move left and climb the face to the base of a left-facing corner. Climb the strenuous, overhanging corner, then exit right to the top (5.10–).

76 Crack of Bizarre Delights 5.11 PG ★
FA: Dave Loeks, John Monten, 1971. FFA: Henry Barber, John Stannard, 1973
Named for a friend of Loeks. A good link-up can be done by climbing the start of **No Exit** (5.10+), moving right and up the **Men-Who-Pause** corner (5.10–), then doing the crux of this route. Climb up the right side of the **Gargoyle** boulder, then move right and up a short corner to a roof. Exit right around the arête, then up a wide crack to a belay at a flake (5.9). Climb the chimney above, then out right through the summit roof (crux) to the top.

77 Three Blind Mice 5.6+ PG
FA: Doug Kerr, Norton Smithe, Ted Church, 1954
Starting 20 feet right of the **Gargoyle** boulder, angle left to a small left-facing corner and up this to a ledge. Belay on the next ledge above on the right. Scurry up to a roof and around this to the left. Up to another roof, which is avoided to the right and the top.

78 Wizard 5.9 PG
FA: Neil Pothier, Chuck Boyd, 1976
Climb the crack just right of **Three Blind Mice**, then up the face to the ceilings (5.7). Over these at a obvious crack (crux) ten feet left of **Giant Chockstone**. Continue over more ceilings on a prow (5.9), then finish on **Three Blind Mice**.

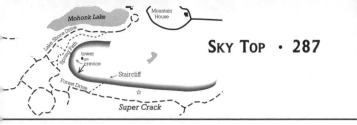

79 Giant Chockstone 5.6	**97 Grey Face 5.5**
83 The Move 5.6	**99 No Holds Barred 5.8**
85 Easy 5.1+	**100 Candide 5.8–**
87 Rear Exposure 5.6–	**102 Vandals 5.13–**
93 Bushmaster 5.5	**120 True Grip 5.11**
95 Greyer Face 5.6	

79 Giant Chockstone 5.6 G

FA: Fritz Wiessner, Edward and Ann Gross, 1945
Climb a chimney 40 feet right of **Crack of Bizarre Delights** to a
belay on the top of the chockstone. Move out left from the belay,
then up and back right to a right-facing corner and the top.

80 All's Well That Ends 5.6+ PG

FA: Ivan Rezucha, Annie O'Neill, Rod Schwarz, January, 1980
Starting just right of **Giant Chockstone**, follow thin cracks to a roof.
Escape left to join **Giant Chockstone** near the top at a tree.

81   Grandstand 5.5 G
FA: Hans Kraus, Ken Prestrud, 1949
Start 80 feet right of **Crack of Bizarre Delights** at the base of a huge right-facing corner. Up the corner, move out left and up a crack to the trees.

82   Unsolicited Advice 5.6 G
FA: Al Rubin, Alan Long, 1973
Start as for **Grandstand**, then climb the huge right-facing corner, moving left at the final ceilings.

83   The Move 5.6 G
FA: Art Gran, Murray and Debby Friedman, 1958
Climb the hidden left-facing corner 25 feet right of **Grandstand** past a block to its top. Exit right and up the face to the top.

V1 5.8 PG FA: Ivan Rezucha, Rick Cronk, 1975. Where **The Move** exits right out of the initial corner, continue up a left-leaning corner past an overhang to the top.

84   MooseStash 5.6 G
FA: Todd Swain, Paul Trapani, October, 1984
Named for Trapani's dog, Stash. Starting on **Easy**, climb the small left-facing corner past roofs (5.6–) to the white face. Climb the short cracks above to the top.

85   Easy 5.1+ G ★
FA: Unknown, 1960s or earlier
Starting downhill from **The Move**, climb a short crack and slab to a small ledge. Traverse right (crux, V1) around the arête and up obvious cracks to the top (full pitch).

V1 Under Easy 5.8 PG FA: Ivan Rezucha, Annie O'Neill, October, 1984. Climb directly up the front of a small buttress to join **Easy** on the arête.

86   Easy Arête 5.6 PG13
FRA: John Mallery, Tom Callahan, 1981
Climb a two-inch crack directly below the obvious, huge arête of **Easy** to a ledge. Move right, go up some cracks, then right again to the arête. Climb the arête, then finish in the left of two cracks.

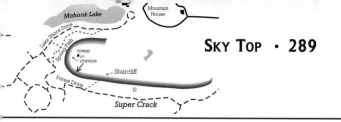

Mohonk Lake

Mountain House

Lake Shore Drive

Spring Path

tower
crevice

Staircliff

Forest Drive

Super Crack

---

87 Rear Exposure 5.6– G ★
FA: Fritz Wiessner, Bill Shockley, 1946
Right around the buttress from **The Move** and **Easy**, is an obvious break. Climb up the arête right of this split (crux, V1), then back left to a belay in the corner above. Climb the face left of the arête to the top.

V1 Climb directly up through the break to join the route in the corner; 5.7.

88 Lip Service 5.11– PG
FA: Ivan Rezucha, Don Hamilton, June, 1983
Climb up into a short corner capped by a roof 15 feet uphill from **Rear Exposure**. Traverse out right to the lip (crux, tricky protection), then back left and up the arête to the shrubs.

89 Slip of Fools 5.7 PG ★★
FRA: Dick Williams, Paul Baird, 1972
Exposed and exciting. Starting ten feet left of **Bonnie's Household**, climb the crack system and face above to the top.

90 Bonnie's Household 5.4 G
FA: Bonnie Prudden, Hans Kraus, 1949
Hopefully her house didn't look like this! Climb the huge, right-facing corner on the left side of the **Grey Face Wall** to the top.

91 Minestrone 5.5– G
FA: Krist Raubenheimer, Ted Church, Summer, 1958
Vegetable soup. Climb the first crack system right of **Bonnie's Household** to a belay at 80 feet, then move left and up a crack. Swing over a small hang to the big roof, which is passed on the right to the top (V1).

V1 Climb the roof direct; 5.3.

92 Linguine 5.6 PG
FA: Ivan Rezucha, Annie O'Neill, May, 1982
Starting 50 feet right of **Bonnie's Household**, climb the second crack system and face above, to the **Minestrone** roof. Climb up, then traverse left (and above) pasta big roof (crossing **Minestrone**) to the top.

97 Grey Face 5.5
99 No Holds Barred 5.8
100 Candide 5.8–
102 Vandals 5.13–
104 Beer and Loathing 5.11–
105 Hidden Piton 5.7–
109 Macramé 5.8+

110 Sky Top Route 5.8
113 Mutt and Jeff 5.9–
114 This Petty Pace 5.9
116 Intermediate 5.1
120 True Grip 5.11
126 Mellow Yellow 5.10+

93 Bushmaster 5.5 G

FA: Dick DuMais, Walt Jones, 1968

Bring a machete. Whack your way up the third crack right of
Bonnie's Household to a belay at 70 feet. Climb up to the roof, and
over this on the left and on to the top.

91 Pale Face 5.8+ PG

FA: Ivan Rezucha, Annie O'Neill, 1985

Climb the face between **Greyer Face** and **Bushmaster** for 40 feet,
then join either route.

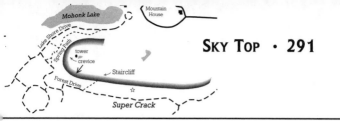

95 Greyer Face 5.6 PG ★★

FA: Art Gran, Pete Vlachos, 1965

Classic face climbing on P1. Starting ten feet left of **Grey Face**,
climb a thin seam past a short right-facing corner (crux) to a belay
as for **Grey Face**. Follow a groove to the roof, then over this at a right-
facing corner and on to the road.

96 Greyest Face 5.9 PG

FA: Joe Bridges, Ed Clark, 1982

The most creditable of the contrived routes in this area. Climb the
face between **Greyer** and **Grey Face** to the first belay (5.9). Angle
right (crossing **Grey Face**) past an overhang. Climb the face past a
bulge to an overhang with a notch (this is ten feet right of a rectan-
gular block). Climb through the notch to the carriage road (5.9-).

97 Grey Face 5.5 G ★★★

FA: Fritz Wiessner, Beckett Howorth, 1940

The classic in this section of the cliff. Romp up an obvious crack
system 80 feet downhill from **Bonnie's Household** and 20 feet left of
the **Candide** arête to a belay at a pine (5.5, V1). Continue up the
crack to the roof, then exit right and up the exposed face to a belay
in the gazebo (5.5).

98 Way Grey 5.9 PG13

FA: Joe Bridges, Faith Aubin, 1986

Climb the face between **Grey Face** and **No Holds Barred** to a belay
in a shallow, left facing corner (contrived, 5.8+). Climb straight up,
pulling the ceiling directly below a pine tree (5.9).

99 No Holds Barred 5.8 R

FA: Joe Bridges, Tom Bridges, Claude Suhl, 1976

The first 20 feet is very nice, but has little protection. Climb the
clean face just right of **Grey Face** past horizontals to easier climbing and a belay at a pine (5.8). Continue straight up the face, then
over the roof at a pointed notch to the road (5.6).

100 Candide 5.8– R

FA: Art Gran, Thom Scheuer, Fall, 1963

Climb just left of the arête at the right side of the **Grey Face** wall,
past the huge roof on the right, to a belay on the face above (5.8–).
Out the roof above at a left-facing corner, then on to the weeds.

101 Kor Slot 5.11+ PG

FA (TR): Kevin Bein, 1976. FA (lead): Dave Loeks, 1978

Top-roped by Loeks before being led. Climb the right-facing corner 25 feet right of **Grey Face** to the huge roof, then out this at the slot (crux) and up to a pine. Rappel, or climb straight to the top.

NOTE: At this point, the trail descends and goes through Bloody Roof Cave.

102 Vandals 5.13– R ★★★

FA: Jeff Gruenberg, Hugh Herr, Russ Clune, Lynn Hill, November, 1983

A climb that required an incredible amount of effort to complete. Climb the blank face just left of **The Pit and the Pendulum** (5.11 R) to the roof, then out thin cracks in the roof (crux) to a short corner and easier climbing.

103 The Pit and the Pendulum 5.11+ PG ★

FA: Russ Raffa, June, 1981

80 feet right of **Grey Face** and on the other side of the cave that the trail goes through, climb a shallow dihedral past the right side of a low roof to a large roof (crux). Move left (1.5 Friend) around the roof, then on to the top.

104 Beer and Loathing 5.11– PG ★

FA: Dave Loeks, Dick Williams, 1978

The bolts were placed on aid for the express purpose of protecting a free climb, even though a no bolt ethic had been communally accepted. The climb has since become very popular. Climb a short corner ten feet left of **Hidden Piton** to a slab on the right. Crank up the face past three bolts (crux), then move left around the roof (5.9 R, very scary to follow) to easier climbing. Rappel, or follow a crack past roofs to the trees.

105 Hidden Piton 5.7– PG

FA: John Lomont, Francis Coffin, 1958

Struggle up the left-facing corner right of **Beer and Loathing** for 15 feet, then move right around the rib and up to a belay in a corner. Stem up the right-facing corner to beneath a roof, then traverse left to the nose (crux) and on up the face to the top.

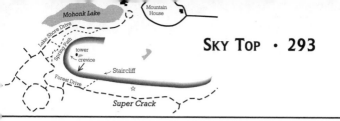

Mohonk Lake

Mountain House

Lake Shore Drive

Spring Path

tower
crevice

Staircliff

Forest Drive

☆

Super Crack

106 Thunder and Frightening 5.11– PG
FA: Mike Freeman, John Myers, Russ Clune, July, 1979
Starting just right of **Hidden Piton**, whimper up the front of the narrow rib along a crack (#1 Hex) to the **Mac-Kor-Wick** belay (5.10). Angle right up an orange face to its top. Move right around the arête (5.10 scary, V1), then back left to a crack out the roof. Climb the crack (crux), then up to a belay at a pine tree. Climb easily to the top.

V1 T&F Direct Finish 5.10+ R FA: Jack Meleski, 1980. Climb directly over the final roof instead of moving right then back left.

107 Fear and Lightning 5.11 PG
FA: Mike Law (Australian), May, 1983
Climb directly up the right arête of the narrow rib mentioned in **Thunder and Frightening** to a belay on **Mac-Kor-Wick**. Climb up left as for **Mac-Kor-Wick**, then into a hanging left-facing corner. Up this and over the roof to a pine tree. Rappel, or climb to the top.

108 Mac-Kor-Wick 5.8 G
FA: Layton Kor, Jim McCarthy, Dick Williams, 1964
A struggle. Up the flared chimney/crack just right of the narrow rib to a belay ledge (5.8). Angle left (crossing **Hidden Piton**) to a left-facing corner (left of **Fear and Lightning**), and another belay (50 feet). Up this, move right, then up the face to the top.

109 Macramé 5.8+ PG
FA: Joe Bridges, Rich Goldstone, 1974
Not much of a line but good moves and clean rock. Starting off a block 20 feet right of the **Thunder and Frightening** rib, weave up the bulging face (crux) to easier rock. Continue up orange rock to a belay under the roof. Up to the big roof, then out the left-facing corner and up the face to the trees.

110 Sky Top Route 5.8 G ★
FA: Willie Crowther, Jim Waters, 1959
This climb was originally rated 5.5! Climb a right-facing corner 30 feet right of the **Thunder and Frightening** rib (V1) past an overhang to a belay ledge (5.8). Angle right and go up a crack to the big roofs. Swing over the roof at a right-facing corner (crossing **Macramé**), then on to the top.

V1 Climb a few feet up the regular route then step left and climb the deceptive, overhanging, thin crack; 5.10.

114 **This Petty Pace** 5.9
116 **Intermediate** 5.1
121 **Sticky Bun Power** 5.12
123 **Up Against the Wall** 5.10–
124 **Burning Bush** 5.11+

126 **Mellow Yellow** 5.10+
128 **Deliberance** 5.10+
130 **Yellow Verschneidung** 5.8
131 **Kalmia Corner** 5.8+
134 **Don Ellisao** 5.3

111 Shake and Bake 5.10– PG ★

FA: Russ Raffa, Laura Chaiten, 1978

Start 15 feet right of **Sky Top Route** on top of blocks. Up flakes and a thin crack past a horizontal to a ceiling. Step right around the ceiling, up a crack, then angle right to a belay at a prominent horizontal (V1). Continue up the face along the prow to a crack, then angle right to a belay. Move back left, then over the large roof in the center. Straight on to the woods.

V1 5.11 (TR) FA: Todd Swain, 1986. It is possible to top-rope the shallow, overhanging groove just right of the first pitch.

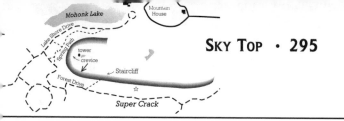

Super Crack

112 Chalk Up Another One 5.8+ R
FA: Dana Bartlett, Russ Clune, June, 1981
Climb the arête right of **Shake and Bake** to where it steepens. Move
left and up past a hidden horizontal (5.8 R) and another horizontal
to easier rock. Climb straight up to a belay beneath a roof, or move
right on a slab (scary) to a belay beneath the right side of the roof.
Climb up the steep, licheny face and arête left of **This Petty Pace**
(5.7+).

113 Mutt and Jeff 5.9– PG
FA: Dave Loeks, Dick Williams, 1974
Starting 45 feet right of **Sky Top Route** and 25 feet left of a small
cave the trail passes through, climb up along a seam, then left
around a nose to a slab (crux, #3 Friend). Up the safer rock to a
vertical crack and a belay on the left (crossing **Shake and Bake** to
the **Sky Top Route** belay). Move back right and over the roof to join
Shake and Bake to the trees.

114 This Petty Pace 5.9 PG ★
FA: Jim McCarthy, Dick Williams, Fall, 1963. FFA: Dick Williams, Dick
DuMais, 1971
The crux moves are quite similar to **Retribution**. Starting at the
base of **Intermediate**, climb up to a shallow dihedral capped by a
roof. Layback over the roof (crux) and up to a belay on the right.
Climb up a groove (5.8) to a dirty right-facing corner and the
woods.

115 Someone Had to Do It 5.8+ PG
FA: Joe Bridges, Faith Aubin, July, 1987
Start left of the **Intermediate** corner (V1), and bypass a ceiling in
the corner, then move out left onto the face. Wander up the face to a
flake 20 feet below the top, then up the left side of a buttress in
white rock to the summit (crux).

V1 Direct Start 5.10+ (TR) Climb up the face between
Intermediate and **This Petty Pace** past a ceiling to the right of a
bush to join the normal line.

116 Intermediate 5.1 G ★
FA: Hans Kraus, Roger Wolcott, Del Wilde, 1940
Climb the lower angled, right leaning corner/ramp 60 feet right of
Sky Top Route to the top.

117 Tear City 5.10+ PG
FA: Mike Robins, Pete Werner, circa 1978
Directly above a small cave and ten feet right of **Intermediate**,
climb a thin seam up to a birch tree (5.10+). Rappel, or climb the
arête right of **Intermediate**, eventually joining that route.

118 Trinity 5.11 PG ★★
FA: Bruce Dicks, Russ Raffa, Geoffrey Ohland, May, 1980
Difficult to protect but great climbing on P1. Dance up a thin
seam/corner ten feet left of **Minne Belle** (crux), then up the face
past a small ceiling at a crack (5.10–). Ramble to the top, or rappel.

119 Minne Belle 5.8– PG ★
FA: Fritz Wiessner, Bill Shockley, 1946
A historical classic that established 5.8 at the Gunks. Climb the
wide crack/flake 35 feet right of **Intermediate** and just left of a
beautiful finger crack to a ledge (5.8–). Climb the chimney above
(5.6+).

120 True Grip 5.11 PG ★★★
FA: P1 John Stannard 1972; P2 Henry Barber 1974
The first pitch is very popular and is known as Fissure Ramins, after
Pete Ramins. Jam up the finger crack right of **Minne Belle** and
behind a large pine tree to a ledge (5.11 G). Climb over a ceiling
near its left edge to a ledge. From the right side of the ledge, Swing
over a hang, then angle left (5.9) to another ceiling. Power through
the final roof near the left side (5.10, small Tri-cams, Friends) to a
short face, and the top.

121 Sticky Bun Power 5.12 R ★★
FA: Hugh Herr, October, 1981
Credit is due to Freihofer's for this one. Who says climbers eat
health food? A crucial hold broke in 1986, making the first pitch
very dangerous. Climb a thin crack just right of **True Grip** past a
bulge (V1), then straight up the face (V2) to a belay below the steep
wall (5.12). Up the crack/flake system in the middle of the steep wall
to the top (5.11).

V1 Burning Buns 5.12+ (TR) FA: Russ Clune, 1986. The blank,
white face just right of the thin crack, utilizing the last part of the
original line.

V2 The original line moved right at the top of the crack, then up.

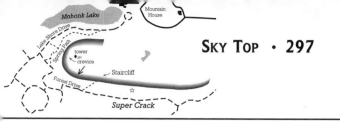

122 Shaffer-Luhan 5.11 PG13

FA: Larry Shaffer, Dave Luhan, June, 1987

Climb the face and small arête just left of **Up Against the Wall**, not using the crack on that route (5.10+). Move left and up to a belay on the arête of the **True Grip** buttress. Hand traverse right along the lip of the roof (crux) to the arête, then up to the top.

123 Up Against the Wall 5.10– PG ★

FA: Arno Vosk, Dave Ingalls, 1969. FFA: John Stannard, Pete Ramins, 1971

The crux is deceptively difficult, and the protection is awkward and strenuous to place. Layback a flake/crack on a small arête 20 feet right of **True Grip** to a belay ledge (5.10-). Rappel, or climb a right-facing corner to the top.

124 Burning Bush 5.11+ R

FA: Steve Wunsch, 1974

On the first ascent, the crux nut was placed using a double nut for reach. Also known as The Troll, after that same nut. Starting 45 feet right of **True Grip** and ten feet left of **Mellow Yellow** on a block, move left around a hang, then up the orange face to a triangular ceiling. Above the ceiling, follow a thin crack to a large flake/chimney, and a belay on **Mellow Yellow** (70 feet). Rappel, or finish with **Mellow Yellow**.

125 Desperate But Not Serious 5.11+ R

FA (TR): John Bragg, 1976. FA (lead): Russ Clune, Jeff Gruenberg, Hugh Herr, Lynn Hill, John Long, March, 1984

Climb the arête and face just left of **Mellow Yellow** (V1), using protection in the left **Mellow Yellow** crack. Usually top-roped.

V1 5.12– (TR) FA: Steve Wunsch, 1974. At the overhang, climb the left side of the arête.

126 Mellow Yellow 5.10+ G ★★★

FA: Roy Kligfield, Dave Ingalls, 1968. FFA: John Stannard, Pete Ramins, 1971

If you are solid leading 5.10, this is well protected. Stem up a shallow yellow dihedral 55 feet right of **True Grip** to a ledge on the left at 40 feet (5.10). Rappel, or climb the large flake past a roof on the right. Move right, then up a crack to the top.

127 Cookie Monster 5.11+ R ★★

FA: Mike Freeman, John Myers, Jack Meleski, 1981; P1 (lead): Alex Lowe, 1982

The first 20 feet were top-roped on the first ascent. Climb the blank face right of **Mellow Yellow** to a horizontal (5.11 R), then past an overhang (crux) left of **Deliberance** to a belay below the huge roof. Up to the center of the roof and out right at a small corner (5.11–) to the easier face above.

128 Deliberance 5.10+ R ★★

FA: Steve Wunsch, John Bragg, Ajax Greene, 1974

It is best not to deliberate on the consequences of a fall from this one. Bring a large Friend, and try to imagine camming hexes instead! Starting 15 feet left of **Yellow V** and 25 feet right of **Mellow Yellow**, climb past a small right-facing dihedral, then wander up the face to a roof and a belay (5.10–). Climb straight up on creaky flakes (crux) to the roof (#4 Friend). Escape right around the right edge of the roof to a ledge, then up the deceptively difficult face above to the summit.

129 Domain of Angels (aka DOA) 5.11 R/X

FA: Mike Freeman, John Myers, August, 1981

Very difficult to protect. Climb the face between **Deliberance** and **Yellow V**, then up the face above to join **Deliberance** as it excapes right around the roof.

130 Yellow Verschneidung 5.8 PG ★★

FA: John Lomont, Francis Coffin, 1959. FFA: Joe Kelsey, Dick DuMais, 1968

A classic. Stem up the yellow corner system 40 feet right of **Mellow Yellow** to a ledge at 40 feet. Climb up to the base of a left-facing corner, then up that to the top (5.6+).

131 Kalmia Corner 5.8+ PG

FA: Joe Bridges, Joan Waltermire, Claude Suhl, 1974

Named for the Mountain Laurel bush (*Kalmia latifolia*) partway up the initial corner. If you are here in June, it'll be in bloom. Starting 25 feet right of **Yellow V**, follow a corner out left around a ceiling (crux), then up a shallow corner to a belay on **Yellow V** under the big roof. Over the roof at a crack on the right edge, then up left along a corner to the top (5.7).

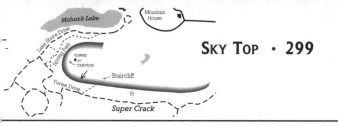

Super Crack

130 Yellow Verschneidung 5.8
131 Kalmia Corner 5.8+
132 A Walk on the Wild Side 5.9–
134 Don Ellisao 5.3
136 The Bull and the Virgin 5.5
138 Burning Fingers 5.12–

141 Fritz's Yellow Face 5.7
142 True Gunk 5.11
143 The Tunnel 5.2+
145 Mixed Bag 5.9
146 Terror Firma 5.9
148 Hardware Route 5.9

132 A Walk on the Wild Side 5.9– R

FRA: Todd Swain, Paul Moores (UK), November, 1981

Climb straight up from the right edge of the **Kalmia Corner** (crux)
to a shallow depression, which is followed to a belay as for **Yellow
V**. Cross **Kalmia Corner**, and climb the roof left of a crack, then up
the steep face to the top (5.7).

133 Men Who Beat Lichen 5.8 PG
FA: Joe Bridges, Bill Swan, 1983
Start 45 feet right of **Yellow V** at a short face that leads to a right leaning ramp and a pine. Climb straight up the face, keeping left of the ramp, to left facing flakes. Step right and climb a left-facing corner to the **Yellow V** belay ledge, below a roof. Join any of the other routes to the woods.

134 Don Ellisao 5.3 G
FA: Art Gran, Rachel Schor, 1959
Starting 45 feet right of **Yellow V**, climb up a gray face past a pine tree to a ledge (5.3, 75 feet). Follow corners up right to the woods (5.1).

NOTE: At this point the trail heads into the woods.

135 The Funnel 5.3 PG
FA: Unknown, 1950s
Swarm up easy, vegetated rock in a gully 60 feet right of **Yellow V** to a belay. Chimney up the edge of **The Tunnel** chimney to the top.

136 The Bull and the Virgin 5.5 R
FA: Joe Bridges, Joan Waltermire, 1974
Climb up the left side of a huge flake leaning against the face 160 feet right of **Yellow V** and 80 feet left of **The Tunnel**. From the top of the flake, traverse left to a shallow corner. Follow the corner to a belay at a pine tree (5.5 R). Charge up another corner to a roof, move right and up through a notch to a big belay ledge. Wander up right across the white face to a ceiling and over this at a crack to the top.

137 Booty and the Beast 5.9 PG
FA: Ivan Rezucha, Rick Cronk, November, 1980
Power up the right edge of the huge **Bull and the Virgin** flake, then up a thin seam to a horizontal (scary, large Friend needed). Move right to a flake, then up left along this to a belay as for **The Bull** (5.9). Traverse out right, then straight up keeping left of **Fritz's Yellow Face** to the big belay ledge. Climb the face left of the final pitch on **Fritz's**, angling left to touch **The Bull**, then back right past the roof at a break.

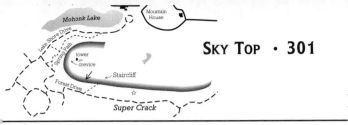
138 Burning Fingers 5.12– R ★

FA: Russ Clune, Russell Ericson, Louis Babin (Quebec), October, 1984

Louis was one of the best climbers to come from Quebec. Unfortunately, he took his own life in 1993. Up a right-facing flake 45 feet right of **The Bull**, then move right and follow a thin seam past a roof (crux, protection difficult). Climb a shallow left-facing corner above to easier rock.

139 Could Be Tough 5.10+ PG

FA: Hugh and Tony Herr, Morris Hershoff, 1979

Climb the thin dihedral ten feet right of **Burning Fingers** and ten feet left of **Mayor of the Gunks**. Join **Mayor** at the first belay.

140 Mayor of the Gunks 5.10 PG

FA: John Myers, Mike Freeman, September, 1979

This climb was named in honor of Kevin Bein. Climb the biggest of three corners 45 feet right of **The Bull** (V1) to a belay ledge that is just right of an orange face. Move up the face past a small overhang right of a crack (V2, 3), then up easier rock to the highest of two ledges. Step right and up a wide crack, then move left ten feet and up right to a roof. Climb the roof at a notch (crux, small units).

V1 The blank-looking corner has been top-roped at 5.11.

V2 Climb the crack on the orange face; 5.9+.

V3 Climb a flake and overhang off the right side of the ledge.

141 Fritz's Yellow Face 5.7 PG ★

FA: Fritz Wiessner, Roger Wolcott, 1944

Starting at **The Tunnel**, move out left along a ledge, up a groove to a ledge and a left-facing corner. Up the corner to a ceiling, move left 40 feet, then up to a belay on the big ledge (long pitch). Climb the very nice crack system past a roof to the top (5.7).

142 True Gunk 5.11 PG

FA: Mark Robinson, Kevin Bein, 1978

Bring large Friends, tape and sturdy clothes for the crux. Move out left as for **Fritz's**, then up a left-facing corner to its top. Angle left to a ledge, then up past loose flakes and a crack to the highest ledge and a belay. Climb a loose corner, then move right and out the big roof at an obvious crack (crux).

143 The Tunnel 5.2+ PG ★

FA: Fritz Wiessner (solo), 1942

A caver's delight. Interesting. Clamber up dirty rock at the base of a huge right-facing corner 80 feet right of **The Bull** and 85 feet left of the Laurel and Hardy Pinnacle to a ledge (50 feet). Tunnel through the cliff (beware of Goblins and Orcs) to daylight and a belay. Stem up the huge left-facing corner to the top (5.2+).

144 Summery Execution 5.9 PG

FA: Ivan Rezucha, Annie O'Neill, April, 1980

Done during warm weather, get it? Starting as for **The Tunnel**, climb a left-facing corner, then up the face above to a ledge on the right. Move back left, then up past a ceiling to angle left to the big ledge. P2 starts at a tree and diagonals up right between ceilings (crossing **Mixed Bag**) to the top.

145 Mixed Bag 5.9 PG ★

FA: John Stannard, Hal Murray, 1969

Climb the face between **Summery Execution** and **Terror Firma** to a ledge, starting 35 feet right of **The Tunnel** (60 feet). Move right and up a bombay chimney, exiting left and up another chimney to the big ledge. Starting on the left, climb to the top of a left-facing corner, move left, then up right across a face to a crack in the final roof. Out the crack to the trees.

146 Terror Firma 5.9 PG ★

FA: Joe Bridges, Claude Suhl, 1974

Lots of exposure on this one. Climb up the left-facing chimney/corner 35 feet right of **The Tunnel** to a niche. Out right, then up a wild overhanging crack (V1) to join **Hardware Route** at the second belay (5.8). Finish on **Hardware Route** (5.9).

V1 5.11 G ★ FA: John Bragg, Kevin Bein, October, 1978 Climb the very exposed layback and finger crack left of the **Terror Firma** crux.

147 Head Over Heels 5.9 PG

FA: Ivan Rezucha, Annie O'Neill, October, 1991

Start at the base of the left facing corner formed by the **Hardware Route** block (below **Terror Firma**). Step right onto the arête just above a ceiling. Climb the face near the arête to a big ledge and belay as for **Hardware Route** (5.7 PG). From the middle of the

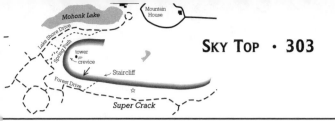

ledge, climb up to and over an overhang, angle left past another overhang, and up to a big ledge. Follow **Hardware Route** to a belay at the right end of the narrow ledge (this pitch may have been done previously; 5.7 PG). Traverse straight right above a large roof with pro at your feet (crux, very exposed) to left facing flakes. Up the flakes to an exciting finish (5.9 PG).

148 Hardware Route 5.9 PG ★★

FA: Hans Kraus, 1946. FFA: Layton Kor, Jim McCarthy, Matt Seddon, 1964

The first recorded aid route at the Gunks involving the use of etriers. A solid 5.9 and a historical classic. Climb an obvious dihedral 80 feet right of **The Tunnel** and just left of the Laurel and Hardy Pinnacle to a ledge (5.8). Around a roof on the right, then left up a corner to a belay at the right end of an exposed ledge (5.7). Traverse out left on the ledge, then up a crack/flake (crux) above a small pine to a ledge and easy climbing.

149 Software Route 5.11 R ★

FA, P1: John Myers, Jack Meleski, August, 1981. FA, P2: Jeff Gruenberg, Russ Clune, September, 1984

Climb partway up P1 of **Hardware Route**, then climb a thin crack on the right, moving back left to the belay on **Hardware Route** (5.11 PG). Up **Hardware Route** to the roof on P2, then move right, then up left along the arête to the trees (5.11 R).

150 Retrogression 5.9+ R

FA: Dave Loeks, Jim McCarthy, 1974

Step off a block to a leaning crack on the arête just right of **Hardware Route**. Climb along the arête, then make scary and unlikely moves right (crux) into a groove. Belay above on a ledge (75 feet). Move 15 feet left and up right along an arête to a corner leaning right. Up the shallow corner, move right and on to the top.

151 Abbott and Costello 5.9 PG

FA: Todd Swain, Annie O'Neill, November, 1982

On the front of the Laurel and Hardy Pinnacle, climb a crack/flake to a horizontal. Up to the next horizontal, move right (crux) and up the thin crack on the crease (V1) to the top.

V1 It's easier if you traverse further right and then go up.

152 Laurel and Hardy 5.10 G
FA: Dick Williams, Dave Loeks, 1974
Midway between **The Tunnel** and **Staircliff** are two freestanding pinnacles. The left pinnacle is the Laurel and Hardy Pinnacle, the right spire is the Crash and Burn Pinnacle. Stem up the right side of the left pinnacle, then swing across onto the face just left of a very shallow chimney (crux) and up the clean face along a crack (5.9) to a ledge. Rappel, or weave straight up a seam to a crack. At the top, move right to a corner and on to the woods.

153 A Comedy of Terrors 5.11– PG13 ★★
FA: Ivan Rezucha, John Bragg, 1975
The first pitch is sustained. Climb the thin crack just right of the Laurel and Hardy Pinnacle to a stance under a small ceiling. Move right and up another crack, then up and slightly right to a stance under an overhang. Over the left side of the hang and up to the **Humpty Dumpty** belay (5.11–, 70 feet). Move right, then up along a vertical seam through overhanging rock to a left-facing corner. Weave right, then left to the top.

154 Divine 5.11 R
FA: Russ Raffa, 1984
Named for the late film star. Climb the thin seam just right of **Comedy** to join the regular route near the belay.

155 Faster Than a Speeding Bullet 5.11 R
FA: Russ Clune, Rich Gottlieb, July, 1986
Climb the face between **Divine** and **Shawangunk Syndrome** to a belay beneath overhangs (5.11- R). Climb the ceilings above at their widest point (crux) to easier climbing and the top (5.11 R).

156 Shawangunk Syndrome 5.10+ PG
FA: John Myers, Mike Freeman, July, 1979
Up the thin seam 15 feet left of **Humpty Dumpty** past an orange bulge (5.10) to the ceiling, then angle right (V1) to a belay on **Humpty Dumpty** at a block. Move out right and up a short left-facing corner to roofs. Follow a crack system through the ceilings to the top.

V1 **5.10 PG** FA: Howard Doyle, Ivan Rezucha, September, 1979. This is a better finish to the route. Climb over the ceiling in the middle of the **Humpty Dumpty** traverse, then over the next roof left of the regular route at a bucket. Diagonal right to rejoin the normal line.

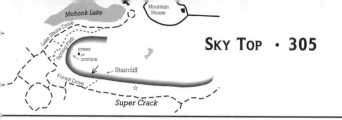

150 Retrogression 5.9+
152 Laurel and Hardy 5.10
153 A Comedy of Terrors 5.11–
157 Humpty Dumpty 5.7–
158 Jekyll and Hyde 5.9

160 Cries and Whimpers 5.11
162 Talus Food 5.11+
163 Half Assid 5.10+
165 Crash and Burn 5.9+
170 The Zig Zag Man 5.8+

157 Humpty Dumpty 5.7– PG

FA: John Lomont, Al DeMaria, 1960

Eggstremely forgettable, if you'll pardon the yolk. Climb the left-hand, left-facing corner 55 feet right of **Laurel and Hardy**, then out left on the face past a flake to a crack (be careful to protect the second, V1). Traverse left 40 feet, then up to a belay ledge. Wade up the dirty left-facing corner to the top.

V1 Climb the crack, then traverse far left to the belay; 5.8.

158 Jekyll and Hyde 5.9 G ★★★
FA: Dick Williams, Dave Loeks, 1974
One of the best 5.9 routes at the Gunks. Climb the overhanging, left-facing corner/crack system 65 feet right of **Laurel and Hardy** to the top. The line weaves back and forth slightly.

159 Comfortably Numb 5.9+ PG
FA: Dan MacMillan, Russ Clune, January, 1983
A little scary and loose in places. Up the pink, left-facing corner system that is just right of **Jekyll and Hyde**. Continue up thin cracks past two left-facing corners.

160 Cries and Whimpers 5.11 R
FA: Steve Wunsch, John Bragg, Kevin Bein, 1974
Scary and hard to protect. Starting 25 feet right of **Jekyll and Hyde**, climb up to an orange left-facing corner and up this to the top. Angle right (V1), then over a white roof to a corner (possible belay here). Angle right and up the arête to the top.

V1 Climb straight through the roof; 5.12- R.

161 Brace Yourself 5.12 R
FA: Russ Clune, Jeff Morris, 1986
A climb that was top-roped extensively, then led after a bolt was placed on rappel. You could get hurt badly if you blew the last clip in. Climb the tricky face left of **Talus Food** past a bolt to a right-facing flake (crux). Up this past more hard moves to eventual salvation.

162 Talus Food 5.11+ X
FA: Jeff Gruenberg, Russ Clune, Mike Freeman, Jack Meleski, Russ Raffa, February, 1983
Even if the talus isn't hungry, you'll probably die if you blow it. An impressive ascent. Wander up the blank orange face left of the **Half Assid** corner, then over the roof to easier climbing, and some protection.

163 Half Assid 5.10+ G ★★★
FA: Pete Carman, Dick DuMais, Burt Angrist, 1970. FFA: Henry Barber, John Stannard, 1973
Strenuous and hard. Follow the obvious crack/corner system facing right 40 feet right of **Jekyll and Hyde** and just left of the Crash and Burn Pinnacle past a huge roof (crux) to a stance. Climb the face and vertical crack to the top.

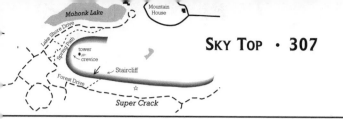

164 Thrash and Churn 5.7 R
FA: Unknown, 1970s or earlier
Climb the left (west) face of the Crash and Burn Pinnacle to the top.

165 Crash and Burn 5.9+ PG ★★
FA: Henry Barber, John Stannard, Ric Hatch, 1974
One of the wildest moves at the Gunks. Start at the prominent pinnacle 50 feet left of the bottom of the Staircliff trail. Bring extra RPs and small Friends. From the back of the pinnacle, climb to the top. Stand on the very tiptop (don't look down), then leap (or lean) across to the main cliff and up to a ledge. Follow the tricky vertical seam to the top.

166 Trash for Burning 5.9 PG
FA: Mike Freeman, John Myers, September, 1979
Starting on **Final Step**, angle left past a bulge to a ledge (right of the **Crash and Burn** ledge above the roof). Climb the heavily lichenated face past the right side of a bulge, then angle left below a roof to join **Crash and Burn**.

167 Final Step 5.4 G
FA: Unknown, pre-1964
Climb the vegetated, left-facing corner just right of the Crash and Burn Pinnacle. The crux is near the top.

168 Close Encounter 5.10 R
FA: Rosie Andrews, Dick Williams, 1984
Climb a short right-facing groove just right of **Final Step** to a belay ledge (5.10- PG13). Move up blocks, then slightly left up the steep wall to another ledge. Climb a crack behind a tree (contrived) to the top (5.10 R).

169 Squeeze and Pump 5.11 R
FA: Jim Munson, Don Perry, Mike Burlingame, 1984
Beware. Climb the difficult face and outside corner 15 feet left of **The Zig Zag Man**, then up easier rock to a belay on the **ZZ Man** belay ledge. Continue up the steep and tricky arête to the summit.

170 The Zig Zag Man 5.8+ PG ★★
FA: Dick Williams, Paul Baird, Walter Baumann, 1972
Boulder up into a shallow dihedral (5.8+) at the very base of the **Staircliff** trail, then move left and up easy rock to a ledge. Climb the steep face to zig zag cracks and up these (crux) to a ledge. Scramble to the top.

171 East Chimney 5.2 G
FA: Frank Carey and Unknown, pre-1964
Waddle up the chimney 15 feet right of **Zig Zag Man**.

NOTE: Approach the next routes by either climbing the first pitch of
No One Keepin' Score, scrambling out left onto a platform from the
base of **Tower Ridge**, or climbing a dirty face ten feet right of **East
Chimney** past ledges to the platform.

172 Flash Dance Arête 5.12– R ★
FA: Russ Clune, Mike Freeman, Jeff Gruenberg, November, 1983
Climb the right side of the arête left of **Shake Your Booty** (V1),
climbing the roof on the right of the arête.

V1 Climb the left side of the arête, moving right at the roof to join
the regular route; 5.12-.

173 Shake Your Booty 5.11 PG ★
FA: John Bragg, Rich Perch, Kevin Bein, 1978
Start on the platform and climb the thin yellow crack and face to the
left to a ceiling. Move right and up, then angle left to the top.

174 Pussy Foot'n 5.9+ R
FA: Dick Williams, Dave Loeks, 1978
A fall on this one could be cat-astrophic. Start just right of **Shake
Your Booty**. Climb up black rock (scary) to a crack in a roof, and up
this (crux) to a left-facing corner and the trees.

175 No One Keepin' Score 5.7+ PG
FA: Dick Williams, Dick DuMais, 1972
Jam up a crack 15 feet right of **East Chimney**, then move right and
up to the platform. Climb the left-facing corners above the right
side of the platform (5.7).

176 Vegetable Grief 5.3 G
FA: George Evans, William Smith, 1973
Bushwhack up the gully left of the stairs on **Staircliff**.

177 Tower Ridge 5.5 G
FA: Derek Price (UK), Todd Swain, October, 1981
Climb the arête left of the stairs on **Staircliff**.

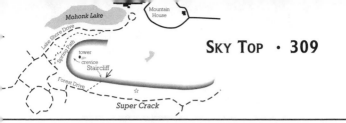

Super Crack

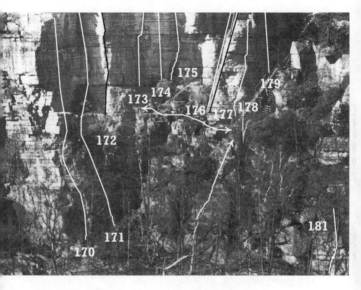

170 The Zig Zag Man 5.8+
171 East Chimney 5.2
172 Flash Dance Arête 5.12–
173 Shake Your Booty 5.11
174 Pussy Foot'n 5.9+
175 No One Keepin' Score 5.7+

176 Vegetable Grief 5.3
177 Tower Ridge 5.5
178 Almost Priceless 5.9+
179 Hystairical 5.10+
181 Flakes in Space 5.7–

178 Almost Priceless 5.9+ PG ★

FA: Todd Swain, Derek Price (UK), October, 1981
Angle right from the bottom of the stairs (V1) to the left-facing corner in the roof. Exit out right (crux), then up the face to the top.

V1 Climb the thin crack off the steps straight up to the roof.

179 Hystairical 5.10+ PG

FA (TR): Todd Swain, Paul Trapani, 1981. FA (lead): Todd Swain, 1986
Climb the short, thin crack and steep face up the stairs from the
Almost Priceless variation.

180 Staircliff ★★★
This wooden stairway makes an interesting ascent or descent trail.

181 Flakes in Space 5.7– PG
FA: Todd Swain, Lizabeth and Chris Taylor, Curt Robinson, November, 1984
Climb a left-facing corner 100 feet right of **Staircliff** to a ceiling, step right and up a cleaned slab along thin seams (crux) to the top. Rappel or walk off left.

182 One Step Backward for Mankind 5.5 G
FA: Dick Williams, Pete Burnes, 1975
Jam up the clean fist crack 130 feet right of **Staircliff** to a ledge (crux), then up the corner to the top.

183 Suzzette's Arête 5.8 R
FA: Todd Swain, Sue Rogers, November, 1984
Starting ten feet right of **One Step**, chimney up a right-facing flake, then up a left leaning groove (crux) to the arête. Climb the rounded arête between **One Step** and **Shitkicker**, moving left around the arête near the top.

184 Shitkicker 5.6+ PG
FA: Dick Williams, Dick DuMais, 1972
Starting 30 feet right of **One Step Backward**, climb a shallow left-facing corner and the face on the right to a slab, then up to the base of two steep cracks (5.6+). Up the wider, left crack (V1), moving left at the top.

V1 Fire up the curving, right-hand crack; 5.7.

185 Through the Looking Glass 5.8 G ★
FA: Mike Freeman, John Myers, 1980
Quite a sight! Climb the nose left of **Hippos** to the **Hippos'** crack. Climb the face left of the **Hippos'** crack, then move left to the arête and up the steep face above.

186 Hippos on Parade 5.8 G ★★
FA: Paul Baird, Claude Suhl, Pete Cain, 1975
A good climb that starts 20 feet right of **Shitkicker**. March up a yellow right-facing corner past a roof (crux), then follow the crack and face to the finish.

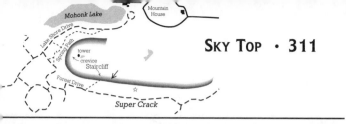
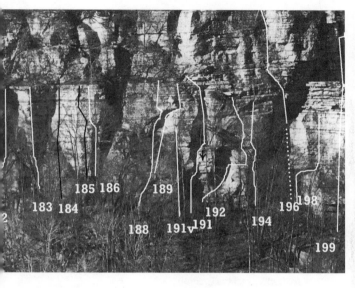

182 **One Step Backward for Mankind 5.5**
183 **Suzzette's Arête 5.8**
184 **Shitkicker 5.6+**
185 **Through the Looking Glass 5.8**
186 **Hippos on Parade 5.8**
188 **Aquavit 5.9**
189 **Aqua Vulva 5.10+**
190 **Dirty Business 5.6**
191 **Frog City 5.9**
192 **Lotus Flower 5.12–**
194 **There Goes the Neighborhood 5.11–**
196 **Hidden Dreams 5.8**
198 **Pop 5.10+**
199 **Pregnant Paws 5.9**

187 Aqualunge 5.10+ G

FA: Ivan Rezucha, Howard Doyle, May, 1993

Rope up ten feet left of **Aquavit** and just right of **Hippos**. Climb past the right edge of a tiny ceiling to a thin flake. Follow the flake up and a bit right to a small tree. Angle left past a grassy ledge, then straight up licheny rock to two trees. Rappel back to your packs.

188 Aquavit 5.9 PG
FA: Ivan Rezucha, July, 1980
The start is often wet. Climb up right-facing flakes on a short wall 35 feet right of **Shitkicker** to lower angled rock (5.9). Climb the steep face ten feet left of the **Aqua Vulva** dihedral to the top.

189 Aqua Vulva 5.10+ PG
FA: Russ Raffa, Howard Doyle, May, 1981
Climb the face right of **Aquavit** to a yellow dihedral, then up this (crux), exiting right to the top.

190 Dirty Business 5.8+ G
FA: Russ Clune, 1982
Layback up the arête left of **Frog City** along a crack (V1) to join **Aqua Vulva** near the top.

V1 Paris 5.6 PG FA: Todd Swain, Sue Rogers, 1984. Climb **Frog City** to the roof, then traverse left to join **Dirty Business** above the crux.

191 Frog City 5.9 G ★★
FA: Dick Williams, Walter Baumann, Paul Baird, 1972. FFA: Dave Loeks, Paul Baird, Pete Cain, 1974
Climb a dihedral 85 feet right of **Shitkicker** to a roof, then move right and up a steep crack/corner (crux) to a ledge and pine tree. Stem up the corner to its top, then up the face (5.7+).

192 Lotus Flower 5.12– R ★
FA: John Myers, Jack Meleski, Mike Freeman, August, 1981
Climb the thin crack just right of **Frog City**, then move right (5.9+) to a ledge. Angle right across the blank face (5.11+ PG) to a belay on **There Goes the Neighborhood** at the nose. Step left, climb a roof (5.11), then up the scooped face (crux, #2 Friend) to the woods.

193 Evenstar 5.8+ PG
FA: Paul Baird, Dave Loeks, 1974
Struggle up a mungy right-facing corner ten feet right of **Frog City** to the ledge, then jam up the overhanging crack (large Friends) to the pine tree belay on **Frog City** (5.8+). Move right to the arête, and up this and the face above, past a roof and flake to the summit.

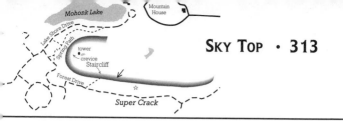

194 There Goes the Neighborhood 5.11– R ★

FA: Mike Freeman, John Myers, June, 1981

The next two climbs start 30 feet right of **Frog City** atop the
remains of a Boy Scout cabin built by the Smiley family in the 1920s.
From the beam on the left side of the cabin, angle left to a left-facing
corner and up this and the face above (crux, slinging the tree growing near cliff makes it a little less scary) to a belay on the arête. Go
up to the roof, step left around the roof right of **Lotus Flower** (long
reach), then up the nose to the top.

195 Burning Shack 5.11+ G

FA: John Myers, Jack Meleski, August, 1981

From the site of the cabin, climb a wide crack, then a roof and bulge
to easier rock, and the trees.

196 Hidden Dreams 5.8 G ★★

FA: Dave Loeks, 1971

Right of **Frog City** about 100 feet, is the **Pinnacle of Suckcess**. In
back of the spire on the main cliff, is a fantastic, left leaning crack.
Exit left around a corner at its top.

197 Secret Hideaway 5.7 PG

FA: Mike Freeman, John Myers, 1981

Climb the somewhat loose crack system right of **Hidden Dreams**.
At the top of the crack traverse left (loose and scary), then up to join
Hidden Dreams to the trees.

198 Pop 5.10+ R

FA: Russ Clune, Jeff Gruenberg, 1984

Start in the cave above and right from the cabin. Hand traverse out
right (crux) to the arête, then straight up the face to the top.

199 Pregnant Paws 5.9 G

FA: Unknown, late 1970s

Not to be confused with **Men-Who-Pause**. On the left front of the
Pinnacle of Suckcess, jam a hand crack over a low roof, then follow
a finger crack above. Angle right to the top of the pinnacle (5.9).
From the top of the spire, climb the left-facing corner, then move out
right at a bush (5.9–), and up the face right of the arête to the top.

196 Hidden Dreams 5.8
199 Pregnant Paws 5.9
200 Pinnacle of Suckcess 5.7+
205 From Here to Infirmity 5.9
206 No Comment 5.11+

207 Tweazle Roof 5.12+
208 Storm Warning 5.10–
209 Blockhead 5.4
210 V Corner 5.3

200 Pinnacle of Suckcess 5.7+ PG

FA: Dick Williams, Dick DuMais, 1972

Climb a short crack on the right (east) face of the spire, then move
around left and up the front face to the top of the pinnacle (5.6).
Leap (or lean) across to the main cliff from the center of the block
(crux), then up a crack system to the trees.

201 Nurdwand 5.8 PG

FA: Todd Swain, Kurt Graf (Swiss), September, 1981

From the right rear corner of the pinnacle, traverse out left to a vertical crack. Up this to the end, exit left to the front face, then up to the
top of the block (5.8). Climb the bushy, left-facing corner above (or
join **Pregnant Paws**).

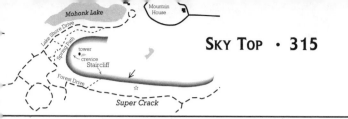

Mohonk Lake

Mountain House

Lake Shore Drive

Spring Path

tower

crevice

Staircliff

Forest Drive

Super Crack

---

202 Crack in the Back 5.4 PG
FA: Dick DuMais, 1970s
Begin at the base of **Nurdwand**. Climb the obvious, chimney/crack
to its top, then step right to a belay (5.4). Angle right to a
crack/seam, then follow this up left to the trail (5.4).

203 Steel Fingers 5.11 R ★★
FA: Russ Clune, Dick Williams, Summer, 1986
Aptly named. Start at a blunt arête 20 feet right of the big pinnacle,
near the left edge of a wide yellow face capped by a roof. Climb up
right on the steep yellow face (V1) past fixed pitons (crux, hard
clip) and a small ceiling. Climb the scary face above, finishing out
an excellent roof (5.8+).

V1 5.11 (TR) FA: John Myers, Jack Meleski, August, 1981. Climb
straight up the arête from the start of the route.

204 Mega Mecca 5.10+ (TR)
FA: Paul Hubbe, 1987
Climb straight up the face ten to 15 feet right of **Steel Fingers**
crossing **From Here to Infirmity**.

205 From Here to Infirmity 5.9 PG
FA: Ivan Rezucha, June, 1980
The protection may be hard to place, even with Friends. From the
start of **Steel Fingers**, move out right into the middle of the orange
face, then up and right along a horizontal to the arête. Angle back
left to a jug, then up right to the belay ledge (5.9). Rappel, or traverse right, then up easier ground to the shrubs.

206 No Comment 5.11+ PG ★★★
FA: Kevin Bein, May, 1979
Probably Bein's best route at the Gunks. He perished on the
Matterhorn in 1988, after over 20 years of top level rock climbing.
Starting 30 feet left of **Storm Warning** (V1), climb a thin dihedral
(V2) to a ceiling. Step right (if you move 15 feet right you can get a
no hands rest), and climb a vertical seam to a ceiling (V3). Move left
to a stance, then up and right to another. Climb more thin seams to
a large ledge with a rappel anchor.

V1 Begin to the right of the regular route and angle up right along a crack to a stance on **The Tweazle Roof**. Move up to the no hands rest on the regular route, then left to rejoin the climb at the vertical seam; 5.11– PG.

V2 Partway up the first corner, move right and climb the scary face to the vertical seam; 5.11 R.

V3 Instead of moving left to the stance, climb straight up past the overhang; 5.12.

207 The Tweazle Roof 5.12+ PG ★
FA: Lynn Hill, 1987
Attempted and protected previously by others. Climb the face (5.9 X) and roof (5.12+) right of **No Comment** past fixed pegs.

208 Storm Warning 5.10– G ★
FA: Dave Loeks, Paul Baird, 1974
70 feet right of the **Pinnacle of Suckcess**, jam and layback up an orange, left-facing corner (crux) to a roof, then move out right and up to a belay. Rappel, or move right and up past two ledges to the trees.

209 Blockhead 5.4 G
FA: Mike Steele (solo), September, 1984
Climb a crack/chimney system around right from **Storm Warning**, joining **Storm Warning** 15 feet below the top.

210 V Corner 5.3 PG
FA: Unknown, 1980s
Climb the bush and tree filled chimney/corner to the right of **Blockhead**.

NOTE: About 150 feet right of the Pinnacle of Suckcess is the Supercrack Pinnacle. The next five climbs and a good descent route are on the main cliff up behind the spire. This section of cliff is known as the Eastern Bloc Wall.

211 Iron Curtain 5.13– PG
FA (TR): Al Diamond, 1986. FA (lead): Al Diamond, Kevin Bein, Russ Clune, Spring, 1986
Scramble up behind the left side of the spire. The two hard routes here are on the left side of the main wall and were pre-protected on rappel with pins and slings. A crucial hold broke on this route, making it harder. Climb the left hand weaknesses to the top.

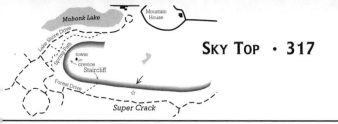

Mohonk Lake

Mountain House

Lake Shore Drive
Spring Path
Forest Drive

tower
crevice
Staircliff

☆

Super Crack

212 Diplomatic Strain 5.12+ PG13

FA: Scott Franklin, Spring, 1986

Top-roped and protected before it was first led. This line takes the weaknesses just left of **Toddling Along**.

213 Toddling Along 5.6 G

FA: Todd Swain, Thom Scheuer, November, 1981

Climb a left-facing corner to a roof, then exit left (crux) to the top.

214 Teeter-Toddling 5.8 G

FA: Todd Swain (rope solo), October, 1984

Teeter directly up the arête between **Toddling** and **Ranger Danger**.

215 Ranger Danger 5.8 PG

FA: Todd Swain, Thom Scheuer, October, 1984

Attempted previously, but due to difficult protection, a second try was needed. Bring a #2.5 Friend and/or a #0 TCU. Up the dihedral right of **Toddling** to the ceiling, then climb up left through the ceiling to the top.

216 Pinnacle Rock Descent Class 4

The descent route follows the chimney 20 feet to the right of **Ranger Danger**, and behind the Supercrack Pinnacle (aka Pinnacle Rock).

217 Genetic Culling 5.7+ X

FA: Todd Swain, Dave Levenstein, July, 1986

Levenstein worked as a Mohonk Preserve Ranger. Climb the black streak to a short left-facing corner on the left (west) face of the Supercrack Pinnacle.

218 Jism 5.10 R

FA: Doug Hall (UK), Louise Shepherd (Australian), October, 1980

Shoot up the scary face right of **Genetic Culling**. The crux is moving past a small ceiling. Descend off the back.

219 Supercrack 5.12 G ★★★

FA: Unknown, 1960s. FFA: Steve Wunsch, 1974

Also known as Wunsch Upon a Climb. Blast up the overhanging finger crack on the front of the spire that is 150 feet right of the Pinnacle of Suckcess.

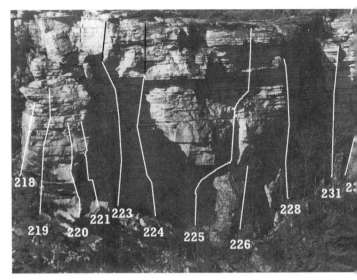

218 Jism 5.10
219 Supercrack 5.12
220 The Sprinter 5.12–
221 Chunky Monkey 5.10–
223 Taste of Honey 5.7
224 Energy Crisis 5.11+

225 October Country 5.9+
227 Blind Ambition 5.11–
228 Great Power Within 5.7
231 Jungle Land 5.5
232 After Birth 5.4

220 The Sprinter 5.12– (TR) ★★
FA: Jeff Gruenberg, Jack Meleski, Spring, 1986
Climb the arête right of **Supercrack**.

221 Chunky Monkey 5.10– PG ★
FA: Paul Baird, Dean Rau, 1977
From the top of a block right of **Supercrack**, climb up to a right-facing corner, then over a roof to the top of the block. The crux is off the block, and rather tricky.

222 Shadow Land 5.8 R
FA: Ivan Rezucha, Annie O'Neill, May, 1994
Start at a tree in the gully just left of **Taste of Honey**. Climb a

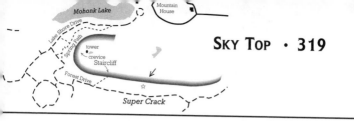

Super Crack

groove, then onto the arête (5.8 R). Move left around the arête to a
ledge (or belay further left on chockstones in the gully). Up the
steep face (5.8) until the angle eases (possible belay here).
Continue up and climb the final overhang just left of its widest point.

223 Taste of Honey 5.7 PG ★
FA: John Waterman, Al Rubin, 1969
Exposed on P2. Up a nice dihedral just right of the Supercrack
Pinnacle to a belay stance under the roofs (5.6). Out left around the
nose (crux, V1), then up the steep face to the top.

V1 Climb up right from the belay along a notch in the roof; 5.9.

224 Energy Crisis 5.11+ PG
FA: Hugh Herr, Russ Clune October, 1981
Fairly scary, especially if you have a crisis. Power up the right arching cracks just right of **Taste of Honey**, then move left and pull the
ceiling (5.11) to a lower angled face. Follow seams to a belay. Angle
right to a spot where the roof is of reasonable size, then over this
and on to the summit.

225 October Country 5.9+ PG ★★
FA: Dick DuMais, Dick Williams, 1969. FFA: John Bragg, Ivan
Rezucha, 1975
Double ropes helpful — the second pitch is a little loose. Starting 65
feet right of the Supercrack Pinnacle, follow a thin crack off a block
to the roof (V1). Move right to the nose, then up a corner to a belay
(5.9+). Angle right past a weakness in the roof (5.8), then up right to
the top.

V1 From partway up the thin crack, step left and climb the face to
the roof. Move back right to rejoin the climb; 5.9 R.

226 Blind Faith 5.11– R
FA: John Myers, Mike Freeman, August, 1981
Climb an orange, left-facing corner 15 feet left of **Great Power
Within** (V1), then traverse just below the ceiling (crux, scary for the
second also) to join **October Country** to the first belay. Move left to
a notch in the roof, then climb the left-facing corner above.

V1 5.12 (TR) FA: Jack Meleski, Jeff Gruenberg, Spring, 1986. Climb
a steep face to an overlap 15 feet up. Pass the overlap on its right
(crux), traverse right five feet, then straight up the face.

227 Blind Ambition 5.11– PG ★★

FA: Rich Perch, Corey Jones, October, 1978

Hard to protect and sustained. Bring lots of small wires. Climb the initial corner on **Blind Faith** until you can move right to another corner. Up this (crux), then right again following a crack to join **Great Power Within**.

228 Great Power Within 5.7 PG ★

FA: Burt Angrist, Dick Williams, 1969

Steep and exciting. Climb the overhanging and left leaning crack system 110 feet right of the Supercrack Pinnacle.

229 The Goobully Gully 5.1 PG

FA: Unknown, 1980s

Climb the dirty chimney right of the **Great Power Within**.

230 Bonsai Buttress 5.9 G

FA: Todd Swain, Annie O'Neill, November, 1981

Starting just right of a gully that is right of **Great Power**, climb a thin crack past a roof (V1), then diagonal right to a belay under an obvious prow (5.9). Swing out onto the front of the buttress, then up this to the weeds.

V1 Climb directly up the thin crack just left of the start of the regular route; 5.10.

231 Jungle Land 5.5 G

FA: Todd Swain, Annie O'Neill, November, 1981

Up the left chimney just right of **Bonsai Buttress** to the belay right of the prow (5.4), then up the right-facing corner above (5.5).

232 After Birth 5.4 G

FA: Al Rubin, John Waterman, 1969

Climb the right-hand chimney/crack 30 feet right of **Great Power Within**. The crux is just below the final ceilings (V1).

V1 Climb the right-facing corner just left of the second pitch; 5.5.

233 Goat Man Rides Again 5.7 G

FA: Dan MacMillan, Ward and Chris Smith, June, 1981

Ride on up the face right of the **After Birth** chimney to a belay ledge (5.4, bushy). Straight up past a roof at a thin crack (crux), then angle right to a pine tree on the top.

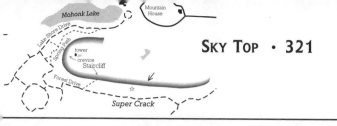

Mohonk Lake

Mountain House

Lake Shore Drive

Spring Path

tower
crevice
Staircliff

Forest Drive

☆

Super Crack

230   232v   233   234   236   239

228 Great Power Within 5.7
230 Bonsai Buttress 5.9
232v After Birth Variation 5.5
233 Goat Man Rides Again 5.7

234 Out to Pasture 5.8+
236 The Jug is Up 5.10
239 Too Steep
   For My Lichen 5.11–

234 Out to Pasture 5.8+ PG

FA: Todd Swain, Annie O'Neill, November, 1981

Climb a corner ten feet left of **The Jug Is Up** to a stance, then left and up a thin crack (crux) to the belay. Up a small, right-facing corner to the woods.

235 Out of Africa 5.9+ PG

FA: Todd Swain (solo), August, 1986

Climb thin seams five feet left of **The Jug Is Up**. Move left, and up to a large horizontal (even with the tree on **The Jug Is Up**). Continue up dirty rock above, or move right and rappel. Crux is the first ten feet.

236 The Jug Is Up 5.10 PG ★
FA: Rich Perch, Bill Ravitch, Mark Robinson, October, 1980
Starting 20 feet left of **Too Steep For My Lichen**, face climb up a thin vertical crack to an obvious pine tree (5.10). Rappel, or move left, then up past a big roof on the left to the top.

237 The Greatest of Ease 5.8 G
FA: Paul Duval, Al Rubin, Summer, 1980
Better than it looks. Climb a slightly right leaning crack/corner 15 feet left of **Too Steep** past a ledge to a horizontal (crux), then move left to the pine on **The Jug**. Rappel, or climb the right-facing corner past the right side of the roof above.

238 Stop Wearing Dresses Mr. Williams 5.8 R
FA: Bill Ravitch, Rich Perch, Mark Robinson, Fall, 1980
Starting on **Too Steep**, climb the left–arching corner to join **The Greatest of Ease** at the horizontal.

239 Too Steep For My Lichen 5.11– G ★★
FA: Sandy Stewart, Mike Sawicky, 1976
And too hard for just hikin'. The taller you are, the easier it is. From the base of a flake 100 feet right of **After Birth**, climb up left, then back right to enter the clean, left-facing corner (V1). Up the corner, then exit right to the same belay as **Wipe Out** (5.11–). Step back left and up the left hand corner to the top (5.10+).

V1 Climb straight up the face into the corner; 5.11.

240 Wipe Out 5.10– G ★
FA: Dick Williams, Paul Baird, 1972
Pump up the short, low, overhanging cracks ten feet right of **Too Steep** to a right-facing corner and up this to a belay ledge (5.10–). Rappel, or climb the dirty corner in the back of the ledge to the top.

241 Wipe Up 5.10+ PG
FA: Darrow and Caroline Kirkpatrick, July, 1986
Climb steep cracks just right of the start of **Wipe Out** to a ledge, then move left and climb the steep corner directly above the first pitch of **Wipe Out**. At the top of the corner, exit left to a ledge, then back right and up a steep, thin crack (hard and exposed).

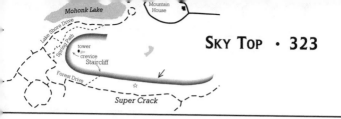

Mohonk Lake
Mountain House
Lake Shore Drive
Spring Path
tower
crevice
Staircliff
Forest Drive
Super Crack

242 The Spider's Lair 5.1 PG
FA: Unknown, 1980s
Climb the cobweb filled chimney right of **Wipe Out**.

243 The Flake Out 5.6 G
FA: Dick and Toni Williams, Pete Burnes, Claude Suhl, 1975
Up a right-facing corner 80 feet right of **Wipe Out**, then right and
up a dihedral to a ledge (20 feet). Move right and climb the left-
hand crack system past a flake to another ledge. Climb the right-
facing corner to the top.

244 Gimme Shelter 5.8– R
FA: Dick & Toni Williams, Pete Burnes, 1975
A little scary on the crux. Climb a right leaning fault 100 feet right of
Wipe Out and 150 feet left of **Pilgrim's Progress**, moving left at 15
feet and up a crack to a ledge. Follow an obvious flake system to its
top, step right (crux), then up past a bulge to the woods.

245 The Polish Connection 5.8 G ★
FA: Dick and Toni Williams, Dave Craft, 1975
Starting as for **Gimme Shelter**, climb up the leaning fault past a roof
on the right to a ledge at 35 feet. Up the right-leaning, right-facing
corner past a roof (crux) to the top.

246 Static Electricity 5.10+ R
FA: Todd Swain, Iza Trapani, Summer, 1985
Top-roped prior to being led. Climb the small flakes and face just
left of **Greased Lightning**, moving slightly right at a small horizontal
then up more small flakes to the ledge.

247 Greased Lightning 5.10+ PG ★
FA: John Myers, Mike Freeman, Jack Meleski, July, 1981
A popular climb for dry days. Climb the clean, right leaning finger
crack just right of **The Polish Connection** past a bulge (5.10+ G) to
a horizontal. Move left a few feet (V1), then up to the ledge. Rappel,
or climb the middle of the face above (5.10 PG).

V1 Continue straight up (5.10++ PG).

248 St. Elmo's Fire 5.9 PG
FA: Mike Freeman, John Myers, Jack Meleski, Danny Costa, July, 1981
Climb the face just right of **Greased Lightning** to the ledge. If you
wish to continue, climb the bulging face above keeping left of the
Down Right Cleaner chimney.

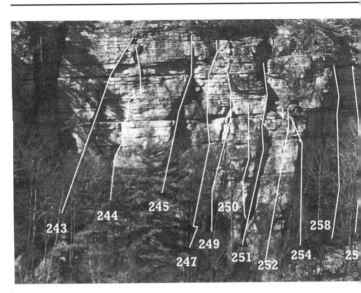

243 The Flake Out 5.6

244 Gimme Shelter 5.8–

245 The Polish Connection 5.8

247 Greased Lightning 5.10+

249 Down Right Cleaner 5.5

250 Rolling Thunder 5.10

251 Crack of Dawn 5.6+

252 LSD 5.11

254 Land of Milk and Honey 5.10+

258 Fallen Monkeys
      Gather No Moss 5.7–

259 Open Casket 5.10+

249 Down Right Cleaner 5.5 G

FA: Dick and Toni Williams, Pete Burnes, 1975

This climb could stand to be down right cleaner. Wade up the slightly right leaning chimney/crack system just right of **Greased Lightning**, starting in a right-facing corner.

250 Rolling Thunder 5.10 G

FA: John Myers, Mike Freeman, July, 1981

Climb **Crack of Dawn** for 15 feet, then layback into a finger crack (crux) to the left of the chimney. Follow the crack past small ceilings to a ledge. Climb past a small overhang to the woods.

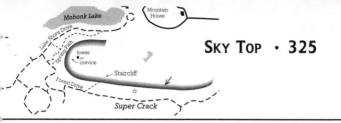

Mohonk Lake

Mountain House

Lake Shore Drive

Spring Path

tower

crevice

Staircliff

Forest Drive

Super Crack

251 Crack of Dawn 5.6+ R

FA: John Myers, Mike Freeman, July, 1981

Struggle up the chimney right of **Down Right Cleaner**, then up the right-facing corners above.

252 LSD (aka Lichen Strikes Direct) 5.11 R ★

FA (TR): Bill Ravitch, 1985. FA (lead): Todd Swain, Bob Hostetter, 1986

Toproped by Swain before being led. Climb a thin seam just left of the **Lichen Strikes** nose to the horizontal, then straight up a slab past a bulge and another seam (crux) to the belay.

253 Lichen Strikes 5.10 PG

FA: John Myers, Mike Freeman, July, 1981

Layback up flakes on the nose just left of **Land of Milk and Honey** (5.10–), moving out left to a ledge. Climb up the left side of the face to the tree on **Land of Milk and Honey**. Rappel, or climb straight to the top.

254 Land of Milk and Honey 5.10+ G ★★

FA: Sandy Stewart, Paul Niland, Rich Ross, Mike Sawicky, 1976

The Horn of Plenty when it comes to good moves. Climb flakes up and left over a small roof. Move slightly left, then up and right to a left-facing corner capped by a ceiling. Exit left to a prominent pine tree belay. Rappel, or follow **Lichen Strikes** to the summit.

255 Abracadaver 5.11+ R ★★

FA: Sandy Stewart, Mark Robinson, Eric Keto, April,1979

Fairly scary. Climb flakes just right of **Land of Milk** to a sentry box about 40 feet up. Exit right (crux), then up the steep face to an overhanging crack on the left. Up this to a roof, then escape left to the **Land of Milk and Honey** belay. Rappel, or follow **Lichen Strikes** to the top.

256 Hocus Croakus 5.11+ PG

FA: Mike Freeman, September, 1982

Kim Carrigan tried this prior to Freeman's success. Being tall is very helpful. Follow a crack just right of **Abracadaver** to a roof, then over this (crux, long reach) to the trees.

257 Acid Rain 5.7+ PG
FA: John Myers, Mike Freeman, 1981
Struggle up a crack system 35 feet left of **Desp-arête** and five feet right of **Hocus Croakus**, then up the left-hand corner to the roof. Over this (crux), then up the face to the top.

258 Fallen Monkeys Gather No Moss 5.7– PG
FA: Paul Baird, Burt Angrist, 1975
Climb a tricky face 25 feet left of **Desp-arête** to the base of an obvious right-facing corner (5.6 PG), then up the right-hand corner (5.7–) to the top.

259 Open Casket 5.10+ R
FA: John Myers, Mike Freeman, July, 1981
An impressive lead. Make sure your health insurance is paid up before venturing onto this one! Start as for **Fallen Monkeys**, then step right and climb the middle of the face (scary 5.10, small RPs) past big ceilings (5.10, #3.5 Friend) to the top.

260 Walter's Route 5.6 G
FA: Walter Baumann, Dave Craft, 1975
Very popular. Climb the obvious left-facing corner just left of the prominent nose of **Desp-arête** to the top. Rappel.

261 Desp-arête 5.8+ PG
FA: Mike Steele (solo), September, 1984
Starting on the left face, climb the prominent arête 35 feet left of **A Pilgrim's Progress** to the top. Steele wrote the climbing guide to Delaware Water Gap.

262 Knot Two Are Lichen 5.5 G
FA: Todd Swain, Thom Scheuer, Karl Beard, Bob Larsen, November, 1981
An enjoyable climb for bad spellers. All of the FA party worked as rangers at the Gunks. Jam up a crack in the corner left of **A Pilgrim's Progress**, then step left and up another crack (crux) to a ledge. Up the steep face to join **Desp-arête** at the top. Rappel from the pine.

263 Three Stooges 5.7 G
FA: Chris and Ward Smith, Dan MacMillan, June, 1980
Starting on **Knot Two**, layback up the flake on the right, then up the easy face to the top.

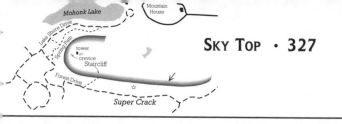

Mohonk Lake

Mountain House

tower
crevice
Staircliff

Lake Shore Drive
Spring Path
Forest Drive

☆

Super Crack

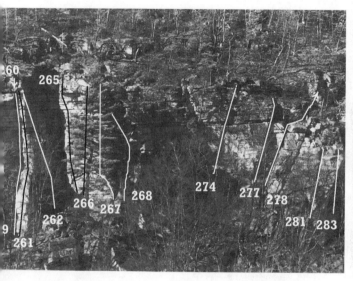

264 Dungeons and Dragons 5.2 G

FA: Todd Swain (solo), November, 1981

Climb up the deep chimney just left of **A Pilgrim's Progress**.

265 Pangallactic Gargleblaster 5.11+ G

FA: Ken Goto, Todd Swain, September, 1986

Also found at the restaurant at the end of the universe! Climb the arête left of **A Pilgrim's Progress** past two pins. Maybe harder if you are tall.

266 A Pilgrim's Progress 5.8 G ★★★
FA: Dave Loeks, Paul Baird, Walter Baumann, 1974
Probably the second best 5.8 at Sky Top. Starting behind a huge
pine tree and 35 feet right of an obvious arête, jam up the finger
crack (crux), then past two roofs to the top.

NOTE: Various descents for this section of the cliff are: Jump into the
pine tree in front of **Pilgrim's**, then down climb that (believe it or
not, its been done!); rappel from the top of **Walter's Route**; or downclimb **Sandstone Chimney** (further right).

267 Purely Psychological 5.11 R
FA: Hugh Herr, Mike Sawicky, 1983
Wander up the blank face just right of **Pilgrim's**, with tricky protection (cliffhanger on flake helpful). The arête to the right has been
climbed, but no more is known.

268 The Scottish Connection 5.5 G
FA: Paul Moores (UK), Todd Swain, November, 1981
Paul Moores owns the only climbing shop in Glencoe, Scotland. Up
the dirty corner 30 feet right **Pilgrim's**, then up the left leaning
crack (crux) to the top.

269 Swineworld 5.8 G
FA: Todd Swain, Bob Anderberg, September, 1984
Start on the previous route, then up into a hanging corner on the
right (crux) to a roof. Climb this at a thin seam to the top.

270 Screw Tape Roof 5.10 G
FA: Dick Williams, Joe Bridges, Anne Fassler, Summer, 1988
Starting at a black birch tree just right of the previous climb, climb
the center of the small buttress to its top (tricky climbing, sling tree
for pro—FA party also tied the tree into cliff for added safety).
Climb the ceiling above in the center at a thin crack (crux).

271 Roast Pigs 5.7 PG
FA: Joe Bridges, Dick Williams, June, 1988
Climb the right side of the buttress 45 feet right of **Pilgrim's** to its
top. Climb a flake to the obvious ceiling, then traverse left to finish
on **Swineworld**.

272 Moore Than We Bargained For 5.8 PG
FA: Todd Swain, Paul Moores (UK) November, 1981
Climb the clean face 55 feet right of **Pilgrim's** to a right-leaning
flake. Up this (crux) past a roof to the woods.

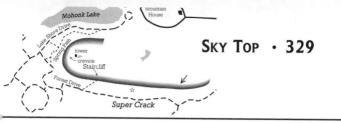

Mohonk Lake

Mountain House

Lake Shore Drive
Spring Path
tower
crevice
Staircliff
Forest Drive

Super Crack

---

273 Est-tu Pret? Arête 5.8 PG
FA: Joe Bridges, Anne Fassler, Dick Williams, Fall, 1988
Be ready for this one. Start just left of **Cresta Climb** at a shallow alcove. Climb the pebbly groove up to the outside corner, then up this to the top. Rappel from the large tree near the top of the corner.

274 Cresta Climb 5.6 G
FA: Paul Moores (UK), Todd Swain, November, 1981
Named for an ice climb on Ben Nevis in Scotland. Climb the obvious, bushy, right-facing corner 75 feet right of **Pilgrim's**.

275 Come Gardening 5.7 G
FA: Paul Moores (UK), Todd Swain, November, 1981
Named for a popular British TV show. Climb a short left-facing corner five feet right of the previous route, then up another left-facing corner to the trees.

276 Whoopla 5.9 PG
FA: Dick Williams, 1988
Cleaned and protected before being led. An expression used by Fritz Wiessner. Start at a large flake on the face between the obvious corner systems. From the top of the flake, angle right on the lichen covered face, then up to the top.

277 Creag Dubh Corner 5.8 G
FA: Todd Swain, Paul Moores (UK), November, 1981
Stem up the clean corner just left of **Sandstone Chimney**.

278 Sandstone Chimney Class 4
A useful descent route. Climb up, or down the chimney 120 feet right of **A Pilgrim's Progress**. This route had a glacial erratic sandstone boulder wedged in it in 1981. The boulder most likely came from the Catskills during the last ice age.

279 November 5.0 G
FA: Todd Swain, Paul Moores (both solo), November, 1981
This was one of 13 first ascents done in a day by Swain and Moores. It's also the name of a terrible route on Cannon Cliff in N.H. Climb the large right-leaning crack and face five feet right of **Sandstone Chimney**.

280 A Stroll With Hot Toddie 5.1 PG
FA: Paul Moores (UK), Todd Swain (both solo), November, 1981
Stroll up the middle of a low angled face 20 feet right of **Sandstone Chimney**.

281 Jordie Bum 5.5 PG

FA: Todd Swain, Paul Moores (UK) (both solo), November, 1981
Moore's nickname for his wife. Climb up a steep corner to a crack, then struggle up an offwidth to the woods.

282 Stupor Man 5.9 PG

FA: Felix Modugno, Mack Johnson, September, 1981
Start up **Stupor Crack** (5.9), then move left at the offwidth and up the face (5.8) to a dirty finish.

283 Stupor Crack 5.9 PG ★

FA: Dan MacMillan, Ward & Chris Smith, June, 1981
Strenuous. Jam up the widening crack on a nose 40 feet right of **Sandstone Chimney** to an overhanging offwidth (crux) and the top.

284 Moore-On Than Off 5.4 G

FA: Paul Moores (UK), Todd Swain (both solo), November, 1981
Starting 70 feet right of **Sandstone Chimney**, clamber up a chimney and crack to a ledge around to the right. Follow a right leaning crack to the top.

285 Clachaig Crack 5.2 PG

FA: Paul Moores (UK), Todd Swain (both solo), November, 1981
Named for the popular pub in Glencoe, Scotland. Climb a thin crack 15 feet right of **Moore-On** to a ledge, then follow the right leaning crack to the trees.

286 In the Heat of the Fright 5.6 PG

FA: Dick Williams, Dave Craft, 1988
Rope up at a right facing corner that is 20 feet right of **Clachaig Crack**. Climb up past a ledge, then move left to a right facing corner. Climb the corner to a broken section of cliff and finish up a narrow face.

287 Scot Free 5.2 G

FA: Paul Moores (UK), Todd Swain (both solo), November, 1981
Swim up a 9" wide crack 60 feet right of **Moore-On** to a ledge, then belay on the ledge above. Move right along a flake, then up a corner and steep face to the summit.

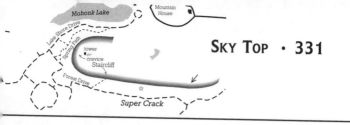

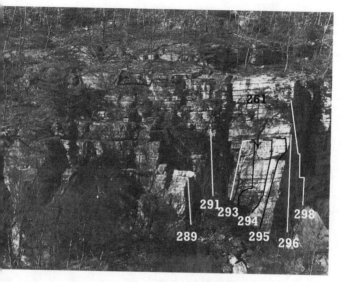

289 Seasonal Positions 5.9
291 Nuclear Arms 5.10–
293 Solitaire 5.9–
294 Trouble in Paradise 5.11

295 Single File 5.9
296 Crank and File 5.11
297 Pumping Pygmies 5.13
298 Max Factor 5.11

288 Tree House of the August Sun 5.9 PG13
FA: Dick Williams, Dave Craft, 1988

Begin ten feet left of **Scot Free** and climb the face to a ceiling. Move right, then angle left to a corner. Angle back right to a belay at some blocks (5.9). From some trees, follow a seam up right to a ledge. Angle left to another ledge, then up to the woods, finishing just right of a pine (5.5).

289 Seasonal Positions (aka Appetizer) 5.9 G
FA: Todd Swain, Dave Levenstein, July, 1985

150 feet right of **Sandstone Chimney** are two buttresses with vertical cracks on them. This route climbs the short crack on the left buttress.

290 Piece-A-Cake 5.9+ R
FA: Dick Williams, Anne Fassler, 1988
Angle right from the top of a large block to a horizontal (5.9 R), then go up past a ledge to the summit.

291 Nuclear Arms (aka Tendon Rip-Air) 5.10– PG
FA: Chris Monz, Ivan Rezucha, 1986
On the main cliff to the right of **Seasonal Positions**, climb a seam and a small corner to the top with difficult protection.

292 Anonymous Climb of the 15th Century 5.9 R
FA: C. Columbus, J. Guttenberg, circa 1450
This climb was first documented by Guttenberg. Start in the back, right corner of the alcove at a short, chimney and corner system. Climb the corner system, eventually exiting right to the rappel tree on **Solitaire**.

293 Solitaire 5.9– PG ★
FA: Unknown, pre-1981
On the right buttress 150 feet right of **Sandstone Chimney**, climb the thin left-hand crack to a pine tree. Difficult to protect. Often top-roped after doing **Single File**.

294 Trouble in Paradise 5.11 R
FA: Todd Swain, Sue Rogers, Summer, 1986
Top-roped in 1985, then led in 1986. Climb the face between **Solitaire** and **Single File** starting on the left.

295 Single File 5.9 G ★★
FA: Paul Sinacore, Harvey Arnold, June, 1980
Jam up the beautiful finger crack 15 feet right of **Solitaire** past a bulge to the ledge with the pine tree.

296 Crank and File 5.11 PG13
FA: Rich Gottlieb, Darrow Kirkpatrick, Jan Schwarzberg, Summer, 1986
Crank up the thin seam on the arête right of **Single File** (crux), then continue up the edge to the tree.

297 Pumping Pygmies 5.13 (TR)
FA: Al Diamond, Russ Clune, Summer, 1986
The route was extensively top-roped and the protection was placed on rappel. An irate local removed the two pins and the bolt soon after the only lead. Ascend the overhung, white wall that is left of **Max Factor**.

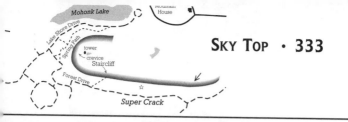

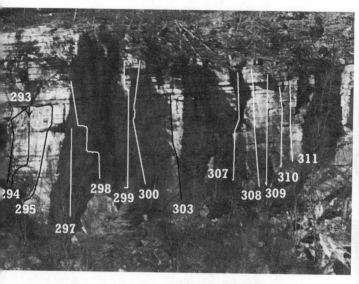

293 Solitare 5.9–
294 Trouble in Paradise 5.11
295 Single File 5.9
297 Pumping Pygmies 5.13
298 Max Factor 5.11
299 Perspiration Point 5.7+
300 She Didn't Show 5.10+

303 Oh Brother! 5.9
307 Shock-ease Ceiling 5.6
308 Fevered Pitch 5.9
309 Packman 5.7
310 Simple Minds 5.10
311 Simple Simon 5.11–

298 Max Factor 5.11 PG ★

FA: Ivan Rezucha, Don Lauber, November, 1981

Many people have maxed out on this one. On the opposite (right) side of the **Single File** buttress, start in a gully below a steep, white face. Traverse out left along a horizontal, then up a thin vertical (crux) to another horizontal. Move up and left, then up another vertical crack to easier ground.

299 Perspiration Point 5.7+ PG
FA: Todd Swain, Peggy Buckey, Randy and Andy Schenkel, August, 1985
Named for the typical August weather in the Gunks. Start 50 feet right of **Single File** at a leaning, right-facing corner on the right side of a nose. Up the corner to its top, then move right across a tricky face (5.7+) to a ledge in a right-facing corner. Up the overhanging left wall past a roof to the top (5.7+).

300 She Didn't Show 5.10+ G
FA: Peter Behme, Rick Cronk, October, 1980
Climb a huge flake just right of **Perspiration Point** until below a big roof in a right-facing corner. Climb over the roof at a flake/crack (crux) to a ledge (touching **Perspiration Point**), then up the right face to the trees.

301 Durango 5.7 G
FA: Paul Sinacore, Harvey Arnold, June, 1980
Up the corner and crack five feet right of **She Didn't Show**.

302 To Go Where No Man Has Gone 5.6– G
FA: Andy and Randy Schenkel, Peggy Buckey, Todd Swain, August, 1985
It's the only reason for doing a route like this! Climb the crack just right of **Durango**.

303 Oh Brother! 5.9 X
FA: (TR) Andy Schenkel, Todd Swain, August, 1985. FA: (solo) Todd Swain, Summer, 1986
Climb the steep arête between **To Go** and **Brothers Left** and (crux, possible blind #1 RP placement), then up the dirty face above (tricky).

304 Brothers Left 5.6– G
FA: Bill and Scott Ewing, Brian Cronk, September, 1979
Ascend the right-facing corner 30 feet right of **She Didn't Show** past a roof.

305 Bellevue is Beautiful 5.9 G
FA (initial crack): Harvey Arnold, Paul Sinacore, June, 1980. FA (complete): Burt Angrist, Dick Williams, 1988
Climb a crack five feet right of **Brothers Left** to a ceiling (V1), then continue through a ceiling at a notch.

V1 5.5 G Escape right to join **Brothers Right**.

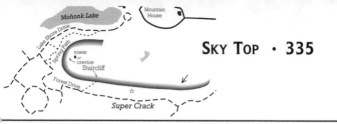

306 Brothers Right 5.5 G

FA: Rick and Brian Cronk, September, 1979

Up a right-facing corner 50 feet right of **She Didn't Show** to a
ledge, then up another corner on the left.

307 Shock-ease Ceiling 5.6 G

FA: Ward and Chris Smith, Mark Nelson, June, 1981

Up a shallow left-facing corner 15 feet right of **Brothers Right** to an
alcove, then up out of this (crux) to the top.

308 Fevered Pitch 5.9 R ★

FA: Todd Swain, Thom Scheuer, July, 1985

Climb the face and arête just right of **Shock-ease** to a horizontal
(5.9), move right, then up thin cracks in a white face (5.8+ R) to the
roof. Out the roof at a prominent left-facing corner (crux).

309 Packman (aka Simple Pleasures) 5.7 G ★★

FA: Burt Angrist, Dick Williams, 1973

Jam up the delightful finger crack 20 feet right of **Shock-ease** past
the right side of a ceiling to the woods.

310 Simple Minds 5.10 PG

FA: Ivan Rezucha, Chris Monz, October, 1985

Up the obvious vertical seam just right of **Packman** (crux), then the
easy face above. Difficult to protect.

311 Simple Simon 5.11– PG

FA: (TR) Todd Swain, Tad Welch, September, 1986. FA: (lead) Todd
Swain, October, 1986

Climb the flake five feet right of **Simple Minds**, then up the dirty
face above.

312 Clumsy Foot 5.8– PG ★

FA: Doug Alcock, Jock van Patten, July, 1986

Start 60 feet right of **Packman** below a large, left-facing corner with
a white arête. Climb a crack just left of the arête (5.8-; easier if you
start further left), then climb the face past two horizontals and a
bulge (5.7 if you keep right) to the top.

310 Milk and Cookies 5.10– PG ★

FA: Darrow and Caroline Kirkpatrick, July, 1986

Start directly below the arête to the right of **Clumsy Foot**. Climb
over a bulge to a ramp. Traverse left above a ceiling to the nose,
then up this to the top.

314 Todd Jobs Class 4
FD: Ned Crossley, Harry Cartland, Summer, 1986
A route right of the **Clumsy Foot** arête.

315 Happiness Is Not a 198 Pound Weakling 5.9– PG
FA: Dick Williams, Dave Craft, 1988
Rope up 20 feet right of **Milk and Cookies** at a dihedral. Climb the corner for 15 feet, then move left and up past a slab and bulge to a stance below a ceiling. Continue up to join **Emanuel Labor** at the left edge of the summit roof. Climb the gully to the trees.

316 Emanuel Labor 5.9 PG
FA: Morris Hershoff, Scott Franklin, 1985
Start 80 feet right of **Packman** below an orange buttress. Work up a slab (5.7+, V1) to a shallow right-facing dihedral. Up the dihedral (crux), then angle left to a gully and the woods.

V1 Start up **Andy Man** and swing left about 15 feet up (5.9) to join the regular route.

317 Andy Man 5.9 PG
FA: Todd Swain, Ned Crossley, July, 1987
Climb the diagonal crack ten feet right of **Emanuel Labor** past blocks to the roof. Traverse left and pull the roof at the nose.

318 Jacques of all Trades 5.9 G
FA: Todd Swain, Ned Crossley, July, 1987
Start at an obvious 4" crack 15 feet right of **Emanuel Labor**. Climb the crack to a flake and the roof. Out the roof at an obvious offwidth (crux, #4 Camalot or larger needed).

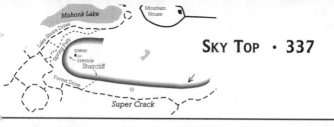

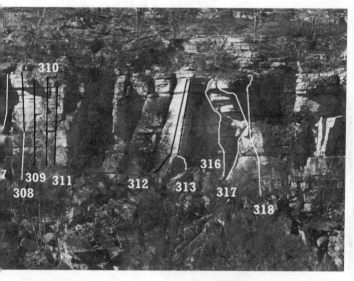

307 Shock-ease Celing 5.6
308 Fevered Pitch 5.9
309 Packman 5.7
310 Simple Minds 5.10
311 Simple Simon 5.11–

312 Clumsy Foot 5.8–
313 Milk and Cookies 5.10–
316 Emanuel Labor 5.9
317 Andy Man 5.9
318 Jacques of all Trades 5.9

Climbing is Dangerous! Stack the Odds in your Favor.

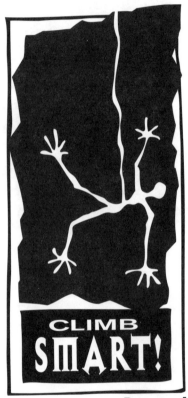

- Check your knots and harness buckle
- Inspect your gear and replace as necessary
- Know your partners and their habits
- Check your belay—are you sure you're on?
- Read all warnings—they can save your life
- Fixed gear is unreli-able--back it up when possible
- Keep an eye on the weather
- Rock breaks—check your holds
- Always double check your rappel system

- Remember -
your safety is your responsibility

Climb Smart! is a public information program of the Climbing Sports Group, the trade association of the climbing industry.

Routes by Rating

Class 4, 5.0 and 5.1

- [ ] **Goldner's Grunge** Class 4 (Trapps) 115
- [ ] **Pigeon and Smegma Garden** Class 4 (Trapps) 104
- [ ] **Pinnacle Rock Descent** Class 4 (Sky Top) 317
- [ ] **Radcliffe** Class 4 (Trapps) **38**, 39
- [ ] **Roger's Escape Hatch** Class 4 (Trapps) 152, **153**, **155**
- [ ] **Sandstone Chimney** Class 4 (Sky Top) **327**, 329
- [ ] **Todd Jobs** Class 4 (Sky Top) 336
- [ ] **Crimson Corner** 5.0 G (Trapps) 37
- [ ] **Dirty Chimney** 5.0 G (Trapps) **30**, 32
- [ ] **Hand Jam** 5.0 G (Sky Top) **271**, 270
- [ ] **November** 5.0 G (Sky Top) 329
- [ ] **Easy** 5.1 G ★ (Sky Top) **287**, 288
- [ ] **The Flake** 5.1 PG (Trapps) 36
- [ ] **The Goobully Gully** 5.1 PG (Sky Top) 320
- [ ] **Intermediate** 5.1 G ★ (Sky Top) **290**, **294**, 295
- [ ] **Jiggles** 5.1 G (Trapps) 33
- [ ] **Silly Chimney** 5.1 G (Trapps) 131, **132**
- [ ] **The Spider's Lair** 5.1 PG **337**, (Sky Top) 323
- [ ] **A Stroll With Hot Toddie** 5.1 PG (Sky Top) 329
- [ ] **Tree Filled Chimney** 5.1 PG (Near) **215**, 218

5.2

- [ ] **48** G (Trapps) 136, **137**
- [ ] **49** G (Trapps) **137**, 139
- [ ] **Casa Emilio** G ★ (Trapps) 152, **155**, **157**
- [ ] **Clachaig Crack** PG (Sky Top) 330
- [ ] **Dirty** G (Sky Top) 281, **285**
- [ ] **Dungeons and Dragons** G (Sky Top) 327
- [ ] **East Chimney** G (Sky Top) 308, **309**
- [ ] **Easy Keyhole** G (Trapps) **23**, 24
- [ ] **Easy Overhang** G ★★★ (Trapps) **47**, **52**, 53
- [ ] **Easy Verschneidung** G ★ (Trapps) **107**, 109
- [ ] **Independence** G (Near) 171
- [ ] **Lemon Squeezer** PG (Trapps) 92
- [ ] **Little Face** PG ★★★ (Sky Top) **283**, 284
- [ ] **Mary** G (Sky Top) 275, 278
- [ ] **Northern Pillar** G ★★ (Trapps) 88, **91**
- [ ] **Petie** G (Sky Top) 274, **275**
- [ ] **Red's Ruin** G (Trapps) 104
- [ ] **Roddey** PG (Trapps) **38**, 40
- [ ] **Scot Free** G (Sky Top) 330
- [ ] **Southern Pillar** G ★ (Trapps) **85**, 87
- [ ] **Sudoriferous** G (Trapps) 26
- [ ] **The Tunnel** PG ★ (Sky Top) **299**, 302
- [ ] **Unnamed** PG (Trapps) 92, **94**
- [ ] **Willie's Weep** G (Trapps) 90, **91**

5.3

5.4

5.4 cont.

5.5

5.5 cont.

- [ ] **Loose Goose** G (Near) 198, **199**
- [ ] **Minerva** G (Sky Top) **283**, 284
- [ ] **Minestrone** G (Sky Top) 289
- [ ] **Obligato** G (Sky Top) 274, **275**
- [ ] **Old Route** G ★
  (Millbrook) 259, **260**
- [ ] **One Step Backward for Mankind**
  G (Sky Top) 310, **311**
- [ ] **Orc Stone** PG (Near) **201**, 204
- [ ] **Overhanging Overhang** G ★
  (Sky Top) **283**, 285
- [ ] **Punch and Judy** PG
  (Near) **221**, 222, **223**
- [ ] **Raindance** G
  (Trapps) 152, **153**, **155**
- [ ] **Ranger's Revenge** PG
  (Trapps) 160
- [ ] **RMC** G ★ (Trapps) **38**, 45
- [ ] **Roman's Climb Next to**
  Keystone Cop PG
  (Near) **223**, 224
- [ ] **The Scottish Connection** G
  (Sky Top) **327**, 328
- [ ] **Scuttlebutt** G ★
  (Near) **207**, **208**, 209
- [ ] **Short and Sassy** G (Near) 231
- [ ] **Simple Ceilings** PG
  (Trapps) **69**, 70
- [ ] **Snowpatch** G (Trapps) **103**, 104
- [ ] **St. Louis** G (Near) 170
- [ ] **Three Generations** G
  (Near) 206, **207**
- [ ] **To Come or Become** G
  (Near) 219
- [ ] **Tower Ridge** G
  (Sky Top) 308, **309**
- [ ] **Triple Bulges** G (Trapps) 90
- [ ] **Under Exposure One Stop** G
  (Sky Top) 284
- [ ] **Updraft** PG ★ (Trapps) **117**, 119
- [ ] **Ursula** PG ★
  (Trapps) **128**, 130, **132**

5.6–

- [ ] **Arrivato** G (Sky Top) **271**, 273
- [ ] **Artichoke** G (Sky Top) 273, **275**
- [ ] **Brothers Left** G (Sky Top) 334
- [ ] **Bunny's Roof** PG (Trapps) 28
- [ ] **Disneyland** PG ★★★
  (Near) **175**, **176**, 177
- [ ] **Hans' Yellow Face** PG ★★
  (Sky Top) 280
- [ ] **Rear Exposure** G ★ (Sky Top)
  287, 289
- [ ] **Rhododendron** G ★
  (Trapps) **30**, 32
- [ ] **To Go Where No Man Has Gone**
  G (Sky Top) 334

5.6

- [ ] **Air for a G-String** PG
  (Millbrook) 264
- [ ] **Animal Farm** G
  (Near) **208**, **211**, **211**
- [ ] **Baby** G ★★★ (Trapps) **47**, 51
- [ ] **Bitchy Virgin** PG (Trapps) **91**, 92
- [ ] **Bulta's Horse's Bloody Elbow** G
  (Sky Top) 270
- [ ] **Contradance** PG
  (Trapps) 152, **153**, **155**

5.6 cont.

5.7 cont.

5.7+

- [ ] **Acid Rain** PG (Sky Top) 326
- [ ] **Baskerville Terrace** PG13 ★★
      (Near) **185**, 189
- [ ] **The Bridle Path** PG (Trapps) 31
- [ ] **Cascading Crystal Kaleidoscope**
      PG (Trapps) 117, 120
- [ ] **Classic** G ★★ (Trapps) **38**, 42
- [ ] **Clover** PG (Trapps) 32
- [ ] **Drunkard's Delight** PG ★★★
      (Trapps) 58, **59**
- [ ] **Emilio** PG (Trapps) 154, **157**
- [ ] **Fitschen's Folly** X (Trapps) 36
- [ ] **Friday the 13th** R (Trapps) **27**, 27
- [ ] **Gaston** PG (Trapps) 64
- [ ] **Genetic Culling** X (Sky Top) 317
- [ ] **Golden Years** PG
      (Millbrook) **258**, 260, **260**
- [ ] **Just For the Record** PG (Near) 218
- [ ] **Laurel** G ★ (Trapps) 32
- [ ] **Mr. P's Wurst** PG13 ★★
      (Trapps) **85**, 88
- [ ] **No One Keeping Score** PG
      (Sky Top) 308, **309**
- [ ] **Perspiration Point** PG
      (Sky Top) **333**, 334
- [ ] **Pete's Meat** PG ★
      (Sky Top) **279**, 281
- [ ] **Pinnacle of Suckcess** PG
      (Sky Top) 314, **314**
- [ ] **Scungilli** PG (Trapps) **52**, 57
- [ ] **Short and Simple** G
      (Trapps) 22, **23**
- [ ] **Snooky's Departure** R
      (Trapps) 84
- [ ] **Something Interesting** G ★★★
      (Trapps) 69, 72, **75**
- [ ] **Sort of Damocles** G (Trapps) 95
- [ ] **Te Dum** G ★ (Near) 176, 179, 180
- [ ] **Tequila Mockingbird** G ★
      (Trapps) 78, **81**
- [ ] **Travels with Charlie** R ★
      (Trapps) 65
- [ ] **The Womb Step** PG
      (Trapps) 85, **85**
- [ ] **Writhe to the Occasion**
      (Millbrook) 246

5.8–

- [ ] **60-40** PG (Trapps) 127, **128**
- [ ] **Candide** R
      (Sky Top) **287**, **290**, 291
- [ ] **Clumsy Foot** PG ★ (Sky Top)
      335, **337**
- [ ] **Day Tripper** G ★
      (Near) **207**, **208**, 209
- [ ] **Gimme Shelter** R
      (Sky Top) 323, **324**
- [ ] **Hyjek's Horror** PG ★
      (Trapps) 89, **91**
- [ ] **Lost Souls** PG (Sky Top) 276
- [ ] **Madame Grunnebaum's Sorrow**
      PG (Trapps) 88
- [ ] **Minne Belle** PG ★ (Sky Top) 296
- [ ] **Morning After** PG ★★
      (Trapps) 59
- [ ] **Nowhereland** PG (Near) 206
- [ ] **Outer Space** PG (Near) 171, **175**
- [ ] **Raunchy** PG ★ (Trapps) 94, **94**
- [ ] **Snooky's Return** G ★
      (Trapps) 83, **83**
- [ ] **Sultana** PG (Trapps) 57
- [ ] **Wonderland** PG ★
      (Trapps) 102, **103**

5.8

5.8 cont.

5.8+

5.8+ cont.

5.9–

5.9– cont.

5.9

5.9 cont.

5.9 cont.

5.9+

5.9+ cont.

5.10–

5.10– cont.

5.10 cont.

5.10 cont.

5.10+

5.10+ cont.

5.11−

5.11

5.11 cont.

5.11+

5.11+ cont.

5.12

☐ **Bone Hard** PG ★★
   (Trapps) 160, **163**
☐ **Brace Yourself** R (Sky Top) 306
☐ **Cinnamon Girl** R ★★
   (Sky Top) **279**, 280
☐ **The Circumcisor** PG13
   (Trapps) 160
☐ **Cluney's Jollies** R (Trapps) 144
☐ **Dark Side of the Moon** PG ★
   (Near) **229**, 230
☐ **El Kabong** R (Near) 193
☐ **Emory Buttress**
   (Sky Top) 283, **283**
☐ **Forbidden Zone** (Near) 192
☐ **Happiness is a 100° Wall** G
   ★★★ (Millbrook) 255, **257**
☐ **The Jane Fonda Workout**
   (Trapps) 77
☐ **Kansas City** G ★★★
   (Near) 171, **175**
☐ **Manifest Destiny** R ★★★
   (Millbrook) 242, **243**
☐ **The Mincer** R ★ (Near) 216, **217**
☐ **The Mohel** (Trapps) 39

☐ **Nectar Vector** R ★★★
   (Millbrook) 240, **243**
☐ **The Numbers Racket**
   (Trapps) 159
☐ **Point Blank** R ★★ (Trapps) 119
☐ **Renaissance** R ★ (Trapps) 159
☐ **Requiem** PG ★★ (Near) **185**, 189
☐ **Slammin' the Salmon** (Near) 194
☐ **Slime World** PG (Trapps) 165
☐ **Sticky Bun Power** R ★★
   (Sky Top) **294**, 296
☐ **Strings Attached**
   (Trapps) 154, **155**
☐ **Sudden Impact** R ★
   (Millbrook) **237**, 239, 240
☐ **Supercrack** G ★★★
   (Sky Top) 317, **318**
☐ **Tiers of Fears** PG ★
   (Trapps) 132, **132**
☐ **To Have or Have Not** R ★★★
   (Near) **191**, 196
☐ **Vanishing Point** R ★ (Trapps) 119
☐ **Yellow Crack** R ★
   (Trapps) 144, **145**

5.12+

☐ **Burning Buns** (Sky Top) 296
☐ **Death's Head Mask** R
   (Trapps) 160
☐ **Diplomatic Strain** PG13
   (Sky Top) 317
☐ **Girls Just Wanna Have Fun**
   PG13 (Trapps) 161

☐ **Iron Cross** PG (Near) 172
☐ **Modern Love** (Trapps) 160
☐ **Organic Iron** PG (Trapps) 78
☐ **The Tweazle Roof** PG ★
   (Sky Top) **314**, 316

5.13 and 5.13−

☐ **Pumping Pygmies** 5.13 (Sky Top)
   331, 332
☐ **Iron Curtain** 5.13− PG (Sky Top)
   316

☐ **Vandals** 5.13− R ★★★ (Sky Top)
   287, **290**, 292
☐ **The Zone** 5.13− R (Trapps) **113**,
   114

Routes by Name

Photo pages are in bold

Do you know this man?

Trivia Answers

These are the answers I found. You may well find more...

1) **Bag's End**, **Balrog**, **Balrog Escape** (**Bridge of Khaza-dum**), **Elf Stone**, **Ent's Line**, **Eowyn**, **Gil-Galad**, **Middle Earth**, **Nazgul**, **Orc Stone**, **Rhun**, and **Ringwraith** (**Dungeons and Dragons**, **Journey's End**, and **The Sting** might also fall into this category).

2) Art Gran (1964), Ivan Rezucha (1981, 84), Todd Swain (1986, 90, 94), and Dick Williams (1972, 80, 91).

3) Henry Barber (White Mountains, N.H.), Rick Cronk (Catskills, N.Y.), Willie Crowther (Quincy Quarries, MA.), Dick DuMais (CO.), Art Gran (Gunks, N.Y.), Ed Grindley (Ben Nevis, Scotland), Joe Kelsey (Wind River Range, WY.), Ken Nichols (CT.), Ivan Rezucha (Gunks, N.Y.), Tom Rosecrans (Adirondaks, N.Y.), Mike Steele (Delaware Water Gap, PA.), Todd Swain (Red Rocks, NV.), Ed Webster (White Mountains, N.H.), Dick Williams (Gunks, N.Y.).

4) **New Frontier**, **Comedy in Three Acts**, **Fat City**, **The Nose**, and **Ventre de Boeuf**.

5) **G String**, and **Mother's Day Party**.

6) Karl Beard, Beau Haworth, Morris Hershoff, Bob Hostetter, Patty Lanzetta, Bob Larsen, Dave Levenstein, Dave Luhan, Ron Matous, Chris Monz, Rich Perch, Larry Schaffer, Thom Scheuer, and Todd Swain.

7) Australia, Canada, France, Germany, Norway, Switzerland, and United Kingdom (possibly Mexico, Spain, and Sweden also).

Photo Todd Swain on **Five Jade**, 5.11 near Moab, Utah. In 1981, and from 1984 to 1988, Todd worked for the Mohonk Preserve as a ranger. During his tenure at the Gunks, he climbed over 1,000 different routes and established over 120 new climbs. With the help of many friends, he wrote the first edition of *The Gunks Guide* in 1986. Now updated and fully revised, this is the third edition of *The Gunks*.